D0854054

William J. Leonard, S.J.

Where Thousands Fell

William J. Leonard, S.J.

Sheed & Ward

Copyright© 1995 by William J. Leonard, S.J.

All rights reserved. No part of this book may be reproduced or transmitted in any form or by any means, electronic or mechanical, including photocopying, recording or by an information storage and retrieval system without permission in writing from the Publisher.

Sheed & Ward™ is a service of The National Catholic Reporter Publishing Company.

◆

Library of Congress Cataloguing-in-Publication Data

Leonard, William J.
    Where thousands fell / William J. Leonard.
       p.   cm.
    ISBN 1-55612-755-3 (hardcover). — ISBN 1-55612-756-1 (pbk.)
    1. Leonard, William J. 2. World War, 1939-1945 — Personal narratives, American. 3. World War, 1939-1945 — Chaplains — United States. 4. World War, 1939-1945 — Campaigns — Papua New Guinea. 5. Jesuits — United States — Biography. I. Title.
D810.C36U485   1995
940.54 ' 78 ' 092—dc20
[B]   94-38767
                                                  CIP

◆

Published by: Sheed & Ward
                115 E. Armour Blvd.
                P.O. Box 419492
                Kansas City, MO 64141-6492

To order, call: (800) 333-7373

Cover photo: William J. Leonard, S.J., Chaplain, U.S. Army, 1943-46.
Cover design by Emil Antonucci.

Contents

For my sisters,
Cath and Eleanor Jean,
in love and gratitude.

Preface

THIS IS A COMPANION VOLUME, IN A SENSE, FOR MY EARLIER BOOK, *The Letter Carrier* (Sheed & Ward, 1993). In fact, it is a much more complete account of my Army chaplaincy in World War II than I had room for in *The Letter Carrier.* There have been few (if any) reports by American chaplains of their war-time experiences, so perhaps, in this 50th anniversary year, an account of "what it was like" to be a priest in uniform, to share intimately—though always as a non-combatant—in the enormous struggle, the terror, the total disruption of normal life, may be appropriate and informative. I cherish, of course, memories of lighter moments, of affectionate comradeships I should have never have known if it had not been for the war; they are precious and I have tried to pay grateful tribute to them here. I hope, however, that the book will witness more particularly to the utter waste and futility of war. *"Jamais encore!"* as Pope Paul VI pleaded. There must be, there *has* to be a better way.

I am grateful indeed to Mr. Bernard Rothwell and Mr. Richard Young of the Trinitas Foundation for their generous assistance in seeing the book through the press. And I want especially to thank Dr. Robert O'Neill, director of the Burns Library at Boston College, for his encouragement and practical help.

CHAPTER 1

A Change of Uniforms

I CALL THEM, SIMPLY, "THE VIVID YEARS." THERE WERE ONLY THREE, but they linger in the memory. I had asked permission several times to offer myself as a chaplain, but had been refused—the last time so definitely that I had gone out and bought the new black suit I needed if I were going to continue in civilian life. It was only a month later that the Rector stopped me as I was coming back from Rocco Canale's wedding.

"By the way, I guess you can write that letter."

"Letter? What letter?"

"Didn't you want to be a chaplain?"

"Oh . . . is that still alive?"

"Yes. You'd better write today. They seem to be in a hurry."

"Yes. Thanks. Oh, is that Army or Navy?"

"Well, there seems to be a greater need in the Army."

"Uh-huh. Thanks very much."

And in that casual fashion I was shipped into the service and into combat. I had seen plays and movies about tight-lipped acceptance of orders: "This will be rough, men. You won't all come back. But I expect every one of you to do a job. Is that clear?" But I had thought all that melodrama. Now it, or something suspiciously like it, was showing up in my own life and mocking my aesthetic theories. It was also taking account of the suddenly empty sensation in the pit of my stomach and mocking my long conviction that as a Jesuit I had a soldier's vocation. All very well so long as the vocation called only to the parade ground; what happened when the dress uniform came off and the dirty side of GI life was uppermost? St. Ignatius, sending St. Francis Xavier to the Indies, had said "Go," but had added words of consolation for an apostolic heart: "Set everything on fire." I had had only the laconic "Go," and though I could supply the unspoken motivation from long years of hearing it, I wished someone had uttered it aloud again just for my benefit. I looked around the quiet campus, taking in the lovely Gothic buildings; life here suddenly became precious indeed. Maybe I wouldn't pass the physical. But then I remembered why the campus was so quiet. Our enrollment had fallen off steadily since Pearl Harbor; in my own class that semester, scarcely a day had passed without my scratching a name from the roster. In a mounting anguish I had seen them go: Gerry Armitage, who was called early and had gone in with the Marines at Guadalcanal. Before leaving he had come to ask me about the morality of volunteering for the paratroops, and then knelt and asked for my blessing. When we shook hands he had looked at me with his serene boyish eyes: "I'm not afraid to die, Father." Or George Malone, home on his last leave before going overseas, who had driven through dark, icy streets at six o'clock on a January morning to serve my Mass. I could still see his grin as he leaned out of the car after Mass and waved: "Be seeing you, Father." I hoped earnestly that he would, one day, but it would not be on this earth; George had gone out from England as a high-altitude fighter pilot and never came back. Tom McCarty, who had planned on becoming a Jesuit, died in a crash on his base in Montana. Bob Muse had said goodbye to Mary and was flying in the Pacific. Jim Sweeney and George Criss, still unseparated, were getting ready for Europe somewhere in Carolina. Joe Dever and Jack Ross and Joe Nolan were writing in from faraway places: lonely letters from wardrooms and USO clubs and BOQ's, full of memories of the *Stylus* and proms and the dramatic society and Lee Bowen's functionalism. Tom Heath had written verse for the *Stylus* that summed it up:

What are you dreaming, soldier,
What is it you see?
A tall gray Gothic tower,
And a linden tree.
You speak so sadly, soldier,
Sad and wistfully . . .
I cannot hear the tower bell

In the swirling sea.
What meaning has it, soldier,
A tower, bell, and tree?
Nothing, nothing — only once
It meant my life to me.

I had wanted to go because these boys had gone, because while they were in college they had "meant my life to me." There were thousands like them: lonely, bewildered by this bloody end to their bright youth, yearning for home and the familiar, struggling tensely to adjust to regimentation and monotony, to forget the queasiness that turned their bowels to jelly when they thought of combat. Many would be Catholics, and to them a priest would mean a counsellor, a tower of strength, a real father. Many others would not be Catholics, but perhaps the presence among them of a friendly older man who stood for spiritual things would prove acceptable and even helpful.

It was December 7, 1943, when I first heard I might go. The days began to whir by, faster and faster. Approval came in from the Military Ordinariate, followed by a commission and orders to report at the Chaplain School on February 10. Only then did I undertake the painful task of breaking the news at home. My father and mother demonstrated once again the fortitude they had shown eighteen years before when I asked if I might go to the novitiate; not by a syllable or a tear did they try to hold me back, and I wonder if I have ever been sufficiently grateful for their making it so easy for me. The first time I wore my uniform home, though, a little chink in the armor appeared. "Pretty snappy, don't you think?" I said. Ma smiled, but she didn't agree. Pa said, "I prefer your other uniform, the black one." Eleanor clapped her hands, though, and encouraged my vanity; I was not to find out until the last day what she was hiding.

There came the last class, and "Midyears"—the last bluebooks. No teacher would regret those, but the word "last" was cropping up too regularly, and I found myself a little breathless at times. The then Bishop Richard Cushing, whose apostolic heart took such a profound and practical interest in the chaplains, obtained for me a Mass kit (paid for by some of his generous Newton parishioners), and I called for it at his downtown office. "The chalice hasn't been consecrated," he said, "but I'll take care of that now." So a moment later, he did: "Adjutorium nostrum in nomine Domini" went rasping out the open window to startle the pigeons and the staid banking offices on Franklin Street. Shortly afterward I picked up the heavy case for the first time. I was to carry it around the world, and its handle was to wear a print on the bones of my fingers. It would be opened again and again, wherever there was an assembly of Christians, wherever two or three gathered together in his name. "Do this," he had commanded. Now I wish I had kept a record of the strange places where I "did this." In a mess hall, after the food stains had been wiped away. On the gray heaving deck of a transport. In hotel rooms. On the roof of the Customs House in Manila. On a pile of ammo cases in a field. On a wardroom piano. On a narrow steel desk under a tent. On the tail-gate of a six-by-six truck. Within earshot of the kitchen, or the Officers' Club, or an all-absorbing crap game. Sometimes, I used to worry whether the setting had even a minimum of reverence, but then I would look at the silent, expectant faces of my small congregation and decide that their need justified my going ahead. There had been beasts at Bethlehem, distractions in the Supper Chamber. There had even been a crap game under the Cross.

The Mass kit summed up my Army vocation. It was at my knee in the jeep, on the swaying, jolting truck. I kept it, locked, in my tent or my field office. It went with me over the ship's side and down the scramble-net into the landing craft when we hit the beach at Lingayen. I spread my poncho over it and got soaked myself by the tropical rain that drenched us while we stood on the little pier at Finschhafen, waiting for the Transportation Corps to make up its silly mind what to do with us. The Mass kit was myself, the man who was useful out there only because he had received Holy Orders, the Christian priest whose graces were for others, not for himself. Sometimes I look at it now for consolation. It's battered; my name, painted on the top, is scuffed and faded; the corners are broken. On it are my serial number and the number of my overseas shipment: RY-003. The device of the 9th Ordnance Battalion is on it too, and the address to which it was to be shipped if anything happened to me. When I open it I catch a whiff of the rancid jungle and the dank South Seas. But I prize it as the most tangible souvenir of my priesthood, of the days when I was mediator between God and fighting men, when I was Christ to Christ-in-uniform.

CHAPTER 2

Count Cadence

WHEN I FINALLY TOOK OFF (THE FIRST OF MANY ARMY PHRASES that found their inevitable way into my vocabulary) on the long-awaited trek to the Chaplain School at Harvard, it was with many dreams of what could be done as a soldier-pastor to "bring the liturgy to the people,"or, better, to make men conscious of their vocation to be members of the praying Church. At home, except for small and isolated groups, there had been apathy, indifference, or misunderstanding. The kindest of our critics had thought us visionaries. They had smiled their tolerant smile. "You have never been in a large city parish." "You don't know what a job it is to get people even to keep the commandments." "I have to clear my church every forty-five minutes." "Let's be sure that our people live up to the *Casti Connubii*, and then we can give them the frills."

So it had run. Liturgy had been rubrics to the priests and poly-syllabic mystery to the laity. In vain we had suggested that commandments might be better observed if given the motivation of the offertory or baptism. In vain we had reiterated the purpose of the Liturgical Movement: "all we are trying to do is to make the Mass and the sacraments the core of our people's living." In my uncharitable moments I had muttered "stand-patters" under my breath; I had wondered about the value of courses in logic; I had recalled ominous hours in history when men had been similarly unable to read the signs of the times. And my wise and patient priest-friend, Father Tom Carroll, had given counsel: "Don't be in a hurry. If the Holy Spirit wants this to grow, it will grow. And if he doesn't, who cares about it?"

"Well," I said to him as he drove me and my luggage across the river and over the icy streets of Cambridge, the penultimate

6

kindness in a very long series, "all that is over the dam. Let's see what can be done in fresh fields and pastures new. If it works with men, with soldiers, that should convince them. They won't be able to call it frills any longer. And maybe if the soldiers get it, they'll demand it when they come home. The old order must change, and maybe this is the way God wants it changed. It will be something to have a chance to try." He laughed as he saw me climb out of the car and give my first clumsy salute to a corporal outside Perkins Hall. I had heard of the tradition according to which a newly-commissioned officer gives a dollar to the first enlisted man who salutes him, but I was already too self-conscious in my new uniform to stop the corporal and explain to him how he had unwittingly earned my tribute.

Well, here I was. Beside the door was a sign reading "Perkins Hall, U.S. Army Chaplain School," and the door stood open. I smiled a little grimly. Seven years' teaching poetry had given me the habit of attaching significance to moments like this. Fragments of allusion ran through my mind. "Abandon hope, all you who enter here." "Tell them that I came, and no one answered." "I am the door. If anyone enter by me, he shall be saved." I entered.

There was "processing"—a mystifying mass of papers to be signed over and over, another visit to the medics ("Heck, we just had a physical!"), an assignment to quarters, a happy identification of brother priests among all these strangers who wore the chaplain's cross, an unpacking of Mass kits on the balcony of the Germanic Museum. This was indeed something. Eighty-eight priests in my class, I was told; Masses would be offered face-to-face across narrow tables. "Don't step back when you genuflect or you'll kick the man behind you." The first set of Masses would start at six, and the second at six-thirty. "And if you want any breakfast you'll have to step on it."

So that was it, and I had always hated to hurry my Mass. Well, I supposed I could do it if I had to. And I did. The rising bell rang at five-thirty, and at six we were on the frozen sidewalk, shivering in the icy blasts that cut their way down Oxford Street. "Where's that O.D.? Let's get out of here." The Officer of the Day finally appears. "Section one, all present or accounted for, sir."

Section two . . . five . . . nine . . . "dismiss!" With that we break ranks and run, lifting heavy GI boots with legs no longer young, down the street, across the yard, over the hedge, through the alley, up the back stairs of Germanic. I take my amice from my box, noting that it is already five minutes past six, and hurry into my vestments, trying desperately to forget the sniffles I picked up on that hike two days ago, the ache in my fallen arch, the fact that by some miracle the man across the table has managed to be vested and well into his collects while I have not yet said my first *introibo*. "All right," I tell myself, "you hurried to get here, but no hurry from now on." But I can't shake my awareness of the flying minutes and the man waiting to take my altar. A general intention must suffice at both mementos; on Ember Saturday I read all five lessons and feel very guilty as I finish at six-forty. But the priest who follows me is reassuring: "I'll be through at seven—I'll say a requiem." I can't serve his Mass—there isn't room for a server between those tables, and besides, I have to make my bed (Army style), and I'm room orderly this week and must sweep the room and tidy up, and I'll need a bit of breakfast to keep me going through four hours of class.

But as I tiptoe off the balcony I look about. It's a feria in Lent, but there are no violet vestments; it's the feast of St. Matthias, but I see no red. There is only the monotonous black or its reverse, the tattle-tale gray that passes for white. And the Masses that are being read are not the Masses of the day; they are the four printed in the Military Missal: Easter, the Trinity, our Lady, or the Requiem. "Imagine," I say to myself, "reading those same Masses over and over through several years of service as a chaplain. What about Advent, or Pentecost, or All Saints? What about the riches of Christ in the liturgical year?" My own complete Missal is an inch thicker, but I wouldn't take gold for it, nor for the three reversible (six color) vestments given me by Tom Carroll, who thought the Army's priest should be as well-dressed as the civilians'. A little more bulky? Yes, but so are bedding rolls, and field jackets, and many other less essential items, and room is found for them. Isn't this an economy more than military; a reflection of that same American tendency to streamline that resulted in twenty-minute Masses and novenas on the half-hour?

At seven-forty all the priests of the class gathered to recite five decades of the rosary in common. It was not required, but if you were not there you were considered a little strange. And it *was* good to be here with your brother priests, asking the Mother of God for her blessing on you and on "all Catholic chaplains, living and dead." But you used to wonder what would be said if you suggested recitation of Prime as a morning prayer instead of the rosary, or whether the almost hundred-percent-attendance would be so perfect if the five decades were not permitted to stand as a substitute for the breviary in case the work-day was long.

On Friday afternoons we were marched to St. Paul's for "Holy Hour." During Lent it was the Stations of the Cross. I hope it was not simply a Gaelic cantankerousness that made me question the obligation. After all, the Stations are a devotion, and the Church leaves us free to choose such devotions as help us. I did not find this helpful—not with the threadbare vernacular hymns, the bellowed *Stabat Mater*, the meditations with their insistence on the exclusive God-and-myself relationship. (The booklet even said, "Lamb of God, have mercy on me," but I always said "on us.") And again I wondered why a group of priests could not sing Vespers and Compline. One day, on a hike, when the order had been given for "route step" and we could talk, I ventured to suggest it to the priest at my side. "Didn't you like it last Friday?" he asked in amazement. "Gosh, I came out of St. Paul's feeling better than I had all week." Which left me wondering whether the first purpose of prayer were to praise God or to "feel good," and why the breviary had in so many cases lost the power it held for centuries to exalt and console the human soul.

All of us found the Chaplain School helpful in introducing us to the military life; we learned customs like "signing out," we learned the first elements of drill, we began to grow familiar with Army terminology and organization. The classes, though, were long and the subject-matter thin; the lectures on how to counsel the soldiers seemed especially superficial after the study of moral theology and much experience in the confessional. But we were discovering that not all the tyro chaplains had had that study or experience. I always will remember one man from Arkansas who, when we came to the subject of identifying the dead properly before burial, seemed to know a great deal about funerals. Finally he explained: "I was an undertaker in civilian life." "But," I said, "I thought you were a minister." "Oh," he drawled, "I used to do a little preachin' on the side."

I'm sure that the Protestants found us priests clannish. The fact was that we did rejoice in one another's company. No matter from which diocese or religious order we had come, no matter what our racial origin, we had a faith and an outlook in common that produced immediate ease and companionship, bantering and high spirits. Somehow we recognized one another as priests on first sight, and there was no secret sign, nothing distinctive about our uniform. This was true even though the little Italian bootblacks in Harvard Square could spot us at once, and I didn't find out how until the very end of my stay in Cambridge. "How's it goin', Fadder?" they would say as they polished our brand new shoes, and we would ask how they knew we were priests. At last one of them owned up, and pointed to the wrinkles in the instep of my right shoe. "Dat's from genuflectin', Fadder."

Our relations with the Protestants were for the most part courteous and polite and diffident. We had not had much to do with Protestant ministers, nor they with us, and none of us knew exactly how to go about building friendships. It seemed to us that many of them displayed a little too much heartiness of manner, an excessive sweetness of speech. How they found us I don't know: clannish, probably, as I said before, and intransigent. My first roommate was Chaplain Bob McCaslin, from Pennsylvania. We shook hands when we met, and sparred politely for a few moments as we unpacked our bags. When Father Leo O'Keefe, a New England Jesuit like myself, arrived and was assigned to us as a third roommate, Bob must have felt outnumbered, but the fact did not prevent us from becoming good friends. Theology rarely came up for discussion; we were together in the room very seldom, and at night we were too weary to talk long. Once in a while we joked about our differences: Leo would say something about the happy days before the Reformation, or Bob would complain about celibates who presumed to give advice to married people.

In the third week of the School, Leo received his orders, assigning him to the Air Corps at Randolph Field; in the fourth week my orders arrived, assigning me to the infantry in Louisiana. The fifth and last week came, and Bob still had no orders. We used to josh him: "Better polish up that old Easter sermon, Bob. The Army doesn't want you, and you'll have to preach again down in Pittsburgh." At last, three days before we broke up, the missing orders came in: Bob was assigned to an "SL" Battalion. But he didn't know—none of us knew—what an "SL" battalion was. Soon we found out: he was to go with the Artillery, in a Searchlight Battalion. That night we had a solemn celebration of the occasion, and presented him with a tiny flashlight, the sort that hangs on the keyring and enables one to find the keyhole, "to get you accustomed to your new duties."

But there were better things. Leo and I would rush back from Mass on Saturday mornings, wondering how we could tidy up the room and our outfits before inspection began, and find that Bob had done the whole job alone, even to polishing our GI boots for us. Charity like that lives on in the memory.

The marching and drilling were pleasant at first. They got us out of doors, for one thing, for hours at a stretch—something I hadn't known since boyhood, except for summer vacations. And it's exhilarating to swing along in step with a moving column, if you have a sense of rhythm. One poor priest had none; no matter how he skipped and changed his gait, we could always see his head bobbing up when ours were going down. Sergeant O'Shaughnessy, our drillmaster, tried to correct him for a time, but finally gave it up as hopeless. In the third week, however, one of my arches fell, and then all the fun went out of drill; I "counted cadence" in groans, and registered a solemn vow to *ride* down Oxford Street when I came home—a vow I have fulfilled many times.

CHAPTER 3

Green in Green Pastures

MARCH TWENTIETH BROUGHT BOSTON A LATE-WINTER BLIZZARD THAT
dumped eight inches of snow on the city and almost made me miss
my train. Farewells are painful enough at any time, but that morning leaden skies and slush added to everyone's depression, and the
great, dreary shed of the old South Station was plunged in gloom.
How much heartbreak there has been on docks, on railroad plat-
forms.

It was like my father that, because of the weather, he should
not have allowed my mother to come, and then that he should have
refused to let the weather prevent him from coming to see me off.
He was beginning to age then, and life had baffled him in many
ways; I know he always felt within himself a capacity for more than
he had achieved. I wish I could somehow have conveyed to him
that morning my admiration of his solid achievement, for what he
was rather than for anything he had accomplished. I wish I could
have told him, for instance, that I sometimes wondered whether I
was more privileged to see at close range his love affair with my
mother through fifty years or to be the fruit and beneficiary of it.
Alas, with the bustle of my departure and our masculine embarrassment over strong emotion, the right words would not come. We
shook hands and I climbed aboard. He wrote to me every day for
the next two years, just as he had written every day during my four
years at the novitiate. They were not long letters, as a rule. They
related some amusing incident, gave me tidbits of family news,
commented philosophically on the headlines. But they were written
every day—of course I often received a bundle of them at the same
time—and they invariably closed with the same phrase: "All well.
Love, Father." It was what I needed to know.

Travel in wartime brings home to one the convulsive effort the country is making. Reservations are difficult to obtain, facilities are tightly packed. The great centers—New York, Washington, St. Louis—are crowded with uniforms. Military police patrol railroad cars, bus stations, airports. The civilians one meets and chats with are all involved somehow in the war: an engineer on his way to supervise a new military installation, a young wife going to a two-room apartment on the fringe of some sprawling camp, hoping to have a few happy weeks before her husband is ordered overseas, an industrialist headed for the Pentagon with a briefcase full of contracts. Insufficient redcaps, Pullman porters, cab drivers, dining cars. Warning posters: "The enemy is listening. Don't talk." Strained nerves snapping if you ask for anything: "Doncha know there's a war on?" Your sense of the lengthening miles between you and the familiar, you and the beloved. And yet a new and exhilarating sense of adventure: you too are in a uniform, streamlined for action. You stand on the jolting platform as the train goes rocketing through unknown towns by night. Those other nights when you lay in bed in the quiet seminary in Weston, listening to the Montreal train whistling in the valley, and yearning to be aboard it, yearning for far places!

St. Louis on a gray afternoon, the train two hours late. I had hoped to see Leo Murphy, then with the Air Corps at Jefferson Barracks, but there was time only to call him on the phone, time only for five minutes' conversation. Leo had been one of the Five who made *The Stylus* a top-flight college magazine. By day he went to class, wrote and acted in the college plays and shouted in the cafeteria. By night he swept out telephone booths in the North Station, courted Mary and wondered about the draft. When he graduated they were married—on a shoestring, and Father Bonn gave them a wedding breakfast in the Dramatic Attic. Not long after our conversation in St. Louis he was assigned to the Ground Forces and went overseas as a sergeant of infantry. Ten years later I drove through Normandy looking at the hedgerows and saying to myself, "It must have been about here." If you could say of a man that he had a sweet nature, you could say that about Leo: he loved much and well, he was patient. I remember how he would declaim the Lyke-Wake Dirge, with its resounding refrain:

"And Christ receive thy saule!"

I've said it often for him. His death was my most grievous personal loss of the War.

The Missouri Pacific's *Sunshine Special* roared on. "Where are we now?" I asked an unhappy GI on the platform. "Beats me," he answered, "Can't be Louisiana yet; it doesn't smell bad enough." On that sour note I decided to turn in. When morning came I raised the curtain in my berth and looked into green pastures. A blizzard had blown me out of Boston two days before, but here was lush, green grass, and blooming dogwood; phlox was out in front of every cabin; black children played along the levees.

Camp Livingston, when I reached it, was just as agreeable a surprise. The streets were paved with concrete, the paths connecting buildings were covered with gravel, flowers were everywhere. The grass was trimmed neatly by German and Italian prisoners of war. Best of all, the trees had been left standing when the camp was built, so the depressing prospect usual in most camps—acre after acre of bleak barracks—was happily missing. The officers lived in "hutments," little cabins large enough for a cot and a foot-locker and a shelf that hung from the wall and served as a desk. The enlisted men had similar cabins, about eight men living in each. When we saw some of the neighboring camps, Claiborne and Beauregard and Polk, we realized how well off we were.

Signing in with a new outfit is quite a process, involving a new physical examination and writing your life history times without number. Baptist Chaplain Bill Bolton, the Division Chaplain, generously gave me most of his time for two days and got me started. He assigned me to the Division Artillery, but the Chief of Staff, Colonel Jones, countermanded that next day. "Infantry needs chaplains more than artillery," he said, and he was right. So I found myself with the 342nd Regiment, and work started with a rush: consultations, confessions, hospital visits, even a choir rehearsal. And three Masses, in different chapels (there were thirteen chapels in camp), the first Sunday. I learned how a pastor feels when he assumes responsibility for his first parish. But I hope most pastors are not as green as I was. Army language was still a foreign tongue, and I knew nothing about weapons, field problems, or standard operational procedures. One evening shortly after my arrival, I decided I'd make an informal visit in a neighboring company area, just to get acquainted. A group of enlisted men were lounging on the grass, but as I approached, bent on cordiality, a sergeant spotted the oncoming brass and ripped out "Ten-hut!" The men leaped to attention. This was disconcerting enough to my democratic sense, but I didn't know how to relieve the situation.

"I know there's some command I'm supposed to give you," I said awkwardly, "but I can't remember it. Is it 'relax?'"

Somebody snorted and got a glare from the sergeant, and slowly the group became comfortable again. The enlisted men in this outfit were pathetically young and grateful for any attention I gave them; if there were any tough nuts among them they kept out of my way. But I was never to find it easy to circulate freely as hail-fellow-well-met. The officers seemed to expect from the chaplain a gush of pumped-up good cheer and stereotyped enthusiasm, back-slapping and the little joke, and I'm afraid I dashed them a good bit by being natural. Even if I had conceived the role of a priest as Chief Morale Officer, I couldn't have managed the artificial respiration they looked for. I had, for one thing, what Conrad called "a confounded democratic sense"—a respect for individual dignity, if it was only a buck private's. I also wanted very much to prove that religion, even in a "professional," was quite compatible with sincerity.

My office was in the rear of the chapel building, quite adequate except that there were no screens in the windows, and after dark all the bugs in Louisiana came in to see me, including some revolting specimens at which I used to stare in disbelief. Almost always I had a stream of men with problems. It had been decided, for instance, that the Air Corps and the Army Special Training Program were overloaded, and many hundreds of men in these relatively pleasant outfits had been assigned to the Infantry. A more disgruntled and resentful crowd I had never seen. Some of them were older men, in their middle and late thirties; they found that long hikes and crawling on their bellies gave them anguish in areas they had never been conscious of before. Some of them were kids who had enlisted in the ASTP believing that they would be sent to medical school or graduate studies. Some of them had highly specialized skills for which, with reason, they foresaw no use in a rifle company. Very occasionally I was able to help by arranging a transfer to the medics or the signal battalion, but for the most part all I could do was provide a sympathetic ear: they were in the Infantry, and that was that.

There was one exception. Colonel Jones sent for me one morning to tell me about a lad who refused to fire a rifle or throw a grenade.

"He says he's a pacifist," the Colonel snapped. "I want you to set him straight, and if you don't succeed, I'll court-martial him and send him to Leavenworth."

"Maybe he's sincere," I offered.

"I don't believe it. He enlisted in the Army, didn't he? He thought he'd get a free ride through medical school, and now that bubble has burst, so he's taking the easy way out. You think I'm hard, don't you? Look, Father, I was at Pearl Harbor the day the Japs hit us. I want to pay off those beggars, and I have no illusions about them. They've been tough and they will be tough. If we're going to survive we have to be tough, and that boy will have to do his part. Knock some sense into his head."

I saluted and went out with a real worry. I respected the Colonel as a man and an officer, and understood his attitude, but the thing wasn't that simple. When the boy in question reported at my office my anxiety grew. He was a blocky, muscular fellow, no sissy. He spoke slowly and softly and without emotion.

"I don't think it's right to kill," he said.

"Then why did you enlist?" I asked.

"They told me I would go to medical school."

"Are you afraid of combat?"

"No, I'm quite willing to go in as a medic."

I gave him all the classic arguments for the legitimacy of a just war. I reminded him that we had been attacked. I pictured as vividly as I could the consequences to us of an Axis victory. I quoted all the theologians I knew. At last, feeling that there must be other considerations I had overlooked, I wrote for help to a theologian at home. The answer, alas, was an appeal to paternalism that even in those days sounded very hollow to me. By what right, I was to ask the soldier, did he oppose his immature opinion to the considered judgment of his country's leaders? I never asked the question. I was afraid it might be the same question that was being put to young men in Germany about that time. We talked, however, far into the night on several occasions, and I found that I could not shake him. It was a very small thing that finally convinced me of his sincerity. We were sitting in my office, very late, and my lights must have been almost the only ones burning in the whole camp. The walls and the ceiling were crawling with insects and I had been killing the most annoying of them. Then one particularly nauseous centipede landed on his arm and started for his face. Very gently, he brushed the repulsive thing away and went on talking. Next morning I reported to Colonel Jones that I was thoroughly convinced of the boy's sincerity and recommended that he be transferred to the medical battalion. The Colonel glared at me, told me I had greatly disappointed him, said he would make sure the lad got twenty years in Leavenworth. But long afterward, when I met the Division again in the Philippines, my boy was with the medics.

Meanwhile it was raining—how it was raining! I had seen tempestuous summer storms in New England, but the sheer weight and volume of the sudden downpour in Louisiana never failed to amaze me. If you were driving in an open jeep you couldn't keep your eyes open, but had to stop and wait for a let-up. The main roads and elevated sections of the landscape dried out rapidly when the shower passed, but the lowlands were largely swamp. The story went around of the soldier recently returned from "manoeuvres" in the back country who, asked to draw a map of Louisiana, complied by pouring a glass of water on the table. I began to think without pleasure of spending days and nights "in the field" when the regiment would go into bivouac again. "Picture me," I wrote to an old friend, "staring up at the Southern Cross or whatever special astronomy they have down here—me prostrate on the good earth, pensive under a poncho." I had once read *Travels with a Donkey* and envied Stevenson his "night among the pines," but that was in the brave days when I was seventeen. And the pine woods of Gevaudan were not the crawling tropical swamps of Louisiana.

We had, thank God, several baptisms, and I learned how much paper work was involved in war-time marriages. A captain in the Regiment was married with a real splash: the Colonel gave the bride away, there was a guard of honor, complete with sabres, and the happy pair toured the regimental area in a jeep decorated with white streamers and dragging tin cans. I liked better the quiet wedding of the young second lieutenant and the very sweet girl from his home town. In comparison with some of the blowsy dames who haunted the streets of our army town, she looked like a spring flower. Her mother and sister were there, but otherwise there were none of those friends and relatives who would have made their wedding day what they had dreamed of. I felt sorry for them (though I don't think they were sorry for themselves), and dressed up our bare sanctuary as best I could, scattering flowers about, draping two crude prie-dieux with sheets, then trying to disguise the obviousness of the sheets with some maroon cloth I found after long searching in that khaki world. When Mass was over I joined them for a wedding dinner at the hotel and waved them off to their three-day honeymoon in New Orleans. When I got back to camp I saw the lieutenant's name posted for immediate overseas shipment, and he left within the week. Poor kids.

The days weren't long enough. The Station Hospital had eighty-four wards, and I remember that one afternoon I got through only five of them: everyone wanted to talk to the chaplain. I was technically responsible, I suppose, for seeing only the men from my own Regiment, but it was hard to pass by boys who looked up eagerly as I approached. And always I was amazed at the tender care taken of these kids so that they might get well and go out to blow up other kids.

I discovered the Camp Stockade and a lot of elementary work to do there. Almost all the prisoners were in for going AWOL—scared, or despondent, or just fed-up. Sentences were long—twenty years in one case. I remember a pathetic boy of eighteen, ridden by fears of every kind since his sickly childhood. He had gone "over the hill" twice to avoid being sent overseas, and was now doing hard labor. I began going there for Mass once a week. Mass was offered on a table in the mess hall (plain boards on a saw-horse); the congregation wore blue denim prisoners' uniforms, stamped with large white letters on the back: "P.O.W." Outside were the guards, the high fence and the floodlights, and the machine guns. There were no knives, I noticed, on the tables set for breakfast, and all the men were searched on their way out for concealed weapons.

Once in a while I had to make some sketchy preparations for exams. All officers were required to know how to read a map and to draw one—complete with streams, roads, hills. It was for me another collision with my perennial bête-noire, the science of mathematics, and I was a dub at it. On one field-problem a group of us were given maps and compasses and I ended up on a hill a mile away from the objective.

In April I was summoned to Regimental headquarters to consult with the Commander and his Executive Officer. The conference went somewhat as follows:

Colonel: "Chaplain, we were planning a regimental review and a dance for a week from Friday, but I understand there might be some objection from a religious point of view. Is that so?"

I: "Yes, sir, that day is Good Friday. I'm sure that the Catholic officers would prefer a different day, and I venture to say that the Protestants would, too."

Lieutenant-Colonel: "Well, it's the best day for us. Of course I don't know anything about your angle, Chaplain."

I: "Good Friday is the day we keep the memory of the death of Christ, and most of us are Christians, sir."

Lieutenant-Colonel: "Hum."

I: "Yes, sir."

Colonel: "Well, maybe it could be arranged for Wednesday. That's all, Chaplain, thank you."

I: "Yes, sir." Salute, Exit.

The dance was arranged for Wednesday. On Good Friday we managed to have the Solemn Mass of the Presanctified in spite of all handicaps, and the little chapel was jammed to the doors. Holy Week in general was very consoling; if I was not much of a soldier I was still a priest, and could do for the men what their consciences told them should be done at this sacred season. They came flocking to confession and to Mass, even though it might have been months since they had frequented either. The result was a lot of elementary cleaning up. I was tempted to be impatient now and then, to upbraid a long-term absentee for his negligence, and then I would remember "there shall be more joy in heaven over one sinner doing penance," and firmly close my mouth. Not all the men were backsliders—I met some whose holiness would rival a saint's—but Army life was not conducive, generally, to sanctity, and absence from home meant the loss of good example and the encountering of temptations which they might never have known except for the war.

I heard confessions for five hours Holy Saturday night. The moon (the same paschal moon that lighted Gethsemane) was shining directly through my office window, and I had turned off the electric light. So when one of the long-termers had finished his story I would look up at the moon for a long minute (I could feel him tensing beside me, expecting a sharp rebuke) and then say quietly,

"Be kinda nice to be at home tonight, wouldn't it?"

There would be a deep sigh, and then, "Oh, boy, sure would, Father."

"Be nice to be home permanently, wouldn't it?"

"You bet, Father."

"Well, maybe we aren't going home until we deserve to. Maybe the reason the war goes on is that some of us are living the way we are."

"Guess you've got something there, Father."

"Okay, so what about it?"

Another sigh. "I'll do my darndest, Father."

Whereupon another absolution, and joy in heaven. Joy, too, in the hearts of priest and penitent.

For Easter we had Solemn Mass at the outdoor amphitheatre, with a congregation of thirty-six hundred. The rain held off, but I was worried about the wind: it threatened to blow the Hosts out of my ciborium as I distributed Holy Communion. There was a horde of photographers from the Signal Corps on hand. One of them came up to me before Mass started.

"Would you mind, sir, if we walked about on the platform during the service, to get some good pictures?"

"Yes, I would," I said. "You'd be a constant distraction to the congregation."

"But these pictures are going to be on the front page of the camp newspaper!"

"Well, I'll leave it to you. Should we think of this as primarily a religious service, a worshipping of God, or as an interesting news event?"

He took his pictures from the front row of the congregation. But he had his revenge: he caught me, during the sermon, in a pose which made me look like an old-time elocutionist reciting Spartacus to the Gladiators. What are the appropriate words and gestures for the magnitude of Easter?

In general I grew conscious of a great isolation. The Division was of course preoccupied with its one objective, the training of soldiers. Toward this objective everyone collaborated, including the chaplain, but I became aware that the chaplain's contribution, since it was in the spiritual order, was the least understood. This should not have surprised me, but it did, and I had to work hard sometimes to conceal my irritation, not at good-humored joshing, for which the delightful banter of community life had prepared me, but at being patronized. The problem I faced, after all, was not essentially different from the one I had wrestled with in my own spiritual life. How could I teach the rightful primacy of the things of God, or better, how was I to show that the immediate and necessary temporal occupation could be inspired and governed by love of God and consecrated to Him as worship?

My men, immersed in Army routine and removed from stabilizing influences at home, gravitated toward the attitude that religion was something for Sunday morning. They would not have admitted it as a theory, but they tended to divide life into incommunicable compartments, one labelled "sacred" and the rest "secular." This, as I saw it, was an abdication of their role as Christians. They were called not to abandon the world, but to live in it and to transform it. They were not to be soldiers who were Catholics, or Catholics who were, however temporarily, soldiers, but quite simply and in an incarnational sense, Catholic soldiers. They had, I used to say in an effort to give them a memorable slogan, to make their worship life-like and their lives worshipful. And I believed that if I could help them to attain the first objective, the second would follow, or at least that they would be much more ready for the second. But a conversion takes time, and time was what I didn't have. No fifty-minute classes running through two semesters now. I was compet-ing with field problems that took a third of the regiment out of camp, with reviews and parades and overnight hikes and furloughs that made me wonder, sometimes, exactly how many of my congre-gation ever listened to me on two successive Sundays.

Anyhow, I started. On my first Sunday in camp I told my assistant that there would be no irrelevant hymns during Mass, much less any doodling on the organ. He was a little shocked, and I set about making my first convert by explaining that the congrega-tion should not be distracted from the Mass, since it was their sacri-fice as well as mine. At the offertory, for instance, they should not be made, by singing an Ave Maria, to think of our Lady, since at that moment they should be offering themselves to God under the symbolic offering of their bread and wine. After the Consecration they should not be singing anything, since they should not be dis-tracted from offering their now sublimated gift, and from answering their great Amen. And at the Communion the "grant us peace" idea was at least as important as "O Lord, I am not worthy."

My sermon that first Sunday was on the need and value of using a missal, and I had copies of Father Stedman's pocket missal for distribution. I began mimeographing a weekly news sheet for the Catholics in my regiment, explaining in their logical order the notions of sacrifice, of priesthood, of the unity of all Christians in the Mystical Body, of Communion as the fruit of the sacrifice and the bond of unity. At week-day Mass I gave five minutes to rein-forcing these ideas in the light of the day's feast. I placed my vest-ments on the altar and vested in view of the congregation, explaining each vestment's symbolism as I put it on. I removed the veil and explained the use of the chalice, paten, pall and purificator. At my Nuptial Masses I emphasized briefly the significance of the union just effected as a miniature of the union between Christ and his Church.

I started a Catholic Action cell, which took for its first project the spread of active participation in the Mass. I also started a weekly "Refresher Course in Catholic Thought," in which I tried to show how a number of subjects—the Scriptures, social thought, the theology of grace and redemption, Mariology, the philosophy of art and literature, peace and post-war planning—could be approached end enriched by a study of the Mass. Believing that, in the words of Pius X, the liturgy is "the primary and indispensable source of the true Christian spirit," I gave the liturgy an undisputed first place in practice as well as in theory, until it might establish its rightful precedence over novenas, Holy Hours, etc., in the minds of my flock. I began nightly recitation of Compline with a chosen group, hoping to open it to all comers when I had a nucleus trained. I launched a choir, trying to let them see how much better for community prayer was the eleventh plain chant Mass than César Franck's *Panis Angelicus,* even when the latter was enhanced with a violin obbligato. I moved obstructing flowers and candelabra off the altar, hoping thereby to make the congregation see it as a table of sacrifice instead of a shrine. More than anything, it seemed, I talked; I began to understand what Paul meant with his "proclaim the message and, welcome or unwelcome, insist on it."

By Ascension Thursday I thought I had talked enough. It was time for action. The chapel that night, since I had taken pains to have all Catholics excused from night problems and details, was crowded to capacity. I went out into the sanctuary and told them that the Mass for this high holy day would be a dialogue Mass; everyone would be privileged to make the responses usually made by the server alone. In addition, they would recite chorally with me the Gloria, the Credo, the Sanctus, the Agnus Dei. There had been no rehearsal, no notice of any kind. "Would they catch on?" I wondered as I began Mass. "Would they catch on?"

From the first response there was no doubt. Former altar boys led the way, but by the time we got by the tongue-twisters in the Confiteor everyone was in it, and the Kyrie and Gloria fairly lifted me off my feet. Of course they murdered some pronunciations, but that wasn't important. What was important was that the long-silent had finally been given a voice, and they rejoiced in its use. No doubt they failed to understand much of the Latin, but repetition might help that somewhat, and since the English translation was printed in parallel columns, they could pick up the central ideas. I would long remember this Ascension Day, the birth-cry of the liturgy in this flock of mine. I began to dream of the next step (not to be taken, however, for some time yet), the congregationally-sung high Mass. My mind went back to that luxury I had had as a civilian when Mother Kenny, the superior of the local Sacred Heart Convent, had given her community, as their Christmas gift, a weekly high Mass, and invited me to sing it. Maybe, I dared to hope, I could have it again.

And then, before the octave of the Ascension was over, I was "pulled out" and sent overseas. The first quarter was over. I was far richer in experience; I now knew what "RSO" meant, and "SOP," and I could tell a musette bag from an S-3. I was not keen on leaving all my work just as it had got started, naturally. Frank Gale, my boyishly eager and generous assistant who collaborated enthusiastically in all my efforts, wrote me sad letters later, lamenting the total cessation of all these efforts after my departure. But, like the woman in the Gospel, I had done what I could, and perhaps these men would be readier than they might have been for the reforms that came with the Second Vatican Council twenty years later. Now, they told me, priests were urgently needed beyond the seas, so I put everything *in manus tuas* and shoved off. But I took with me an exultant conviction that it could be done, and a burning desire to see it done where, perhaps, it was needed most.

CHAPTER 4

Hurry Up and Wait

"STAND NOT UPON THE ORDER OF YOUR GOING, BUT GO AT ONCE," was Lady Macbeth's injunction. "Hurry up and wait," was the GI's weary summary of everything relating to Army movement. Does something happen to an efficient administrator once he puts on a uniform, so that everything he touches goes wrong? A civilian handled our embarkation at San Francisco, from Camp Stoneman to the transport, and there wasn't a hitch. With one phone call a civilian in London put me aboard the *Lake Charles* at Southampton for the last leg of the long trip home. But when the Army took care of its own troop movement, things were usually in chaos from start to finish. Prodded by orders demanding the most urgent haste, you raced madly to get somewhere, discovering on arrival that no one knew who you were or why you were there or what all the fuss was about. Over and over the pattern was repeated until finally you developed the GI's cynical resignation, but in the beginning it was a rude shock.

Rumors about my transfer began to reach my ears in the middle of May, and shortly afterward I was "alerted"—notified officially, that is, to prepare for overseas shipment. I went to see the Adjutant.

"Don't get any steam up," he said with a yawn. "You'll have to wait at least two weeks for orders, maybe longer. Then we can probably give you a leave home: ten days or so, plus travel time."

"Would it be OK if I visited New Orleans?" I asked. "Just overnight? I'd hate to leave this part of the country without seeing New Orleans."

"Oh, sure," he answered. "No problem. Just leave me an address where I can reach you if I should have to. I won't, of course, but just in case."

So I gave him Loyola University as my address, and took off with Father Bob Walton, the genial and generous chaplain of the 343rd Regiment next door. But when we reached New Orleans we found that there was a convention of some kind in session, and there was no room at Loyola. So we registered at a hotel and sallied forth to see the sights. It was very pleasant to be in a city again after two months in the back country; we strolled through the narrow, lamp-lit streets of the French quarter, studded with night clubs and antique shops, pushing our way through companies of sailors and girls, and arriving finally at one of the well-known restaurants. They seated us outdoors in a palm garden. It was quaint: brick walls left purposely in a state of disrepair, French and Spanish dishes, a very sweet string orchestra, and so on. On a chance, I ordered "chicken à la bonne femme," surmising that a good Frenchwoman should know how to prepare chicken. And I wasn't disappointed. We sat there by the splashing fountain, with turtles and goldfish swimming in the pool at our feet, listening to the muted strings in the corner and the subdued laughter of many young people at the tables. We watched the flame leap up in the old-fashioned oil lamps and gleam on the glossy palm leaves, and it seemed that I was reading Joseph Conrad again. At last we returned to the hotel, finished the day's Office, and went to bed.

In the morning we went back to the Quarter, this time to the Cathedral, where we offered Mass. The Oblate Fathers, who were very cordial, had us in for coffee and toast and a chat afterward, and we explored the Cabildo at our leisure. It was about eleven when I suggested to Bob that it might be good to call Loyola and see if any messages had been received for me. He pooh-poohed the idea. "You won't hear anything for two weeks yet." So we took pictures of the square and several doorways. I bought a crucifix for my Mass kit. We looked into a shop where I yearned for a few hundred dollars to buy for my nieces the magnificently costumed dolls they had for sale. We went to a Catholic book store for some pamphlets Bob wanted, and gradually we worked our way back to Canal

Street. At noon I decided to call Loyola, but all the booths in the hotel were occupied. It was nearly two when I thought of it again. Then came the shock. I got the switchboard operator at Loyola.

"Father Leonard? Father William Leonard? Oh, Father, I've been trying everywhere to find you. Camp Livingston called at eight o'clock, and then at ten, and again at twelve. You have to be in California tomorrow night."

"Tomorrow night?"

"Yes, Father, and you're to call Colonel Williams right away."

I called Colonel Williams and had the shock confirmed.

"How soon can you get back here?"

"Well, it took us six hours to get down."

"Six hours! Look, Father, this is a must. Get back here as fast as you can travel."

Bob and I checked out of the hotel and went tearing up country. And then, of course, it happened. The engine boiled over. We drained the radiator and filled it again, but with the fierce Louisiana sun on the hood and the evident choking up of the water circulation, we had to hold it down to forty an hour, and I knew that wasn't good enough. At Baton Rouge Bob started to read the Office and I, driving, edged up the pace a little; then Bob drove while I read the Office, and doggoned if it didn't rain—a typical Louisiana cloudburst. We pulled the cover of the convertible down over us, the motor cooled off, and we splashed along at sixty through the storm. Opelousas, Lecompte, Alexandria, Livingston, and Sheridan two hundred miles away. At eight-forty-five we pulled up in front of regimental headquarters. The adjutant dashed down the steps.

"Boy, am I glad to see you. Come in here. Sign these three papers. Here are six copies of your orders. All your stuff is packed and loaded on that recon car. Send me sixteen dollars for your mess bill. Here are your tickets, all the way to Marysville. Goodbye. It's a hundred and twenty-five miles to Shreveport, and you have three hours to make it."

I shook hands with him, with Bob, with Bill Bolton, with my very blue assistant, Frank Gale, and swung into the recon car. Thirty seconds later we were doing fifty an hour, and the needles dropped below fifty only twice from then until 11:45. What a ride!

That old wagon had a front-wheel drive that ground the heart out of it every time the wheels turned. We pounded along through the swamps, swaying around the curves, passing oncoming traffic with a six-inch clearance, listening to the hoots and whistles of the wild life under a moonless, starless sky.

At the airport I had to fight to get all my luggage aboard.

"You can't take that."

"Sorry—Government authorized. Priority. Overseas shipment."

And then the plane came in, and I looked it over. My first flight. She was a pretty job in silver and red but, I thought, awfully small to be venturing out into that endless expanse of sky, that journey to the end of night. Some twenty people went aboard, squired by a solicitous and efficient stewardess. I found my seat, the plane taxied out a few hundred yards, paused, then her propellers really started to spin. With a tremendous roar she trembled all over, seemed to gather all her energies together in an enormous resolution (I had the ridiculous image of a scholastic gathering up the skirt of his cassock to race some of the boys in his class), and rushed forward in a run that seemed at first clumsy and then grew sleek, swift, and confident. Before I realized it we were looking down on Shreveport, a blotch of tiny lights. For a moment I was bewildered, for another moment I wanted very much to get out. Then the resemblance to an ordinary train interior, the passivity of the sleeping passengers, put me at ease. I had the new thrill of seeing the earth as God sees it. There was nothing but the darkness and the stars and the steady hum of the engines. My seat was so comfortable, and I was so tired, and—bump! I woke up to find that we had landed in Dallas. It was one-thirty in the morning. Ten minutes later there was that swift taxiing, the pause, the gathering up of skirts, the rush, and then the sudden ease, like that of a proficient swimmer, boring through the air. I didn't sleep this time, but was wide awake, and had the thrill of circling over Fort Worth, swooping down on the runway, bouncing down and up and down, but with remarkable gentleness, and swinging up to the waiting room. Here, between planes, I noticed the ten-gallon hats of the Texans, the loud talk and boisterous laughter. Then we were gone again, winging toward El Paso; a long hop this time, so I slept an hour or two, waking to stare down at the bad lands of West Texas, the desert barren and yet somehow honest after the lush jungles of Louisiana. It was almost the difference between a prim Yankee schoolmarm and a plump, meretricious, overdressed southern belle. El Paso at eight and off again—miles and miles of grassless, treeless desert. At eleven the Colorado River, a messy, scummed affair, lolling along between slender fringes of green after (I knew) pouring in tumultuous torrents through the Grand Canyon; rather like a dirty old man who, after a misspent youth, has nothing left but an existence.

It was then that I remembered my orders, and took them out to read carefully. As I did I whistled. The orders, despite their length and detail, had been telegraphed. And they came direct from the War Department. I was to report to the Commanding Officer at Camp Beale and then to the Commanding General at my overseas station. It was evident that the latter must have some delicate and highly significant assignment for me; there would be no reason for all this rush otherwise. The orders . . . but the reader should judge for himself:

DA64
WBI14
DCL V WARH NR 115 P
FROM DUNLOP WAR WASHINGTON DC 200534z
TO CO CP LIVINGSTON LA
PRIORITY

WILLIAM J LEONARD CHAPLAIN FIRST LIEU-
TENANT 0544318 USA RELD FR ASGNT AND
DUTY 86TH INFANTRY DIVISION CAMP LIVING-
STON LA ASSIGNED TO PERMANENT STATION
OUTSIDE CONTINENTAL LIMITS OF US TROPI-
CAL CLIMATE SHIPMENT RY 003 PAREN A
PAREN HE WP FR PRESENT STATION TO CAMP
BEALE CALIFORNIA PAREN WAR 39028 PAREN
REPORTING NOT LATER THAN MAY 23 44 TO
COMMANDING OFFICER ASF PERSONNEL RE-
PLACEMENT DEPOT TO AWAIT CALL OF PORT

COMMANDER UPON ARRIVAL FINAL DESTINA-
TION WILL REPORT TO COMMANDING GEN-
ERAL FOR DUTY PCS TDN 1-5000 P 431-01
COMMA 02 COMMA 03 COMMA 07 COMMA 08 A
0425-24 CLOTHING TROPICAL AND EQUIPMENT
AS PRESCRIBED IN TE 21 COMMA DECEMBER 15
43 AND CHANGE THERETO WILL BE TAKEN EX-
CEPT THAT ONE SET OF WOOLEN OUTER GAR-
MENTS WILL BE TAKEN FOR COMFORT EN
ROUTE PONCHO WILL BE SUBSTITUTED FOR
RAINCOAT SERVICE HAT RAYON CORD AND
CHIN STRAP ARE NOT AUTHORIZED HERRING-
BONE TWILL CLOTHING ONE OR TWO PIECE AS
APPLICABLE AUTHORIZED AT RATE OF THREE
SUITS PER OFFICER CANTEEN MAY BE
ALUMINUM PLASTIC OR STAINLESS STEEL AD-
DITIONAL EQUIPMENT AUTHORIZED ONE
TRUNK LOCKER MAY BE TAKEN OR SHIPPED
ONE MATTRESS COVER ONE FIRST AID PACKET
CHOLERA AND TYPHUS IMMUNIZATIONS WILL
BE ADMINISTERED TO OFFICER IMMEDIATELY
TEMPORARY ADDRESS CARE ASF PERSONNEL
REPLACEMENT DEPOT PROVISION POR AP-
PLIES.

Well, I hadn't been in the Army very long, but obviously I had made quite an impression if I could be singled out in this fashion, if all this meticulous care could be expended on my clothing and equipment. I was too exhilarated even to wonder much about the responsibilities and possible dangers involved in my new, mysterious assignment. It was clear that the top brass thought I could handle them and, by George, I could.

At last we came down into Tucson, flat and brown. We stretched our legs, looked into the uncompromising sun, and took off once more. As we neared Palm Springs the going became rougher, and I was suddenly aware of a revolt in my interior. The stewardess gave me half a lemon to suck, and opened a ventilator that blew a stream of fresh air in my face, but to no avail. As we stooped over Palm Springs I was humiliated. And, since it was a military airport, they wouldn't let us out of the plane, where I might have walked about for a few minutes and put down the revolt. However, there were no more outbreaks; just an uneasiness which I gradually forgot as we circled around, gaining more and more altitude and passing finally over the last range of mountains. Then came the great thrill. We were above the clouds, flying down the San Bernardino Valley in California. It was superb. All about and under us were white puffs that curtained off any view of the ground. It was like lying on a limitless counterpane of fluffy, immaculate white balls. I looked out and thought how aviation had answered the dreams of the generations, from Icarus and the Magic Carpet to Leonardo da Vinci and the Wright brothers. I waited for the moment when we would plunge down through those swirling clouds and break into the smiling valley I knew lay beneath. I was not disappointed. We pointed our nose down, there was a long moment of fog, then we were clear, and the green of the country around Los Angeles was in full sight. Square miles of orchards, long ribbons of roads, an air of peace and blessed abundance. At Los Angeles one noticed the welting and fake foliage camouflaging the airport against possible Japanese air attack, and wondered if that rouged creature were one of the stars of Moviedom. Dinner was served on the last hop of the journey (compliments of the airline), and finally we came down into South San Francisco, where all the buildings were gleaming white stucco, and the afternoon sun was mellow.

Aboard the bus for Marysville, I talked with a Chief Petty Officer going home to Oakland after two years in the South Seas. He hadn't notified his wife that he was back in the country; "wanted to surprise her," he said. I've often wondered if she survived the surprise. After Oakland we cut north toward Sacramento and the end of the long trail. I sat and smoked, looking out into the placid evening; it was good to see hills again. Across the aisle a brazen thing gave up her giggling conversation with two GI's and turned the battery of her charms on me. She couldn't see the cross on my left collar wing, just the bar on my right, and thought that I was better game than the rankless privates. I continued to admire the scenery, and after three attempts she gave up.

"You and your pipe," she snorted.

I chuckled and the bus rolled on. Marysville at last, and the Army bus to Camp Beale. I signed in at eleven-forty. My orders read: "not later than 23 May 44," and I had made it. But at what a cost. No leave home, no chance to say goodbye to good friends at Livingston, no opportunity to do more than cast yearning glances at cities and country I should have loved to explore on foot. Well, it was necessary, no doubt, and probably I'd be rushed out of Beale in a day or so to whatever urgent work awaited me. So I sat at Beale for three weeks, and spent three weeks on a slow boat to Guinea, and languished in a casual camp for six weeks after that. "Hurry up and wait," said the GI's.

"Long Ago and Far Away," Jerome Kern's last popular song, was a hit that summer, and its melancholy thirds kept pouring out of every radio. I shall always associate it and the brown grass, burned early by the California sun, with this period of waiting. There was little to do. We had a "seminar" forsooth, on the duties of the chaplain overseas, another gas mask drill, a drill in pitching tents and the use of the compass. To forestall boredom I went out on the range and fired the carbine. The company of other priests in my group was the saving feature. There were five besides myself in Shipment RY-003(A). Two diocesan priests, Father Bill Galvin from Little Rock and Father Joe Durney from St. Louis; a Dominican, Father Frank Regan; a Benedictine, Father Bede Michel; and a Precious Blood Father, Father Harold Roth. We hadn't the remotest notion where we were going, or when, or what would happen to us when we got there, but we were together for nine weeks, and the gaiety of the group kept any one of us from thinking long thoughts. When yet another lecture was announced, and we groaned, the irrepressible Rothy would grin and say, "Hup two, boys. On the ball or on the boat." So we'd grin, too, and go. When we had been in the kunai grass and the mud of the Fifth Replacement Depot for two eternal weeks, with no orders, no mail, no baths, no hope and little charity for the Army brass, Father Ed Tanski, with unforgettable generosity and thoughtfulness, came down from Oro Bay in his jeep and drove us to Cape Sudest for a swim. We wallowed in the salt water for hours, not knowing when we'd get another bath, and at last Bede swam in and stood up, water streaming off his bald head and bushy eyebrows.

"War is hell," he said, "but it's improving."

Among the official papers I took away from Livingston was one signed by the Regimental Adjutant. "To whom it may concern," it read, "This is to certify that Chaplain (1st Lt.) William Leonard, 0544318, is POR qualified except for the running of the infiltration course day and night." I was the person most concerned, as it turned out. One day all of us who hadn't run the course were herded into trucks and driven some miles to a level area about eighty yards long, with a dry ditch at either end. Opposite us were two machine guns mounted on concrete emplacements; we were told that they would fire live ammunition over us at a height of thirty inches. "Keep your head down, and your tail, too, if you want to save them." Then they told us we'd have to go through two barbed wire entanglements, and showed us how it was done: you turned on your back and lifted the wire strand by strand over your body, inching along meanwhile until you were through. Oh, yes, and at intervals along the course there were craters, in which charges of dynamite would be set off to simulate exploding shells. "Don't go too near those craters." It was all quite convincingly realistic.

Before we started I had a funny feeling in my stomach, and made an Act of Contrition in case the bullets went astray. Then the order was given; the guns began to chatter. We slid very cautiously out of our ditch and began to creep toward the far end. The young boys in the group went along with a speed that discouraged me; I was using muscles I hadn't used since I was in rompers, and never had I had a sharper reminder that my youth was over. I hadn't covered fifteen yards before I forgot the whining bullets and the dynamite. I had only one anxiety: how could I possibly get to the other end of that course? It ran across dry, dusty red clay, littered with small sharp rocks that dug into you, cut your hands, lacerated your forearms and your knees. But the worst thing was the sun. It was a little after noon, and the temperature was over a hundred—how much I didn't know. After a while I got to the first barbed wire, and found that lying on my back was an agreeable relief. How I crossed the fifty yards to the second entanglement I couldn't now say. Several times I had to quit and wait till the exhaustion passed. I hadn't known I had so many muscles that could ache. At long last I rolled into the ditch at the far end, sixth-last in a group of a hundred, and lay there waiting for the guns to stop. One by one the other tail-enders arrived, but the most pathetic case was our Jewish chaplain, forty-one years old, who finished last. He had not worn his glasses, poor chap, and his vision was so poor that he lost his direction and kept crawling this way and that over the course. He must have covered twice as much distance as we did. I had to lift him into the truck, and he simply sat there, huddled and silent all the way back. He needed a good stimulant but it couldn't be bought on the post until evening, so we poured cokes into him and left him on his bunk. *Postume, Postume, labuntur anni.* Those kids who were with us were done in temporarily, but fresh as daisies in the PX that night. The rabbi and I agreed that we would kill in cold blood any radical fool who, after the war, uttered a syllable about the clergy who stayed home instead of fighting.

On the night of June 5th I returned from the Officers' Club, where I had been writing letters, to the barracks, and found a knot of men around a tiny radio, very intent. "The invasion is on," they told me, "at least according to a German report." I sat on my bunk, listening. News commentators were stretching their fragments of information as far as they could, warning at the same time that no Allied confirmation of D-Day had been given. NBC would broadcast through the night. We finally gave up and went to bed, but next morning everyone's morale was sky-high. We, of course, were headed in the opposite direction, but the fall of Rome and now the Normandy invasion gave us hope—not, we prayed, illusory—that it would not be too long for us, either. We speculated not so much on the success of the assault on Europe (we took that for granted) as on the speed with which our full power could be concentrated against the Japs, so that the last mess could be cleaned up, and we could go home. "Home"; that was the magic word for every officer and man. "Let's finish the business and go home."

At the Officers' Club, between news bulletins, I talked to a private who swept the floors and washed the glasses. He was thirty-seven years old, had emigrated from Germany in 1928, become a citizen, struggled for a few years to make a living during the Depression, and was now in the Army. He had three brothers in the German army, and a brother in the American army in England. Fratricide, literally. All he wanted to do, he said, was to get out, make a little money, go back to visit his mother and father in Leipsig, and live in peace. In 1923, he told me, twenty-two of his forty-four schoolmates had died of malnutrition (he called it starvation). He talked of his visit home in 1936, when he went to see the Olympic Games in Berlin.

"Fifty-two nations combeted, and were at beace. Why not now? Vite beople in the vorld, ve kill each other. Bretty soon yellow beople, black beople, they kill us."

Quousque, Domine?

One week-end Father Bill Galvin and I visited San Francisco. We were given a warm reception by the Fathers at the University, and I found it delightful to be back in a Jesuit community—a home away from home in more ways than the hotel advertisements dream of. But I had another mission. Our family had cousins in the city whom we had never met, and one of them, I knew, was a priest. So Bill and I went down to the waterfront, to a club for sailors called "The Apostleship of the Sea," and there we found Father Edward Lenane, a big man with currents of energy pouring from him and an exceedingly genial laugh. We shook hands all round and sat down; he was P.O.E. Chaplain for the Navy, and was used to having chaplains drop in from nowhere. After a while he said to me,

"What did you say your name was, Father? Leonard, eh? Almost the same as mine, eh?"

Then he talked about something else, while Father Galvin, who was in on the joke, winked at me. At last I asked him if he had ever visited the East.

"Not much," he said. "We have some distant cousins there, though."

I stood up. "Father, let me introduce one of them. I'm your long-lost cousin."

He stared. "You're pulling my leg," he said.

"No, really. It's a fact."

"Tell you what," he said finally. "My cousin—my real cousin—Mike Scanlon is coming in any minute, and he knows the whole family tree. I'll just give him your name and we'll see what he says."

A few minutes later in walked Mike. Gray-haired, spare of figure, direct and unsmiling, a real Irishman if ever I saw one.

"Hello, Mike," said Father Lenane. "I have a couple of friends I'd like you to meet. This is Father Galvin, from Little Rock."

They shook hands.

"And this is Father Leonard."

Mike cocked his head on one side. "What did you say your name was?"

I smiled, "Leonard, Mike."

"Would you be from Boston?" he asked.

"I would."

"Would your father's name be William?"

"It would."

"Would you have an Uncle Phil, in the weights and measures?"

"I would indeed."

"Then you're my cousin," he said with finality, and sat down. How we roared. This was the anagnorisis of Greek drama, the "I see it all now" of Dion Boucicault.

"And to think," Father Ed spluttered, "that I was on the point of calling you a fake."

Our enforced idleness at Camp Beale ended at last, and we moved to Camp Stoneman for three days. Then, on the day we were to board the transport, all the chaplains in the shipment (six priests, six ministers, and a rabbi) were sent into San Francisco on a truck to pick up supplies at the P.O.E. Afterward I went to see Father Ed again.

"Why don't you call home?" he asked.

"No," I answered. "My father might be working late, or Eleanor might be out, and they'd feel badly if they missed my call. Besides, we haven't time; I have to report in an hour, and you couldn't get Boston in less than five hours. And anyhow, I'm afraid. I'll break down if I have to say goodbye, and I can't tell them I'm going."

"Nonsense," was all he said, and reached for the phone. "Operator, this is Father Lenane, at the Apostleship of the Sea U.S.O. I have an emergency call I simply must get through to Boston, right away. Can you help me out?"

He hung up and I shook my head, but ten minutes later the phone rang and there they were. After a while my father's voice dropped to a strictly-in-confidence, I-won't-tell-your-mother-and-sister tone.

"When are you sailing?"

"Yes," I answered, "and it's very warm out here, too." I'd have been court-martialed if I'd told him over an open wire that a transport was sailing in an hour. Then Father Ed took the phone out of my hands and wouldn't let me say goodbye. I'd have made a very bad job of it.

On the way to the pier in Oakland I was assigned to sit in the cab of a truck which was carrying our luggage. To my amazement, a young lady jumped up into the cab and started the engine.

"Hey, what goes on?" I exclaimed.

She laughed, "I'm the driver."

"Egad," I said, "what next?" She told me many women were doing that sort of heavy work on the Coast; the men were all in the shipyards or on the docks. Then she looked curiously at my cross and asked what church I belonged to. I had noted her Italian features, so I said,

"Roman Catholic, of course." Well, she was one, too, though she admitted she didn't work very hard at it. I had only the length of time it took to cross the long Oakland Bridge, but I was glad that the last conversation I had on American soil gave me that opportunity to witness to my faith.

We stood on deck and watched as the San Francisco waterfront slipped by. We passed under the Golden Gate Bridge and strained our eyes to catch a last glimpse of it as it faded over the horizon.

How salt the severing sea!

CHAPTER 5

Blue Distance

"NOW HEAR THIS," RASPED THE LOUDSPEAKER. "IT IS NOW OFFI-cial black-out time. Close all portholes and black-out screens. There will be no more smoking on the open deck. The smoking lamp is out." For the next three weeks our lives were ruled by that P.A. system. "All troops report to boat-stations on the double." "Submarine watch begins today at eighteen hundred."

I had my own turn over the loudspeaker. There were, as we suddenly realized, no morning or evening newspapers, so each day I got the news bulletins from the captain and wrote my own presenta-tions for broadcasting to the ship's company. There was little to give beyond war dispatches and baseball scores, but I tried to spread it as far as possible, inserting wisecracks and local references. I couldn't give, of course, what the men wanted most, news of their own home towns.

We were on a Dutch ship, the *Noordam*. In peacetime she had carried passengers and freight; now the officers on board were the passengers—at least they had the cabins—and the GI's were the freight, stowed in the holds. We six priests were crammed into a cabin designed originally for one, or at most two. It was thoroughly uncomfortable, but palatial when compared to the lot of the enlisted men below decks. We saw almost nothing of the ship's officers, who were Dutch, because we had our own troop commander with staff, but the Javanese stewards interested us, especially when we saw them squatting on their heels on the deck, hour after hour, in a position which we could not maintain without cramps.

We had no idea where we were going, and speculation, though it went on constantly, was profitless. Amateur navigators on board tried to establish our position, but could give us no certainty within a thousand miles, so they were not much help. Most of us knew very little about the South Seas. Some reading of novels and the National Geographic had given us vague images of coral beaches fringed with palm trees, outriggers manned by brown natives who harpooned fish and were fascinated by trinkets from Woolworth's. We had no very clear ideas, most of us, about the geography of the South Pacific, or the general plan of attack that was steadily winning back the islands the Japs had conquered on their first overwhelming thrust to the very shores of Australia. The tireless publicity of the Marines had made Guadalcanal a household word, of course, but names like Sanananda or Buna meant little to us. To this day the superb march of the 32nd Division over the Owen Stanley Mountains, catching the Japs from behind and driving them into the sea at Buna, is still looking for its historian, a Livy for its Hannibal.

One opinion that was widely accepted on shipboard for a time was that we were to be assigned to garrisons on outlying islands, relieving troops that had been over here from the beginning. I reflected wryly that of the books I'd always said I'd take with me to a desert island—the Bible, my Breviary and Missal, Shakespeare, and a good anthology of English poetry—I had only the Breviary and Missal. These two, of course, contained many passages from the Bible, but I regretted not having the complete text. As for the poetry, I was to learn how little time a chaplain, even in a rear-echelon unit, can claim for leisurely reading.

As our flight across the very placid Pacific continued, curiosity about our eventual destination was dulled by the steady routine of life on board. The ship's engines never paused, and the days began to blur, so that we had to count on our fingers in order to remember how long it was since we sailed. Occasionally, with a sinking of the heart, one recalled that all this blue distance would have to be traversed again before we saw loved faces and heard loved voices. And occasionally, too, one realized that this was anything but a pleasure cruise; once or twice the watch thought it saw a periscope, "General Quarters" was sounded, and I could feel my scalp prickling. Would all one's fine theories about the brevity of this life, the worth of eternity, and so on, collapse in the face of imminent death? I prayed not; I prayed against panic. Life could suddenly grow dear, though. And then, in a swift slide from the tragic to the farcical, I thought of Father Faber's truly Victorian, truly bombastic hymn to Our Lady,

> "O Mother, I could weep for mirth,
> Such gladness fills my soul . . .
> I think of thee and what thou art . . .
> O could the transport last!"

This transport had better last!

Looking off, day after day, across the tranquil, limitless sea made prayer easier. The engrossing, but really petty concerns of everyday living began to assume their true proportions, and one's spirit, delivered from trifles, was free to soar a little, to warm itself in the sun of God's love. At the same time, remembering how difficult I found it to be conscious of God's presence in ordinary circumstances, I used to feel some embarrassment. Why could I not turn to him more easily, even in the midst of absorbing occupations, and especially when I was perplexed or troubled or fatigued?

Religion has for its ultimate purpose union with God. Holy men of all ages and varieties of opinion have, like Enoch, sought to walk with God, to live in his presence. Life has been good when God was close, arduous and dreary when He seemed absent. We have all looked back wistfully to Eden, when God walked with his first creatures in the cool of the evening. The Jews, once settled in the Land of Promise, looked back nostalgically to the days of the patriarchs, when the uncluttered sky arching over the desert seemed to betoken his presence hovering over and enveloping them. Latter-day Christians are tempted to think longingly of the infant Church, when signs and prodigies on every side confirmed the faith and made God very near indeed. And how many of us, afflicted and lonely in our adult years, have remembered sadly the childhood days when faith was untroubled and God, approving and solicitous, was as close as our parents? If we could recover that vivid sense of his presence, it would be easy to pray again, and confidently, the 23rd Psalm:

> Yea, though I pass through a dark valley,
> I will fear no evil, for you are with me.

There are obvious values for the spiritual life in being aware of God's presence. One may turn to him at any moment of the day to adore, to give thanks, to ask for what one needs. He is not Majesty enthroned in the distant heaven so much as the gracious Companion in life's ways. A union of my will with his is more likely, much easier, if I am conscious that he is here now, loving me as he always has ("with an everlasting love," as Jeremiah says). Anxieties and fears, the twentieth-century neuroses, dissolve and melt away in the radiant assurance of his fatherly care, and I can be contented, even merry, as I move with him across the years. We less spiritually sensitive men are puzzled sometimes when we read how the saints, who could endure almost every anguish, found "the dark night of the soul," when God seemed to have abandoned them, so distressing. I remember reading a pathetic prayer composed by the Greek Gregory, Bishop of Nazianzus:

> Alas, dear Christ, the Dragon is here again.
> Alas, he is here; terror has seized me, and fear.
> Alas that I ate of the fruit of the tree of knowledge,
> Alas that his envy led me to envy, too.
> I did not become like God; I was cast out of paradise.
> Temper, sword, awhile, the heat of your flames
> And let me go again about the garden,
> Entering with Christ, a thief from another tree.

But it would be easy to find similar passages in the writings even of the most seraphic of the saints. They knew better than we that the most terrifying sentence a man or woman could hear from the lips of the Lord is "Depart from me."

It occurred to me that certain trends in contemporary thought were making it easier to realize that God is present to us in love. We have become aware, for instance, that there is a valid theology of history, which ponders the entire sweep of human experience and sees a design in it. Our renewed study of sacred history, of God's activity in his world, has restored to us (even as modern science makes us acknowledge how enormously complex the world is) our confidence in the purpose and pattern of things, in the serene dominion of the Lord of history who attains his ends *suaviter sed fortiter.* Even our return to scriptural and liturgical language, with its emphasis on the sovereignty and majesty of the most high God, has served to remind us that it is precisely these attributes which should give us confidence.

> Aeons ago, you laid earth's foundations,
> The heavens are the work of your hands;
> All will vanish, though you remain,
> All wear out like a garment;
> Like clothes that need changing you will change them;
> But yourself, you never change, and your years are unending.

> Glory to God in the highest, and on earth peace to men of good will. We praise you, we bless you, we adore you, we glorify you; we give you thanks for your great glory, Lord God, heavenly King, Father almighty.

> O God, who give unity to the minds of the faithful, grant that your people may love what you command, and desire what you promise, so that among the changing things of this world our hearts may be fixed where true joys are to be found, through our Lord Jesus Christ your Son, who lives and reigns with you in the unity of the Holy Spirit, forever and ever.

From the oaks of Mambre and the burning bush down to this year's paschal candle, sacred history, I knew, provides a succession of signs that God is present to the world he made and active in the human souls he loves. He calls Abraham out of Chaldea across the Fertile Crescent into Canaan. He suffers himself to be wrestled and even to be pinned by Jacob. He sends Joseph into Egypt so that the brimming granaries of that country may one day feed his starving people. When the people have been enslaved, he summons Moses to lead them, the saving blood still wet on their doorposts, across the impassable sea to freedom. He goes before them in a pillar of cloud and fire, gives them food from heaven and water from arid rock, punishes them when they are disobedient with a plague of serpents. In their own land at last, he gives them judges and prophets, and anoints their kings. At last, in the fullness of time, he sends them his living portrait, Christ, "the image of the invisible God." And as if to prove that the power of evil has not banished his presence from the world, he raises his dead Son from the tomb and makes him "both Lord and Christ" over that world until its consummation. He is here still, and the signs of his presence are bread and wine, water and oil and lifted hand, candle flames that leap up in the darkness and beckon to his altar or simply the coming together of two or three in his name. Christians are beginning to long, as the first Christians did, for his coming again, for the fullness of his visible presence, when the dawn shall have broken and the shadows fled away. But they are sustained meanwhile by the knowledge that he, the strong, the immortal, the gloriously living and reigning Christ, is present to them now.

Among my favorite passages in Isaiah was the prophecy that in Christ, God would be "Emmanuel," "God-with-us." To prepare the way for that stupendous presence, the Jews had been instructed to erect a tent and later, a temple which would indicate that he was their God and they his people, that he dwelt in their midst and would protect and prosper them. Solomon knew that the temple itself was only a symbol of the divine presence; on the day of its dedication he stood before the altar in the sight of the assembly of Israel and prayed aloud:

> Yet will God really live with men on the earth? Why,
> the heavens and their own heavens cannot contain you.
> How much less this house that I have built!

Nevertheless, the temple became the heart of Jewish religious life:

> How lovely is your dwelling place,
>   O Lord of hosts!
> My soul yearns and pines
>   for the courts of the Lord.
> I had rather one day in your courts
>   than a thousand elsewhere;
> I had rather lie at the threshold
>   of the house of my God,
> Than dwell in the tents of the wicked.

The Jews for centuries converged in pilgrimage upon the holy city, singing their "songs of ascent":

How I rejoiced when they said to me,
    "Let us go to the house of the Lord!"
And now our feet are standing
    in your gateways, Jerusalem.

Jerusalem restored! The city,
    one united whole!
Here the tribes come up
    the tribes of the Lord.

They come to praise the Lord's name,
    as he ordered Israel,
Here where the tribunals of justice are,
    the royal tribunals of David.

Pray for peace in Jerusalem.
    "Prosperity to your houses!
Peace inside your city walls!
    Prosperity to your palaces"

Since all are my brothers and friends,
    I say, "Peace be with you"
Since the Lord our God lives there,
    I pray for your happiness.

Our Lord's earthly life was intimately bound up with the Temple. It was there, forty days after his birth, that he was presented by his mother and St. Joseph. He "went up" to it each year in accordance with the Law. During the Judean phase of his ministry he taught there daily, after casting out from its sacred precincts the buyers and sellers who had been making it a public market. He scandalized the Pharisees by predicting its destruction, and at the hour of his death the veil that had closed its inner sanctuary was torn asunder, indicating that the Presence which had dwelt there was departing forever. For greater than the Temple, he himself, "in whom dwells all the fullness of the divinity," had come, and people "saw his glory" as they had once seen it in the Tent of Meeting in the wilderness. God had "pitched his tent" once more on the earth. Now they might enter through the veil of Christ's flesh, as the Letter to the Hebrews tells us, and approach with confidence the throne of grace. In Christ, God came to meet human creatures visibly, to be present to them. They could ask "through Christ our Lord" and it would be granted to them.

But Christ has joined to himself a multitude past counting. Christians are, as both Peter and Paul assure us, "living stones," built on Christ the cornerstone "into a house where God lives." So the Temple that betokens God's presence in the world is now his Church; not a structure of wood or stone, obviously, but that sacred fellowship which will abide "always, yes, to the end of time" precisely because it is the sacrament of his presence to the men and women he has loved. The Church is the sign of his presence, and therefore we shall find him in the Church. Prayer offered in and through the Church will gain a hearing. Sinners are reconciled with the Church (whom they have offended, also) and through her. To whom shall we go, then, out of the cold and dark? To whom shall we cling, believing against belief, if not to her? "Love the brotherhood," Paul tells us, for this is to love Christ, to love God.

> Jerusalem, if I forget you,
> May my right hand wither!

The Church, more truly than Eve, is "mother of all the living." Through her sacraments God prolongs the history of salvation; they are, in Schillebeeckx' fine phrase, "the pledge of God's availability." In the "character" imparted by baptism, confirmation, and holy orders there is a "brimming presence," as Carré says, never drained, never withdrawn. In the Eucharistic meal we have a foretaste of that eternal communion when "God shall be all in all."

But the individual Christian is himself a temple of the Most High. "If anyone love me," our Lord said, "He will keep my word, and my Father will love him, and we shall come to him, and make our home with him." The mystery of this indwelling, this pervasion of our being by the loving God, is so overwhelming that it may even have frightened us away from pondering it very much, but surely we should pay more hospitable attention to the Guest in our house. He comes not to inundate our own personality but to transfigure it, to lift it to the plane of his mode of living.

It was abundantly clear to me, after six months in the Army, that scholarly seclusion, cloistered solitude, even decent privacy were things I had bade farewell to "for the duration." If I were to pray I should have to find God in my situation, and above all in my companions. Well, was not this what my training had prepared me for, and in a measure was it not the kind of life I had already been living for many years? Mine was not a monastic vocation. My teacher and exemplar was Ignatius of Loyola, whose distinguishing grace had been the ability to see and contemplate in every object, action, and conversation the presence of God, to remain a contemplative even in the midst of action. His broadly sacramental approach to God was the one he wanted his sons to use, too, for in the Constitutions he wrote for the Society of Jesus he sets it down that in their dealings with one another they are to

> show no signs of impatience or pride, but are to seek and desire to yield to others the better part, esteeming all in their hearts as their superiors and giving to each one outwardly the honor and reverence which everyone's state requires, with simplicity and religious moderation, and so it will come about that, considering one another, they will increase in devotion and praise our Lord God, whom everyone should strive to recognize in another as in his image.

In solving the difficult problem of how much time the young Jesuits should spend in prayer during their training, St. Ignatius explained his thinking on the presence of God at greater length:

> In view of their goal of study, the scholastics cannot have prolonged meditations. But over and above the exercises which they have for the sake of virtue, namely, to hear Mass daily, an hour for saying prayers and for the examen of conscience, and confession and communion every eight days, they can exercise themselves in seeking the presence of God in all things, such as their conversations, their walks, in all that they see, taste, hear, and understand, and in all their actions, since it is true that the divine Majesty is in all things by his presence, power, and essence. This

manner of meditating, which finds God in all things, is
easier than raising ourselves to the consideration of divine things which are more abstract, and to which we
can make ourselves present only with effort. This good
exercise, by exciting good dispositions in us, will bring
great visitations from the Lord, even though they occur
in a short prayer. In addition to this, one can frequently
offer to God our Lord his studies and the effort they
demand, seeing that we undertake them for his love
while sacrificing our personal tastes, in order that in
something we may be of service to the divine Majesty
by helping those for whom He died.

The *Noordam,* after all, was a symbol, like the Ark of Noah.
The community aboard her was a miniature of the human community that rides our planet. Most of us, I think, had no great taste for
our adventure, but we felt constrained to see it through, and this
created a bond of solidarity that overrode our individual differences.
It also created a mutual respect, an appreciation of the courage that
enabled each man to govern his anxieties and to carry on with a
resolution which, if it was not heroic, was at least sturdy. We might
break and panic in the face of imminent danger (I suppose it was
one of our anxieties that we might do this), but we didn't want to,
we hoped we wouldn't, and meanwhile we intended to keep going
on. In spite, therefore, of certain unlovely outcroppings of human
selfishness that became occasionally visible at close quarters, it was
possible to love all these men, to find God in them at least as surely
as one might find him in a sunset. And in many of them, of course,
his face shone forth with a beauty and winsomeness that won the
heart forever.

On week-days we offered Mass on the grand piano in the officers' lounge; young Clyde Nash, from Kansas, never missed a
morning as my server. I doubt that my Mass has ever been graced
by more real innocence and more single-minded love of God than
he brought to it. When we landed in Guinea, he went off to fly
C-47's out of Nadzab, and six months later—though I myself did
not hear of it for a full year—he was shot down somewhere near
Biak. There could be only one inscription for his grave, I felt: "Of
such is the Kingdom of Heaven."

On Sunday one of us offered Mass on the open deck. I remember, on the Fourth Sunday after Pentecost (Old Style) wondering almost with amusement if the Mass had been composed for our situation. It opened, for instance, with an act of faith for wartime:

The Lord is my light and my salvation: whom shall I fear?
The Lord is the defense of my life: whom shall I dread?
When evildoers assail me, to devour me,
My enemies and my foes, they stumble and fall.
Though an army should encamp against me, my heart
shall not fear.

The Collect asked for the gift that, as a matter of fact, we wanted badly.

"Grant, we beseech you, Lord, that the affairs of this world may be peaceably ordered for us by your direction of them, and that your Church may find joy in untroubled devotion."

The first reading laid great stress on the meaning of waiting, that Army word, that human word. "Brethren," said St. Paul, "I think that what we suffer in this life can never be compared to the glory, as yet unrevealed, which is waiting for us . . . From the beginning till now the entire creation, as we know, has been groaning in one great act of giving birth; and not only creation, but all of us who possess the first fruits of the Spirit, we too groan as we wait for our bodies to be set free."

I took the text for my sermon from the Gospel: "He began to teach the multitude from the boat," and it was an easy development: the many things about himself and about ourselves God would teach us on this voyage if we would listen to Him. But the sermon I was preaching to myself dealt rather with the apostolic commission given to my ancestral bishop, St. Peter, and through him to me: "Let down your nets for a catch." I was beginning to see that this chaplaincy was my own greatest apostolic opportunity—perhaps the best opportunity the Church would have in my century. I could say, with much more truth than Peter, "I am a sinful man, O Lord." But Peter, though he booted things egregiously, could and did come through in the clutch, when it counted. Maybe the Lord would help me to do likewise. I found that some verses from the Psalms kept coming to my mind:

> "God, you know how foolish I have been,
> My offences are not hidden from you,
> But let those who hope in you
> not blush for me,
> O Lord of hosts,
> Let those who seek you not be ashamed of me,
> God of Israel."

At such times it was very comforting to remember the morning of my ordination at Weston, the pressure of the bishop's commissioning hands on my head. "But Jesus said to Simon, 'Do not be afraid; from now on it is men you will catch.' "

I never knew that men wrote so many letters. The number of correspondents on the ship exceeded even those engaged in crap games, sun-bathing, or comic-reading. One day, sitting on a bench on the port side, out of the sun, I glanced absently to my right and saw, before I could look away, a sheet of stationery headed "My darling wife." On my left was a boy who would write a paragraph and then stare at the sea. He looked pretty blue, poor lad. Would these lads be better off without the ties that bound them so tight? What would it be like to be thick-skinned, nonchalant? I could remember envying such Olympian beings sometimes—until I learned that men were better than gods, at least the gods of Olympus, and that the true God, who created men to love, punished sinners who abused love by taking love away from them, here as well as hereafter.

Letter-writing was, at any rate, the great sea-going occupation, whether it served simply to chase ennui or to remember happier things. I myself found it curious and a little difficult to write without the usual taking-off from circumstances. "Let me see; what can I tell you without violating any of the rules of a very rigorous censor? I am on a ship. I have not, thank God, been seasick. I am well and more-or-less happy. I hope you are the same. The sunsets are lovely. The food is wonderful. I hope we shall have a safe voyage (oh boy, how I hope it)." Beyond that, I wasn't always sure, when I looked in on my material for writing (the raw material inside my head and heart, I mean), how accessible it would be. Sometimes I could get at it, and again I couldn't. Sometimes I had to wrench and tear at it for a long time before it came tumbling out to be shipped home in parcels neat or ragged according to my ability at the moment to wrap it up in syllables. Sometimes I would look at it and decide that it was just too fluid or too unruly for packaging. Why burden those at home with one's own moods? When one couldn't describe the immediate circumstances or narrate interesting incidents the perpendicular pronoun tended to exclude all the others from one's vocabulary. And the net effect on oneself was not healthy, either.

About this time I borrowed Tom Wolfe's *You Can't Go Home Again* from the ship's library, hoping that I might now reach a more sympathetic understanding of him and of some of my former students, who had idolized him. But I couldn't finish the book. Perhaps it was my early exposure to the classics (*"meden agan"* said the Greeks; *"ne quid nimis,"* said the Romans). I wanted strong feeling, but I wanted the lid kept on. Wolfe exhausted and bored me with his incessant spoutings; even the self-confessed romantic poets had shown more reticence, more art. I reflected that this reticence, this objectivity, was one of the beauties that drew me to the Roman liturgy. No spouting in those exquisite, chiseled collects, that said so much in so few words, and with such rhythmic perfection that one dared not add or subtract a syllable when the climactic cadences died away. No spouting in the majestic Prefaces, or in the great doxology that concludes the Canon and catches the very accent of adoration: "through him and with him and in him, in the unity of the Holy Spirit, all glory and honor is yours, almighty Father, for ever and ever, Amen." "Amen" indeed. There is nothing one can add to that.

My loafing went on into its fifth week. Life at B.C. was never like this, I told myself. I noticed how my memory began to play games with me. One day I found myself staring over the water and remembering a summer evening when I was about ten years old. I was meeting my father as he came home from work. I could feel under my hand the texture of the cement wall I was leaning against; I could see my father crossing the field from the train, wearing his straw hat and carrying his folded newspaper. "Now what brought that up?" I asked myself. Another picture, flashed into my mind with no apparent association or cause, was of a boyhood Christmas morning; I could see the snow on the hill outside our home, and I was fondling a new pair of skates. In the kitchen, where my mother was, I could hear the preparations for dinner, and my sister Cath (what a little tow head she was then!) was admiring that big doll of hers. My brother Fran must have been off on one of his surreptitious expeditions; he doesn't appear in the picture. In still later images I was driving Father Carroll's car around the bend of Beacon Street, by the Reservoir, looking up at the towers on the Heights. Or I was walking up and down under the lindens outside the Library, reading my Office, and the coaches were shouting to the football team down on Alumni Field. It amused and perplexed me; I didn't call up these pictures, they came unbidden—things I thought had forgotten.

I got to wondering one day about writing the story of all this. It couldn't be a novel; I have no "invention," as the old rhetoricians used to call it, for plot or character. It would have to be autobiography; "The Mountains Were in Labor," I might call it, or "The Foolish and the Weak" (things God chooses to confound the wise and the strong). The advantage would be that I would need no reference library, and I'd certainly have none for a long while. Memory would provide the library—not, alas, too well catalogued, and much of it inconsequential stuff, and some rooms very definitely closed to the public. Come to think of it, why should I parade my intellectual and spiritual poverty at all? If I kept quiet fewer people would suspect the truth.

I used to break off such idle ruminations and join the crowd in the lounge. Someone was usually at the piano in the evening, with a crowd about him shouting "I've Been Working on the Railroad" or trying for close harmony on "When You Were Sweet Sixteen." I'd stand at the pianist's elbow suggesting tunes from the twenties (I could never think of the later songs). One night he broke off and stared at me.

"Say, how old are you, anyway?"

"Older than I look," I said demurely. "Do you remember 'Kalua' from 'Good Morning, Dearie'"?

"Now you're back in the Middle Ages," he grumbled. "What about 'I've Got Sixpence?'"

"OK, or 'The Beer Barrel Polka,' maybe? The B.C. band used to play that when we made a touchdown, in the Sugar Bowl days."

"Are you from B.C.? I've been waiting to ask somebody; what happened that day when Holy Cross beat you 55 to 12?"

"Well, er, it's a long story. Let's try 'Genevieve'—and pitch it low so I can hit the tenor."

"You'll hit it all right. Just try not to hurt it too much."

Our third week at sea began. The blue life preservers we were required to carry with us everywhere were becoming filthy, and we ourselves, putting on damp clothes in the morning and washing in salt water, didn't feel especially clean either. There was only one gallon of fresh water each day for the six of us, and it's a neat trick to shave and wash your face, hands, teeth, and laundry in a sixth of a gallon a day.

We were definitely in the tropics now. Little did I think, singing "The Road to Mandalay" on a picnic in my seminary days, that "somewhere east of Suez" might one day be my mailing address. Little did I think, assigning Conrad's *Youth* to a class in Contemporary Literature, that I, too, might drift into some port across a world and see the Orient staring inscrutably back at me. Why, I asked myself for the thousandth time, why couldn't it have been gondolas instead of sampans? Everything I was interested in lay in the opposite direction. But, I reminded myself, Dante had a dream of travel, hadn't he? And it was in "the midway of life" for him. I tucked the dream away in a safe corner of my mind and kept it warm.

On the morning of the twentieth day we were sitting at breakfast when somebody glanced through a porthole and shouted "Look! A house!" We leapt to our feet: "a house?" Then we ran to the deck, where we hung over the rails and watched the land go by with starved eyes. Everything looked good: trees, greenery, even human beings who were not on the ship. It was Milne Bay, New Guinea. Pushing out from the beach were several small jetties and docks; ashore, among the palm trees, were bungalows with thatched roofs and tents on wooden floors. It looked, especially to us who were so weary of the sea, cozy and pleasant—rather like a summer resort back home, with a few interesting novelties of its own. We had scarcely anchored, for instance, when an honest-to-goodness outrigger canoe, with a bamboo mast, came alongside. It was piloted by two young natives, very dark brown in color, with bushy hair, and clad only in a pair of shorts. The GI's greeted them with characteristic American wise-cracks, good humor, and generosity; they were showered with coins, apples, and packs of cigarettes, and they caught everything thrown to them with a skill that would do honor to Fenway Park. It was an hour and a half before they pushed off, the outrigger laden with their spoil. I suspected that to the natives the war must have been the best thing that ever happened. Well, it's an ill wind that blows nobody good, and with the coconuts hanging in the palm trees ashore, and the jungles steaming in the far distance, I began to feel that at last I was really seeing the world, and to have a taste for this adventure.

But Milne Bay was not, after all, our destination. We were only pausing here to pick up orders. The exaltation of the landfall gave way to restlessness, and the men griped in true Army fashion.

"Wouldn't you know this would happen?"

"If there's a hard way to do it, the Army can find it."

"We come away the hell and gone over here, and when we get here the Army doesn't know what to do with us."

That night was pleasant, though. We hadn't seen lights for a long time, and even at home there had been black-outs or at least brown-outs in the cities and towns along the Atlantic coast. Here the whole installation was lighted, and jeeps ran along the roads with headlights blazing. We had the relief of keeping the porthole open and enjoying a bit of a breeze while we slept, though the breeze was damp. We didn't have to brace ourselves in our bunks against the roll of the ship. Someone said, just as we were dropping off, "Did you notice how much that hill looked like Bear Mountain? You know, up above Yonkers?"

CHAPTER 6

All Experience Is an Arch

NEXT DAY THE TROOP COMMANDER CAME BACK WITH OUR ORDERS. We were very curious as to their content, but no information was divulged; we up-anchored and chugged steadily all night. When we awoke again it was to look into a gorgeous morning, the sunshine pleasantly warm, a lively breeze stirring up white-caps across a wide bay. Ashore was an installation that looked very attractive, with tents and semi-permanent buildings. We noticed electric light wires, and men swimming in the surf. "Not bad," we told ourselves, "not bad at all." It was Oro Bay, two hundred miles north of Milne Bay.

At nine o'clock the long-awaited disembarkation began. Amphibious trucks, aptly called "ducks," came out from shore and began to take men off the float that had been moored next to a wooden ladder running down from B deck. The "ducks" were fascinating. They chugged shoreward with the power and speed of a heavy motor-boat, and when the beach shoaled up the driver shifted gears, his wheels began to turn, and he rolled up and away as if he were driving a limousine. They were most amusing at the moment when they emerged from the water—like prehistoric monsters waddling out of the ooze.

Our own disembarking did not come until three in the afternoon. We priests had our problem staggering down that heaving ladder, Mass kit in one hand and duffle bag in the other. On the float at last, I threw my duffle bag into the duck and tenderly passed the Mass kit to Father Regan before leaping aboard myself. Then we pushed off, and had our first good look at the ship that had been our home for so long; at San Francisco we had simply gone up the gangplank from a covered wharf, and there had been no chance to see the ship from a distance. Now she rode at anchor, a noble vessel, and we looked back at her with the affection born of long association and with gratitude to her officers and crew for a safe voyage. The *Noordam* is still reported periodically in the harbors of New York and Boston, and one of these days I shall have to go and have a look at her for old times' sake.

But then the future beckoned, and we stared curiously ashore. At the beach things were in good order. We looked at the tropical barracks, wondering which would be our home, praying that there might be fresh-water showers and a GI laundry. But a laconic officer glanced coolly at us, said "Fifth Replacement" to the driver, and off we went. Now what? Deeper and deeper into the lush vegetation, where the kunai grass waved eight to ten feet high, and the trees and vines were locked in interweaving embrace everywhere except where bulldozers had lowered their powerful heads and chewed out a wide lane and a hard-packed, excellent dirt road. We spun along at forty an hour. Now and then there would be intersecting roads with wooden signs reading "Sunset Boulevard," "Madison Avenue," and so on: the omnipresent GI humor, rather grim but getting chuckles just the same. The Jewish chaplain, Marcus Kramer, leaned back-to-back against me; Ted Mundeloh, the Lutheran chaplain from the Midwest, smoked reflective cigarettes nearby; Jack Traweek, the Baptist chaplain from Oklahoma, swapped wise-cracks up front with Rothy and Frank Regan. And finally we began, through the dust and our sweat-filled eyes, to see "home." We were in Dobodura, fifteen miles from Oro Bay. On this plain, a year and a half before, the 32nd Division had learned with blood and sweat the savage principles of jungle warfare, had driven the Japs back into Buna Mission and built an airstrip. Nothing else was there until the Fifth Replacement Depot came up from Goodenough Island three weeks before our own arrival. Then the bulldozers had pushed out on all sides of the road, bowling over trees and kunai grass, and the GI's had followed, pitching four-man tents in the mud, marking off company streets, digging ditches to drain off the pools, dragging in Army cots and setting up housekeeping. They grinned at us as we whirled by, shouting "You'll be sorry!" We found that this greeting took the place of "Hello" in New Guinea, and with reason.

At last we drew up in front of a tent where an officer sat at a home-made desk (four sticks and a packing-case). He demanded two copies of our orders and had us sign the inevitable register. Then a weary supply sergeant handed out two blankets, a mosquito netting, and a cot, and we took up our beds and walked out into the mud. I was assigned to N Street, Tent 2, and I made the discouraging discovery that I was the odd man in our shipment of thirteen chaplains and was all alone. Nor was I cheered particularly by the appearance of my happy home, once I had located it. Neighbors had "borrowed" the tent poles and cut lengths off the ropes, so that the flaps trailed dismally in the mud. I was to learn that out here the seventh commandment had been repealed. Everyone committed larceny with "don't get caught" as the only inhibition. You appropriated tent-stakes, shovels, axes, poles, mosquito-bombs, gasoline— everything the supply sergeant had in stock. Survival seemed to depend on your ability to make off with and conceal your ill-gotten gains. It was called "moonlight requisition," and the sergeant could only swear. He did that, of course, with a fluency and a pictorial quality that would curl your hair.

But to return: I lifted the sodden tent-flaps and peered in. A puddle looked back at me. It was fed by a brimming ditch, and I realized that it would take a miniature Boulder Dam to divert it, so I chose the only dry corner, parked my cot there, dropped the duffle bag next to it, and cast about for some scraps of wood I could use for stakes to set my Mass kit on. This done, it was time for chow. I pulled out my mess kit and went off to stand in a long queue known as the chow line. You stood in line for everything; some wag remarked that even the mosquitoes out in the jungle had picked up the habit, and stood in line to bite you. Into one half of the mess kit went beef ("Corned Willie," the GI's called it), boiled rice, and dehydrated potatoes; into the other half went a chunk of bread, a slab of synthetic butter, and some canned pineapple. The cup was successively filled with sugar, evaporated milk and steaming coffee. We squatted in the mud or at the fender of a jeep and stowed it away, and it tasted very good, too.

It was almost dark then, so I went back to Suburban Heights, where, by the light of a solitary candle, stuck in my versatile helmet to protect it from the breeze, I rigged up over my cot a temporary support for my mosquito netting. When I looked out again, the darkness was thick; the men, I was to learn, went to a movie at night and then to bed. Once in a while a foursome could be seen, with heads close together as the poker chips clicked under the candle. I decided my own day had been long enough. But going to bed was not a simple process, even after some experimentation. You picked up your pajamas; they were damp and ugh. Then you undressed and climbed in, pulling after you the ends of your mosquito netting. Then you went over the inside of your netting with a flashlight, to be sure you had no anopheles mosquito for a bedmate. At last you stretched out; it was snug there under your canopy of netting, and you remembered those lines of Bryant's,

> As one who draws the draperies of his couch about
> him, And lies down to pleasant dreams.

After a moment or so, though, the hard reality of that army cot began to make itself felt, and you thought rather of Gray's line,

> Each in his narrow cell forever laid,

because there was only one narrow trench in that cot, and you could not roll out of it, and when you tried to roll there were no springs to cushion bony protrusions. Besides, you had no pillow except your own contrivance of a shirt and a pair of pants inside a laundry bag. But you clutched your rosary and asked to be rid of all "vain, perverse, and alien thoughts," and you told yourself that you "held the gorgeous East in fee," and you sent a blessing in the direction of San Francisco. And all of a sudden it was dewy morning, and your undershirt was wet instead of your pajamas.

The next day it poured rain until noon; mean rainfall in Papua is two hundred inches a year. For breakfast we stood in our ponchos, looking like a group of traffic cops in a storm, and the rain beat down on our scrambled eggs and diluted our coffee. The eggs were powdered, and the coffee was weak as dishwater, so that if we had added a few tears to the raindrops it would have been quite fitting, and might have supplied some of the missing salt. Morale was generally low that day. I went back to my tent and dug a ditch to carry off the puddle; meanwhile a truckful of sand was being dumped on our company street, and I persuaded the sergeant in charge of the detail to drop a load outside my tent. When I had scattered this around my floor, the results were consoling, but the operation cost me an hour's heavy labor and much sweat, and I learned that in this climate one did well to distribute his energies wisely.

When it did not rain, the mornings were very lovely. My spirits were high as I walked to the chapel to offer Mass at six-thirty. It was cool, and the mountains, their tops shrouded in mist, were violet in the sunrise. I could see that in spite of all foreboding, all wrenching separation, I should have been infinitely poorer for having missed this.

> And all experience is an arch where through
> Gleams that untravelled world whose margin fades
> Forever and forever as I move.

I was beginning to be ashamed of my greed for new experience. But I had been shut up for so many years, and I had read so much. Now I could verify what I had read. It was really rich: the coconuts growing in clusters at the top of those arrowy palms, the GI's assisting at Mass by candlelight, the ground won from the Japs a year before with how much American blood, the almost violent contrast as a group of soldiers listened to a transcription of *Professor Quiz* over the Armed Forces Radio while a family of Melanesian natives marched by single-file along the road. Every so often I would pinch myself and say,

"Old boy, do you know that you are really in the South Seas, that the land-locked bookworm is having his belated Odyssey, that this is almost ten thousand miles from little old Boston?"

The Sunday after our arrival I preached at Father Van Holme's Mass in the Depot chapel, and heard a great many confessions. In the afternoon Father Bill O'Connor, of the Hartford Diocese, generously took us swimming at Cape Sudest. We walked about in the neighborhood, staring at a Jap cemetery (all graves unidentified save one), at crumbling pill-boxes and overgrown barbed-wire entanglements—grim reminders of what Americans had had to face when they came in here. Just as we were leaving Father Roth spotted a native selling coconuts and gleefully shouted,

"Hey, George, bring us a couple of those."

All the natives were called "George," and all the women "Mary." George wanted a shilling apiece for his coconuts, but at that moment a jeep-full of Australian soldiers for whom he was supposed to be working yelled at him, and when the Aussies yelled the natives jumped. He ran off, crying "me come back" over his shoulder, but we knew he wouldn't, so Roth kept his "bob" and we hacked the coconuts open with our versatile knives, drinking the milk and eating the white meat.

The natives were a study. The men were tall and brawny, and dressed only in loin-cloths. Their hair stood up like wire, and they wore it like a bush, very high; the lower hair was black, but the top was red, because they bleached it—the best present you could give a native, we were told, was a bottle of peroxide. The women wore no more than the men, but were very shy and modest. The children ran about stark naked. It was quite a sight to see a fuzzy-wuzzy family on the road: Daddy stalked ahead with his spear, his several wives followed after in single file, carrying all the burdens on their heads, and the children brought up the rear. They matured very early, the girls often becoming mothers at ten, but their life-expectancy was only thirty-five. They didn't seem to have any of the million diseases of the area, but we concluded that they must have had them with suppressed symptoms. We ourselves had plenty of trouble with tropical diseases: jungle rot, elephantiasis, scrub typhus. When I first landed I used to see men scratching themselves, and concluded that in this primitive life, with no refining feminine influences, the male simply reverted to type. But we were not ashore long before we, too, were scratching. Jungle rot wasn't pretty, and the gentian violet smeared on it by the medics made the victim a really sorry sight.

One morning we got up to find that it had snowed during the night—well, what they called New Guinea snow, at any rate. A volcano several hundred miles away had erupted a day or two before, and the clouds of very fine ash thrown up by it had reached us. Everything lay under a layer of powder; the jeeps and trucks made a choking fog of it; the sun was obscured and headlights were on for daylight driving. We rubbed our necks and the dirt came off in folds. There were no showers in our happy home. As a substitute, we put large cans out to catch rain-water, and then stood under a home-made scaffold while our buddy poured the water into another big can on the scaffold over our heads. The bottom of this second can was perforated with a hatchet, so we had a shower of sorts. Of course in that man's world one stood in the open just as God had made him—privacy was only a word derived from the Latin, with no meaning whatever. We were shucking off our civilization.

I opened my bed-roll one day for the first time since leaving Camp Beale, and groaned. Everything in it was damp, even wet, and blue mold had begun to gather on my brand-new (and as yet unused) sleeping-bag and blankets. I put the blankets up on a rope to be aired; the other items went into a ten-gallon can of rain-water and Rinso, and thence into my helmet for scrubbing. It was the first skirmish of a long battle with tropical dampness. I learned to put talcum powder on the gummed flaps of envelopes, to keep them dry, and to keep the breads for Mass in a box heated by an electric bulb. But books and anything made of cloth or leather took a licking.

It was a base order that everyone had to wear canvas leggings, heavy and hot though they were, for protection against insects. In addition, we had to take a tablet of atabrine every day as a specific against malaria. It was queer that an officer had to be appointed in every outfit to see that the men actually swallowed the tablet; they invented and firmly believed the weirdest ideas about its eventual effects on their health. The tablet was a very bright yellow and contained a powerful dye which after a time changed the hue of everyone's skin somewhat, the dark-complected chaps being much more affected than the blonds. It was popularly known as "Guinea Gold."

One other seemingly inescapable pest had found its way here. At night rats came in and scurried about the tent. Even when I had nothing like peanuts or crackers to attract them, they seemed to enjoy playing football under my cot. Sometimes I would reach out and, using my heavy GI shoe for a weapon, break up the game by crowning one as he made an end run, but for the most part I didn't bother. The mosquito netting kept them from running over me, and that was all I cared about. Still, anyone who had read *Rats, Lice, and History* would not have objected to a wooden, elevated floor and some really effective rat poison.

Over the P.A. system they used to play, daily, a current song-hit: "This is a lovely way to spend an evening, can't think of anything I'd rather do . . . " The absence of electric light made our evenings long and monotonous. I tried reading by candlelight, with half a tin can rigged up in back of it as a reflector for the candle, but my eyes protested. Darkness fell at six-thirty (it was July, but midwinter in those latitudes); after dark you could go to whatever Special Service was providing in the way of entertainment—a movie, a news broadcast, a transcription of some stateside radio program, a card of boxing matches. Being snobbish, or hyperesthetic, I didn't care much for that sort of thing, but either you went there or you went to bed. We saw Bing Crosby in *Going My Way* three times, and chuckled at Barry Fitzgerald, but the picture made us GI priests a little homesick for a black suit and a Roman collar and people to call us "Father" instead of "Chaplain." One night Jack Benny and Lanny Ross and some Hollywood movie queens made a personal appearance on our crude stage. The men were well received and their double-entendres elicited whoops, but when one of the girls began to tell smutty jokes, there was a noticeable falling-off in laughter and applause. Even from an amoral standpoint, I wondered why that woman couldn't understand that as a reminder of the girl back home, the wife or sweetheart every GI wanted to go back to, she was damaging morale more than she was lifting it.

Like all exiles, we wanted news from home. Twice a day we would hopefully approach the mail orderly's tent, but for six weeks our visits were fruitless. Then one day I saw one of the Protestant chaplains coming out of the tent with a letter in his hand, and guessed that if he, who had come over on the same shipment as myself, had received mail, my own would not be long in arriving. So I hailed him eagerly.

"Got a letter, George, eh?"

"Yes," he answered with deep disappointment, "I thought it was from my wife, but it's only from my church."

I have wondered since if he ever reflected on his contribution to the four-hundred-year-old controversy.

One day I was watching the C-47's roar down the Dobodura airstrip, laden with paratroopers from the 11th Airborne Division, who were practicing jumps, and I began talking with a GI from the same outfit.

"Who's your chaplain?" I asked, hunting for a conversational gambit.

"His name is Dunne, Father."

"Dunne, eh? Is he a diocesan priest?"

"No, he's a Jesuit, I think."

"Is he? What's his home town, do you know?"

"Well, I've heard some of the boys kidding him about Brooklyn."

"Dunne from Brooklyn? Lead me to him, will you?"

To our mutual wonder and delight, it was Father Ed Dunne, with whom I had studied philosophy years before at Weston. Neither of us had known that the other was in the Army, much less that we were neighbors in this far corner of the world. We talked so long into the night that Ed had to escort me past the sentries and over the strip into the casual area where I belonged.

We were all spoiling for action, so Father Dunne invited Father Regan and myself to give a mission in his regiment, each of us to take four sermons and four instructions. That must have been a "first" of sorts: a Dominican and a Jesuit giving a mission together. The attendance was pretty fair, about half the Catholics in the regiment. Ordinarily this would have seemed a poor turnout, but the men in this regiment were very young and scatterbrained, so we were content to have so many. Each evening I celebrated a dialogue Mass, with Father Ed leading the responses. The men liked it, and said so in such numbers and with such enthusiasm that I was convinced all over again of their desire to take an active part in the Mass. The Signal Corps was on hand to take pictures of the closing of the mission; one was a shot of Father Regan in his white habit, myself in cassock, surplice, and stole, and Father Dunne in khaki shirt and trousers—the hard-working pastor. The best one, though, was of Father Regan offering Mass in the red vestments Father Carroll had given me; the amice, draped as the Dominicans wear it, and the white alb set off the flaming chasuble magnificently.

It was good to run across, in one of the chapels on the Base, four back issues of *America,* and to enter once more into the world of Catholic ideas I had known before enlisting. I read everything, including the letters to the Editor, and realized that the academic, not the military, was my field. How, I asked myself, did I get into this? It must have been a case of God's lifting me by the hair of the head and dropping me into a uniform, even as He had dropped me into a cassock before I had had a chance to look over the world. *Misericordias Domini in aeternum cantabo.* But the chaplain, as I began to see clearly, has the function of a surgeon at the battle-front: all he can do is staunch and bind up wounds. He cannot build up with vitamins and calories. We absolved, offered the Mass, anointed; there was no chance to inform, to rear a structure.

One night Father Dunne took me to visit some friends of his, lieutenants in the Air Corps. I was amazed at what could be done for civilized living in the jungle. Their cabins were built three or four feet off the ground, with wooden floors, and were screened in. On the back porch was a shower. They had a short-wave radio that could pick up about any broadcast anywhere; we listened to San Francisco and Moscow, and heard for the first time the famous Japanese woman called "Tokyo Rose," or "Madam Tojo," who broadcast propaganda every night in excellent English. When our boys were isolated on Guadalcanal she used to tell them, crooningly, how silly they were to be fighting out here, and sing American love songs. Her favorite stunt, the story ran, was to learn through spies the name of some soldier and tell him over the air that his wife was running around with another man at home. We listened as she suavely explained the loss of Saipan and the insignificance from a military standpoint of our invasion of Guam. We shut her off finally and had another round of grapefruit juice. One of the lieutenants tasted his drink appraisingly and shook his head.

"It would be better with ice," he said.

"Ice?" we answered. "What's that?"

He produced real cubes of ice, from a refrigerator, and we gaped. This Air Corps! They had everything!

A story went the rounds one morning about a GI at the Base who seemed to have rather remarkable powers. It seems that he dreamed, before sailing from the States, the name of the ship his outfit would sail on, the place at which it would disembark, and the day of its arrival, and he hit all three squarely on the nose. Then he dreamed about D-Day in Europe, and he missed the exact hour of the invasion by only thirty minutes. Now he had had another dream: Germany would surrender on August 6th and Japan on August 22nd. It sounded wonderful to us; everyone who heard the story perked up instantaneously, then looked foolish for having betrayed his credulity. We wouldn't have been surprised if the prediction had been verified with regard to Germany, especially since the news had just come over about the attempted assassination of Hitler, but we didn't feel so confident about the Japs, in spite of Saipan. It was an interesting study in the psychology of wishful thinking to see how our bunch snapped up the story. Alas, the GI "seer" was looking into a clouded crystal ball. There would still be the Bulge in Europe, and Manila and Hiroshima in the Pacific.

The GI language one listened to all day was indescribably foul. Back in the States one could close his door against it, at least occasionally. But canvas is not soundproof, and I used to say the Gloria at Mass and the Te Deum in my Office in reparation for the blasphemy that dinned into my ears all day long. The vulgarity was not sinful, but it turned my stomach, especially since the repertoire of the average GI was limited to four or five expressions. I knew that for most of the men the practice was sheer habit, unreflecting and unintentional, and I liked the way men in both the Army and the Navy would see me coming and pass the word: "Here comes the chaplain, boys; clean it up." The only exception I found to this rule was the Merchant Marine, who very decidedly did not clean it up no matter who was present. And I got so that after a while I paid small attention unless it was the Lord's name that was involved; that I could never hear without wincing. It seemed to me that if the men had some clearer concept of the Lord himself, some intimation of his majesty, they would not have tossed his name about so thoughtlessly. I used to look forward to Thursday, when the marching, exultant cadences of the 72nd Psalm occurred in the Office: what a piece of regal poetry. I had always loved it as an *apologia pro vita mea,* a pledge of that vindication which will surely be given, one day, to the sacrifices of the priestly life, when "He shall rule from sea to sea, and from the river to the ends of the earth." I loved, too, its breathtaking pageantry:

> His foes shall bow down before him,
> And his enemies shall lick the dust.
> The kings of Tharsis and of the islands shall offer tribute,
> The kings of the Arabians and of Saba shall bring
>   gifts.
> And all the kings shall worship him,
> All nations shall serve him.

The solemn tramp of those syllables stirred me profoundly, and I reflected sadly how few of our people were acquainted with the gorgeous prayer-book which is the Psalter, how many of them seemed to prefer prettiness and sugar to strong meat and majesty. The Byzantine concept of Christ, as Watkin pointed out, was of such a royal, satisfying Person, every inch a King. Oh, we needed the Christ of the Agony, too; the almost weak, almost vacillating, almost panic-stricken Christ, but this Christ would be ultimately meaningless and profitless to us without the Christ of the Resurrection, the King of glory.

> His name shall be blessed forever;
> As long as the sum shines, his name shall endure.
> And all the tribes of the earth shall be blessed in him,
> All nations shall proclaim him blessed.

On St. Ignatius' Day, as I walked to breakfast, the hill that walled the jungles from the ocean was green-gold in the morning sun, and the jangling of the knife and fork against the plate of my mess-kit was strange accompaniment for the memories that crowded their way into my mind. At the novitiate, nineteen years before, there had been a curving hill like that; it swept away across the Berkshire valley and took the eye with it to the far reaches of the lake and the hazy distance that was, they said, Connecticut. It certainly was a lovely sight on that first St. Ignatius' Day morning, when all things were new in the dancing sun of one's seventeenth summer, and the great adventure lay ahead. We had arrived the previous afternoon, eight of us fresh out of high school, and the dew on our shoes as we strolled across the lawn on that first morning was no more fresh than we were: spirited, immature, cocky, bringing to the religious life little but the faith our sturdy parents had given us and a desire to be like the teachers who had formed us. The second-year novices appointed to be our "angels" and to guide us through the first days of our orientation were shocked at the flip way we joked, in the slang of the mid-twenties, about the sacred customs of the novitiate, but they smiled a grim smile when they voiced the warning, "The Long Retreat will fix you." It did, indeed, in the sobriety of October three months later, but on that glorious midsummer morning, facing that incomparable valley, there was no room for seriousness. Even the little gray man, who radiated such vitality, and who was introduced to us as "Father Master," did not in his wisdom attempt to sober us then. He shook hands, stepped back and surveyed us in a way we came to know as characteristic, and said with an enigmatic smile, "Postulants are very precious."

We had no notion of his meaning, but one of the group shook his head wonderingly years later and speculated how he could have seen in us the hope of the flock. "What blind kittens we were!"

After dinner we met the men who had pronounced their first vows at Mass that morning, and their ecstatic happiness was stirred into the elixir of our own gaiety. It was a heady draught, and it sent us to bed confused and sleepy, but dimly realizing that St. Ignatius was mighty yet, and that his Day would in all the years to come hold a significance uniquely its own.

Remember our own vow day, two years later? Remember the calculated coldness with which we pronounced the formula, striving to get into each word the deliberate, irrevocable decision we were making? Remember how, after Communion, the cold deliberation took fire in a delirium of joy, and how we did not realize until late afternoon that it had been raining all day? Remember the feel of the strange new biretta, and the silence in the chapel as one of the eight sang the "Suscipe" at Benediction? Yes, and remember later years, when the annual appointments would be published on St. Ignatius' Day, and we would crowd around the bulletin board to see who was going where in the Province? Remember the genial banter of the community at dinner, and how we walked the seminary road afterward, laughing with classmates now scattered to the far corners of the vineyard? St. Ignatius' Day, more than any other feast of the year, was always the family day, the day when humdrum routine and petty dissatisfactions yielded to the overwhelming realization, Lord, it is good for us to be here.

But, however lovely that New Guinea hill, it was not one of the Berkshires, and the chow line bore small resemblance to the refectories at home. The C-47's roared by unnoticed on the neighboring airstrip. The chaffing of the officers, who noticed that I looked abstracted and advised me, if I had worries, to "see the chaplain," were heard as from afar. St. Ignatius' Day. Had it not been for St. Ignatius I could never have dealt with the arguments brought up in a two-hour discussion last night with a neo-pagan whose epistemology and natural theology were riddled with non sequiturs. Had it not been for St. Ignatius there would not have been those young second lieutenants from the University of Detroit and Santa Clara and Holy Cross, who had assisted at my Mass daily on the transport. Huh! Had it not been for St. Ignatius there would have been no Mass on that transport—at least none of my celebration; I wondered if St. Ignatius would feel a twinge of memory could he have stood in the chow line this morning. Maybe he, too, waited restlessly for orders in a casual camp before moving on Pampeluna.

Breakfast was not well over when there was a call from the Filipino Jesuit several miles away.

"Say! We should celebrate! I have Father Stretch from the California Province and Father Dunne from the New York Province, and we'll run over and pick you up for dinner. Right?"

Right, very right. Things were looking up. But, one reflected, why make this an exclusive affair? St. Ignatius had been as insistent as St. Paul on particular solicitude for those of the household of the faith. So the Dominican and the Benedictine and the Precious Blood Father and the two diocesans were duly apprised of their obligation to make merry on the Jesuit high holy day. The jeep that Father Verceles drove groaned and protested, but finally, in the teeth of regulations about jeep capacity and under the noses of MP's, deposited seven padres at the Filipino area. They inspected the chow, the like of which had never been seen at the casual camp, and agreed that they were glad for St. Ignatius. They went swimming off the broad Pacific beach and admitted that perhaps St. Ignatius had had something on the ball. They returned to drink deep of coffee brewed out of GI beans but with Filipino artistry, and conceded that while his sons might still have to be regarded with caution, St. Ignatius himself would henceforth be above suspicion.

But Father Dunne had not been able to come, after all; he was attending jump school in his paratrooper regiment. So when the New Guinea hill was turning purple in the swift tropic twilight, Father Verceles' jeep pulled up at the paratroopers' motor park. Father Dunne was sitting on the edge of his cot, tenderly caressing strained muscles, when we walked in. His tent-mates, the major from Arizona and the captain from North Dakota, had never heard of St. Ignatius, but they were very happy to celebrate his memory, especially when they saw what we carried. A trench knife sliced the cheese and the pineapple cake, a scout knife opened the Australian wine. We sat in the white effulgence of the Coleman lamp while Typhus, the mascot pup of the regiment, ran over our feet and snapped at crumbs. Maybe there was some rhyme or reason to this, after all. We wondered. The other day, for instance. That hulking boy from Tennessee, with the childlike smile, who told blood-curdling tales of the Buna campaign and death in the jungle, and who said, quite suddenly,

"Y'know, my father used to go to church. He belonged to some New England religion—begins with a 'P.'"

"Presbyterian?" I asked, helpfully.

"Nope."

"Not Puritan?"

"Nope," He scratched his big head. "I got it—'Piscopalian."

And then the matter-of-fact Aussie I had met, in charge of a detail of natives cutting logs in the hills. I asked him what the fuzzy-wuzzies made of this war business.

"Oaow," he answered. "They don't mind. The Jap wanted to tyke the country, and we're stoppin' 'im."

Was it as easy as that? I didn't know; it was too big. Better leave it, like everything else, *in manus tuas.*

Father Verceles, Father Dunne and I stopped at the edge of the airstrip and looked up at the Southern Cross. We were very far from classrooms and libraries and domestic chapels. We would be parted very shortly. But we had caught, for an hour or two, the savor of home and the spell of the family. Perhaps the officer in Ignatius might overlook some of our shortcomings if we could show him, some day, our khaki, our leggings, our regulation field uniform. At any rate, we had celebrated his Mass and prayed his Office and rejoiced in his memory, because, though we might have had many instructors in Christ, we had not had many fathers, whereas he, through the Gospel in Christ Jesus, had begotten us.

CHAPTER 7

Dry Run Gets Wet

IT WAS TIME TO TANGLE ONCE MORE WITH THE TRANSPORTATION corps. And the pattern hadn't changed. On three mornings we were roused from sleep in the small hours, hustled through breakfast, lined up for movement—then the whole thing was called off and we unpacked again. In the vivid slang of the GI, these mystifying undertakings were known as "dry runs."

On the fourth day, we left the Depot in trucks at ten o'clock in the morning, although we had been called from sleep seven hours earlier, and arrived on the beach at Cape Sudest at ten-thirty. Nine LCI's—small vessels designed to carry two hundred soldiers and the operating Navy personnel—were waiting to take us aboard. They had steam up and were ready to sail; the tide was out and it would have been easy to go aboard. But for some reason known only to the troop movement officers, we squatted on the beach until four in the afternoon. No one had thought to provide food, of course, so we went hungry. At last, when the tide was full and a stiff wind was rolling the breakers in, we were ordered to go aboard. I stripped to my shorts and managed to heave my luggage up the gangplank without getting it too wet. The next problem was to see that the men, burdened with rifles and full packs, got up the plank before they drowned. One by one they charged down the beach into the water, trying to reach and scramble up the slippery plank before the next breaker shook it. Six of us officers hung precariously on the side of the plank, catching them as they came up and passing them on to the next officer above. No one went into the drink, but almost every man came within an ace of it.

The little ship was like a toy. Eight of us officers were in a tiny cabin and the men were below, in four tiers of bunks. The air was indescribably stuffy down there, with only one bulkhead between them and the engine room, and a single hatch open after dark. It began to rain heavily, and the ship heeled over in a forty-degree list as the storm struck her. I found that the executive officer, Lt. John Kelley, was a BC man; we chatted pleasantly over a welcome supper, and then I went on deck, where I discovered the GI's hanging over the rail in misery. "Poor kids," I said to myself. "Glad I don't feel that way." So I stood watching the horizon bob up and down between the crests—no one had ever told me that the worst thing to do in rough water is to watch the horizon—and after some minutes my supper, too, went over the rail. At eight I went to the cabin and slept for two hours; at ten I was hopelessly awake, sliding back and forth and trying to brace myself against the roll of the ship; at midnight, I decided that fresh air was imperative and went on deck and lay in a drizzle on a heap of duffle bags. A piece of a moon showed occasionally through rags of rain-clouds. I could see a beacon on shore when the ship rose to the crest of a wave. The running lights of the other LCI's in our convoy tossed up and down, burning green and yellow. My nausea subsided gradually and at last I dozed until about three o'clock, when the air turned raw and I went below. At seven I awoke; we were offshore, and the ship's captain was inspecting the beach to learn whether it was too rough to land. Word was finally passed that we would attempt a landing, so I ate a fairly good breakfast. But when I came on deck I was dismayed to see that we were heading for open water again; the decision had been reversed, and we were going to put in at a pier ten miles up the coast. As we rounded the point I lost my breakfast!

At ten we went ashore in a torrential rain. I succeeded in keeping my Mass kit dry under my poncho, but everything else was drenched through. On the pier confusion reigned; no one was expecting us or knew what to do with us. At last a couple of troop movement officers came, shouted into the telephone, blustered a bit to the Navy, and ran aimlessly about. We stood under a dismal roof that kept off half the rain, and Jack Traweek, the Baptist chaplain, voiced everyone's opinion when he wondered aloud with great sincerity how the hell we were winning the war.

Then I got an idea, and after an hour managed to reach the Ninth Ordnance Battalion by phone. A very pleasant voice (I found later that it belonged to Captain Paul DeGrieck, the supply officer) asked where I was, and said a jeep would be right over.

"I don't suppose you've had your dinner?"

"No."

"We'll hold dinner for you."

I put down the phone in a fine glow. After twelve weeks of being pushed around as an unwanted casual, here was someone interested in me, claiming me! But then we discovered that the bridge between our dock and the base had been washed out, so my outfit could not get through to me. I rejoined the desolate group in the shack, and at four in the afternoon those jokers finally got together with the Navy officers; we were herded back on the LCI's, this time for a ferry ride to the beach we had originally put into. There, at six-thirty, I called the Ninth, a jeep appeared at once, and I was whisked off to a dinner of steak, potatoes, bread, and fruit. After the chow at the Fifth, I couldn't believe my eyes. Then I was shown my quarters, a raised tent with a wooden floor and excellent electric light. Everyone was most cordial and helpful. I would have a jeep, and an office, and a typewriter if they could get one, and a clerk, and anything else I wanted, and they were as good as their word. In the Division at home the chaplain had seemed to be either a fifth wheel or a matter for joking, but out here he and his work were taken seriously, and the attitude helped much.

My new home was Finschhafen. The name doesn't appear on most maps of New Guinea, even the detailed ones, and the place couldn't have been very important in pre-war days. It lay in north Papua in the territory called Northeast New Guinea, where that island bulges toward New Britain. There had been a short, sharp fight with the Japs for its possession; the favorite swimming place when we were there was still known by the grim and sadly apt name of Scarlet Beach. But now it was far behind the lines, an enormous supply base sprawling along some fifteen miles of coast. From the high country to the north, the view was majestic; at one's feet were the coral cliffs bordering the sea, and the mountains swept away inland. It looked like an undeveloped tourist's paradise. But when one went down among the palm trees he found it hard to remember the beauty of the landscape. All the difficulties of tropical living were here in force—the humidity, the rains, the insects, the disease. On December 1st the thermometer stood at 104 degrees—in the shade. Humidity averaged eighty per cent. Malaria control teams in every unit had done a splendid job in eliminating mosquitoes; oil was spread every day on any standing water that could not be ditched away and men went through the company areas kicking over cans or other containers that might afford breeding surfaces. But ants and termites and other pests crawled everywhere. They told me that before my arrival it had rained forty-four days straight, and the rains were like those in Louisiana, heavy and unremitting, giving the area an average rainfall in excess of two hundred inches a year. The resultant mud was, in the wet season, rich and deep; men frequently went in over their shoes, and I remember watching what I thought must be one of the most frustrating tasks that could be given to a man: the uncrating and assembling of a six-by-six truck in a soggy marsh where the work and the workers sank at every movement six to twelve inches. Dengue fever, scrub typhus, jungle rot, and hepatitis kept the hospitals full and the medics busy.

I had been assigned to the Ninth Ordnance Battalion, consisting at that time of a headquarters and eleven companies, or about eighteen hundred men. There were two other battalions nearby, not as large, and with no Catholic chaplains, so that I would try to serve them as well, at least by providing Mass in their vicinity, but my first responsibility was to the Ninth. Originally set up to supply weapons and ammunition, Ordnance, with the coming of the motor age, was given charge of all vehicles as well: jeeps, command cars, trucks, weapons-carriers, tanks, half-tracks, ambulances, ducks, motorized field kitchens. Some of my companies dealt with small arms like pistols and rifles, some with mortars and Long Toms, but most were "grease monkeys," as they called themselves, and spent their days assembling new vehicles or servicing old ones. Their talents ran to the mechanical rather than the theoretical, and there were few college men even among the officers. I was shocked to discover several enlisted men who could not read or write, and to find that they did not come from the less literate States back home.

Well, there we were. It looked like a long stay, too. The Information Service and the base newspaper kept us up to date on the progress of the war as it was fought, but of course they could reveal nothing of future operations, and no one could give us an answer to the great question: how long before it's over and we can go home? "Golden Gate in '48," said the pessimists. "Back alive in '45," said the optimists. Meanwhile the sweat rolled off our backs, the trucks rolled off the assembly lines, and the days began to merge into months. We were not fighting men, strictly, but the fighting men could not fight without us. Ours was an essential job. And if there was no danger, there was loneliness and tedium and all the problems common to humanity. The chaplain would not be idle.

I began visiting the companies one by one. The C.O. would introduce me after the evening meal, and I would speak to all the men for about three minutes, then meet the Catholics separately and ask them to fill in a questionnaire. The tabulated answers were not encouraging; the men openly admitted that they did not go to Mass regularly, and in too many cases the length of time away from the sacraments varied from three to ten years. I began to be skeptical about the alleged spiritual revival in the armed forces.

"What happened?" I would sometimes ask one of these long-termers.

"I dunno, Father; just got careless, and nobody was around to give me a shove like I needed—but it was my fault just the same, Father."

The humility and honesty of these big children silenced any rebuke I might have been thinking of giving them, but I decided, all the same, that the first thing I would have in my chapel, once it was completed, would be a mission, and it would be the old-fashioned kind of mission, too, aimed at waking up the sleepers.

Meanwhile, without a chapel, the peerless worship of God which is the Mass went on, though the setting was something less than ideal. On Sundays Bill Graham, my assistant, and I arrived at the Officers' Club about seven in the morning, and set to work to sweep up the place and make it look a little less like the morning after. We washed the beer stains off a long table and set it up on water cans so that it would be nearer the usual height of an altar. Out of the Mass kit, then, came the three linen cloths, the crucifix, the chalice and paten and ciborium, the vestments, candles, and cruets. When the congregation had arrived I put on the vestments, explaining the meaning and history of each and the use of the sacred vessels. I asked all the men to come up around me, so that they were kneeling practically at my feet; then I began Mass. After the Gospel, I made announcements and spoke of little matters that had come to my attention in my cruises through the area and the shops during the week—foul language, for instance, or the pin-up girls in so many tents, no help to Christian chastity surely. Then I read the Gospel in English and preached. I wanted to institute active participation in the Mass when the chapel opened, but I knew that if it were to be more than a novelty I had to tell my men why it was better than what they were used to; I had to teach them certain fundamental doctrines that would make the new practice seem natural and reasonable.

I began by explaining the unity of Christian men. They were one in the mind of God before creation, they were one in Adam, their common father, they were one in the redeeming death of Christ, and they were now one in the Church, the Body of Christ, into which they had been incorporated by baptism.

I went on, then, to talk about the worship these unified Christians offer to God. I tried to show that when men seek to adore God they naturally look for something they can place before him that will stand for themselves. It's the same impulse, I said, that prompts a man to give flowers or candy or a ring to the girl he loves; the gift itself is nothing, but it stands for him. So men have always offered to their God some symbol of their lives, of their work, their ambitions, their hopes and sorrows. The thing they chose most frequently was food, because what they ate and drank in order to stay alive would be a natural symbol of themselves. The ancient Egyptians, for example, offered little cakes to the god of the River Nile. The American Indians killed buffalo in honor of the Great White Spirit. The Greeks and Romans poured wine on the ground and killed a bull or an ox. The Jews killed the Paschal

Lamb and offered its life-blood. When Christ our Lord directed us to use bread and wine for our worship, then, he was bidding us follow a deep-seated human instinct. We could have eaten that bread and drunk that wine, and it would have sustained us in life. Instead, we give it to God, and in the sign-language we are giving him ourselves. But at the Consecration of the Mass, Christ our High Priest takes these poor gifts of ours and gives them a value and dignity they could never have of themselves: they become nothing less than the flesh and blood of the Son of God. Now there is really something to offer, something of unimaginable worth. God could not refuse this gift, any more than he could have refused it when it was offered on the cross by the Son in whom he was well pleased. But we offer it, too, because at baptism we were made one with Christ and deputed to adore with him, and because by providing the bread and wine we made the gift possible. So our gift is united with his, and the Father sees and accepts them as one.

Then in Holy Communion, God, as a sign that he is pleased with our offering, gives it back to us so that we may live by it and become holy by means of it. It is also the means of consolidating our union with one another; in fact, it proclaims to the world the fraternal love Christ came to establish and invites others to share its warmth. "Because the bread is one, we, though many, are one body, all of us who partake of the one bread." Here, I used to say, is our hope of a better world after the war, a chance for "peace in our time."

About two weeks after I arrived at Finsch, my mail caught up with me. The mail clerk, full of wisecracks but impressed in spite of himself, dumped eighty-one letters on my desk, and I went on a four-hour binge of reading that threatened to leave me with a hangover of homesickness. How did I ever land out here, anyway? This rough-and-tumble world was never meant for me. I belonged on a campus, near a library, among people who argued about books and ideas. When the mood was at its darkest, something reminded me of a parody I had composed for the popular tune, "Mairsy Doats," which everyone was singing that summer. It attempted to satirize the ardors of some dithyrambic young Catholics whom we had all known at home, and it went like this:

Maisie Ward and Frankie Sheed,
And Belloc and Guardini,
America, Ronald Knox, Dotty Day;
John L. Bonn and Chester-ton,
And rural-life Ligutti,
Liturgical books and such move me much.

I laughed, and the mists lifted, and at that moment the jeep I had been allotted arrived at my office. It was far from new, but the boys had cleaned it up, and to make sure everyone would know who was coming, had painted "CHAPLAIN" below the windshield in letters four inches high. While I was thanking them an idea occurred to me.

"Look," I said, "All the jeeps I've seen have personal names, like 'Susie Q,' 'Mudbug,' 'Mrs. Occasionally,' and so on. I'd like one, too—and I don't want 'Holy Joe,' either."

They scratched their heads. "Got any ideas, Father?"

"Yes," I said, "How about 'Pater Noster?'"

After I had written it out to prevent misspelling, they drove off, and returned a little later with the new name duly inscribed below the "CHAPLAIN." It seemed to me not only a unique name but a good joke. But after some weeks, when a number of the GI's had asked me, "What's that Latin on your jeep mean, Father?" I began to think long thoughts about the alleged universality of our ecclesiastical language and the advisability of using the mother tongue in our worship of God.

That was a memorable day in other ways, too. I had an ice-cold coke, for one thing, and learned that the coke syrup was shipped over from the States and carbonated by my Ordnance men, whose ingenuity seemed equal to anything. Then Steve Brennan, adjutant of the next battalion, invited me to his company mess, and for dessert produced a soup-plate full of better ice cream than I had tasted since the War broke out, home-made in an improvised freezer. The day had been another scorcher, and it hadn't rained for two days before that, so that the nearby road, built of coral, was deep in dust, and the countless trucks, bulldozers, half-tracks, ducks, jeeps, and AA guns that rolled by all day had swirled the dust all over us. The coke and ice cream went down well, and I walked contentedly to my tent as night came on. The tent was located on a low cliff overlooking the sea. I let my eye range over the Pacific to the far horizon, thought briefly of those I loved beyond it, prayed Compline, and called it a day.

CHAPTER 8

I Go A-Fishing

THE ARMY OFFERED ME AN EXCELLENT PROVING-GROUND FOR some of my theories. One night after chow, I gathered some twenty of my best-disposed men.

"You've been listening patiently while I've been explaining the Mass," I said, "and I'm grateful. But now it's time to do something. If we Christians are a corporate unit, we ought to pray together, and our best prayer is the Mass. So from now on we're going to recite the Mass together. I asked you to come here tonight so that we could rehearse it a little, and then you can be the leaders when we start next Sunday. OK?"

There was much nodding of heads.

"Good," I went on. "Let's try it. I'll begin the prayers at the foot of the altar, and you make the responses. Page 5 in your Stedman missals. Ready? *Introibo ad altare Dei . . .*"

There was a silence, and I looked around questioningly.

"What's the matter?"

"You mean in *Latin,* Father?"

"Sure," I said easily. "If those little altar boys at home can do it you should be able to. No problem, really."

Well, they tried. They stumbled and fell, repeatedly, over *laetificat* and *confitebor* and *vivificabis,* but they went gamely on, and I told myself that all they needed was practice. The odd part of it was that not one of them asked the perfectly obvious question, "What's the point of this? Why recite words when you don't know what they mean? Can you pray when you don't understand what you're saying?" It was just as well that they didn't ask because I couldn't have answered them—then.

The dialogue Mass never really caught on in New Guinea, in spite of my encouragement and the good will of my congregation. At the time I don't think I ever grasped how utterly unintelligible it was to the men. I had begun studying Latin in 1921, twenty-three years before. During the twelve years of my seminary training, our prayers, lectures, textbooks, and oral examinations had been in Latin. We had, except on holidays, spoken Latin in ordinary conversation around the house; it had become a second language, and I loved it. I think I even believed that there were things you could say in Latin which English could not express. But by the time we reached Manila my disillusionment was complete, and I instituted a dialogue Mass in which the congregation responded in English. Just after I had said *Dominus vobiscum* my leader would shout "The Lord be with you," and the men would reply (whole-heartedly and with full voice), "And with thy spirit." The practice bothered me, because the men were responding to my leader, and not to me as the president of the assembly, but there seemed no alternative at the time.

I remember a lieutenant-colonel who came up after Mass one Sunday to introduce himself. He was a convert, he told me, and wanted to say how much he had liked the sermon.

"Well, thanks," I said. "How do you like the dialogue Mass?"

"Oh, gosh, Father," he answered. "I was hoping you wouldn't ask me that."

"OK," I said. "Try not to make up your mind about it yet. Just keep doing it for a while."

Three months later he came up again to say good-bye. He had been ordered home.

"And by the way, Father, I've changed my mind completely about the dialogue Mass. I just hope my pastor back in California will start it."

But we couldn't know then that it would take twenty more years and a General Council of the Church and much ponderous head-shaking before the change was made.

On August 15th, we kept the ancient feast of the Falling Asleep of Our Lady as best we could. There was no procession with her image on the vigil, as there had been in tenth-century

Rome; the only procession that ever passed along our one road was the weary column of fuzzy-wuzzy laborers returning single-file at evening to their compound. They trudged along barefoot, at the very edge of the road, their bleached top-knots sticking up cut of black hair that reminded one of Medusa, keeping a wary eye out for the six-by-sixes which careened dizzily by them. We walked that road very seldom; it was too risky, and even if the trucks missed us, they left in their wake such clouds of coral dust that we choked and wept.

But for the Feast we offered the Holy Sacrifice twice—once at the 496th Port Battalion area, where thirty-seven sweating stevedores came out of the holds of Liberty ships and tried their best to be recollected in fatigues at eleven o'clock in the morning; and again at the Ordnance Officers' Club, a cool verandah overlooking the sea and designed to resemble as much as possible a night club at home, where at six in the evening two hundred and five "grease-monkeys" assembled in sun-tans. The short homily dealt with the exalted privilege of our Blessed Lady and her love for us who had been baptized into brotherhood with her Son; afterward, when chalice and linens and white vestments had been packed into the Mass kit and the place looked again like Dew Drop Inn, we sat and talked. Skinny from Sheboygan liked to be kidded about his one-horse town; he was a welder, and wanted to make something that could be used at the altar in the new chapel we were planning. Tom from Brooklyn had a new picture of Annie, whom he would go home and marry if the Japs would only lay off. Leo, whose patient good nature was later to accomplish so much in getting palm logs upright for the chapel walls, said little, but smiled eloquently with his dark Italian eyes. He cut the company's hair in his off-hours and sent the proceeds back to help support Ma in Mamaroneck.

No conversation ever ran very long without the question, "How long do you think it'll be before we get home, Father?" "Beats me," was my staple answer. I thought privately we might be camped on those blessed islands for two years or longer, but there was no point in saying so—especially not when we could look out on the salt acres of the Pacific that tossed and ran between us and those we loved. In that faraway, unreal war on the other side of the

world, the boys had still not got very far off the Normandy beach-
head; out here, the stepping stones between us and Tokyo seemed
numberless. We hadn't even control of all New Guinea yet, and then
there were the Admiralties, and the Marshalls, and the Russells, and the
Philippines, and a succession of Jimas bristling with enemies who had
to be killed before they stopped fighting . . . how could any of us have
known that our next celebration of the Assumption would be one of
frantic relief and delirious gratitude?

There were nine hundred Catholics among the Ordnance troops
in the area, but my best attendance on any Sunday amounted to only
a little over three hundred, so I decided that I should conduct an
old-fashioned "mission." I announced it at Mass on three consecu-
tive Sundays, and broadcast throughout the area a mimeographed
program, giving the time of the services and the titles of the sermons. These last, as I look at them now on the yellowing paper,
seem dated and melodramatic, but I suppose that at the time and in
those circumstances I thought they might have a particular drawing
power: "True North or Magnetic North?" "Allies and Enemies in the
Combat Area," "A Tracer in the Dark," "Total Defeat," "Escape
from Captivity," "This Way to Victory." There were two instructions and two full-dress sermons each night for eight nights; by
Thursday I felt utterly drained, and managed to keep going only
because I had written rather complete outlines of all the sermons
before the mission opened. About supper time I would groan to
myself over the effort it was going to take to become oratorical.
My years in the classroom and my long habit of explaining rather
than exhorting had to be abandoned in favor of highly charged oratory, because of the nature of a "mission" and because of the nature
of the GI. My purpose was not to perfect the good Catholic but to
remind all and sundry of their fundamental obligations, and especially to win the backsliders to a good confession. The purgative
way would have to be the road taken by most of these men, and the
rest of the program of Christian perfection would have to be incul-
cated through the power of the liturgy Sunday after Sunday during
the rest of their lives.

Attendance at the "mission" was disappointing; my largest
crowd was only two ninety five, whereas I had thought to break five

hundred before the week was out. Many of the men who needed it most did not appear, of course, at all. But the net results were consoling beyond my deserts: three First Communions, seven or eight rectified marriage cases—rectified as well as they could be over there, with promises to go the rest of the way when the men returned home—and a large number of long-term confessions, ranging all the way from three to eighteen and twenty years. One man was forty years old and had never made his first confession, though he had been baptized. Less conspicuous but genuine advances were seen in the improved recitation of the dialogue Mass and the growing familiarity with the missal, not to speak on the grace in the lives of those who received Holy Communion for eight straight days.

We closed the "mission" with a High Mass. My rough-hewn choir had been reinforced through the discovery of two men who had actually sung Gregorian chant before; one was an ex-seminarian and the other an officer who had, astonishingly, attended Pius X School of Liturgical Music. I chose the *Missa de Angelis,* and while they did murder, slay, and leave wallowing in its blood the *Sanctus,* they got through everything else creditably enough. No one except myself had ever had anything to do with a High Mass, so I had to remember things which good sacristans had always done for me, like lighting the charcoal for the incense. My acolytes and thurifer, who were making their very first appearance in the sanctuary, got by with a minimum of whispered admonition. The GI's were vastly impressed with the ritual, especially when they saw their own buddies taking an active part. One boy was particularly taken with the Asperges. "Never saw that before, Father. Did you dream it up yourself?"

A glance through the "monthly reports" I made out each month for the Chief of Chaplains in Washington shows that the number of regularly practicing Catholics was never impressive except at the time of an invasion. I used to hunt down my backsliders during the week. They would see me coming, of course, and try to slip out of sight. But one by one, I caught up with them, and then there would be great surprise on both sides.

"Hello, Tom! How's it going?"

"Oh, hi, Father! Pretty good."

"What do you hear from home?"

"They're OK, I guess."

"Say, Tom, haven't seen you at Mass lately."

(Much embarrassed pawing of the ground.) "Guess I been sleeping over lately, Father."

"Uh-huh. Sleeping over the evening Mass, too?"

(Great surprise.) "Do you *have* an evening Mass, Father?"

"Yup. We've been having one for three months now. See you there next Sunday, eh?"

"You bet, Father."

I didn't worry too much over these boys; their spirit was willing even though the flesh was weak. The ones who gave me pause were the ones who coolly told me they had no intention of changing their ways.

"I gave it up, Father. I've been going to Mass all my life and never got a thing out of it."

How do you answer that one? I used to say, "Look at it this way. You don't go to Mass primarily to get something out of it. You go to put something into it. You're there to worship God, to thank him for life and health and all the other blessings he's given you, and to ask him for what you need and what all of us need—his grace. You'll come away with plenty, but you have to make your own contribution first. Try that next Sunday, will you?"

When the 959th Company was alerted for action in what turned out to be the invasion of Leyte, I made a last appeal to the hold-outs. Several of them responded, but others remained adamant. I suppose I'll always remember one, a "Cajun" from Louisiana, who said firmly,

"No. I used to believe, but they knocked all that out of me at L.S.U."

The transport carrying the 959th into Leyte was bombed, but the bombs fell on the bow (killing several men), and he was on the stern. I often wondered if the incident made any change in his thinking.

There was so much to do that the days blurred one into another, and suddenly it was October. Back home, I thought, there would be a chill in the air and maybe a film of frost on the lawn in the morning. The maples would be in their glory about now in the Blue Hills, the crowds would be pouring into Fenway for football, the sea would have that incredible autumn blue, seen from the rocks at Cohasset. Here, nothing changed. The jungle grew as lush in October as it did in May. The temperature varied little; on October 16th, at nine-thirty, it was ninety-six in the shade. The screaming of the kookabura bird, the New Guinea crow, was just as raucous. Colonel Motz observed one day that its cry, repeated until we wanted to throw stones at it, sounded like "This is the last straw; this is the last straw; this is the last." A perennial source of amusement was the way America had been imposed on the country by the GI's. A sign over one mess hall read, "Ye Old Fat One's Greasy Spoon." On the bank at Scarlet Beach was another sign, "Guinea Wash-wash. No credit." I saw a tank one day with the cabalistic letters "IITYWYBAD" on its side, and wondered if it were the name of some South Pacific Campaign or battleground; later I learned that it meant "If I tell you, will you buy a drink?" Another day Len Stack was shifting some of the heavy Ordnance crates in the blazing sun of midday. He was sweating profusely, and had to stop every few minutes to clear his eyes. Suddenly he stopped again, took off his cap, and shouted "I *hate* wah! *Eleanor* hates wah! My whole *family* hates wah!"

There was the night the mess sergeant produced steak, french fries, and apple pie out of the blue heaven, and morale was high for a week. Most of the time we ate bully beef, Australian style, or Spam with powdered eggs and "tropical" butter (grease, pure and simple), griddle cakes and diced carrots and dehydrated potatoes. Far more important to morale, though, was mail. Air mail from home took about ten days and the Army tried very hard to keep it coming. "V-mail," a photographic process, was a little faster, but a distich in *Yank* summed up the average GI reaction to it:

> V-mail is quicker,
> Air mail is thicker.

Sometimes, especially when there was an invasion up ahead and planes used for mail had to be diverted to other uses, letters stopped coming, and then morale really slumped. More than anything, we wanted mail; as the camp newspaper put it, when asked what he wanted for Christmas the GI would promptly say "lots of air mail stamps, with letters stuck on 'em."

The morale problem was a real one in New Guinea. In other theatres there were things to see and do in off-hours. (I remember telling a group of men one night that a classmate of mine, on duty with the Fifth Army in Italy, had had an audience with the Pope. One of the boys spoke up, "Write and tell him you had an audience with a palm tree.") One day, feeling fed up with things in general, I decided a good long ride would clear my head and change my perspective. I climbed into the jeep and drove down the road (the only road), past the Base Headquarters, past the air strip, past the 33rd Division—and then the road ended. There was nothing ahead but jungle, and if you were bent on exploration you would have to do it by sea or by air.

After eighteen months in New Guinea men were theoretically entitled to leave in Australia, but no one in my outfit ever got it. I remember talking, shortly after I arrived, to a fine young officer who had the blues.

"Why don't you put in for a leave in Australia?" I asked.

"Nothing doing," he replied.

I persisted, "But you've been here for twenty-two months. You're entitled to it."

"Nope."

"But you'd come back a new man. Why not?"

"Look, Father," he burst out. "I love my wife, and I want to be faithful to her."

I hope Marge found out, somehow, sometime, how much she was loved.

We would get a week of intense heat, then a week of torrential rains. Everything made of metal rusted, everything made of leather or cloth picked up blue mold. The most frequent sight in the area was uniforms or Valpacks hanging on the clothes-lines. My typewriter, after two months, began to stick; it was rusting. And my fingers stuck to the keys. I thought that if I could draw, I would send a cartoon to the *New Yorker* showing a GI leaping from his bed and standing at the flap of his tent, slapping his chest and breathing the invigorating air. We were never completely dry; five minutes after putting on a fresh undershirt it would stick, and everyone had heat rash or jungle rot.

Radio helped pass the evening hours. The announcer began, "This is Station WXNG, the Jungle Network. The Information and Education Section, Headquarters USAFFE, brings you late news bulletins from San Francisco. We take you now to the United States." (Chorus from the listeners, "If you only could!") Then there were growls and squeals from the loudspeaker, sounding like mid-Pacific storm winds, and a faraway voice began, "This is Armed Forces Radio, San Francisco . . ." or Jimmy Durante's well-loved voice would come through his nose and across the miles. Just after the news, as a rule, we would have fifteen minutes of "GI Jive," presided over by "GI Jill," who had a voice of absolutely liquid sweetness, and who signed off at the end of her programs with

"And so, until tomorrow, this is your GI Jill saying 'Good morning' to some of you, 'Good afternoon' to some more of you, and to the rest of you, 'Good n-i-g-h-t!'" Such syrup.

My own best morale-builder was the weekly meetings with the other priests on the base. We called them our diocesan synods. By a rare grace, I had two old friends at Finsch; Father Bernard Boylan, a fellow-novice, was the chaplain at the Navy base, and Father Jerry Collins, a diocesan priest from Boston, was with an ack-ack outfit high in the hills to the north. Father Collins had a "mission" for his men several weeks before mine. He was fairly content with the results, but sighed over the "other nine" who were missing; his estimate was that he reached about a hundred and sixty of his three hundred men. After Mass on Saturday evening, Bill (my assistant) and I jumped into the jeep and drove up to his place, about four miles away. There had been a cloudburst just before supper, so the roads were in bad shape, and we were glad we had the four-wheel drive. At Scarlet Beach the tide was washing over the road, but we got through. When we arrived, Father Collins was sitting in his T-shirt, drinking a can of beer with Father Marquette, of the New Orleans archdiocese, and his assistant. Confessions had been rained out. So Bill and I ordered a can of beer each, and Father Collins grumbled about visiting firemen, and I told him that was fine gratitude for my heroic efforts to help him with confessions. He and Father Marquette proceeded to thank God piously that they were diocesan priests, members of the Order of St. Peter, and not scrounging Jesuits. And so far into the night.

Not all nights were so pleasant. One of the officers asked me to talk with a boy who, he said, had a real problem. He had just discovered that his wife, the mother of his two baby daughters, had been living with another man, and he had sued for divorce. But the thing had been eating into his heart so much that he was thinking of applying for transfer to a combat outfit so that he would not have so much time to brood over it. I talked to him for a long time, gradually edging around to the idea that he should think of the two babies. At least he had them to go home to and to work for, and, their mother being what she was, they would need him to bring them up right. I liked the boy a lot; he made no bid for sympathy, but he talked in such a slow, painful way that anyone could see how deeply wounded he had been. Then, quite without any prompting of mine, he began to ask about the Church.

"I kinda think I'd like my girls to be brought up Catholics. They'd hear the right thing and be taught what's right, and then maybe they wouldn't do the same as my wife done to me. I ain't been anything myself, but the Protestant churches say divorce is all right, and so girls naturally get to thinking they can do this sort of thing to their husbands. And I got to figuring that if I was a Catholic I could bring up my babies that way. I'd like to start now, so when I go home I wouldn't feel like a stranger in church. We got a big Catholic church back home."

So he went away with a catechism, and we discussed it several times thereafter, but when we moved out his company was separated from our battalion, and he became one of the hundreds I met, liked enormously, and never saw again. God be with them all.

When I went to bed I looked the cot over carefully. Insects were everywhere, and they gave me the horrors: woolly grubs, long-haired, multi-legged things that throve in the hot damp. Tom Jones had managed to lay hold of a pillow—it could be done if you knew a sergeant who knew another sergeant who had an "in" with the supply sergeant in the medics—and he offered me half of it. For a while I slept luxuriously, but one night there was a very noisome aroma in my tent, and next morning I discovered the cause—a defunct lizard which had crept in between the pillow slip and the pillow and died there, violently, no doubt, when I bounced my bony head on him. If only he had chosen some other cemetery! I burned my pillow, and when came such another?

CHAPTER 9

Building a House

IN THE NATURAL COURSE OF EVENTS, I SHOULD NEVER HAVE BUILT A church. Only bishops, pastors, and, occasionally, college presidents do that. The teacher must be content to erect a building "not made with hands," and hence not visible except to the eyes of faith.

But this does not mean that the teacher has no ideas as to how he would build a church if he got the chance. Accordingly, the bishop and the pastor should take counsel with parishioners before signing contracts. Someone at a little distance from the problem might have better perspective. Someone just might ask what the overriding purpose of a church is, and whether the building could not be designed with that in mind.

The Second Vatican Council in 1963 ordained that "when churches are to be built, great care must be taken that they be suitable for the celebration of liturgical services and for the active participation of the faithful." But, for too many hundreds of years before the Council, churches (especially cathedrals) had been built as signs of faith, or as monuments of a city's devotion, or to proclaim the triumph of the Christian idea. Great gray piles of stone tower over Chartres or Exeter, Rheims or Cologne or Siena; they do attest genius and dedication, they do capture the aspiration of the human heart for the eternal majesty of God. But in those cavernous vastnesses the tiny community is scattered and its dignity is lost. The Lord of the Universe, awesome and frightening, is there, to be sure, but it is hard to find the Word made flesh, the Lord who would be with his brethren when two or three of them gathered together, and who would say to them in the intimacy of the Supper, "Let not your heart be troubled, nor let it be afraid."

Parish churches, it is true, could not and did not attempt to match the grandeur of the cathedrals. But they, too, located the altar, the focus of parish life, as far away as possible from the community. The activity at the altar took on the character of a spectacle—admittedly a sacred and salutary spectacle—which the faithful were privileged to watch but in which they had no active part. Further, even after the "Ages of Faith" had passed and the society that had expressed its genius in Romanesque or Gothic or Renaissance architecture was long vanished, parishes continued to build churches in those dead styles. Pastors said that a church was not "devotional" unless it had mullioned windows or flying buttresses or niches peopled with saints in medieval costumes. Churches, and by implication all religion, came to seem quaint, to have a Christmas card quality, and to be utterly divorced from the realities of contemporary life.

Our government was generous in providing chapels for all its stateside posts and bases. There were thirteen of them at Camp Livingston. But they were "regulation," built from the approved blueprint, noncommittal in that with a minimal adjustment they could be used by Protestants, Jews, or Catholics. They had the long nave that placed the worshippers far from the sanctuary and kept them spectators. When we got overseas the Army often duplicated such chapels, especially if it was foreseen that the base would be a permanent one. But on the Pacific islands, where we did not plan to remain indefinitely, the chaplain would often be permitted to erect a chapel of his own designing. This was the situation I found myself in at Finschhafen. In fact, when I look back, I wonder that I was allowed to build at all. As a supply base, "Finsch" was fading in importance as the attack moved northward through New Guinea, Biak, and Halmahera toward the Philippines, where, according to the strategy, the assault on the Japanese homeland would be mounted. Finsch would be, ultimately, a deserted village, or the bush mission it had been before the War. As a result, by the time I joined the Ninth Battalion, lumber and roofing (galvanized iron or native thatch) had been "frozen," and I had to spend ten weeks on the road, scrounging what lumber I could from areas that were being evacuated by troops moving up. I lugged four-by-fours and six-by-sixes, begged salvage canvas for the roof, and sometimes watched in despair as my hardly accumulated stores were commandeered by the Base Service Command. The project that should have been three weeks in the building took, actually, fourteen weeks. And then we had only ten weeks to enjoy it.

On the other hand, there was one great advantage which probably would not have been ours if the base had been intended to be permanent. Army Regulations provided that unit chapels should be available for services of all faiths, and that there should be nothing in the way of decoration peculiar to any one religion or offensive to others. But we were fortunate inasmuch as the Protestant chaplain had his own chapel—too small for our use—only a few hundred yards away, and the Jewish men were cared for at the Base Chapel. We could go ahead, with the sanction of the authorities, and make our chapel a distinctively Catholic church. My congregation liked that, of course; they were tired of the usual Army chapel, which was so carefully neutral that it stood for almost nothing except the vague idea of "religion." Besides, the GI longed for home and normal life. He yearned for his wife and the child he had never seen, or the girl-friend, for Mom's solicitous love, for freedom to walk the streets without a pass and to drive a car without a trip-ticket. These represented normal life for him, and anything that savored of it or brought it closer won his heart.

He did not change on Sundays and holy days. In the field, of course, he recognized as unavoidable the Mass on the tailgate of the truck or the piled-up cases of ammunition, but once the area had quieted down he wanted a chapel, and the more it resembled a "real church" the more he felt that he was worshipping as he used to back home. His tastes in decoration were usually dictated by what he had known from childhood; he liked the conventional representations of God and Our Lady and the saints; he was impressed by soft lights and sentimental music; he looked askance at any departures from the methods and customs of the home parish.

All of which had to be weighed by the new pastor before he introduced any of his "liturgical" ideas and practices. He had to walk softly and explain at length the reason for each step before he took it. He had to be prepared for the objection, "we never did that in our church" or the more subtle "we used to have a nice thing at home; after Benediction the lights would be dimmed and we'd sing 'Good Night, Sweet Jesus,'" ending in an upward inflection of the voice which asked why it couldn't happen here.

From the first sermon to my new congregation I tried to throw out hints that might prepare their minds for accepting a different kind of chapel. Architecture had never been included among my formal studies, much less structural engineering, but I remembered a plan drawn by Barry Byrne for *Liturgical Arts,* and a friend sent me a picture from *Time* of St. Mark's Church in Burlington, Vermont, that helped me explain to my puzzled draftsman, Lieutenant Bob Hauser, what it was that I wanted.

"I dunno," he said, "It looks more like a boxing ring than a church to me."

"Well," I said, "A boxing ring has certain advantages. Everyone can see what he came to see. In the conventional sort of church, poor Joe Doakes, down in the last pew, can't see and has a hard time hearing. It's almost impossible for him to take an active part in the Mass."

"OK," he sighed, "And you don't want any center posts?"

"That reminds me," I answered, "of the fellow who went up to the ticket-seller at the theatre and asked what he had in the way of good seats. The answer was, 'Several large posts.'"

"You win," said Bob, "But I'll be hanged if I know where we are going to get beams over here strong enough to support a forty-foot span without center posts."

I grinned at him. "Work on it, Bob."

As it turned out, Bob's work was designing an intricate set of trusses that would hold up the roof without posts. We had to find and cart the lumber. Tom Jones from Brooklyn and Ben Gorski from New Jersey volunteered their day off and helped Bill and me carry wood (crates in which trucks and jeeps had been shipped over from the States) from the battalion assembly line to our site. Next day one of the company commanders gave me four men, two more volunteers offered their day off, and we broke up the crates into usable two-by-fours and two-by-sixes for flooring. Meanwhile Steve Brennan was arranging with his usual mysterious resourcefulness to get us palm logs for supports and roof-trees. This evidence of action generated interest among the company commanders, and each gave me one man every day thereafter. But the assembly line could not supply our needs, so I went out scrounging. Six hours on the road and I came back empty-handed. The Air Corps had nothing, the Division had nothing, the Base Engineers had nothing— nothing, that is, that they would part with. But there was some consoling news for me when I returned disappointed and weary: a friendly supply sergeant had obtained for me three huge tarpaulins which would serve for a roof. He had also laid hands on some salvage parachutes which would be effective in the later decoration of the sanctuary. With this encouragement I led out my trusty detail next morning in the opposite direction; I had been notified officially that "several thousand" logs had been cut by native labor and were available to anyone who would take them away. We thrashed the bush and splashed through cuttings in the jungle until my jeep stalled in the ruts. Then I sent the truck ahead, but the boys were able to find only twelve logs, and these were on the far side of a stream that was too swift and wide to ford with the truck. Two days later, however, we located the place the officials had really meant to send us to. Thousands of logs lay on the banks of a small river, and near them, taking their ease, lay some twenty fuzzy-wuzzies. They were supposed to be working for the Australians, but there wasn't an Aussie in sight, so I inquired for the "boss-man" and said to him, "You carry um logs, huh?" He said "Huh," and in fifteen minutes the truck was loaded with logs we could use for rafters and joists.

I learned rapidly to stay away from "the brass" when I wanted something and to hunt up instead the sergeant on the job. By and large, whether they were first sergeants, master sergeants, tech sergeants, staff sergeants, supply sergeants, mess sergeants, or personnel sergeants, the race of three-stripers was a kindly, obliging one, and they seemed to take the chaplain, who, like themselves, was a kind of buffer state between the higher-ups and the lower-downs, under their fraternal protection. This is not to decry the interest and real cooperation of an occasional captain or lieutenant, much less the whole-souled generosity of the corporal, the PFC, and the lowly buck, but when you wanted something you went automatically to the sergeant, and infallibly you came away with it.

I wanted the chapel to be, specifically, a place where men of the Ordnance Department could worship God. As I told them in my sermons, we were not Infantry, or Air Corps, or Artillery; we were Ordnance. As such, I felt, we had a gift to offer God that was peculiarly our own—the work we did in our shops and offices. So many of our waking hours were spent at work, and in New Guinea there was so little recreation to divert us, that we might say our work was our entire life. In dedicating our work to God, then, we were dedicating our lives to Him in a manner more exclusive, perhaps, than we ever did at home. We were giving Him these years of our life, laying our youthful energies on his altar as an acceptable sacrifice.

Again, for most of us, life in New Guinea was a hardship. The heat, the rains, the inconvenience of the chow line and life in the open, more than anything the loneliness of separation from those we loved—these were real difficulties, but they could be accepted as God's present disposition of us; they could be offered to Him in union with the eternal sacrifice of his Son.

It seemed to me that if these two ideas, Ordnance and New Guinea, and their relation to the Mass could be given expression in the design of the chapel and all its furnishings, the men would have before them a vivid reminder of how they could participate actively in their worship while they were in the Army and might apply the lesson to their new circumstances after the war. My idea for the altar, which more than any other feature of the chapel should symbolize their work and difficulties, was to use a large log of native wood for the base, two 90-millimetre shells for the legs, and native planks for the table. So one morning, when the corner posts had been set and the floor-supports were going in, I fought my way (a good thing the jeep had a four-wheel drive) through mud and ruts and along a plank road far into the jungle, where I found a huge sawmill, piles of sawdust and a crew of Forestry Engineers snaking trees down from the hills and turning out lumber by the ton. What was the wood? It was mahogany and rosewood, beautiful stuff, enough to supply cabinet-makers in the States for generations. And what was it being used for? For such things as tent-floors, latrines, crates for ammunition, and even the road I had come in on. Of course it was not seasoned or polished, but even so the splendid red grain shone out in the sun. I told the sergeant what I wanted: three planks eight feet long and a heavy log. I got the planks, solid mahogany, but he hadn't a log of the dimensions I wanted. I went back next day; still no luck. But when I drove in again he casually pointed out a five-hundred-pound log, squared on three sides but with the bark still on top and the crimson grain bright as blood, and asked if that would do. I contained my delight as well as I could, got the log on the back of my truck as swiftly as its weight would allow, and drove away before someone appeared with bars on his shoulders and second thoughts in his head. Bill Graham and Tom Jones sandpapered and lacquered the face of the log, and strove to enhance its glow with shoe polish, which was the nearest thing we had to furniture polish. And "Skinny from Sheboygan" made a gleaming map of New Guinea in steel which we affixed to the log in order to make its meaning unmistakable. The shape of the island is roughly that of a turtle and we knew it well. So with the shells we had both New Guinea and Ordnance in our table of sacrifice. Then, instead of putting the table at the far end of the chapel, we set it on a generous platform, twelve feet by twelve, reached by three broad steps, against the long wall rather than the short one. The altar itself was forty-two inches high, so that it concentrated attention on itself, and we seated the congregation about it on three sides and brought the main aisles down from the vestibules at the rear so that they converged on the altar like two searchlights picking out a target. There was no mistaking what was the principal furnishing of the chapel or its reason for being.

By this time my men had entered into the spirit of the thing and begun to come forward with inspirations of their own. Lieutenant Bob Carracher made six candlesticks of brass shimstock, shaped in the likeness of the Ordnance Department insignia, a flaming bomb. The missal stand was of heavy brass wire, and had a crossed hammer and a wrench, typical Ordnance tools, worked into its back. The credence table (made of mahogany and a single shell) was a replica of the altar, and on its base, cut out of plywood, was the Chi-Rho emblem, the monogram of Christ. The holy water stoup was the base of a shell, and the aspergill or sprinkler was made of Ordnance brass and New Guinea mahogany. I wanted a censer for High Mass, but no one could come up with an idea for that. Then, one morning, Steve Brennan put his head into my tent.

"I've got your censer," he said.

"Good! What's it like?"

"You'll see."

So, not long after, I did. Steve had taken a jeep piston, cut slits in it, and hung it from chains on three sides. He had even fitted it with a removable cap. It was far and away the most ingenious contribution to our furnishings, and also the most pedagogically effective, for when the men saw that commonplace item of their daily work used for the worship of God, I think they really understood for the first time what I had been trying to say in my sermons.

We were proud of the tabernacle, too. When a group of us were discussing it one night in my office, someone said,

"Why not make it look like a tent?"

"Of course!" I cried. Every Army installation overseas was a tent city; we lived and worked and slept in tents. We would put the Lord in a tent, too.

"Then," I added, "It would be a wonderful symbol of the Incarnation and the Eucharist itself. We say 'The Word was made flesh and dwelt among us,' but what St. John actually said in the original Greek was 'The Word was made flesh and pitched his tent among us.'" So one of our amateur but clever carpenters made to scale a pyramidal box, sixteen by sixteen inches (our tents were sixteen by sixteen feet) and we hung about it a close-fitting drape of parachute silk with a fly in the front, and the resemblance was plain.

Easily the most impressive feature of the sanctuary, however, was the crucifix suspended over the altar. From the beginning I had wondered what I could do for a suitable crucifix. The tiny one from my Mass kit would have looked absurd on that long altar, and if I sent for one to Australia or the States I might be waiting still. Then I heard that in one of my companies there was a lad who amused himself with wood-carving. "He's really good, Father." Should I ask him? If he produced something bad, would I have the heart to tell him I couldn't use it? On the other hand, how could I use it if it were not good? At last I decided to take the risk, and the artist and I went to the Engineers' lumber yard, where he looked carefully about and finally selected a piece of rosewood that had come in as ballast, they told us, on a ship from Australia. Without adequate tools—what he used chiefly, as he told me later, was a jack-knife and broken beer bottles—he went to work in his spare time and in some extra hours that his C.O., Captain Richman, who became interested as the work progressed, gave him. The only suggestion I made was that the figure on the cross be crowned and royally vested. I was thunderstruck, then, several weeks afterward, when he brought me his handiwork. The cross was three feet long, the corpus two feet. The face was strong and serene, the figure majestic. "God," as the prophet said, "reigns on the tree." In this crucifix was not only the suffering Servant of Good Friday but the risen Conqueror of Easter. In my sermons thereafter it was easy to point out that all the sorrows of our Lord had ended in victory and peace. I could hold out the promise that our Army privations and our New Guinea miseries would have a like glorious end when we returned home, and that if we kept faith with him we would come eventually by his passion and cross to the glory of his resurrection. My artist's contribution to the chapel ensemble was immense, and I felt that he could with justifiable pride carve his name on the back of the cross (where it may still be read): "Clarence Staudenmayer, Portage, Wisconsin. November, 1944."

The actual building of the chapel was going on meanwhile. The names of my carpenters represented pretty much our multi-racial Army: Jones, Spinelli, Dupont, Stack, Mangiaracina, Jensen, Galucci, Scannell, Paluch. During the last week they worked especially hard, setting the rafters and the roof-tree and swinging the heavy tarps up and over the whole. Then the critical moment came. We had to pull out the posts that up till now had supported the cross beams. Would they hold up without the posts? Bob Hauser, who had designed them, asserted that they would. We said a Hail Mary and Tony Galucci picked up a sledge-hammer. The rest of us crouched apprehensively, looking up at the rafters. Bang! One post out, and no suspicious cracking. Bang! Two posts out. Heck, this is gonna be OK. Let 'er rip. They all came out, and nothing even quaked. A moment later the boys were walking all over the roof like cats. Johnny Mangiaracina—such music in these Italian names—shook his head doubtfully, "We have had some bad storms here." And I gave the answer Brother Glennon, years before, had made familiar to a whole generation of novices at Shadowbrook: "Johnny, ha' ye no faith?" Well, the boys finally picked up their caps and departed, but I stayed there in the growing twilight, revelling in the finished building. Finally I went looking for Steve Brennan, and found him pitching horseshoes.

"Want a real, authentic thrill?"

"Any time," he answered.

"Well, come over here."

Steve felt it, too. The chapel, by our standards, was spacious, generous, yet it swept so unerringly up to the altar that the high purpose of the building was never in doubt.

I needed one more item to complete the sanctuary: red cloth to cover the canopy and the wall behind the altar. It was the custom to hang salvage parachutes of various colors as decorations in Officers' and Noncoms' Clubs. I had seen them, also, in Air Corps chapel. But we were not Air Corps, and I didn't want parachutes as such. However, parachutes were made of cloth—fine silk cloth, as a matter of fact. I went hunting. People assured me, one after another, that there wasn't a red parachute on the base, but at last I made a strike, and came away with four. Ah! Softly, now: one more step. At the Quartermaster Salvage Company, where they repaired shoes, clothes, tents, and the like, I found Sergeant Sammy Shapiro from New York. Apologetically, and with a tear in my voice, I asked if it would be at all possible to rip out the petals of my parachutes, turn them around and sew them together again in huge squares. I explained that if he could do that they would no longer look like parachutes, which was what I wanted. Sammy saw my point, got interested, and said he'd do all he could.

"When would you want it?"

I said, "Er—by Saturday night?"

He whistled and scratched his head, then grinned. "Well, we can try. Come back on Thursday and we'll show you how we are making out."

I couldn't get back until Friday, but by that time they had finished the drapes for the wall and were working on the canopy. Then I had the bright idea of asking them to cut out a Chi-Rho monogram in white parachute silk and sew that to the drapes. On Saturday night Sammy came up to help Bill Graham, Jimmy Scannell, Steve Brennan and myself hang the drapes, and kept us roaring with laughter by telling one Jewish story after another. Bill and Warrant Officer Chris Spicuzza, from Providence, had in the meantime given the altar a final polish, had sanded, oiled, and shellacked the altar platform, and provided kneeling benches behind each row of chairs. At eleven-fifty the last wrinkle in the canopy was smoothed out; we had a bottle of beer and went off to bed, very weary indeed.

Sunday was the Feast of Christ the King, the day we had set for the dedication of our chapel. The men gathered for Mass at six-thirty in the evening; six of my fellow priests generously came and graced the occasion in cassock and surplice; the battalion C.O. and his adjutant and several other Protestant officers gave us the courtesy of their presence. I heard confessions until the hour of Mass, when Father Dietzel took over and finished up while I vested. Before Mass I went to the foot of the altar and read a prayer I had composed myself, patterned after the blessing in the Ritual of a new house. There was no blessing of a new church in the Ritual, I suppose because such blessings are properly reserved to bishops. But our nearest bishop was in Australia! Then I intoned the Asperges, not being optimistic about the response I would get from my make-shift choir, but they rose to the occasion and came through nobly. I walked up and down my two broad aisles, sprinkling the building and the congregation with holy water, and returned to the rear of the chapel to put on maniple and chasuble, and faced the altar once more.

Outdoors, night had fallen by this time. The altar, in consequence, rose up before me like the "holy hill" of the 43rd Psalm, which I would recite in a moment at its foot. We had hidden in the canopy "seal-beam" jeep headlights, and in their radiance the brass of the shells and the candlesticks glittered and flashed, while the mahogany smoldered somberly beneath. Overhead and behind hung the crimson drapes, suffusing the sanctuary with a red glow—the color of devotion, the color that symbolizes blood and life and love. It was an appropriate setting for the perfect Sacrifice which we were now privileged to offer and to which we were invited to join our own.

Mass began. I was profoundly moved as I ascended the wide steps, bowed and kissed the altar I had myself designed, looked up at the crucifix I had suggested. This was almost certainly the only church I would ever build. It would never rival the great churches of the world, but much planning and ingenuity and toil—yes, and frustration—had gone into it. It was such a gift as men give when they want to prove their love; it was the best we had and the best we could do.

But it was not too much, for as the Entrance Chant of the Mass reminded us, "Worthy is the Lamb who was slain to receive power and divine honors and wisdom and strength and honor and glory and blessing. To him belong glory and dominion forever and ever." And the purpose of this chapel was that in it we might do as the Epistle bade us, "give thanks to the Father, who has made us worthy to share the lot of the saints in light. He has rescued us from the power of darkness and transferred us into the kingdom of his beloved Son, in whom we have our redemption, the remission of our sins."

Ideas like these were the ones I put before my congregation when, after reading the Gospel of the Feast to them, I explained the design of the chapel and the symbolism of its furnishings. Here in the middle of our encampment, I said, in the center of our lives and our work, stands a sign that gives them meaning and value. Here we might come individually to find strength and comfort and forgiveness, and here we might assemble to witness to our faith and to praise God. Here, as they could see from what lay before them, it was possible to bring a gift fashioned from the everyday commonplaces of life that would sanctify us and please our Father in heaven. Here we had a house and a table where we might eat and know that we are sons and brothers. And we could ask earnestly, as one of the prayers of the Feast put it, that he whom we offered in our sacrifice might himself give the blessings of unity and peace to all men.

One of the advantages of preaching from that platform was that no one was more than twenty-four feet away from me, and I could make what I said very direct and personal indeed. Dialogue Mass, too, in such surroundings was not the disturbing innovation it might otherwise have been; the men seemed to feel that the departure from custom was sanctioned by the other new things they had made and had grown to like. It would have been going too far in those days to celebrate "facing the people," but at least my congregation surrounded me on three sides, and I had a vivid sense that I was, in the words of Justin Martyr, "the president of the assembly."

But the Army teaches unremittingly that central Christian idea, "we have not here an abiding city." Five weeks after the dedication, the altar and the furnishings disappeared into crates, and five weeks after that they went into the hold of the transport. I looked back across the open water and saw the frame of my chapel melt into the jungle. What happened to it later I never heard. Some other outfit used it for a time, no doubt, but then? Perhaps the Aussies made it into a pub; perhaps the termites took over and brought it crashing down, one night, when the high winds blew. It would have been good to have lived through one complete liturgical year there—if it had not been New Guinea, and if the Philippines had not lain ahead—a long stride toward victory and peace and home for war-weary GI's. Maybe, I thought, there would be other Ordnance chapels north of the Southern Cross. After all, the sergeants were going with me. So was man's innate yearning to understand his worship of God and to share in it.

CHAPTER 10

Long Ago and Far Away

MY STAY ON THE UNREGRETTED ISLAND OF NEW GUINEA WAS NOT very long as the calendar reckons time, only six months. And the amazing spectacle of the shotgun marriage between American industrialism and the jungle provided novelty enough to speed the hours—to say nothing of a schedule that left few minutes open for brooding. But I felt while there as if I were living in a clearing in a forest, surrounded by stealthy enemies who grew always more numerous and crept closer. There was something sinister in the New Guinea atmosphere—something invisibly malevolent toward us, who were not, like the fuzzy-wuzzies, children of the jungle. And if I was prompted by common sense to shrug off this hostile presence, or to think of it as the effect of over-indulgence in Joseph Conrad, a visit to the hospital would always bring it back. You don't shrug off jungle rot or scrub typhus.

For that matter, you don't shrug off the mud, or the choking coral dust that blows in the dry season from the one busy road and sifts over everything, or the blue mold that ruins leather and linen alike, or the omnipresent, centipede insects. In particular are you conscious of the tangled jungle behind you, with its sour, vinegary smell, and the wastes of open water before you, stretching eight thousand miles to the Golden Gate and home.

I know that if I had never seen New Guinea I could not have imagined it. Oh, some features, to be sure. I remember how, when the weather cleared, the full moon would look down through waving palm trees on the surf, and the scene was pure Hollywood. But visible moons were rare; the rains were never far away. When the War was over and we had been at home for some years, tunes from the musical, *South Pacific,* were immensely popular. The first time

I heard the lyrics of "Bali Hai," they seemed impossibly sentimental, and then with a start I recalled the evening we were going over to the mess hall for chow, and everyone stopped to stare out to sea at an island, quite distinct, that we had never seen before and, as a matter of fact, never saw again. Even when the sun was shining on shore the rain clouds hovered densely over the sea, lowering and raising curtains, suddenly opening long corridors to the eye or building up fantastic Saracen castles of mist.

The movie-makers at home certainly seemed to have no idea of what the real New Guinea was like. One night Bill Graham and Jimmy Scannell, insisting that I needed a break, hauled me by main force off to the evening show. We sat in the open, swaddled in ponchos, with the steady rain cascading off our helmet liners and making it difficult at times to see the screen, which was the only thing under shelter. The picture was called "A Guy Named Joe," featuring Spencer Tracy and (I think) Irene Dunne. According to the story, Tracy, a flyer of some experience, has been killed in action, and then assigned as a kind of guardian angel to sit behind novice fliers on their first solo flights and whisper directions in their ear that would prevent them from cracking up. It was a clever idea, lightly and fancifully handled. Then one of his protégés, having won his wings, is given his overseas orders—to New Guinea! We sat up—so far as we could without exposing our faces directly to the rain—and took an even greater interest. This should be good. But Hollywood's version of New Guinea made it a sun-drenched paradise of white beaches and lovely gardens set in palm groves, bungalows with every convenience, beautiful girls in party frocks strolling with immaculately groomed officers toward pagodas hung with lanterns and filled with the music of Guy Lombardo's orchestra. A swelling chorus of groans, hoots, and horse-laughs broke out around me, and the audience, wrapping their ponchos around them, went off disgustedly through the rain and mud to play poker or finish the letter home. A piece of verse called "Thoughts of a Troppo Trooper" appeared about this time in *Yank Down Under* (the South Pacific service magazine) and gave a humorous but more realistic picture of our life on that ineffable island:

Thoughts of a Troppo Trooper

Oh sing a song of Guinea-land, a pocket full of slime
    Sixty billion blowflies, a-buzzin' all the time,
Snakes and ants in front and back, and lizards on my flank;
    Say, isn't that a dainty dish to set before a Yank?

Behold, in all his truculence,
    the wallaby connubial,
A pocket-book edition of a
    pocket-book marsupial.
He bounces and he bounces with a
    shock-absorbent ease,
And gaily bouncing with him are his
    fifty thousand fleas.
He bounces 'round my tent at night;
    he bounces out again.
I wake up and I look, and think,
    "Why, wasn't he a dear?
There—see? Within my shoes he's left
    the nicest souvenir!"
God bless thee, little wallaby;
    God bless thee, bouncing fauna,
I bless the day we met,
    but I'll be glad the day you're gone-a!

Oh sing a song of Guinea-land, a barrel full of mud,
    Leeches and mosquitoes in a bacchanale of blood,
Fungus in the lister-bag and termites in the tank,
    Say, isn't that a dainty dish to set before a Yank?

— T5 Norman Lipman, *Yank Down Under,* 1944

Long after I had moved on to the Philippines it occurred to me that I had not seen a single flower or any bird except the raucous Kookabura during my six months in New Guinea. It was perhaps understandable that the noisy, teeming Army may have frightened the birds away, but where were the gorgeous orchids, the trailing bougainvillea and other exotic blooms that the *National Geographic* had prepared us for? Actually, there were very few tropical birds or flowers in the Philippines, either, and I had to wait almost fifteen years before I visited Jamaica and saw what the escapist painters and poets had been talking about. Perhaps at Finschhafen we were in the right church, but the wrong pew. Perhaps we should have seen the Fijis, or Hawaii, or Tahiti. In any case, we had one more compelling reason for "wanting out."

Psychiatrists, guidance directors, and other professional counsellors must have, I imagine, sanctuaries to which they can retreat sometimes in the interest of their own sanity; hideaways where they can lock a door, pull down curtains, and have a good cry of their own. At Boston College, when the pressures threatened to climb beyond the toleration point, I could hide behind a suave switchboard operator who had the knack of saying "I can't seem to locate him at the moment" with just the right accent of despair. But at Finsch there was no place to hide—not, surely, in a tent where the flaps were necessarily kept up to encourage the entrance of any vagrant puffs of fresh air, and certainly not in the shops or company areas where the chaplain discovered he had magnetic qualities that attracted every problem in the battalion. The working day for officers and men ended at supper, but his went on into the small hours, and to so many of the problems—loneliness, tedium, the dragging uncertainty of how long it would be before we could go home, anxiety about parents or wives—he could only try to lend a sympathetic ear, knowing they were not solvable except through the patience that is born of trust in God. I had letters—and I suppose the men did, too—from friends in other theatres of the war, telling of leaves spent on the Riviera, or the Amalfi Coast, or Paris, or New Delhi, or some other diverting place. Here, even if leave were given (it wasn't), there was no place to go except to "another part of the forest," and our jungle was no Arden.

It took me thirty-five days to re-read *Crime and Punishment,* and though I bought from the PX copies of *Henry Esmond, Gulliver's Travels,* and some of George Eliot, I might have spared myself the expense; the books were never opened. Well, C. S. Lewis asked by what title we Christians thought our time was our own—a reasonable question except that periodically one must have a bit of solitude, one must fill up the tank a little in order to have something to give. I remember thinking one day that if I could only talk to God quietly for half an hour I might be a calmer man and a better counsellor. So I left my office and took up a position in the far corner of our area, my back to a palm tree, looking off to sea. But so many of the men stopped as they went by to ask solicitously, "Whatsa matter, Father? Got the blues?" that I finally laughed and gave it up as a bad job. On another day, though, I simply fled. It was a clear morning; I threw my breviary, a copy of the *Divina Commedia,* and some stationery into the jeep and drove to an unoccupied cliff overlooking the ship-filled harbor. The day passed blissfully; I prayed, read, wrote home, and thought long thoughts with the help of a reflective pipe. The day was so refreshing that I sang aloud all the way back. Luckily the jeep had no muffler, so the men in the outfits I passed did not hear me and rush out to see who the new Paul Revere was, spreading the alarm.

Judith Anderson visited the Base and gave us several scenes from *Macbeth.* It was rather heady stuff for the general run of the GI's, but several near me, I noticed, enjoyed it thoroughly, and I myself came away in a state of starry-eyed intoxication. God bless the lady for having come so far and into such an unladylike world to entertain us. Some weeks later the natives provided another type of entertainment. The Australians, who ruled the natives' lives pretty completely, would sometimes allow them to have a "sing-sing" in their compound, which was usually off-limits to us, but which we were permitted to visit on such occasions. The "sing-sing" went on for at least two days; the native men would go round and round tirelessly in circles of about twenty, crouching and chanting a monotonous anthem or dirge that varied only in volume. Bill Graham, Tom Jones and Lou Baker, our supply sergeant from Ohio, went with me to the top of the highest hill in the neighborhood, where we found the compound and, by the light of a huge fire and the flashlights held by a multitude of curious GI's, watched the chanting rings of fuzzy-wuzzies. They wore skirts of rainbow colors and long earrings, but it was their headdresses that caught our attention. On top of their already ample bleached hair-do's they had set superstructures as much as two feet high, made of feathers, bits of wire, and palm twigs, and decorated with covers of *Yank* magazine (a vivid red), labels from cans of grape juice and pineapple, and even burned-out electric bulbs. We watched the weird and tireless cotillion until the musk from their bodies drove us away. Could it be that in this twentieth century there were still people like that? Then I thought of our New Year's Eves, our football and political rallies, our jam and jive sessions, and wondered how deep the difference really was.

Thanksgiving came and went, providing a half-holiday for the battalion and a miraculous dinner that made us forget for a few days the "corned willie" and dry flapjacks that by this time had become staple fare at Finsch. I was invited by three companies to share their festivities, but Captain Richman of the 523rd had asked me first. Before going to his mess hall, though, I made a short speech and offered a prayer of thanks for the 959th Company, at their request. The Company didn't know it, but the prayer was appropriated from the Votive Mass of Thanksgiving in the missal. At the 523rd Company I found a literally groaning board; the mess sergeant was what we then called a Big Time Operator, and had managed to put his hands on every delicacy traditional on this day at home. Of course our provident Uncle Sam had achieved a few minor miracles in getting all those perishables across so many thousand miles to us. They could scarcely be classified as strategic items, indispensable to the war effort, and in our thanksgiving "the folks at home" deserved a place. We dined extremely well, in an atmosphere of relaxed conviviality, and afterward sat at ease on the back porch of the officers' quarters, overlooking the sea from a height of forty feet. Some of the men played touch football and volleyball, though I wondered how, with a dinner like that inside them and the thermometer standing at 103° in the shade, they could play anything except, perhaps, water polo.

Early one morning Steve Brennan came rushing in, waving a yellow sheet on which was a news item transcribed from a short wave broadcast from the States. "The Apostolic Delegate announced today in Washington that the Most Reverend Richard J. Fussy has been named Archbishop of Boston." It took only a second to translate this perplexing communiqué, and then I dashed for the phone to tell Father Collins.

"Jerry," I said. "We're in!"

"In what?" he asked. "The soup?"

"No, you old grouch. In clover! Bishop Cushing has been given the Archdiocese!"

All of us priests in the service had reason to rejoice. To each graduating class of the Chaplain School at Harvard, Bishop Cushing, as a token of his interest in our apostolic opportunity, had given a send-off dinner at which he personally played the generous host; many of us were indebted to him for Mass kits and other necessities. And I knew the stupendous things he had already done for the missions; whenever I had met a missionary in the Pacific area and mentioned that I was from Boston I had got the same reaction,

"Boston? You must know Bishop Cushing."

What we could not foresee then, of course, was how much reason our Archdiocese and Latin America and indeed the entire Church had for rejoicing. The doctrine of the "collegiality" of bishops, according to which a bishop is consecrated not for his own diocese only but for the needs of the faithful everywhere, would not be defined until the Second Vatican Council, twenty years later, but it was exemplified with shrewd foresight and prodigal generosity during the interval by the craggy, great-hearted Archbishop of Boston. We used to smile when we read, on the feasts of the Apostles, that there was "no speech and no utterance whose sound could not be heard; into all the earth their sound goes forth"—it was literally true of our Cardinal's booming voice, whether from his episcopal throne or from the Inauguration Day platform in Washington or in the chamber of the Council in Rome. But if his voice and his munificence went out to all the earth, it was because his heart had gone there first.

Up to this point in our experience, none of us had seen a Japanese, alive or dead, and I used to wonder whether our enemy knew how little zest we had for our war with him. I suspect that he may have guessed; the propoganda of "Tokyo Rose" certainly tried to exploit it. I could see no parallel in this war for the rollicking mood of the country in World War I, when we went overseas to knock off the Kaiser and bring home a king or two as souvenirs. Most of the popular songs in those days of my early boyhood had been gay, cocky, exhilarating. In 1944 we sang "Mairsy Doats" and other nonsense rhymes like Bing Crosby's "Would You Like to Swing on a Star?" and "Is You Is or Is You Ain't My Baby?" but the real favorites were the wistful, sad songs of loss and longing. "Lili Marlene," which our troops in Europe had picked up, oddly enough, from the Germans and made their own, never caught on particularly in the Pacific, though it expressed the prevailing mood. The popular songs with us were "I'll Be Seeing You in All the Old Familiar Places," "I'll Never Smile Again Until I Smile at You," "Long Ago and Far Away," and similar pieces. I used to wish that we Catholics had some strong hymns we could sing to counteract, at least once a week, the aching ballads of homesickness and craving. But the time was not yet ripe for borrowing from the Protestants as we now do, to our profit, and our Catholic repertoire was small indeed. "Tantum Ergo," in its best-known setting, was good, but was generally so dragged that it sounded like a dirge, and the long pause inserted after "ergo" showed—if one needed evidence—that no one really understood even the drift of the Latin words. "Holy God, We Praise Thy Name" was good, too, but pretty threadbare from excessive use. Many hymns the men might have been familiar with were sentimental (and set to music in three-quarter time!) or theologically weak. With considerable diffidence but in desperation I translated the "Salve Regina" and taught it to my congregation. A real musician, and especially one with any knowledge of Gregorian Chant, would have winced to hear it sung ("Mo-o-other of mercy"), but the men liked it.

Though my friend Father Joe Nolan was later to write a much more successful translation, I can't escape the conviction that our English does not lend itself to Gregorian neums. I thought of trying my hand at "Christus Regnat," that fine, virile litany which one can imagine the barons roaring at Chartres a thousand years ago, but I'd have needed a stronger choir than the one I had to introduce and support it. In those pre-Gelineau, pre-Howell days we hadn't one singable psalm, and so that lovely book of aspiration and comfort was closed to us. Now that the Second Vatican Council has given us the vernacular and insisted on popular religious singing, composers have carte blanche to experiment, to write new melodies, to adapt old ones. One hopes that they will not compose only for trained choirs, that they will not think it beneath them to provide music in which the whole People of God can express their praise and love.

Ordinarily we saw little of the traffic in the harbor, being too far away, but one Sunday I received a message inviting me to dinner aboard a hospital ship, and managed to board a launch going out to where she sat in the stream. At the top of the ladder was Father Jack Shea, a New York Jesuit who had been in my class at Chaplain School. We shot the breeze, as the GI's put it, for three hours, and I tried not to look envious as he told me about his cruise in the Mediterranean, how he saw Oran and Corsica, Naples and Rome, and was in on the Marseilles invasion. Dinner was, well, amazing. We were served, for one thing, and there were tablecloths and napkins, silver knives and forks. They brought us, then, fruit cup, soup, our choice of capon or broiled swordfish, peas, candied yams, ice cream, cake, cheese, coffee.

"Just an ordinary dinner," said Jack. "Too bad you didn't come aboard yesterday."

I smiled painfully.

About this time there fell into my hands the first copy of the *London Times' Literary Supplement* that I had seen since leaving the States. Reading its leisured, civilized pages was balm to my soul, though I marveled how the English, in view of the past five years, could maintain their academic tranquility. It took courage of a very high order to get out fifteen crowded pages weekly and say so little about the war. In this issue they reviewed a biography of Francis Quarles, that inconspicuous 17th-century Metaphysical, with the scholarly concern that Alfred Tennyson, in the midst of his Victorian calm, might have bestowed on it. Unfortunately there was no one with whom I could share such interests. At our headquarters mess the meals were garnished with discussions of generators, trucks, M-l anti-aircraft fire directors, and so on—a world I never knew. Once, I remember, a conversation on psychology got somehow started, coughed, spluttered along for a moment, then died, and defied my efforts to resuscitate it. Never, before or since, have I lived with a group of such pleasant fellows and had in common with them only the topics of everyday routine and good-natured chaffing. Both sides found it, I think, tolerable but a little wearing.

By December first we knew we were moving. Our tools and heavy equipment were crated and hauled to the docks, and our shops closed down almost entirely. Speculation was the order of the day; would it be Leyte, which the workhorse 32nd Division had finally wrested from the Japanese and where one of our companies had already gone? Or would it be some island closer to the front than New Guinea now was, yet far enough behind the lines to set up our maintenance and supply functions in safety? It was taken for granted that we would not be charging up any beach-heads or digging any fox-holes; after all, we were Ordnance troops, not Infantry. And, aside from the usual personal considerations, I found this an agreeable idea. My men had all had basic training, of course, but that was long ago, and I couldn't envision most of them in a combat situation. It seemed to me that they would do more injury to themselves than to the enemy.

Speculation came appropriately for the season; it was Advent. And there were, for once, none of the preoccupations we Americans have brought into December to distract us from the real meaning of both Advent and Christmas. I have often thought what a disenchantment must result from the contemporary celebration of this season. It begins very early downtown—any time after the first of November. And it rises in a steady crescendo of anticipation until, by Christmas Eve, it has crowded out every other thought. Gifts must be bought, in bewildering numbers and lavishness, greetings must be written and mailed, business must be wound up. We are reminded each morning exactly how many days remain before the consummation. The carillons ring out from the department stores; radio and television reiterate the Christmas theme and the Christmas music. At last, and at last, the Great Day dawns. Everyone, except the children, is exhausted. The Day slips by and is gone in a sixteen-hour puff. Back to the office we go, back to the shop; the morning-after traffic is a worse snarl than ever; the guard on the subway throws an extra savagery into his unintelligible announcements of the stations. Nothing in prospect now except the tag-end of December and an avalanche of bills.

It would have been impossible for us to celebrate the season in this fashion in New Guinea. There were no shops except the PX; if we had any gifts to send home—Australian coins hammered into rings, or bracelets of sea shells, each with its delicate pink inlay that reminded the beloved recipient of her dentist, or should have, since the filling came by devious ways from our battalion dentist's office—if we had gifts of this sort to send home they would have had to be in the mails before the end of October. Our own gift packages (sticky, many of them, from candy that melted in the tropical heat) might arrive any time from Thanksgiving to the following Easter, depending on when they were sent and how many times they had to be forwarded in order to catch up with us as we moved. The sun grew hotter and hotter; the only snow was the coral dust drifting in from the road; we couldn't look for Santa Claus to attempt a landing on a pyramidal tent. As I said in a sermon on the First Sunday of Advent, this might be the only chance we'd ever have to celebrate Christmas undistractedly for what it really is, the birthday of our Redeemer and the "expectation of his visible return."

I asked on that Sunday for volunteers to man a choir that I hoped would sing the Midnight Mass on Christmas. It was a happy request, for it brought me a choir but, even more important, it introduced me to Tippy Maher. Tip was an Engineer from Trenton with an absolutely infectious Irish grin and a simple rectitude of soul that must have delighted the angels. He waited for me after Mass and offered to recruit a choir from his outfit.

"They're pretty good, Father. Honest. 'Course they don't know the Latin, but you can teach 'em."

So on the following Wednesday evening he appeared with a dozen diffident but willing choristers. A couple of them remembered from parochial school vaguely some cadences of the "Missa de Angelis," but most were quite innocent of any acquaintance with the Chant. It didn't matter, I told them, we'd do our best; as St. Augustine had said about worship, "God seeks you rather than your gift." So we set to work, and it may have been ironic that the truest and strongest voice belonged to a Protestant lad whom Tippy introduced to me with a pre-ecumenical plea for tolerance:

"The poor guy is a Protestant, Father, but it ain't his fault. He's OK."

I wonder where all those good fellows are now. I hope that when Christmas comes around some memory of our New Guinea caroling is with them still, and that they draw from it gladness for what has been and support for what yet must be. For the liturgy of both Advent and Christmas makes it clear that at this season we look backward and forward. Of course we recall the weary centuries of waiting (St. Paul compares them to the long months during which a mother is in travail for her child) when the whole creation groaned for its Redeemer. We ponder the great, sweeping design of God, who loved us even when we were in our sins, and devised a way to free us from them. We turn and turn again the pages that tell us how persistently, how delicately he sought our love, as a man might woo the girl he has set his heart on. We trace the Promise as it comes down from the Garden to Abraham, from Moses to David, from Isaiah to Malachy. "God Himself will come and save you."

What a prodigious story this is! Abraham's faith, and God's promise that in him all the tribes of earth would be blessed. The shadowy figure of the priest Melchisedek, with his prophetic gift of bread and wine. Joseph sold into Egypt that he might feed his brethren. The lamb that was slain at the Passover, and the mediating blood on the doorposts. The covenant in blood, the manna, the water from the rock, the brazen serpent lifted up to shield the people. The centuries roll on, the generations rise and fall; always, from father to son, the promise is held in remembrance:

> "My soul waits for the Lord, my soul waits . . .
> More than watchmen for the morning.
> O Israel, hope in the Lord!
> For with the Lord there is steadfast love,
> And with him is plenteous redemption,
> And he will redeem Israel from all his iniquities."

David is anointed, and the pledge given that from his line the one will come whom they call the expectation of nations, the desire of the everlasting hills. Solomon follows after strange gods, the kingdom is torn asunder, the prophet, weary of wrestling with a stubborn ruler and a stiff-necked people, falls to his knees crying:

> "Oh, that you would tear the heavens open
> and come down . . .
> Send justice like a dew, you heavens,
> And let the clouds rain it down.
> Let the earth open for salvation to spring up."

The Holy City is sacked, the people led off to exile, but Jeremiah, to give them faith in their return, buys a field at Anatoth. The people do return, and if the Assyrians sweep down from the north, the Babylonians from the east, the Egyptians from the south, the Greeks and Romans from the west, still, when the tide of invasion has receded this People of God bob up again like a chip on a wave:

> "We hoped in you, Lord,
> Your name, your memory are all my soul desires.
> At night my soul longs for you
> And my spirit in me seeks for you."

As the weeks of Advent pass we look back through the ages, into the dead hearts that prayed for the coming of the holy night. We hear the voices of the prophets, the saving remnant, the "anawim," rising and falling like a surging ocean at the feet of God, begging that in their day he who was to come might be given. John the Baptist is our teacher now, the gaunt herald who comes running from the desert with his vision and his warning: "The Lord is near! Make straight his paths!" Mary of Nazareth is our model as, full of grace, and the Lord with her, she consecrates herself more unreservedly still to his purposes.

It pleases me to think that it was a fellow-townsman of mine, the Protestant minister Phillips Brooks, who gave to the climax of all this waiting an utterly simple and lovely expression:

> O little town of Bethlehem,
> How still we see thee lie.

> The hopes and fears of all the years
> Are met in thee tonight.

Christmas was that night, the fullness of time, when God crowned his prodigal gifts to our race by giving himself, and it's small wonder that Christian men have sung their alleluias and their God-rest-you-merry's ever since. Christmas would be Christmas even in New Guinea, though there would be no falling snow in the lamplight and no frosty breath of carolers at the door.

But if our celebration paused at this it would lack the fullness of the Christian feast. For Advent looks forward as well as backward. It is the period symbolic of all our human waiting, waiting for Christ to come again to take us to himself forever, waiting for full redemption in body and soul. It is the time of patience, of faith, of fidelity in trial, of hope deferred but burning as brightly in the night as ever did the torches of the virgins who waited for the Bridegroom, and went in with him at the last. The Jews of old time praised God for his faithfulness—"He said He would do it and he did!"—and the Advent of this life is a confident waiting for the final fullness of time, when the faithful God will again make good his promises as He did at Bethlehem. "Maranatha Jesu!" said the early Christians, "Come, Lord Jesus."

And Christmas, too, is not just a looking back, however happy, to a past event. Even at the Midnight Mass St. Paul tells us that we are to "give up everything that does not lead to God, and all our worldly ambitions; we must be self-restrained and live good and religious lives here in the present world, while we are waiting in hope for the blessing that will come with the appearing of the glory of our great God and Savior Christ Jesus."

As one grows older it is not as easy, perhaps, to keep the feast with the same childlike ardor; the burdens of life weigh more heavily, and one thinks with wistful love of those who kept it with us in earlier years and are with us no longer. It is then, perhaps, that this deeper meaning of Christmas begins to come home to us, as a pledge of our full redemption and an end to perplexity and pain. Until that day dawns, and the shadows flee away, Christmas is the rich, warm assurance that "God loved the world enough to give his only Son." If, as St. Augustine argued, he loved us enough to give this more precious gift, will he not love us enough to give a lesser one, eternal happiness? The best part of celebrating the feast in this way is that its import is not lost when the Christmas lights burn low; it carries over into the octave and into the New Year, sustaining our hope and our Christian serenity and giving us new reason for loving as we have been loved.

Our Christmas, actually, turned out to be wonderful. We were not sure, up to the last moment, whether we would go aboard ship before the day, but we went ahead with our preparations anyway. I obtained a quantity of white target cloth and hung it as I had hung my drapes before, against the back wall of the chapel, behind the altar, and over the canopy. Red cloth was almost impossible to come by, but, after fruitless appeals at the Special Service Warehouse and the Red Cross, I got a couple of yards from the Signal Corps. We cut symbols out of orange canvas—caskets of gold and myrrh, and a smoking thurible filled with frankincense—and my friend Sammy Shapiro sewed them to the red cloth, so that we had an appropriate and handsome antependium to clothe the nakedness of our temporary wooden altar. Then one of the boys from the 211th Company came in to tell me that a buddy of his, a Protestant, had painted a Madonna and Child and had offered it to the chaplain for use on Christmas. I went with much misgiving to see it, but actually it was pretty good, and I accepted it with thanks to the artist, Sergeant Johnson from Boston, whose business in civilian life had been painting stage sets in the theatres. Considering that he had no oils, but only flat house paints to work with, the picture was amazing. Odd how many skills were dressed up in uniforms in those days. I vetoed firmly several suggestions to set the picture behind the altar and placed it instead against one of the posts of the side wall, near the sanctuary. The men gave it a border of target cloth, and then one of them brought in branches of evergreen and set them about it. Evergreen! It was the last thing I had expected to see in this pine-less, spruce-less, tropical country. It was a frail species; the needles crumbled at the touch, so we had to be careful. Then the men focused a spotlight on the ensemble; I had to countenance that, because most of my large bulbs were packed, and the lighting in the chapel was dim except about the altar. Well, everyone loved it, of course. The Colonel, whose religious convictions had not up to that time been very apparent (he once told me that in his family the men were either religious men or engineers, and he was an engineer) insisted that the picture be packed and taken with us, and so it was, though it vanished and what became of it after the invasion we never learned. Maybe it's still on display in some Filipino barrio.

About seven o'clock on Christmas Eve I had a phone call from Father Collins.

"I'm celebrating your Midnight Mass," he said.

"You're what?"

"Come, come," he said impatiently, "I'm celebrating your Midnight Mass."

"Oh," I replied at last, "I get it. Okay, sure. Let me know if you need a ride down."

He couldn't say so over the phone, but his outfit had received orders to move, and if he didn't offer Mass at midnight he might not have a chance to do so at all. Actually, I was relieved a little; the choir that Tippy Maher had recruited for me from the Engineers had had only three rehearsals, and now I could direct and steady them to some extent. Everything went splendidly; we sang carols from eleven-thirty to midnight, and then the Mass of the Angels. About four hundred and fifty men, many of them non-Catholics, assisted, and although my inexperienced thurifer waved the censer right under Father Collins' nose, so close that I feared he might take it off, the rookie acolytes acquitted themselves nobly. My homily, preached from hasty notes made in the one half-hour I had to myself all day, was listened to patiently. Afterward we had beer and cookies for the choir, and then Father Collins, Bill Graham, Jim Scannell and I, all Bostonians, talked until three o'clock about the caroling in Louisburg Square and how cold it must be on the Mall along Tremont Street, and how after the war we would get together at Father Collins' parish and do all this again.

I was up again at seven-thirty for Masses in my chapel and in the Port Battalion's mess hall. Dinner was as good as it had been for Thanksgiving, and the men were in high spirits—only one or two were a little blue. Of course "Jungle Juice" helped many to develop an appetite and forget their loneliness. That stuff could be really potent; the men used to cut a plug out of a coconut, drain off the milk, and pour in swamp water (crawling, as we found out when we went swimming and developed earaches and other ills, with bacteria). They would then replace the plug, and let the coconut stand and its contents ferment—assisted by generous additions of "GI alky" from the surgeon's stores. The net result neither looked nor acted like Coca-Cola.

It was after five in the evening when a young sailor came to my office.

"Sir, are you the Catholic chaplain?"

"Yes, I am."

"Say, Father, I'm on a ship that came in here today. We don't have a chaplain, and I couldn't get to Mass. But I've been fasting since midnight, and I'd like to receive Holy Communion."

I looked at him. "You've been fasting since midnight?"

"Yes, Father, but I haven't been able to find a priest who has the Blessed Sacrament."

"Well," I said, "I'm not able to reserve it here, either. But we'll find a place where it is reserved if we have to drive all over the Base. Let's go."

It took a little hunting, but at last we found that the Catholic chaplain at the Base Hospital had a tiny oratory where the Blessed Sacrament was reserved. I gave the boy Holy Communion, and then a Catholic nurse to whom I explained the situation put together enough left-overs from the Christmas dinner to make a festive spread for both of us. I dropped him, finally, at his ship, and drove rejoicing back to the Ninth. It was things like that—or rather, boys like him—who made a priest's Christmas happy and the whole Army experience worthwhile.

A few minutes after I had gone to bed, or so it seemed, Bill was shaking me.

"Father! Get up! We're leaving! We have to clear the area by seven o'clock!"

I threw everything I could reach into a duffel bag, perspiring madly, and we piled into trucks and drove away to the dock, where we were herded aboard a transport as if she were going to weigh anchor any moment. But the Transportation Corps ran true to form. It was two days before we sailed.

Life is full of leave-takings, and most leave-takings have at least a stab of pain in them. I would not miss New Guinea; I was glad when open water appeared, at last, between me and the malignity I sensed there toward me and my kind. I was happy to have done with the heat and the mud, the insects and the disease. I was glad to be moving up, to something that should be cleaner, to something that could promise more than this endless squatting in the jungle. And yet, and yet. The last thing I did in our area was to run into my chapel and glance around once at the altar platform, at the empty chairs, at the trusses that held up the rafters. From the tailgate of the three-quarter-ton truck, as we lurched away down the coral road, I caught a last glimpse of the canvas pitch of my roof. *Sunt lachrymae rerum.*

CHAPTER 11

Invasion

I DON'T REMEMBER THAT I THOUGHT OF THE WAR, WHILE WE WERE fighting it, as just another episode in the history of salvation. The convulsion it brought into all our lives was too gigantic. And if we had been able to grasp the full dimensions of the horror at that time—in particular the demonic things associated now with names like Dachau and Auschwitz, Katyn Forest and Bataan and Lubyanka Prison—it would have seemed such a sickening concentration of misery that we could not have endured it, much less seen it in perspective against the panorama of cosmic human history. It was not a pretty time to be alive. We had known the bread lines and the stagnations of the Depression, and as the Thirties drew to a close we heard Mussolini ranting in the Piazza Venezia and saw the Stormtroopers go goose-stepping into Prague and Vienna. The lights went out, then, all over the world; it was the scorched earth of the Ukraine and the Nine Hundred Days of Leningrad; it was disaster at Dunkirk and death raining from the skies over London; it was, finally, Pearl Harbor and the Murmansk run, Anzio and the Kokoda Trail and Omaha Beach.

> We who lived in that day, who heard the grave voices, who listened to the words: Bataan, Corregidor, the varying pronunciation: Spanish, American,
>
> Guadal or Guathal: the strange syllables Buna, Gona: the flat main street sound of Henderson Field: the autumn football sound,
>
> We who saw the pictures: the foxholes, the blasted trees, the wash of dead bodies along the shallow beaches, the curved hand, the boy asleep after fighting,

> We who looked into their faces: the smiling lips, the
> dark eyes less manageable, filled with the broken
> nights: the sudden sounds, the silenced voices,
>
> We, who looked on their faces—may never again drink
> water free of the taint of the foxholes, never again, the
> water sweet, unclouded, leached
>
> free of their suffering: must never again: for only the
> communal cup, the shared suffering is pure: can as-
> suage, is dipped from the living water.

The convulsion, they said, was the birth-pangs of a new order,
the kind of thing that happens about every five hundred years. But
this was too cataclysmic; no new order could be worth that much
wretchedness. One claps his hand to his mouth and falls silent in
the presence of an evil so hideous, so enormous.

Go out on deck now. You open one door, close it securely
before you open the next so that no glimmer of light will escape,
feel your way out on the iron plates to the dim rail which is the only
thing between you and the swirling water twenty feet below. Except
for a very faint murmur, there is no sound, and yet you are forging
north with all the merciless purposes of a footpad, and all about you
is your gang—the other ships in the convoy, dim blacknesses some
hundreds of yards away, grim, heads down, plowing on and on, day
and night. A peculiarly bright star peers through racing scraps of
cloud, you feel the heave and swell under your feet. Behind and
below that double door are light and conversation and glowing cigarettes, but here, on the outside, all that is shut in, it doesn't exist. A
Jap submarine could fire one torpedo . . . just one. A foaming track
across those lightly phosphorescent waves, a roar, an eruption of flame,
a swirl of closing water over a periscope, an SOS, an acre of bobbing
heads supported by blue cork . . . whoa, imagination! And yet, not
too long a stretch of the imagination, either, though the real danger
is from planes by day rather than subs by night.

Hail, Star of the Sea!

The forty-millimeter guns loom over your head, their mouths
gaping. You see the watch on the bridge lift binoculars and stare

steadily—at what? Those dark wastes could be concealing so much. And then you begin to think of what this pack of hounds is hunting, what you are being carried to regardless of your wishes. And rebellion surges up in you:

"I wasn't consulted about this! What's the rush? Let me think it out. I have a right to think it out."

But the pack slips silently on—the worst feature of it is the silence—like wolves running on soft snow, and you know that you are committed, that you have as little to say about your destiny as the man who whirls in narrowing circles close to the brink of Niagara.

> Mary, mother of grace,
> Sweet mother of mercy,
> Protect us from our enemy,
> Receive us when we die.

We had sailed north from Finschhafen to rendezvous in the spacious harbor of Manus Island, in the Admiralties, with the other ships that would make up our convoy. When we saw them—destroyers, aircraft carriers, other transports—we knew we were in for it. Maybe we were only supply troops, maybe we should be taking part in such a business only after everything was well under control, but quite obviously things were not going according to the script. There was a strange feeling down where our stomachs used to be, but I liked the way the men shrugged, set their jaws a little, and said, "This is it, I guess." No heroics, but no flinching, either. Good stuff.

Manus was a desolate atoll, sand-swept and burned dry by the pitiless sun. A small Navy contingent of bored officers and men operated the installation as a supply and signal station. When we dropped anchor there the word was passed that no one would be given shore leave, but I had noticed on the way up that our ship had no library, no supply of magazines or paper-backs or playing cards—nothing the men could use to while away the endless hours. They did have dice, of course, and shot crap for the highest stakes I had ever seen, but as an officer I was not supposed to see such forbidden recreations. At any rate, I asked for and received permission to go ashore and find, if possible, reading material and any other means of entertainment that might be available and portable. The first Navy officer I met turned out to be Lieutenant Paul Power, a Boston College alumnus and a brother of Father Will Power of the New England Jesuits. Together we toured the officers' and the CPO's clubs, and even begged at the doors of the officers' quarters, but our harvest was small; I was able to bring back to the ship only two hundred paperbacks, and what were these among so many? On the following day general permission was given for shore leave, and a large delegation from the Ninth took advantage of it. They had quite a day. It was the last day of the year, and—as they told me afterward—the Navy clubs wanted to dispose of the liquor on their shelves so that accounts could be started afresh. I didn't quite grasp the economics of this, but no matter—the point was that everything was on the house, and in any quantity. Our men, who had had nothing better to drink than Jungle Juice for many months, looked incredulously at the free, full decanters that were pushed toward them, and yielded to a temptation that was almost certainly beyond their strength. Late in the afternoon their boat came alongside, and we hoisted them aboard in various stages of liquefaction. One, a dear friend of mine, held up an empty canteen and moaned:

"Where'sh Fa' Leonard? I brought thish back for Fa' Leonard, but thoshe guysh drank it all. Dirty trick. Where'sh Fa' Leonard?"

We got him below and tenderly poured him into his berth. His last words were, I knew, addressed to his wife, "Mary, I love you." Poor old boy. No one saw him for a couple of days, and he shamefacedly avoided me for a week.

Now we were off. Maps of the beach we would land on and of the area the Ninth would occupy were passed around and studied; debarkation exercises were held daily. We were going, we learned, to Luzon; we would go in—as the Japanese had gone in three years before—at Lingayen; a Regimental Combat Team would push the Japs back through Rosario toward Baguio, and hold them there while the Sixth Army raced down the corridor to Manila. The RCT was on the convoy ahead of us, the 37th Division was with us, and the First Cavalry Division would come in a day or so behind us. In our approach to Luzon we did not, for some reason, swing outside Mindanao into the South China Sea. Instead, we ran inside, through the Visayan Sea and on up between Mindoro and Batangas, and finally outside to Lingayen. Probably it was better so; by this time our planes were flying out of air fields on Leyte and could cover us; on the other hand, we knew that Panay and Mindoro were still in Japanese hands, that our position was known to the enemy, and that an aerial sortie from one of those islands could appear at any moment. Every night, in fact, we heard from Radio Tokyo a threat to that effect, delivered in hard, flat, clipped but very intelligible English:

"There is an American convoy proceeding north at such a latitude, such a longitude (giving our exact position each day). But the Japanese Special Attack Corps will make certain that the American convoy never reaches its destination."

We had no assurance that the Japs would not make good this threat. Alerts and calls to General Quarters were frequent. Steve Brennan and his buddy, a young Protestant officer whose name, alas, I now forget, used to come around early in the morning to inquire whether I had read Lauds and Prime, the morning prayer of the Church, in my breviary. Toward noon they would appear again.

"How 'ya doin' on that book, Father?"

"Oh, fine," I used to say casually, "I just finished Sext. We're all set until three o'clock."

Father Nolan, the ship's chaplain, and I offered Mass on deck each day, he in the morning and I in the afternoon, and every man aboard, it seemed, attended both Masses. I had never known such fervor back at Finsch, nor would I see it again once we had landed and things quieted down. In those days I used to wonder and even be irritated by this see-saw piety—how much superstition was there in it? Did we worship God only when our necks were in danger? Wasn't he worth our attention even if we got nothing out of it? Nowadays I am grown more tolerant and see how human such fluctuations are. We were playing dangerously in the enemy's back yard, and he did give the convoy ahead of us a bad time, as we learned later. Besides, I remember that I, too, was very glad there was another priest aboard. I knew that Holy Orders was a sacrament I had received for others, not for myself, but I was a sinner, also, and if I could not bless, absolve, or anoint myself I wanted someone around who could do it for me. All in all, that trip was a good rehearsal for our last exit—and entrance. It's salutary to rehearse now and then so that one can get over stage fright and do it gracefully.

Army life was full of vivid contrasts and violent juxtapositions. We had on board a former concert violinist, who had played for ten years in Paris after graduating from the conservatory there, later with the Baltimore Symphony and on concert stages all over the States. He was now a corporal with an Engineer Depot Company, passing out spare parts for bulldozers and the like—one of those wartime perpetrations that make you want to knock your head against a wall. On Twelfth Night he played for an hour in the officers' wardroom—magnificent stuff—and I talked to him afterward. He was an Armenian named George Sisanian, born in Constantinople; he spoke five languages and was, he was careful to assure me, a Roman Catholic, not Orthodox. We talked for an hour and a half on the little I knew about his part of the world: Turkish persecution of the Armenians (I had read *The Forty Days of Musa Dagh*), and the *Hagia Sophia,* Justinian's Church of the Holy Wisdom, an enthusiasm of mine. He had been in and out of the church all during his boyhood. And all during this music and good talk we were slinking swiftly through infested waters, with war of the bloodiest lying ahead. I wanted to shriek my protest at the insanity of it.

Not much longer now. It will be good to get off this ship; you can't dig a fox-hole in a steel deck, and, especially at night, you feel like a big duck in a very small pond, a perfect target. Dusk and dawn are the bad times, although the Jap has developed a new trick of dropping flares that light up the convoy at night, while he hovers above, invisible. The Navy has done a grand job so far; we haven't seen a hostile wing in the sky, and that means that the boys from the flat-tops must be out sweeping around the clock. Two or three times there have been submarine scares, but we dropped "ash cans" over the fantail and heard no more. Another day or two ...

The Colonel asked me what I was going to carry ashore in the way of side-arms. He showed me the tommy-gun he intended to take. When I replied that I planned on carrying only a bolo knife, to scrape out fox-holes and to cut through the underbrush, he remonstrated strongly.

"The Japs won't respect the Geneva Convention, Chaplain!"

"Well, maybe not," I said, "But it's under the terms of the Geneva Convention that I'm here at all."

"A dead chaplain is no good to the troops," he reminded me.

"Sorry, Colonel," I answered, "My profession makes me a man of peace."

"You're asking for eternal rest, not peace," he snorted.

I grinned. "Maybe I can have both."

When we got up on the morning of January 11th the ship was shrouded in mist; at least we thought it was mist, and had to be told that it was a protective smoke-screen. Black cylinders, shell-cases from the Navy bombardment of the coast, floated in the water. As we anchored, about three miles offshore, the light breeze began to carry the smoke away, and we could see the beach glittering in the sun and the green, low-lying hills beyond. A destroyer was standing offshore a mile north of us, throwing broadsides at something we couldn't see. Buoys marked the graves of a few sunken ships; we could see the mast of one of them sticking up ten feet above the water, but there was no way of telling whether they were Japanese or ours. Now the idea was to get to the beach as fast as possible; there was no telling when enemy planes might come over in strength from Formosa. It was "D plus two," or two days after the initial landings, so a tremendous Navy bombardment and the infantry invasion had prepared the way for us.

Father Nolan and I exchanged blessings and I went over the side, down a "scramble-net" into a LCVP—a motor launch the Navy officially categorized as a "Landing Craft Vehicle and Personnel." There were twenty-five of us aboard; we took off for our assigned beach, got an approval from the control point to come ashore, and ran the boat up on the beach. The bow fell out and we slogged through a couple of feet of water to dry sand. The beach was apparently in chaos, but there was order underneath. We moved inland on foot about five hundred yards, and dug fox-holes at once in the sandy soil, then broke open our K-rations: canned sausage meat, "energy crackers," tropical chocolate, a pressed prune bar, a packet of four cigarettes. Our orders, after landing, were to push inland to a palm grove near a railroad spur that came down from the hills and joined the main line at San Fabian. Captain Clune, Warrant Officer Falkenburg, and I reconnoitered a little and found the road to San Fabian, then decided to get the men there as soon as possible, inasmuch as the Japs had shelled the beach the night before, and we didn't like the looks of the shell holes and the jagged pieces of shrapnel. As we heard the story later, the Japs knew we would be invading at Lingayen (it was really the only place where a large force could be landed and then deployed), so they moved our own naval sixteen-inch guns from Corregidor into caves high above the beach and mounted them there on railroad tracks, pulling them swiftly back into the caves after firing. Our planes could not silence them by bombing, and it wasn't until some days later that we used anti-aircraft guns, which have a level trajectory and could penetrate the caves and so put the sixteen-inchers out of business. Meanwhile they gave those of our men who had to stay on the beach at night a bad time.

The road to San Fabian was a very pretty one that reminded me of country lanes in New Hampshire when I was a boy. The ground was firm, not like the spongy earth of New Guinea; the vegetation, except for the countless palm trees, looked like home. Filipino huts stood up on stilts at intervals, and we heard sounds we hadn't heard for months, like the cackling of hens and the crying of babies; it sounded good. All along the road grown-ups and children smiled and bowed and held up two fingers in the V-sign for Victory. They wore indescribably tattered rags; the Japs, they said, had taken all their clothes. Next morning, however, several girls blossomed out in pretty print dresses, and told us they had buried them three years before and had just dug them up. The people had had no soap for many months, but were uniformly clean—even their rags were spotless. We never learned what they washed with.

The railroad junction, when we reached it eight miles further on, held out the familiar long, black-and-white arm to warn road traffic of a grade crossing, and we cheered it as another welcome sign of civilization, even though at the moment we were hot and tired, and the musette bag on my back, with the essentials of my

Mass kit in it, was getting very heavy. The palm grove we had been assigned to was nearby, however, and proved to be a very pleasant place. We got some water from a neighboring well; the men put their decontaminating halizone tablets into it, but the dentist and I took the further precaution of boiling it in our helmets; the local sanitation didn't look too good. By this time it was growing dark, so we hastily threw some bouillon cubes into the hot water, ate a little cheese and crackers, and set about digging fox-holes with the miniature shovels we carried. The ground here was a hard clay, and the palm-tree roots were close to the surface, so night was on us before I was able to scrape out more than a foot of earth. Then I was soaking wet from the exertion, and after I lay down and scooped out special adjustments for my bony shoulders and hips, I shivered so much that sleep was impossible. The stars were interesting: we were back in the Northern Hemisphere now, and it was good to see the Dipper and Orion and the Pleiades instead of the Southern Cross and a skyful of unfamiliar constellations. About four o'clock Sergeant Eddie Cullen, from Fall River, the only man among us who had a blanket, went on guard, and threw the blanket over me as he went by, so I slept for three hours. Morning brought a sound that raised everyone's spirits: the crowing of a rooster. More than the stone buildings, more than the railroad or the cement highway, the crowing spoke to our hearts and told us we were out of the jungle at last.

The Colonel, our C.O., went off in the morning and did not return until late afternoon, when he announced that he had found a much better bivouac area and that we would move to it at once. The truck took us into the town of San Fabian itself, and as darkness fell we were digging foxholes again. This time the ground was quite soft, but we soon discovered why when we struck water three feet down. We were in a swamp, and the Colonel's popularity, never very high, sank a few more points. I shoveled back some of the earth I had dug out of my hole, looked at the damp result, and had an idea. That sleeping bag I had bought in the States and brought over with me! It had never been used, but surely this was the destined moment, and it had come from the beach today with the rest of my gear. I tucked it into the hole, rolled a couple of palm logs over the top, and slid my body under them into the bag.

"Good boy!" I told myself exultantly, "Snug as a bug in a rug."

But other less pleasant comparisons soon presented themselves. The hole, except for depth, had the dimensions of a grave.

"So this is what the New York World's Fair, six years ago, called the Century of Progress," I meditated, "Before my time comes, and to save my skin for a bit, I must crawl into a hole in the ground. My fellow men have made so much progress that they can stand miles away and kill me where I lie."

And as if to prove the truth of this, the first Japanese shell came moaning through the air. There isn't a great deal to choose between them, but I think I'd rather be bombed than shelled. If you are in a hole, especially a covered hole, a bomb will not hurt you unless it's a direct hit, and the chances are good that none will fall exactly where you are. But shell-fire methodically combs an area: the first shot goes beyond you, the second falls short of you, and you cower and cringe waiting for the third to land on your back. That night (as we learned next morning) the first shell destroyed a Filipino home beyond us and killed a baby; the second exploded harmlessly in a ditch behind us. For some reason, known only to the Father of mercies, there was no third. We also learned in the morning that a Jap force of about two hundred men had infiltrated our lines a mile away and set fire to a jeep before being driven off. The interesting aspect of this was that they had come straight through the pretty palm grove where we had bivouacked the preceding night. Had we fifteen stayed there a second night, they would have made mincemeat of us. The Colonel suddenly became more popular.

On the third day we moved to a lovely coconut grove overlooking a shallow, narrow river—an ideal location except that the infantry had by-passed this area and we didn't know how many Japs were still hiding in it, or how much to believe of the Filipinos' stories about snipers. We were also several miles away from any other troops, but one of our companies had joined us, so we were no longer just a headquarters detachment. We set up a reinforced perimeter, hoping our inexperienced service troops would not be "trig-ger-happy" and shoot one another. We officers sat up all night, try-ing to pierce the darkness every time the breeze stirred the palm leaves or one of the guards coughed. It was a very long night, an uneasy peace. But nothing untoward happened, and next day we had a chance to set up machine guns and warn the innocent Filipi-nos not to move out of their huts after dark. They swarmed all over the area the first two days; we had to clear them out to get anything done. Gradually they were organized into labor gangs, working on the roads, which our heavy equipment had smashed, putting up bamboo offices, headquarters, and the like. They were an extremely polite people, almost embarrassingly grateful for their deliverance from the Japs; small and looking much younger than their years, they smiled with a readiness and cordiality that was very winning indeed.

It was Sunday afternoon before I was able to offer Mass, and then, in a ploughed field nearby, I set up an altar on some ammuni-tion cases and gathered about me a congregation of about thirty GI's and over a hundred Filipinos. The latter, including men, women, and children down to babes-in-arms, assembled in wonder and curi-osity; they had never seen Mass celebrated in the afternoon, or out-doors, and almost certainly would not have associated it with the American Army. I was happy that they could see how religion was not only tolerated but even supported and in a sense promoted offi-cially by the invaders who had just manifested their military power so convincingly, and I wished that my GI's had turned out in larger numbers. I think, in fact, that the disappointment of this Sunday may have been a kind of turning-point in my attitude toward the Ordnance men of my outfit. It was irrational as well as lacking in true apostolic spirit; I struggled against it and I don't think I ever consciously let it be seen, but from this day I began to feel a dis-couragement about this group. Since coming among them I had preached the Mass, in season and out of season, as the epitome of Christian life, the best possible expression of our Father's love of us and our love of Him. Our chapel in New Guinea had given this idea a concrete embodiment, and on the transport when they had turned out to a man, I fondly believed that the lesson had been

learned. Of course I had to take into account the indisputable fact
that there was much work to be done in these first days ashore. I
had to recognize that the tingle of danger and anxiety was no longer
there to provide the spur that many of us—especially young men—
need in order to think serious thoughts. I had to acknowledge, in
myself first of all, the human ability to rationalize, to postpone with
the promise of atoning soon, to forget in the face of the moment's
attraction. But as the weeks turned into months and my weekday
congregations amounted to only five or six on the average, while
my Sunday congregations were only a fraction of the Catholic
troops in my area, my disappointment was keen.

Did it occur to me at that time, I wonder, that something serious might be wrong with the Mass itself, something that prevented
it from attracting the young men? Yes, I believe I did think of this.
I was beginning to realize that the Latin language was a serious
barrier to understanding, and I knew that the symbolism of many
rites and gestures was simply mystifying. Yet any substantial
change in these matters was undreamed of in those days; even the
very moderate proposals that were put forward by "liturgists" were
pooh-poohed as visionary or condemned out of hand as savoring of
heresy. The Mass was an utterly lovely rite, enshrining the supreme
moment of the Consecration when God deigned to descend among
men, and giving to God, by the very fact of its objective offering,
peerless praise, thanksgiving, and impetration for human needs. It
did not matter a great deal whether the congregation understood the
rite so long as they were aware of the value of what was done in
their presence. There was certainly no need of their taking any active part outwardly; all that was required of them was a certain interior identification with the purposes for which the sacrifice was
offered. I should not have been surprised that so many found the
Mass dull, remote from their concerns. But I was surprised, and, I
suppose, hurt somewhat, or at least considerably dashed. And for
the first time I began to wonder whether I should not try to shake
the dust of Ordnance from my shoes and see if I could find a readier
response elsewhere.

That first Mass in the Philippines was memorable on other
counts, too. I preached after reading the Gospel of the day, and was

struck by the fact that my congregation had assembled in two sharply differentiated groups. There were the GI's, white, confident, big men, tracing their ancestry to every racial stock in Europe. Then there were the Filipinos, the most completely westernized of any people in the Far East, yet still unmistakably Orientals: brown, small, outwardly impassive, diffident as civilians are in the company of the military, as peasants are in the company of city-dwellers. How, I thought subconsciously as I talked, could these two ever be made one? Was East East and West West, and never the twain should meet? If so, how could the dream of peace in our time ever be realized? Were we destined to permanent segregation, with periodic wars flaming out like the one we were now fighting?

I turned back to the altar and went on with the Mass. But at the Consecration, when I lifted the chalice, I saw my congregation again, reflected this time in the polished surfaces of the chalice as in a mirror. And it came home to me that only thus would men be united, in the blood of Christ.

It was "in Christ Jesus," as St. Paul put it, that "you who used to be so far apart from us have been brought very close, by the blood of Christ. For he is the peace between us, and has made the two into one and broken down the barrier which used to keep them apart, actually destroying in his own person the hostility caused by the rules and decrees of the law. This was to create one single New Man in himself out of the two of them and, by restoring peace through the cross, to unite them both in a single Body and reconcile them with God. In his own person he killed the hostility."

To be sure, it would help in the post-war days to exchange students, to visit one another's countries and become acquainted, to realize that with a shrinking world and fantastic advances in our ability to kill one another we must strive for self-restraint or perish utterly. But these were half-measures that could not be trusted to create the new society we needed, a brotherhood that would brush aside as irrelevant the surface differences that up till now had divided men and look instead to the essential humanity that united them. The selfishness that precipitated wars could not be defeated by high resolves, treaties, non-aggression pacts. We needed to acquire an esteem of one another as persons of value, for whose restoration to dignity God had not thought the blood of his Son too high a price. We needed a patient, great-hearted love which we could have only if God, moved thereto by the sacrifice of our Priest and Mediator, gave it to us.

Our new Group Commander showed a distinct personal interest in the plans for our new chapel. One day he told me he had located a bell which he would like to see installed when we had the chapel built. So I asked for help from one of our companies, and was given two men, a block and tackle, and a ride to the wrecked schoolhouse where the bell had once called the neighborhood children to class. The ride was the amusing part of the incident. The company had just finished repairing a 1938 Chevrolet sedan which a Filipino had taken apart and buried in sections when the Japanese invaded Luzon; he had dug it up after our arrival and sold it to the Red Cross. Now the car had to be given a road test, and Lieutenant Olson suggested that the test could be my bell-hunting expedition. We drove away, and it was fun watching the GI faces along the road. They had seen nothing but olive-drab jeeps, trucks, half-tracs, and trailers for years, and their jaws dropped as the sleek black sedan slid by them. At the intersections the MP on duty as traffic cop would snap to attention and throw a real highball salute at the back seat, where I was ensconced, certain that I must be a four-star general. We got the bell, a brass one weighing about forty pounds. Shrapnel had punched two small holes in it and made it look like the Liberty Bell, but it still had a pretty fair tone. Then we went back, and as we drew up to our headquarters the Adjutant came tearing out on the dead run, but stopped, disgusted, when he saw me.

"Heck," he said, "I thought I had MacArthur on my hands."

Rumor had reached me that there were some Irish Columban Sisters living in the vicinity, so Bill and I went looking for them, thinking they might be in need. We found them safe and sound in their convent about fifteen miles away. As soon as I announced my ancestry I was accepted, but Bill couldn't remember whether his people had been Irish or if they were, from what county they had come, so he was accepted only on probation. They were a very merry group. We listened to some of their tales about life under the

Japanese; they had been hungry at times, but were otherwise unmolested. However, most of them were fairly well along in years, and two were definitely old, so it could not have been any picnic. At the end of their story I said,

"Well, Mother, it seems to me you've been very heroic about all this."

The Superior's eyes twinkled, "Ah, sure, Father," she said, "We're all martyrs."

That remark, and the self-effacing, bantering tone in which it was made, comes back to me often as the best summary I have heard of the gallantry I have been privileged to see in the nuns I have known.

A few miles from our area, at Santa Barbara, was the new cemetery, and Chaplain Hardin and I, as the nearest chaplains, were appointed to carry out the religious rites there. I understand that the bodies interred there have been long since removed, either to Manila or to the States, in accordance with the desires of relatives. Compared with other military cemeteries, it was not large, but we were kept busy. During four months I read the prayers for thirty-five hundred men, and those were only the Catholics. Chaplain Hardin and the Jewish chaplain from the Base took care of many others. Most of the dead were pathetically young, boys in their teens or early twenties, but there were older men, too, battalion and even regimental commanders, and, once or twice, general officers.

The first impression one receives on arriving at such a place is, sadly, the unmistakable odor in the air, sweetish, sickening. It was a hot country, there could be no embalming, and sometimes three or more days elapsed before these coffinless bodies could be laid to rest. The next impression is of the silence. No one shouts, and the GI's assigned to supervise the work, the Graves Registration Section of the Quartermaster Corps, seem to have been chosen for the gentleness of their natures. Perhaps it was the work they did that subdued and softened them.

Chaplain Hardin and I left the registration tent and moved out into the great open field, past the bodies lying mute in their shrouds of blankets or shelter-halves and waiting for burial. Filipino laborers were digging graves as fast as they could, and they, too, were hushed and quiet in their speech and work. We walked among the graves that had already been filled, trying to learn from the lists we had been given, and the numbers of the graves, which of these newly dead belonged to us. But GRS hadn't had time to type out the religious faith in every case, and there were some unknowns, and the graves were too fresh to have been adequately marked, so all I could do was read the prayers and sprinkle a little holy water here and there. It would have been impossible, anyway, for me to make distinctions among them, to say that some of them belonged more to me than others. I could only ask their common Father to give them all the joy of knowing and possessing Him forever.

Ever since Guadalcanal, the papers, magazines, newsreels, and radio back home had been filled with the exploits of the Marine Corps. By contrast, General MacArthur had seemed to frown on glamorous publicity for Army campaigns. I often thought, after see-ing Buna and some of the Kokoda Trail, that if it had been the Marines who had driven the Japs back over the Owen Stanley Range and into the sea, instead of the stouthearted 32nd Division, we should never have heard the end of it. The average GI, I think, being by nature generous and not fancying himself a hero, particu-larly, would have been quite willing to give the Marines credit for their achievements—if they hadn't taken so much. As it was, he grew understandably a little tired of hearing and reading about Iwo Jima and Saipan and the intrepid Leathernecks, while his own re-spectable accomplishments in New Guinea, the Admiralties, Biak, Kwajalein, Leyte, and Luzon went unsung. He could not have guessed at the time that—as President Truman later said in a mo-ment of imprudent but delicious candor—the public adulation of the Corps was planted and nourished by techniques learned on Madison Avenue. At any rate, a deep and satisfied chuckle rippled through the Army's tents when the story of the Marine invasion of Lingayen became known. It went like this:

A detail from an Engineer Supply Battalion (it was Tippy Ma-her's outfit, actually) was sent one day down to the beach to uncrate machinery dumped there by an LST. It was a glorious morning: the Gulf was as placid as a wading pool; the sun shone out of an un-troubled sky; the battle by this time was many miles away. The detail had been working for an hour or so when suddenly one GI nudged another.

"Hey! Get a load of this!"

A flotilla of landing craft had materialized from nowhere and was bearing down on the beach. The boats were crowded with helmeted men, each with his bayonet at the ready. The ramps fell down as the boats struck the sand, and the fighting men stormed ashore. The GI's were at first perplexed, then alarmed. Were these the Japs coming back? Then one of them heard a whirring noise behind him, and spun around to see a battery of movie cameras trained on the invaders. On the cameras were the letters "U.S.M.C." The Marines had landed at Lingayen. It was D plus fourteen.

CHAPTER 12

Mangaldan

I'VE OFTEN WONDERED HOW WELL I MIGHT HAVE WITHSTOOD THE monotony of imprisonment if I'd been captured. Perhaps I could have settled down to it. After all, I had survived, in our houses of study, eleven years of what most people would call incarceration. Aside from an occasional visit to a dentist or an oculist and, during the time at Weston, one day at our parents' home each year, we stayed in the same house and followed the same routine. Our motto was "Here today—and here tomorrow." It wasn't good for us spiritually—unless dogged endurance has some value—and it certainly wasn't good for us intellectually. We went without the immense stimulation that might have been afforded us by contact with scholars outside our seminary and by association with non-clerical students. Our library was not only poor but even closed to us except at stated times. We had few visiting lecturers, and our teachers were content if we learned what was in the manuals that served us as textbooks. We lost touch even with the people whom we expected to serve in our ministerial works later, so that, for example, we did not really know at first hand the value of money or the problems, especially during the Depression, of earning it. We were in danger, since we had no responsibilities, of growing up without becoming genuinely mature. Happily, all that has changed now, and will change even more radically in the future, but one wonders at the mentality which considered such a training ideal for future priests, pastors, and professors.

My Army experience was very different. It began with movement, the steady, massed movement of the marching battalion at Chaplain School in time to Sergeant O'Shaughnessy's "Hup, two, heep, hour."

"Count cadence!" he would shout, "Count!"

And the deep growl would answer him from the ranks: "Hup, two, heep, hour!"

From that time I kept moving: Cambridge to Louisiana to California to New Guinea to Lingayen to Manila, and after that out of all whooping.

Among the American military prisoners taken by the Japanese after the fall of Corregidor, I knew there had been quite a few priests. One of them was a New England Jesuit, Father John Dugan, who had been very kind to my family in the days before he had joined the Army and been posted to Manila. I wanted very much to meet him if he were still alive, but could learn nothing about him until, almost a month after our landing at Lingayen, I visited a hospital and got into conversation with a soldier who, after three years' captivity, had just been liberated in a spectacular raid behind the Jap lines by the Sixth Army Rangers. Without much hope of an affirmative answer, I asked him if he had ever known a Father Dugan.

"Sure I know him! He came out with us."

"He did? Where is he now?"

"I don't know. They brought some of us here because we were sick, but I couldn't tell you where the rest went."

I spent the following day on the telephone, trying to get some information, and had to give up when the time came to drive to Caloocan for evening Mass with the Engineers. But on the way I picked up a hitchhiking Air Corps Lieutenant who was on his way to meet his cousin, just freed; he gave me the location of the camp where all the liberated prisoners were staying. So after Mass four of us set out. At the camp headquarters they didn't want to let us in; they were trying to protect the former prisoners from being badgered by the merely curious. I managed to persuade the commander that I was not in that category, and, since everyone was at a movie, he had Father Dugan paged. A moment later a thin figure came out of the crowd and, blinking in the light, looked questioningly about. I stepped forward.

"John, I'm Father Bill Leonard, from B.C. Remember?"

He threw his arms around me, gulped, then shook it off.

"I haven't broken down yet," he said. "I don't want to."

"Sure," I said rapidly. "Meet some friends of mine: Bill Graham and Paul Heffron from Boston, and Jim McGinnis from Binghampton."

Father Dugan had always been a quiet man, but that night he positively bubbled. So did the other officers he introduced us to as we stood for hours in the kitchen, drinking coffee. An air raid alert was sounded about eleven o'clock, but we just put out the lights and went on listening. It was a good thing the Japs did not materialize.

Father Dugan, as we suspected, had been on Bataan, and was captured there early in 1942. He missed the "Death March" only because he had contracted malaria and was a hospital patient. We asked if what we had heard about the "Death March" had been exaggerated, and everyone assured us solemnly that whatever we had heard was an understatement. No food or water was given to the American captives for two full days; their hats were pulled off and they were made to march, weak and malaria-ridden, in the blazing sun; any who fell or even lagged (and they were many) were bayoneted. From May until October of 1942, they told us, there were fifty deaths a day in the camp at Cabanatuan, from disease and malnutrition. One medical officer estimated a total of forty-four hundred American graves in the vicinity of the camp. The prisoners were assigned to groups of ten called "execution squads"; if one man escaped the other nine were shot. They were given two bowls of rice a day and an ounce of meat a week. Usually the meat was horse or the native caribao, but several officers talked of eating dogs and cats, and Father Dugan of cooking and eating snakes. Everyone, from high-ranking officers to privates, had to work; a beating was the price of malingering.

They had received some letters from home, and twice the Red Cross was permitted to bring in packages from the United States. Through the help given by neighboring civilian priests and the Chaplains' Aid Society in Manila, the priests had wine and altar breads for Mass, and so were not deprived of the richest consolation they could have enjoyed. As for news, for a long time all they heard was Japanese propaganda; several officers were very bitter about the labor strikes back home that Tokyo Rose had made so much of. But two medical officers managed to steal enough parts to construct a small radio inside a standard GI canteen; this they kept buried except twice a week, when they would secretly dig it up and listen to American broadcasts. The majority never had any doubts that we would return and rescue them; the only difficulty was the waiting. The months lengthened into years, and some gave up hope. The older men, more patient and philosophical, stood it better than the young fellows. Father Dugan said he forced himself to expect nothing; even when the Rangers were conducting them to safety, he would not allow himself to hope. It was the only way, he said, to preserve sanity.

On January seventh, when our artillery began its bombardment of the Lingayen coast preparatory to the invasion, the Japanese dazed the prisoners by telling them that the camp garrison was leaving and that they were no longer prisoners of war, but warned them that if they left the compound they would certainly be killed as enemies. Then the Japs departed. The prisoners seized the opportunity to raid the stores they had left behind, and found four hundred cases of evaporated milk in American cans—the remainder of the loot the Japs had taken when they captured Manila in 1942. They drove two caribao steers into the compound and had a barbecue. The effects of this feasting were magical: everyone put on at least twenty pounds in the next three weeks.

Meanwhile our divisions were rushing on Manila, but the spearhead passed some forty miles away from Cabanatuan, and the prisoners began to think they had been forgotten. The Japs evidently thought the same thing, and were lulled into a false security. On the night the Rangers attacked, although the official garrison had departed, there were about seventy Japs in the camp, using it as an overnight bivouac. At seven o'clock, just at dusk, bullets began to whine around the stockade. The prisoners concluded that at last the Japs had decided to finish them off, and fell into ditches, waiting for death. But at that point soldiers rushed into the compound, shouting,

"Run to the gates! Everybody run! We're Americans! Get down to the gates!"

Father Dugan said that he was in his stocking feet, having been suffering from an ulcer on his toe, but he left his shoes and everything else behind him and ran. In thirty-two minutes every prisoner was outside and on his way, even bed-patients, even those the Japs had declared unfit for travel to Japan. One poor fellow, who had been the victim of hallucinations, kept clinging to Father Dugan, insisting that it was a trap, that the Japs were up to another of their tricks. They walked from seven-thirty that night until early the next morning (the very sick rode in native carts); they forded four rivers where the water was waist-high and the slime on the river-bed was up to their knees. At one point along the way guerrillas warned them that eight hundred Japs, with two tanks, had an ambush prepared for them, and they had to strike off in another direction. At last, in the small hours, they found the trucks that had been concealed two days before, still behind the Japanese lines, and made their last dash for freedom. In all, five hundred and eleven Americans were brought out. Everything, Father Dugan said, was providential: if they had not had that food during the previous weeks, they could not have made the forced march; if it had been raining, they could not have forded the rivers; if the Rangers had come in the night before their actual attack, they might have been overwhelmed by a large number of Japs who had bivouacked in the camp.

Father Dugan kept making references to the two other Jesuits who had been freed, especially a Father O'Keefe from the New York Province, but somehow I did not make the proper associations. At last we went to meet them. Father Dugan slipped under the tent-flap and I heard him say,

"Here's Father Bill Leonard from New England."

Then I heard "Gosh! I know him!" and I went under the flap, saw the face in the flickering candlelight, and shouted, "Gene!"

We had lived next door to each other at Weston, fifteen years before.

He explained that he had been teaching in Mindanao when the war broke out, had volunteered as a chaplain, and been captured in May of '42. After that it was the same tale of brutality and wretchedness. Father Hugh Kennedy, also of the New York Province, came in at this point; I had never met him before, but it made no difference. We listened for another hour, and I gave them all the news I had from home. They were full of questions about class-mates and friends, so that it was nearly one o'clock before we left, and we would have stayed longer except for our fear that our own sentries would take us for Jap night-prowlers and fill us full of holes.

Two days later I went over to the air strip to see the three off on the first leg of their long journey home. I was touched as I saw in the eyes of all these men, who had suffered and survived so much, a pathetic admiration of the new American Army. They stared goggle-eyed at the B-17's, the P-38's, the ducks and buffa-loes. And though they didn't say it, they must have been thinking, "If we had had this stuff on Bataan!" I watched them hoist their wasted bodies aboard the C-47's and an elephant stood up inside my throat.

From our first days ashore we priests managed to have the weekly meeting which we called "the diocesan synod" and which all of us enjoyed so much. The meeting place was the "convento" or rectory of the local pastor, Father Juan Sison, with whom Bill and I had become very friendly, and whom I was trying to convert to my liturgical ways. He laughingly confessed that the first evening I celebrated Mass in his church he nearly jumped out of his seat, thinking I was calling for help. It was only my way of reciting the prayers in a voice that could be heard. In those days, at home no less than in the Philippines, the Mass-text was usually kept a deep, dark secret so far as the congregation was concerned; even the serv-ers, three feet away, had to strain sometimes to hear it, and the faith-ful, doing their best to follow in their missals, could often only guess how far the celebrant had progressed. Father Sison and I maintained a correspondence for a long time after the War; he would give me the news of Mangaldan and San Fabian and con-clude with "greetings from your small Filipino friend." But one day I received a letter which had a slight variation in its ending: "And now," he said, "you must pray for your small Filipino friend, be-cause on the Feast of St. Peter and St. Paul he is going to be made a bishop." And so, in truth, he was, and later became Archbishop of Vigan in northern Luzon.

General MacArthur had ordered, after the Luzon campaign had been officially declared a victory (there was still much dirty fighting ahead for the 25th and 32nd Divisions in the hills) that a religious ceremony of thanksgiving be held in every town. When I mentioned this, Father Sison and Bill came up with a bright idea. Father Sison suggested that we have a High Mass in his church, and Bill enhanced the suggestion by proposing that we ask the Bishop of Lingayen to come. So I got the appropriate military sanction and we went to see the Bishop. He was enthusiastic, overrode all the difficulties, and made further suggestions of his own. We asked him to sing the Mass, but then there arose the canonical question of whether he could, inasmuch as he was not a military chaplain and could not, in the terms of the law at that time, celebrate Mass in the evening.

"Tell you what, Monsignor," I said with a grin. "I'll delegate you to offer the Mass; I can do that in virtue of my faculties, and I'd like to have it on my record that I once delegated a bishop to celebrate Mass."

"That would not exactly do," he smiled. "I know, we shall have a Solemn Mass *coram Episcopo.* It is even more colorful than the Pontifical Mass itself. I shall wear my cappa magna, we shall have the Mass outdoors, on the steps of Father Sison's church, you will get your soldier choir and they will sing with the parish choir. We can get rugs at Dagupan and dalmatics at San Jacinto . . ."

So we left, with lots of problems for the supply officer (myself), but very happy about his reception of our idea. Waiting for me when we returned to our area were two Jesuits. One was Father Pacifico Ortiz, who, as chaplain to the late President Quezon, had escaped from Corregidor just before the surrender there, spent several years in the States, and had recently come home to the Philippines. The other was Mr. Jaime Neri, a scholastic who was about to begin the study of theology when the war broke out. He was interned, then confined in Santiago Prison, tried by a Japanese court-martial for suspected cooperation with guerrillas, let off with a reprimand but kept in prison, finally managed to escape and lead a hundred other prisoners to freedom. Father Ortiz wanted to see his Superior, Father John Hurley, in Manila, and to be of any assistance he could to the Jesuits there, and he asked me to drive him. I was doubtful, but the Colonel approved; the major's leaves on Father Ortiz' collar (he was acting Chief of Chaplains of the Philippine Army) had a certain persuasive value. We bought a quantity of shirts, trousers, and shoes from the Quartermaster and set out. The ride was a long one, since the Japs had blown up many bridges and our planes had destroyed some of the road in strafing the retreating enemy, but we got along well until about four in the afternoon, when the jeep went dead. Bill tinkered with the condenser and the carburetor to no avail, and at last we were glad to accept a thirty-mile tow from a passing truck that belonged to the 37th Division. The dust had been bad before we were taken in tow, but the dust that the rear wheels of that six-by-six truck threw into our faces from ten feet out was choking.

It was after six when we were dropped at an Ordnance Company in San Fernando, where we not only got a temporary repair job done on the jeep, but also wangled a square meal and a much-needed bath. Alas, the jeep stalled twice more before we got into the outskirts of Manila, and then, because of rumors that Rizal Avenue had been mined, Father Ortiz took us through side streets to the gates of the University of Santo Tomas. During the Japanese occupation, American and European civilians had been interned either here or at another camp at Los Banos about thirty miles to the south, which was still in enemy hands. It was now after dark, and the MP's didn't even want to hear of letting us in, but Father Ortiz' golden leaves again came in handy, and we pushed the jeep through the gates. The ex-prisoners were enjoying their first movie in three years, and it would have been difficult to pick out any individual in the crowd, so we walked on and ran suddenly into Archbishop O'Doherty, the Archbishop of Manila, with whom we had a long conversation. He told us of all the maneuvering and chicanery he had had to resort to in order to avoid being forced into a public approval of the Jap regime, and of his many narrow escapes from imprisonment in Santiago. At last I said,

"Your Excellency, where are the Jesuits?"

"Father," he replied, "Over behind that building, which used to be a girls' dormitory, you'll find a big chicken coop. That's where all the priests are living."

Well, in that shanty we found Father Hurley, the Superior, Father Vincent Kennally, later Bishop of the Caroline Islands, Fathers John and Vincent McFadden, Father Anthony Keane, Brother Abrams, and a number of Columbans, Oblates, and Maryknollers. It was a wonderful reunion, particularly since Father Dugan had told us horrible stories he had heard by grapevine about atrocities involving Father Hurley and Father Keane, and it was glorious to find that they were simply not true. There were plenty of horrors without those. In the middle of the excitement a priest came up to me with his hand extended.

"Hello, Bill."

I was embarrassed. "Er—hello, Father," I said uncertainly.

"Don't know me, eh?"

I looked again, but nothing registered. "I'm sorry."

"Buck Ewing!" he said.

I was staggered. The last time I had seen the distinguished Fordham anthropologist he had been a burly figure of two hundred and fifty pounds. The skeleton I was talking to could not have weighed more than ninety. Father Ewing had been looking for relics of prehistoric man in Mindanao when the war broke out, and had been interned at once. The food ration, which was never substantial, dwindled to a thin gruel of rice and water during the last four months. The Japs in this case had not been deliberately barbarous. Our Navy had effectively blockaded the Philippines and prevented Japanese supply ships from bringing in food—if, indeed, there was anything they could bring after feeding their own teeming millions at home. Had it not been for the loyal devotion of the Filipinos in the city, who threw bundles of food over the walls to the prisoners, there would have been few survivors in Santo Tomas when we got there.

Sometimes I wonder, in these days when we Americans are so cordially disliked abroad, when our flag is insulted and our consulates burned, whether we have ever been sufficiently grateful to the people of the Philippines for their loyalty to us through the three years of the Japanese occupation. We had been ignominiously defeated and driven out of the islands, and it must have looked—in spite of General MacArthur's famous promise—as if we should never return. It would have been easier for the Filipinos if they had welcomed the invader, if they had joined the "Greater Asia Co-prosperity Sphere" which the Japanese were sponsoring. Instead, the young men took to the hills and became guerrillas, harassing the enemy incessantly, while those who stayed in their homes maintained a steady policy of non-cooperation with the Japs and clandestine assistance to the guerrillas. Our administration of the Philippines must have been, one thinks, a singularly enlightened and beneficent one during the years between our arrival there and the Japanese attack; otherwise we should never have won so staunch a friendship. And there has been no comparable expression of gratitude elsewhere in the world, although American wealth and blood have twice been prodigally spent to keep Europe from going under.

The erstwhile prisoners told us how respectful the men of the First Cavalry had been when they first came into the camp, and I thought I knew why. I myself felt a sense of awe in the presence of these Americans who had undergone so much. Somehow the word "internees" (a clumsy word in any case) had always held for me an exclusively masculine connotation; I was shocked when I saw women and girls among them. And the babies! Some of them had been born inside the wretched compound; others were so young when they went in that they never knew anything else. Father Ewing told us of a conversation he had overheard between a little boy and his father.

"Daddy, when we get out I'll stand in the breakfast line and get your food for you."

"But there won't be any breakfast line outside, son."

"No breakfast line? Well, how can we eat?"

All this time I was looking expectantly about, and finally I asked,

"Where is Father Doucette?"

Father Doucette was a New Englander like myself, and his family and mine had been intimate friends for years. They told me he was living in another building, and Brother Abrams volunteered to get him.

"Don't tell him who it is," I said.

Meanwhile we went out to push the jeep a little closer to the shanty, and while we were at it Father Doucette arrived. He peered at me in the darkness, and I had to tell him who I was. It was a most delightful meeting for us both. I gave him all the news I had from his family and from the Province, and he spoke of his confinement in Santiago Prison. Because he had directed the Observatory at our college, the Ateneo de Manila, the Japs were convinced that he was working secretly with the American Navy, and had imprisoned him. Though he showed no bad effects, I suspected that he had had more to put up with than he told us about. The great loss for him, he said in his self-effacing manner, was the Observatory; he had managed to remove and hide the lens of the telescope, but everything else was gone.

The worst thing that night was the bombardment of Intramuros, the original Manila, an area of narrow streets surrounded by the thick, high walls of the ancient fortifications. Many of the Japs had pulled back into this area and were holding out. An American ultimatum giving them four hours to surrender, or at least to release the civilian population, had been ignored. Now some six or seven thousand civilians, including at least one community of cloistered nuns, were trapped there, and our artillery was shelling it heavily. Behind us the 155's would roar, we would hear the high whine of the shell above our heads, then there would be the dull thump in the distance, and a column of flame and smoke would slowly lift itself over the stricken area, while one grew a little sick. The wall was breached next day, and our troops went in. I never saw what they found there, and I'm glad I didn't.

Next morning we offered Mass on improvised altars, using an eye-dropper at the offertory so as not to take more wine than was absolutely necessary for validity. Father Ortiz and I reproached ourselves because we had not thought to bring any altar wine with us. There was more talk then, and we left to see the other Jesuits at La Ignaciana, a retreat house where seventy-six novices and scholastics and a few priests, plus more than two hundred refugees, had been housed during the last months of the occupation.

We drove through cluttered streets and across hastily improvised substitutes for bridges. It was destruction beyond description. One had the impression that a mad giant had stalked through the city, swinging a bloody, flaming scythe. The buildings were mere walls about eight feet high, filled with rubble. The Post Office and other government buildings had been blown in and shattered by artillery fire. Escolta Street, the heart of the business and financial section, was a sagging ruin. On every side a sickening stench filled the nostrils, and we saw dead and decaying bodies of Japs and Filipinos lying in grotesque postures, some half-burned, with clouds of flies rising above them. We knew that our Ateneo was in ashes, that San Jose, our seminary for diocesan priests, and our novitiate at Novaliches were empty shells. Here and there a building had escaped and stood intact, drawing its skirts, as it were, away from the universal ruin about it. St. Sebastian's Church, for instance, a building entirely of steel brought in sections from Belgium and set up here, lifted its twin towers without a scratch. But far beyond it stretched the wrecked city.

We drove on in awed silence, and came to La Ignaciana. Here the Filipino Jesuits, who had not been interned as the Americans had been, were living. There were glad reunions for Father Ortiz and Mr. Neri, and cordial welcomes for Bill and myself. We were introduced to the Apostolic Delegate, and to Bishops Hayes and McCloskey. They told incredible tales of Japanese brutality—the most recent and inexplicable being the bayoneting in cold blood of sixteen La Salle Brothers the day before the Japs left the city. The Brothers were Germans, and had not been molested in any way during the occupation, since they were subjects of an "ally nation." But at the end some insane hatred of all white men must have driven the Japs to include them in the holocaust.

Dinner with the community was a homecoming for me. My last meal in a Jesuit dining room had been in Grand Coteau a year before. I enjoyed the familiar graces, the reading of the Scripture and the Martyrology, far more than I could ever have imagined in the days when they were routine. The food was scanty; a little rice and fish were all they had. But the atmosphere of gladness and the warm handclapping for us after the Rector had given permission to talk moved me deeply.

On the way back to Santo Tomas we noticed that the traffic had thinned out and that we were alone in the street. So we pulled up to an MP and asked if we were in safe territory. He was a long Southerner with a drawl, and he said,

"Naw, Ah doan reckon it's too safe. We just got three snipers rah chere."

We did a right-about-face and scooted.

Back at the University, Bill and I went on listening to the stories. We heard how the prisoners, when they were first confined in 1942, had set up a government for themselves, how they had built on the campus the shanties and the lean-to's which were the only shelter they were permitted to have. The months wore on and turned into years. Hopes that flamed high at first began to burn low. But in September of 1944, the first American planes appeared over the city; the prisoners ran out of their huts and cheered and hugged one another until the Japs threatened to shoot them. But October passed, and November, and December, bringing no further raids, and hope waned once more. Then came that wonderful night in early February when the prisoners heard a column of tanks in the street outside. They thought nothing of it, since the Japs often moved their armor from place to place. But suddenly the leading tank swung in and butted its snub nose against the campus gates, and they screamed,

"Americans!"

The First Cavalry had sent in a spearhead of only three hundred men, but they took the gate and swarmed in. The prisoners rushed on them, careless of the Jap snipers in the upper stories of the buildings, flinging their arms about them until the soldiers themselves urged them to go back for safety's sake.

It's probably far-fetched, and I shall be accused of preaching when I say it, but when I think of the Redemption, especially the Resurrection of Christ, or of his coming again at the end of time to "wipe away all tears from our eyes," as the Book of Revelation says, it's actually this story that returns to my mind. The long waiting at Santo Tomas—longer because no one could say when it would end—the perplexity, the hunger, the need to bolster others' courage at the same time that one's own is languishing, and then the swift, incredible release, the mad joy, the freedom, the friends, the food, the going-home—it seems to me the best parable in my experience for what will happen when our Lord returns to claim his own.

Before we left I took pictures of all the priests and promised to send them to their families as soon as possible. As soon as possible, too, I promised to return with as much material assistance as I could gather, but there was no way of predicting when the chance might come. The ride back to Mangaldan was a long and wearisome one; we had to thread our way between the ox-carts of refugees, and the jeep was still acting like a stubborn donkey. Bill and I got in about six-thirty that evening; eight hours for ninety miles. I took a shower and headed out again for a choir rehearsal fifteen miles away, returning at midnight considerably the worse for wear. Next morning I had to run about getting lights, a generator, a P.A. system, a ride for the bishop and another for the seminarians. The publicity had not been taken care of as I had expected, so I had to get word around as well as I could. Lastly, the chaplains had delegated me to deliver the sermon. I held myself to my desk for an hour and a half and managed to throw something together in a more or less coherent outline. But it was all worth it.

When the Mass began there were almost two thousand there, soldiers and Filipino civilians. The altar had been decorated very tastefully by the ladies of the parish under Bill's vigilant eye, and was in pleasant contrast with the riot of over-ornamentation one saw in most of the churches, while my red drapes made the bishop's throne look really princely. Father Joe Monahan of Boston, chaplain with the Amphibious Engineers, sang the Mass. The deacon, the sub-deacon, and the bishop's chaplains were Filipinos. The master of ceremonies was a professor at the seminary, a German. Even within the sanctuary we had an exemplification of the unity and the diversity of the Mystical Body of Christ. The bishop was wonderful: dignified, fatherly. And no one threw stones at the preacher, who went his garrulous way for nearly twenty minutes.

The Signal Corps photographers were on hand to take pictures, and afterward I managed to get copies. There is one in particular that touches and amuses me when I look at it now; it shows a long line of GI's approaching the altar for Holy Communion, while a number of Filipino men are staring at them open-mouthed. The soldiers, God bless them, are so big, so undeniably manly, and yet so candidly devout and reverent that the Filipino men, who in the Latin fashion find it difficult to associate virility with piety, are astounded. Sometimes the most effective witness we give is the one we are not aware of.

After Mass I insisted on presenting the choir, whose GI members towered over the parish men and girls, to the bishop. When I explained that I had instructed and baptized one of them on the transport, the bishop asked,

"And when shall I confirm him?"

So that would be the next thing to arrange—a confirmation of all the men who for one reason or another had not received the sacrament, with as much splendor as we could possibly have. But that would be another day. I was done in, so Bill took the bishop home, and said he was tremendously happy about everything. So were we all.

CHAPTER 13

Rear Echelon

OFFICIALLY, THE CAMPAIGN IN LUZON HAD BEEN DECLARED A VICtory, but the war dragged on. Walter Cassell, who had been in my first class at Boston College, dropped out of the blue one day and told me that his Division, the 25th, had had a hundred and sixty-five days in the line. I remembered Walter well because, at the end of his freshman year, he had accused me of ruining his batting eye with my reading assignments, and he had been considered a prime prospect for varsity baseball. We laughed over that memory, and after some conversation I asked him what he was doing while he was on leave.

"Reading," he said with a grin.

On another day I came back to my tent and found a long, gaunt man asleep in my chair. He started to his feet when I came in, and introduced himself with apologies. It was Father Callistus Connolly, a Passionist who was with the 32nd Division in the hills. He had run out of altar breads and hoped I could give him some. I had never seen a man more exhausted, but when I urged him to stay the night, or at least to stretch out on my cot for a couple of hours, he gently refused.

"Must get back," he said, and drove his jeep off into the gathering darkness.

The Japanese soldier was tough. He must have known that his cause in Luzon was hopeless, but he would not quit. He had developed a tactic of digging gun-pits and fox-holes into the slopes, so deep that he could sit in them while our planes and artillery blasted the area, and then come up and pour fire into our advancing infantry. It was in those hills that Father Owen Monaghan, a Passionist like Father Callistus, and like him attached to the 32nd Division, met his death. The Japs had the section pinned down under heavy mortar fire, so it was several days before Father Owen's body could be reached and brought out. I had made plans for a Solemn Mass of Requiem in my chapel, but the arrangements went awry, and we had to settle for a low Mass at the cemetery. The Bishop of Lingayen presided, and there were twenty-nine priests who came from all over the island. I had not known Father Owen, so his death, that of a martyr to charity, did not touch me so closely. There is, too, an appropriateness in a priest's giving his life for his flock.

I did not find it so easy to accept the news of Leo Murphy's death in Normandy, which reached me at this time. I had so many memories: Leo sleeping in my Contemporary Lit class because he had been working most of the night, Leo clowning with Joe Dever, Leo waving a handful of manuscript and shouting that he had something really good for this month's issue of *The Stylus,* Leo and Mary and Joe and Frances and I walking down Newbury Street to the Black Goose Restaurant for dinner, and Leo's crack that we looked like the cover of one of Father Lord's pamphlets, Leo and Mary at their wedding breakfast in Father Bonn's "Dramatic Attic," Leo standing by in St. Elizabeth's Hospital the day I baptized his Mary Abigail . . . "Blessed are the dead who die in the Lord," but that realization dawns only after time has dulled a little the pain of separation. I was heartsick then.

Two young officers asked me after Mass one evening if I would conduct the funeral rite for their elder brother, who had just died in a hospital near Tarlac. It was very unusual that three brothers, especially since they belonged to different units, should have been in one area at the same time. The one who had died was about thirty-seven years old, and had been serving with the medical battalion of one of the infantry divisions. His brothers told me he had been a fervent Catholic, that, as a matter of fact, the last time they had been together was at Mass on Ash Wednesday. At that time he had said how much he hated the infantry (older men found it pretty hard, as I knew from my days in the 86th Division), but he ended with a quotation that summarized beautifully his concept of the work done by the medics: "No greater love has any man, than that he lay down his life for his friend." He was killed, actually, by a

Before the war. William Leonard, S.J.: Boston College, October, 1940.

Finschhafen, New Guinea, 1944: crucifix carved of rosewood by Clarence Staudenmayer of Portage, Wisconsin, for chapel of Ninth Ordnance Battalion. Held by chaplain's assistant Bill Graham of Newton, Massachusetts.

Finschhafen, New Guinea, 1944: William J. Leonard, S.J., Chaplain, Ninth Ordnance Battalion, "Pater Noster."

The crew that built the Ninth Ordnance Battalion chapel (rafters in the rear) at Finschhafen, New Guinea, 1944.

W.F. Leonard, S.J., Finschhafen, New Guinea, 1944.

Left: W.F. Leonard, S.J.;   Right: Frank Gale, of Philadelphia, Chaplain's
Assistant. Camp Livingston, La., April-May, 1944.

Fr. W.J. Leonard, S.J.   Fr. Tom Shanahan, S.J.
Luzon, after the invasion; January, 1945

Ordnance Chapel, Mangalden, Pangasinan, Luzon, Philippines.

January-April, 1945.

The Ordnance motif was expressed not only in the altar but in its appurtenances. A Jeep piston (left) made a thurible for burning incense; a hammer and wrench, typical Ordnance tools, were worked into the design of the Mass book stand (center); a 90 millimeter shell made a holy water stoup and New Guinea mahogany provided material for the sprinkler.

sniper when he ran into the middle of the road to help a wounded Filipino. He didn't die at once, and Father Bill Rogers of the 33rd Division anointed him on the spot. As he lay dying in the hospital he begged for water, and when his brothers wet his lips he murmured something about "a cup of cold water in my name" and went off into unconsciousness; it was the last thing he said. One of his brothers was a captain and the C.O. of a black Quartermaster company; the dead man had often visited the QM company and was well-known to its personnel, so they asked if they might sing at his funeral. I hesitated a little, fearful that they might choose some sentimental piece that would be out of keeping with the dignity of Christian death, but I needn't have worried. After the ritual prayers, six of the men, while they held the flag over the grave, sang "Steal Away to Jesus" and "Swing Low, Sweet Chariot," and nothing could have been more appropriate or formed a more sincere tribute.

I remember that at the time I wrote an old friend in Boston and described all this, expressing the wish that something could be done to improve our funeral rites. They were too grim, I thought; there was, especially in the "Dies Irae" and the "absolution," almost a theatrical exploitation of the Last Judgment. We needed something that would express joy in the course well run and the fight well fought, praise and gratitude for the graces given and the victory won. The "Dies Irae" might have literary merit as a lyric setting forth the highly personal emotions of a sinner in dread of punishment, but it reflected a subjective, introverted type of spirituality common in the late Middle Ages rather than the mentality of apostolic and patristic times. No Christian would deny, of course, that we are all sinners in need of pardon, and that we should ask it for ourselves and for one another, especially for those who have just gone to God. It's a question of emphasis. To halt the entire action of the Mass while the choir sings a hymn of fifty-seven lines enlarging on the theme of terror seems a little disproportionate. The Second Vatican Council, in its Constitution on the Sacred Liturgy, instructed the commission charged with reform of the liturgy to draw up a rite that would "express more clearly the paschal character of Christian death." In other words, the new rite should express more of the joy of the resurrection—our Lord's resurrection and the one we Christians can look forward to because he has joined us to himself in baptism and the eucharist. As St. Leo put it long ago, "Where the glorious Head has gone before, there is the hopeful Body called to follow."

Sensitivities are very delicate in this area. When death comes and mourning is intense, people do not welcome changes in the rites and customs they have become familiar with and from which they draw consolation. However, changes gradually come about. When I was a boy there were no "funeral homes," or if there were a few they were not patronized by Boston Catholics, who would have thought it a cold, malicious sin against family piety not to bury the dead from their own home. Some one of the family, also, had to sit up all night while the body remained in the house, even though it was precisely the members of the family who might have been exhausted from nursing the invalid through his long, fatal illness. The "wakes" that turned into revels had gone out before my time, and so had the practice of keening, or wildly lamenting the dead. But wakes were still occasions when you went on one knee and whispered a prayer for the deceased, expressed your sympathy (quite genuine, be it said) for the bereaved who kept vigil around the bier, and then joined the distant relatives and the neighbors in the kitchen for a long evening of story-telling and jokes. When the funeral Mass was over, there was the long ride to the cemetery—in horse-drawn carriages, freezing in winter, at first, and later in huge, black Packards and Cadillacs supplied by the undertaker—and the painful ceremony at the graveside, which did not end until the laborers began to fill up the grave, and one heard the stones rattle on the coffin lid six feet below. No one could regret the passing of such pointlessly painful customs. On the other hand, it would seem that no Christian could be content with the reading of "Crossing the Bar," which was the only contribution of the chaplain at one funeral I attended in New Guinea. Tennyson's faith, judged at least by "In Memoriam," was not especially vivid, and no merely human composition has the charismatic power of the Holy Scriptures to console and strengthen us. The new funeral rite leaves room for some expression of legitimate sorrow and some earnest petition for the

Christian soul now in God's presence, but there is a strong affirmation of faith in the risen Christ and an evoking of peace.

We had not been ashore more than twenty days when the chapel for Ordnance was finished and in use. Thanks for this were due to the new group under which our battalion was now working, and especially to Captain Gerry Dalton of New York, who gave me his master carpenter, a sergeant, and twenty of his best Filipino workers. It was another "cathedral," larger even than the one we built in New Guinea, though it lacked some of the features we had there. There was no floor, for instance, just the well-trodden earth, and there were no chairs, but bamboo benches instead. In fact, the whole structure was of bamboo poles, roofed over with a thatch of leaves. The Army used so much bamboo for its installations that I have often wondered how long it was before a new crop was grown. This chapel was more imposing outwardly; it even had two miniature towers, and was quite pretty. There was a large bay that afforded much more seating space and enabled me to accommodate the civilians who worked at the Base, and there were offices for both the Protestant chaplain and myself. My altar, crated and left behind in Finschhafen, did not arrive until much later, when I was expecting a transfer to Manila, so it was never set up in this chapel, but I did have my crucifix and red drapes, and they relieved a little the bareness of the sanctuary. Although it was in some ways a more satisfactory and attractive building, I could not take as much interest in this chapel. I did not have to work so hard for it, and I was reasonably sure that we would not be using it for very long. And in any case, it's first love, they say, that is deep.

Chaplain Martin Hardin, of Elmira, New York, was the Group Chaplain. We hit it off at once, and had a most happy association. He was a Presbyterian, like my roommate and friend Chaplain Bob McCaslin at Chaplain School, earnest and eager to do all he could for the men, and equally eager to cooperate with me in any way he could. We shared the same tent, and used to chaff each other unmercifully, so that the other officers were sometimes hard put to decide whether we were serious or not. One morning, I remember, we were shaving outside the tent, using our versatile helmets as wash-basins. I had an English Rolls razor—the kind you can strop in its case—and I was vigorously slapping it to and fro when another officer, who had never seen this type of razor, happened by and asked,

"What kind of a gadget is that?"

Before I could reply Chaplain Hardin cut in with a conspiratorial whisper,

"That's one of those things the Catholics use."

The officer looked his embarrassment at this raising among gentlemen of *odium theologicum*, but I laughed and said,

"Marty, I'll get you for that."

My chance came unexpectedly at lunch a few days later. The officers had been asking Captain Lowell, our battalion surgeon, about modern methods of detecting mental illness, and Chaplain Hardin gave examples of the questions he had been asked when he applied for a commission. Then he turned to me.

"What did they ask you?"

"They didn't ask me anything," I said. This happened to be true, although I had never reflected on the fact before.

"They didn't ask you *any* questions?" Chaplain Hardin repeated.

"No," I said, "They ask those questions only of Protestant ministers."

For a moment there was a blank silence. Then the officers saw that Chaplain Hardin and I were both laughing, and joined in.

Somewhere among my souvenirs I have a picture taken outside our chapel, next to the sign which announced the various services and the hours at which they were held. In the picture Chaplain Hardin is standing on one side of the sign, pointing to the Catholic services and sneering like the villain in an old melodrama. I am on the other side, pointing to the Protestant services and doing my best to sneer more fiercely than he. The days of genuine ecumenism, of a dialogue intent on understanding opposing views, were still far distant then, but at least we buried the ancient hatreds and found each other's company very agreeable. A particularly grateful memory is that when Chaplain Hardin returned to the States, as he did about six months before I did, he telephoned my mother from New York and told her that when he had last seen me I was in excellent health.

This was an unprompted act of charity that placed a generous fare-well seal on our association.

We were definitely rear echelon by this time. The noise of battle receded, and our routine began to resemble the one we had followed in New Guinea. I made several friends among the Filipino people in the town, who were very cordial and generous, and whom I tried hard to understand because so many of my Jesuit confreres had been stationed among them and had talked about them. It seemed to me—of course my judgment was not based on anything like sufficient experience—that they were Orientals after all. Their ideas might have been Western where democracy and freedom were concerned, but when certain elemental issues came up, a certain Ori-ental stolidity made itself evident. It was not because they were a peasant people, either, I thought, because their reaction to death was very different from that shown by the Irish or Italian or Polish peas-ant. On several occasions I tried to help relatives of civilians who had been killed in accidents involving military vehicles. One fam-ily, I recall, was from Manila; as a city family its members had had more education and were a little more sophisticated, and they did show to a greater extent the reactions we would expect to see at home. But the country people were, outwardly at least, stoical or phlegmatic. In one sad accident a man was killed who had a wife and four small children, and the family came to ask my help. The wife's eyes were a little red, and her face was certainly sad, yet she gave no sign of being close to prostration, nor did her brothers, though they were very considerate of her, seem to expect any nerv-ous collapse or violent outbreaks of grief. She sat in my chapel nursing her baby in silence while her brothers with the utmost po-liteness tried to make arrangements to have the body transported to the grave.

"We do not like to ask much, Fader, but any kind con-sider-a-tion would be ap-pre-ci-a-ted."

Then they shocked me by saying almost casually,

"Our mother and our sister and our nephew were also re-cently killed, Fader. Yes, Fader, in the shelling when you came here first."

No visible resentment, no outcry against war or the Japanese or God; simple acceptance. And not, so far as I could tell, a religious acceptance, either, but I had not known the people long enough to be able to analyze it.

The fact that we were now far behind the front lines and out of danger began to make itself felt in many ways—none of them pretty. The élan of the crusade vanished, and selfishness reared its ugly head. There was an enormous amount of pilfering, and much traffic in the black market, and at last we had a memo from headquarters which threatened dire punishment for anyone caught stealing government property. I had no sympathy for the big-time operators who highjacked truck-loads of cigarettes and sold them to civilians, but I was afraid that some of my men might take some little thing and be given a heavy sentence in order to deter others, so one Sunday I talked about the matter. I emphasized the immorality of stealing, then pointed out that it was delaying our return home, and finally made an appeal to common sense. What amused me, when I thought about it later, and convinced me that I had indeed come very far from my academic cloister, was the language in which, without any forethought or preparation, I couched the last appeal. It went something like this:

"You might as well realize that the brass intends to throw the book at you. You fellows haven't much chance to operate in any big way, but you're just the mugs who will be caught pinching some little thing, and they'll make goats out of you. So I'm telling you before they turn the heat on: let the stuff alone."

"Egad!" I said to myself, "I don't speak English any more."

But they listened to that sort of thing. Many years later, after I had returned to Boston College, I was walking across the campus after class and met Vin Wright, who was then Dean of our Graduate School of Business Administration. He remarked that I did not look very cheerful, and I explained that I was reproaching myself for becoming impatient with my students and laying down the law.

"You've got to do it sometimes, Father," Vin said. "When I was in the Navy I was in charge of keeping the deck clean. So I'd say to my men, 'Look, boys, let's straighten things out a bit, shall we?' The next day I'd see that nothing had been done, so I'd say, 'Men, I asked you yesterday to clean up the deck. How about a little cooperation?' Then on the third day, when things were still untouched, I'd let go: 'If you blankety-blank so-and-so's don't get off your tails and clean up that mess, I'll clap you in the brig. Now get started!' Then they'd do it. Same principle here, Father."

Not that the enlisted men were the only ones who displayed the ancient human vice of selfishness. Some high-ranking officers, by seizing on palatial homes for their quarters, or by maneuvering to have additional units attached to their commands so that they could qualify for another star, set an example. "Empire-building," we called it. The tendency toward selfishness was more indulged in the "S.O.S.," the Service of Supply, than in the combat outfits, which had a better esprit de corps and a greater dedication to the war effort. The cynics among us used to say,

"Take down the battle flag, mother; your boy's in the S.O.S.!"

And I was reminded how the ancient Jews relaxed after they had been delivered from slavery and from the imminent peril of death at the hands of the Egyptians, and how God made the sad comment,

"The beloved has grown fat, and kicks."

The three Irish Columban Fathers at Lingayen lost almost all their possessions at the time of the invasion, and we Army priests, in the course of making sure that they were taken care of, came to know them well. One night a group of us, including several who had just been liberated in Manila, spent several pleasant hours in their house. When we were leaving, Father McDevitt told us we were all invited for dinner on St. Patrick's Day. I turned to the assembly and said,

"Remember, Fathers, keep the thirteenth of April open."

Father Ford looked at me in dismay. "Oh, Father dear," he said, "That's not Patrick's Day. Sure, don't tell me you don't know that day."

"To be sure," I said. "My mistake. Fathers, keep the twenty-seventh of March open."

He was really distressed until Father Tom Crump, an Oblate from Roslindale with the 40th Division, assured him that a Bostonian knew the day as well as any man from Ireland.

"I don't know," said Father Ford. "You can't tell about these F.B.I.'s."

"These what?"

"These Foreign-Born Irish, Father dear."

We gathered again on St. Patrick's Day, about sixteen of us, and the bishop joined us. The Columbans provided chicken, rice, and a sort of custard, tasty but very rich, made of steamed egg-yolks, and we provided a supply of what had made Milwaukee famous. Father Ford sang Irish ballads, and Father Joe Monahan, from Boston, kept us in roars with his clowning at the GI organ he had transported from his chapel. Father Joe was a good ventriloquist, and had the bishop turning around all evening to see who was talking behind him. It was a good evening, topped off when I drove my jeep into the motor pool at Mangaldan and found a GI wandering about in an alcoholic haze, looking for his outfit. I managed to get him into his tent without arousing any of his officers, and he was very grateful.

"Thanks a lot, old man—I mean, sir."

There was an amusing yet pathetic incident in camp one night. I was sitting on a log, talking to Captain Lowell and Captain Firman, our doctor and dentist, when Jim Scannell suddenly appeared, carrying a baby in his arms. With him was a young couple. The two medics, who had small children of their own and missed them sadly, were on their feet in a jiffy, open-mouthed.

There was a sensation all over camp. The GI's crowded around, holding the baby, playing with her, gurgling their delight. She was only nine months old, but amazingly bright and good-natured. Jim had met the couple on the road, and after asking if he could please hold the baby, found that they were Catholics and knew many Jesuits in Manila, so he brought them over to meet me. The husband was Lithuanian, but had spent part of his boyhood in Russia, gone to college in Italy, taught school in China, and had been in business in Manila when war broke out. Since that time he had been in the hills, one step ahead of the Japs. His wife was Spanish, from the Pyrenees, but had grown up in the Philippines.

I felt a lump in my throat when I looked at the soldiers around the baby. Jim Scannell, for instance, had a son he had never seen. The tributes laid at the baby's feet were touching.

"Can she drink pineapple juice?" they asked the mother.

"Sure-lee," the mother answered.

Whereupon hitherto carefully hoarded cans of pineapple juice appeared from nowhere, followed by tomato juice, and canned pears, and evaporated milk, and even a bottle of rubbing alcohol for the baby's heat rash. The young parents had lost everything they owned except what they could carry in two suitcases. They talked so confidently about God's protection of them and their hopes—in spite of their destitution—for the future that I'm sure they did much more good in the camp than all my preaching. I drove them, finally, to the thatched house where they had found hospitality, but not before the medics had entreated and extracted a promise from them to come again the next night.

I pondered awhile before I went to sleep. I had no children, and wouldn't have any. Did I miss them? No, I couldn't honestly say I did. Wasn't that odd, even unnatural? Perhaps it was.

There was one time, I recalled, when I had felt a real pang. I had been visiting my brother, and because I was there, my niece Mary Lou, who was ill as a child, had been allowed to leave her bed and spend some time downstairs. But at last my brother picked her up, saying, "Time to go back to bed, Mary Lou." At that moment the phone rang, and he turned to me. "Hold her a moment, will you?" She stretched out her arms to me, and realization went through me like a sword. She—or someone like her—might have been mine. I remember that I left the house quite shaken, and that the pang lingered for some time. But it was eventually forgotten in the press of work. I had ruled out the possibility so definitely and so long before, and my students filled the vacuum at least to some degree. I hoped I could say that the natural desire had been sublimated by my very real wish to serve these boys and to deserve the title "Father" by which they called me.

Toward the end of my stay in Mangaldan I decided to take Father Sison on a day's outing. We left about ten in the morning with no particular destination, but with an idea in the back of my head that we might be able to make Cabanatuan, the prison camp where Father Dugan and the rest of the American military prisoners had been confined. We stopped at the 43rd Field Hospital in Urdaneta, where Father Herve Trebaol, of Los Angeles, was stationed, reminisced over dinner about Finschhafen, where he had been Base Chaplain, and then set out again, over some of the worst roads I had ever driven on. Eventually, some ninety miles away, we reached Cabanatuan, only to learn that the camp was six miles out of town, and that there was very little of it left. But, having come so far, we decided to go on. The last stretch of road was like a goat trail, but the jeep took it somehow, and at last we bumped across a wide, open plain to the posts which had been the gates of the camp. There was an earthen enclosure which had been the guard post for the Japanese sentries, and behind that the ground rose in a slight incline to a little crest. The camp had been built on the slope and the top of the hill. It had been burned after our men were freed, and the civilians, who seemed to be much poorer in that neighborhood than elsewhere, had carried away every scrap of bamboo and thatch for their own miserable hovels. So the only things we could see were the bare spots, already beginning to grow over, where the prisoners' huts had been, outlined by the ditches that had been dug around them to keep the water at bay during the rainy season. The GI's had also combed the place, looking for souvenirs, so the aspect it presented was one of complete desolation. I stood there and tried to imagine what it must have been like to live for three years in such a waste. To the east the mountains rose up; behind us, to the west and south, there was nothing except the plain. A couple of scrawny trees grew on the hill; otherwise there was no shade, no protection from the glaring sun or the rain. An ideal place, I thought, to go quietly mad. No freedom, no food, no hope. I stared about until an overwhelming depression began to lay hold of me, and then suggested that we take off as soon as possible. I think Father Sison was of the same mind. But at the guard post a last surge of curiosity moved me to look into the area surrounded by the earthen wall, and there I saw a pathetic souvenir which meant more to me than anything else I could have found. Our liberated prisoners had told us how, when the Jap garrison moved out, they left behind them hundreds of cans of evaporated milk, which the prisoners devoured, and without which they would not have had the strength for the march which led to liberty. My souvenir was a label from one of those cans.

At Cabantuan itself I persuaded the chief of police to part with his copies of the proclamations issued at the time of the invasion by General MacArthur and President Osmena. He had tacked them up on his town hall bulletin board, and didn't want to part with them, but I talked him into it. He stood disconsolately by as I took them down; there was nothing else to grace his bulletin board when I finished. But I planned to make them part of a collection that would have permanent historical value, whereas in his possession they would only dry up and blow away.

Another item of interest was that on the road we had given a ride to a hitch-hiking Filipino guerrilla, a very pleasant kid of about twenty. When we reached his destination, he asked us where we were going.

"Cabanatuan," I said.

"I go with you," he said simply. We were definitely interested in knowing why. "Are there any Japs there?"

"No."

"Then why do you think we shall need protection?"

"May-be others."

"Who? "

"Huks."

Hmm. "Do you really think they are there?"

"May-be."

Father Sison and I looked at each other. The Huks were Filipino Communists, anti-Jap and anti-American; they masqueraded at this time as guerillas, but in fact were nothing better than bandits, pillaging the countryside. They were not very numerous, but they had a nasty record.

"Oh," I said finally. "Let's take a flyer on it."

The boy had a sub-machine gun, and looked as if he could handle it efficiently. So we drove on. Nothing happened, but as we were taking pictures of the gate we saw a civilian car, a pre-war Plymouth sedan, bearing down on us, and out of the corner of my eye I saw the Filipino boy cock and half-lift his gun. For a moment the hair on the back of my neck rose; it was too late to run, and all we could do was wait. I had visions of rifles being poked through the windows and riddling us, but instead there were only very pleasant smiles and bows from several Filipino civilians, evidently of the wealthier class. My sign of relief was deep and genuine.

Late in March one of my Christmas gifts reached me, a copy of D.B. Wyndham Lewis' *Ronsard,* sent by my friends Mary and Phil McNiff, and delightfully garnished with Mary's penciled marginalia. How well they knew my tastes! The book was a feast of all the things I loved. What a fresh lyric breath! I went around for days repeating in its original form that thing that Yeats paraphrased, *"Quand vous serez bien vieille, au soir, a la chandelle"* . . . It was when I had such a book that the lack of leisure and of privacy hurt most. Life in the field reminded me, not pleasantly, of my first four years as a Jesuit, when we lived all day in a study hall and slept in an open dormitory. The tensions that build up when one can never be alone are considerable; I am by temperament fairly gregarious, but sometimes I must have solitude. At the old Shadowbrook there were no private rooms, not even curtained cubicles, and it was not until I went to Weston to begin philosophy, and for the first time could close a door behind me, that certain unconscious nervous tensions relaxed and I began to feel my own man again.

For the thousandth time I speculated on how I had got into the Army. It was not, I knew, out of any love for the great outdoors or for fresh-air activities; I had enjoyed sports when I was young, but now I never hesitated between a book and a golf club. It was not because I was attracted particularly to the adventure of war or to the exhilaration some men derive from life in camps. I could only conclude that for once my motives in volunteering had been pure; I wanted to be useful as a priest, and in the early forties a priest had his most obvious and fruitful apostolate with the Army or Navy. Still, I had the impression that, just as long ago I had been lifted by the hair of the head, so to speak, and deposited at the novitiate, so my being in the Army was the result not so much of a reasoned choice on my part as of a direct intervention in my life. The patriarch Jacob, when he was near death, spoke of "the God who has been my shepherd all my life." There is such a thing as a vocation, even a temporary one, within a vocation, and one does well not only to listen attentively for the voice of the Spirit but to obey it with alacrity.

I hope it was under such an impulse of grace that, when the opportunity of making a change of unit came my way, I took it. For some time I had been feeling that my usefulness to the Ninth Battalion was waning. The headquarters officers were not a bad lot, but I had failed, even after steady effort, to get on any easy footing with them. We had almost nothing in common, and our association was a growing strain. It was the Vicar of Wakefield, I believe, who said that genuine cheerfulness is never produced by an effort that is in itself painful. Two of the officers were Catholics who, since our arrival in Luzon, had ceased to come to Mass or the sacraments, so there was bound to be a little embarrassment when we were together. The Commander, who was not a religious man, seemed to feel that a chaplain's job was to cruise about smiling brightly at all and sundry and lifting morale by the bootstraps, and, though I tried to be consistently pleasant, this did not strike me as my chief function. So far as the men were concerned, I had to acknowledge, also, a sense of failure. Their attendance even at Sunday Mass had fallen off woefully, and on weekdays I saw very few; twelve was an exceptionally large number even during Lent. They would not be abandoned; even if no other priest were assigned to the battalion, the neighboring parish church could always care for their essential needs. It seemed that, without exactly shaking the dust of Ordnance off my sandals, I could legitimately look for "fresh fields and pastures new."

On April 20th orders came through transferring me to Headquarters, Philippine Base Section, in Manila. The news was received with cool politeness by the officers of the Ninth, not unmixed with curiosity as to how the deal had been managed, and the Commander blustered a little over the fact that it had not been done "through channels," which was true enough but not very unusual, as he well knew. Harry Curtis, an old friend whom I had met in Manila, and who was then an aide to the Commanding General at PHIBSEC, had put in a good word for me. A few of my loyal friends among the enlisted men were distressed, but in general my departure caused little stir. Goings and comings were the order of the day in the Army.

My faithful assistant, Bill Graham, would not go with me. We had got on well together, but he was not overly fond of the assistant's job, and felt he would not care for the office work that my new assignment would entail for him. So I managed to have him transferred into one of the companies, where we both felt he would be happier and where he would have a chance for the promotion which the Battalion had denied him even though his position called for it.

My last sermon was a bit of an effort. I wanted above all else not to seem disappointed, much less bitter. I said that since coming among them I had regarded our Mass together as the best service I could offer, and therefore I had talked in season and out on the meaning and value of the Mass. Not only was it the supreme adoration of God, I said, but it was the way to make something of our watery lives by blending them with the wine which was Christ. I hoped that in after years the Mass might mean more to them because we had offered it together so many times, and I promised to remember all of them every time I went to the altar, wherever that might be. And so, like St. Ignatius' famous Letter on Obedience, my discourses ended where they had begun. Looking back, I had no regrets. A priest could have a worse epitaph than that "he tried to bring the Mass to the people and the people to the Mass."

CHAPTER 14

Tropical Ministry

IT WAS ANTICIPATED THAT MANILA WOULD BE A GREAT BASE where the invasion of Japan would be mounted, so when I arrived there I found several headquarters already well established: General Headquarters, Armed Forces, Pacific (this became AFWESPAC), Philippine Base Section, and Base X. I was to be shifted back and forth between the latter two as the tempo of the war accelerated and hasty readjustments had to be made.

PHIBSEC and Base X were located in the Customs House, a large office building opposite Pier 7 on the waterfront. Hundreds of officers, enlisted men, and WACS put in long hours here, trying to receive, dispose, feed, shelter, and prepare for new moves the troops that were landing every day, as well as to reorganize the national government and economy, feed and employ the Filipino people, hospitalize and send home American prisoners of war and their dependents. Personnel (G1), Intelligence (G2), Plans and Operations (G3), and Supply (G4) all had their offices, and under them were ranged such diverse subsections as Quartermaster, Signal, Medical, Sanitary, Ordnance, Air Corps, Chemical Warfare, Finance, Engineers, Transportation, Special Services, Chaplain, and so on, not to speak of Navy liaison, Red Cross, War Shipping Administration, Military Government, and any number of related agencies set up for the multitudinous needs of a vast army and a disorganized civilian population. It was a new experience for me to be thrown into the midst of all this, and it took me some time to learn my way about and to overcome the diffidence of the new arrival.

It was a problem to find housing for the headquarters personnel itself. Field grade officers (major and up) were entitled to live "off the base," in a house or apartment of your own choosing; company grade officers (captain and down) lived wherever they were billeted. "Home" for me turned out to be a former automobile showroom a few doors away from the Customs House. There, where four or five cars had been displayed in pre-war days, two hundred officers had cots. We were so close together that, as one wag said, you had to ask permission of the man next to you before you turned over in bed. There were no shelves, closets, or lockers, so our belongings were all over the floor. Above each cot was a mosquito netting which was necessary and welcome, but two hundred nettings prevented any vagrant breeze from getting around the room, so sleep was restless and unsatisfying in the humidity which by the end of April had descended on Manila like a heavy blanket. We were just across the street from the docks, and all night long the big QM trucks gunned their engines thirty feet from our heads. Every so often, too, someone came home late in a merry or pugnacious mood, and the chaos that prevailed before he was quieted down and put to bed was destructive of peaceful slumber.

There was no chapel, and no civilian church nearby, so services of all faiths were held on the roof of the Customs House. The heat there was intense, but we stuck it out until the rains came. Indeed, I remember the first Sunday of the rainy season, when four GI's held a tarpaulin over the altar and me while they and the heroic congregation got thoroughly soaked. After that we repaired to a room in the cellar that at best was dimly lighted. On our first day there the rains had short-circuited the electricity, so we did not have even the dim lights. We used four extra candles and I somehow made out the text of the Mass in my small missal, but when I faced my congregation I could see only vague shadows. So I scrapped the introduction I had prepared for my sermon and talked instead about the Catacombs and what the Mass had meant to the early Christians.

In our district, the Port Area, we were very close to Intramuros, the old Walled City, and in time we became quite accustomed to the devastation that lay about us on every side. At first it was overpowering. The solid walls of the old city, in some places so wide that the kids used to play basketball on top of them, were breached and shattered by our shells. All that was left of the ancient cathedral was the facade, and what kept that standing was hard to see. Near the cathedral had been several other churches, including the Jesuit San Ignacio. Nothing whatever was left of them. The only church still in use was the Augustinians', at the corner of the enclosure; I was told that it had survived two earthquakes, a tidal wave, and several invasions, so I used to grin as I passed it and read the inscription over the door, "This is the house of the Lord, strongly built." On the whole, the Walled City was no great loss; much of it had been slum or worse. Visitors were not allowed to enter it while I was in Manila; the Army was afraid of booby traps or accidents from falling walls.

Manila is divided fairly equally in two by the Pasig River, so that if you go any distance you must cross it somewhere. The bridges had all been wrecked either by our shells or by Jap demolition, but as soon as we entered the city our Engineers erected Bailey bridges where the Jones and Santa Cruz bridges had been. However, when the Army moves, it moves everything, including huge trailers, cranes, tanks, and the ubiquitous "six by six" trucks; it needs room. Traffic was always snarled near the bridges. A little further removed from us were the City Hall, the ruined Post Office, and the Botanical Gardens, which were so utterly destroyed that when I first saw them I took the area for a parking lot used by patrons of the theatre next door. Just beyond Santa Cruz Bridge there was one office building which had not fallen, but which leaned at about a sixty-degree angle; I kept wondering when it would topple and join its neighbors in the dust.

The main street of the city was Rizal Avenue, named for the Filipino patriot. Some sections of it must have made, formerly, an impressive white way, but now much of it was ruins, and much of it must always have looked like Skid Row. Soldiers, sailors, a few American or other white civilians, and swarms of Filipinos jammed the sidewalks. Small stores had been opened in the shells of crumbled buildings, offering everything from watches to peanuts, old copies of *Yank* and *Life,* American cigarettes obtained through the black market. Every second doorway opened on a cafe: "The GI Joe Rendezvous," "The Lingayen Successful Landing Cafe." Blackboards, looted from some half-destroyed school, stood or hung outside these bistros and solicited patrons: "Wine, women, and song!"

"Joe! You're tired! Come in and rest awhile!" (At ten pesos per rest.) "Whiskey—government inspected." (There were twenty two Army deaths by June from poison liquor.) The more exclusive clubs, patronized by the officer-nurse trade, or the officer-Spanish mestiza trade, were out in the suburbs. The girls on the Avenue looked much like the girls at home except that they wore gaily pointed wooden sandals; they did not, like the girls in the Provinces, soak their hair in evil-smelling coconut oil. Businessmen wore white linen jackets, but the young blades blossomed out in lavenders and pinks and exquisite white silk shirts. No one wore a hat except the laborers; these never appeared without a uniformly dirty and tattered sombrero that had a very wide brim to keep off the murderous sun.

The street simply roared with traffic, and the civilian pedestrians lived dangerously, jay-walking without so much as a glance in either direction. We madly blew our horn just as it seemed that we were going to crush them, and they skipped nimbly back, laughing. It was no wonder, I thought, that even the very old among them hadn't a wrinkle; they didn't worry. They drove tiny cabs the size of a Volkswagen, and I saw as many as ten passengers crammed into them. Their trucks and cars were of course in pretty bad shape by this time, but they still limped along Rizal, and the quantity of cargo, human, animal, or inanimate, that they were required to transport would have taxed a freight train back home.

I tried hard to speak deliberately when I talked with the Filipinos, but never managed to make myself easily understood. They were very precise in their pronunciation of English; I wondered if they had caught from the Spaniards the habit of articulating exactly every syllable, and I used to tease the Filipino nuns by getting them to repeat over and over the name of their chaplain, "Father Mac-Ni-cho-las." They never used possessives; it was always "the house of my father," not "my father's house." After a while I gave up trying to make the mess-boys understand me, and resignedly accepted a cup of coffee when I had asked for water. It was so hot at night that to drink coffee was to invite a shower of perspiration.

When I arrived in the city I found that the chaplains had planned a huge celebration of Mother's Day in Rizal Stadium for all the troops in the area. I was something less than enthusiastic about this.

"What are you planning to have on the following Sunday?" I asked.

"Why, what's the following Sunday?"

"Oh, just Pentecost."

They thought me, I know, a little odd. But when they told me that they were going to have a low Mass, followed by solemn benediction, I wished them well but said I'd have no part in it. Mother's Day was sentimental enough, but the reversal of values involved in a coupling of benediction on to Mass, especially solemn benediction on to low Mass, was too much.

Of course I went to the celebration. Some thirty-five hundred soldiers, nurses, and WACS were there. There was no participation, and I wondered all through Mass how much the congregation understood or shared in it. The local superior of the Australian Redemptorists preached the sermon; he had a fine voice and a cogent presentation, but the clichés about Mother made me wince, and when he finished I felt like standing up and singing "Give a Little Credit to Your Dad." It struck me, too, that at least some of the congregation must have felt as I did. I had met a surprising number of men in the Army whose mothers, unfortunately, were not what they should have been. And if the preacher gave as almost the only reason for being a good Catholic the motive of being worthy of one's mother, what were these fellows going to think?

There was a species of pragmatism in the attitude of some of us Army priests which I could never quite accept. Crudely stated, it came to this, that any means of getting our men to turn out for Mass, especially if they went to confession and communion, was good. I suppose it was a consequence of the emphasis that was laid during our formative years on the *ex opere operato* aspect of the sacraments and the "fruits" derived from the celebration of Mass. Simply being at Mass was the important thing; not only did you "satisfy your obligation" but you were bound to be better for the experience. It reminded me uncomfortably how during the later Middle Ages superstitious people believed that while you were at Mass you did not grow older, that after Mass your food tasted better,

and you would not die a sudden death. None of the chaplains believed this nonsense, of course, but many of us had the quantitative
approach to "grace" and the Christian life. Even the Army made us
submit, each month, a report of our labors that was made up of so
many services held, so many counseling interviews granted, so
many personnel visited in hospital, etc. Perhaps the Army had no
other way of determining whether a chaplain was industrious or
lazy. How *does* one measure his effectiveness as a mediator between God and human creatures?

More and more, the question of language in the liturgy bothered me. Every time I offered Mass I was conscious of how the
plebs sancta was excluded. Once, after another priest had celebrated while I led the dialogue, I asked him to slow down during the
Offertory and Canon; I myself could not keep pace with him. He
was a devoted priest, but had no awareness whatever of the people's
share. With much diffidence I proposed to the priests of the area
that instead of the "Holy Hour" we had scheduled for the first of
each month, we have a Mass with choral responses, with the confer-
ences becoming a homily on the Epistle and Gospel, and possibly
Vespers or Compline to conclude our meeting. The suggestion was
given only one supporting vote besides my own. I was learning day
by day how irrelevant the liturgy was considered, even by professional liturgists, to the practice of virtue, to the apostolate, to the
social mission of the Church, to the attainment of Christian holiness
in oneself and others. After the War I encountered the same attitude
among priests of outstanding intelligence and zeal; the moralist who
assured me that really, he had "nothing against the liturgy," he simply "prescinded from it"; the economist who teased me, saying,
"Now, Bill, if you had only taken up something practical"; the soci-
ologist who, returning from a conference in the South where he had
spoken courageously for racial justice, told me on the train that he
knew nothing about liturgy; the journalist who said, in the course of
a discussion about the position of the layman in the twentieth-century Church, "Look, I don't want to step on anyone's toes, but what
has the liturgy to do with this question?" It was the same priests
who, after the Constitution on the Liturgy had been promulgated by
the Second Vatican Council, wrote letters-to-the-editor asking when

the "liturgists" were going to "come out of the sanctuary" into "the highways and byways of life." Well, it was nice to know that we were now being missed.

About this time I was beginning to be a little self-conscious about the solitary silver bar on my collar. I had been commissioned sixteen months, and overseas for a year, and I was still a first lieutenant. People would say, brightly,

"Just come over from the States, Chaplain?"

"Er—no," I would reply, "Matter of fact, I came over a year ago."

"Oh, is that so?" they would say, looking at my single bar and thinking, "What did you do that you shouldn't have?"

Actually, a recommendation for my promotion had been submitted by the Ninth Battalion on Christmas Eve, but in the confusion after our invasion at Lingayen, the Battalion changed headquarters and reverted from Sixth Army to Services of Supply, which had a different form of recommendation for officers' promotion. Mine "bounced back," therefore, in February, and not long afterward I was transferred to Base X, and then to PHIBSEC, and back again to Base X. So the double bars—"railroad tracks," as the GI's called them—did not come through until June. Most Army chaplains were captains, so my embarrassment was at an end. So were my ambitions. I came, in fact, to believe that it would be in the best interest of the Chaplain Corps if the Chief were a major and everyone else were a captain. Some rank would seem to be necessary if we were to be considered really members of the Army, and if we were not to be brushed off by officers unsympathetic to our work. But field grade rank on a chaplain's collar frightened away the GI's, and the possibility of attaining it made for a degree of political finagling that was, at the least, unedifying and diverted energies that might have been better spent in apostolic effort. We were not exempt from the human hankering for distinction, or from the heartburn that comes when rank is conferred on someone less deserving (of course) than ourselves. Nor is ambition ever really satisfied. Give a man a gold leaf and he begins to pine for a silver one; give him the silver one and he dreams of an eagle. I wondered sometimes, especially in the Services of Supply, if we were in the war in order to finish the dirty business and get out or whether we were interested in making a good thing of it for ourselves. For me, at any rate, it would be best, spiritually, if I kept the rank I had. I'd have hated to wake up some day and find that I'd been preening myself over a trinket on my collar. The bishop had put a chasuble over my shoulders in 1937. That would be ornament enough, and it wouldn't frighten the men away from me, either.

Most of the American Jesuits who had been imprisoned at Santo Tomas or Los Banos had been sent home for rest and recuperation, but a "token force" had remained. They included Father John F. Hurley, the Superior, and Fathers Harry Avery, John McNicholas, Austin Dowd, Leo Cullum, Henry Greer, and Anthony Keane. Since most of our houses had been destroyed in the war, the Fathers were living in four rooms in the back of "La Consolacion," a girls' school now operating at only a third of its capacity. Here they set up a "Catholic Welfare Organization" which was adopted by the hierarchy and became for the Church in the Philippines what NCWC is to the Church in the United States, disbursing food and other necessities of life to the civilian population, acting as liaison with the Army, providing information to the newspapers, assisting refugees, and in general getting the wheels of normal civilian life turning once more. Quite incidentally, their rooms became a haven, too, for Catholic chaplains assigned to or visiting the city, as well as for alumni of Catholic schools, especially Jesuit schools, in the States. It was a rare night that there wasn't a group reminiscing about old professors at Georgetown or Holy Cross or Campion or one of the Loyolas. And we all listened with fascination and roars of laughter to Father Hurley's stories of smuggling food and medicine during the occupation to American prisoners at Cabanatuan and to guerrillas in the hills, of his efforts (successful until six months before the end) to outwit the Japs, to keep the Ateneo from being taken over, and to remain himself at large in spite of Japanese suspicion that he was not wholly sympathetic to their aspirations. But it hadn't been altogether a matter for humorous recollection. Father Hurley once showed me a tabulation of the debts he had incurred from December 8th, 1941, to July 31st, 1945. It cost him $282,354 to support for three and a half years one hundred sixty seven American, Filipino, and Spanish Jesuits and one hundred ten diocesan seminarians—a figure which averaged out, he said, to about 98 cents a day for each man—"and this in the blackest of black markets." In addition, there were these debts:

> For helping to support, in the Provinces of Pampanga, Bataan, Cavite, and Laguna, small short-term camps of American officers and soldiers who had escaped from the Death March,
>
> For helping American prisoners in work gangs in the Manila Port Area with medicines and food,
>
> For helping Filipino guerrilla units in the mountains with medicine,
>
> For helping families of guerrillas in Manila, and wives and children of officers and men who were hiding in the city,
>
> For helping widows and orphans of dead Filipino soldiers,
>
> For helping some soldiers and two officers hiding for a time in Manila,
>
> ... $51,347
>
> For housing and feeding an average of about 70 internees (ill and therefore released from Santo Tomas Internment Camp to the Ateneo de Manila, where living conditions were better and the help of doctors was more readily obtained) from December, 1941, to April, 1943,
>
> For helping with food and quarters the Red Cross Hospital no. 7, established in the Ateneo de Manila with a patient list of sometimes nearly 100,
>
> ... $24,118

The debt came to something over $350,000—enough to gray the hair of any mission superior.

What with the clamorous trucks outside and the all too frequent hubbub inside, I wasn't getting much sleep in my billet at the Base. I was, moreover, homesick for Jesuit community life. My visits to Consolacion made me pine for the company of men who shared my background and purposes, who followed the same Rule and lived according to the same customs. Finally I asked Father Hurley if I might move in with the community, and he made me very welcome. I kept my bed in the billet, in case anyone should be inquisitive, but I lived happily at Consolacion, and to this day I cherish bright memories of my days with those Jesuits, all of whom are now dead. They were weary from the war and imprisonment and suffering still from malnutrition, but they were cheerful and graciously kind; they prayed much and gave themselves selflessly to the Kingdom of God.

There was a jibe going about that if you wanted to get your letters back to the States in a hurry you could either send them by air mail or give them to someone in the Navy, since Navy tours of duty overseas were much shorter than ours. My office was on the waterfront, so I saw a good deal more of the Navy personnel than I might have if I had been stationed elsewhere. And, since so many of my former students had become naval officers, one or another was always bobbing up to our great mutual delight. Joe Bellissimo came in, and Carl Lucas and Eddie Doherty of our Sugar Bowl football champions, Frank McGuire, Frank Moran, Charlie Rogers, and then—most delightful reunion of all—Sandy Jenks and Joe Nolan. Mike Holovak was skipper of a PT boat, both at Finschhafen and in the Philippines, but I never quite caught up with him. I had no scruples about enjoying civilization with the Navy whenever an invitation came my way. I would go aboard a ship or visit the Navy base (the Philippine "Sea Frontier") and eat excellent Navy chow, drink iced Navy fruit juices, lounge in comfortable Navy leather chairs, stop sweating in the Navy's air-conditioned wardrooms, look over the Navy's well-stocked library, buy a good pipe at the Navy's ship's store, and enjoy myself without ever pausing to wonder at the widely divergent standards of living in the two branches of the service. At the Navy base, where later on I was Joe Nolan's guest on several occasions, cocktails were served outdoors before dinner. It's true that there was a choice of only two, but that was two more than the Army offered. Then we sat down at tables gleaming with snowy linen under candlelight and picked up the day's printed menu. Our dinner was brought us by soft-footed and obsequious stewards in black ties and white coats. On September 21st, 1945, the menu read thus:

FRIDAY EVENING
21 September 1945

Cream of Vegetable Soup
Melba Toast

Pig en la Blankette—Spanish Sauce
Whipped Potatoes   Buttered Asparagus
French Stringbeans

Bread—Butter

Stuffed Banana Salad

Caramel Sundae—Sugar Cookies

Coffee

"Why do you never invite me to dinner with the Army?" Joe demanded after one such evening.

"Joe," I said, "You're right. I've been very negligent. What about next Tuesday?"

So Joe came over for Mass on Tuesday evening. After it I took out two steel mess kits and handed him one.

"What's this for?" he asked wonderingly.

"Bring it along," I said.

We entered the huge mess hall and attached ourselves to the end of a long line; while we were moving up I showed Joe how to put the collapsible mess kit together. Then, in swift stages, the mess sergeant and his crew filled one half of our kits with corned beef, a woolly gravy, a scoop of synthetic potatoes and a dash of wrinkled peas. Into the other half of the kit went some watery jello and half a canned pear, while one GI poured steaming coffee into our cups, and two others administered in rapid succession a shot of powdered milk and a spoonful of sugar. I led Joe to a naked table supported by two wooden horses and wearing some fairly conspicuous stains and rings from a previous meal.

"It's efficient, Joe," I said, "and you won't starve. And now that you know the way you must come often."

I got acquainted with the Navy Port Director and spent a pleasant evening at his house in the suburbs. Not surprisingly, since he administered the arrivals and departures of supply ships, his table was bountiful, and when he invited me again some weeks later I was glad to accept. I told him I'd be a little late, since I had evening Mass, but I was sure I could find the house. However, my wretched sense of direction played me false once more. I drove up and down the streets in the neighborhood but found nothing familiar.

"Well, there's an easy solution to this," I told myself. "They'll be sure to know at the Navy base where an important officer like the Port Director lives."

So I presented myself to the sentry at the Base gate and asked him.

"Sir," he said, "I really don't know. But if you would step inside and ask the O.D., he would certainly be able to tell you."

The O.D. was a brisk young lieutenant j.g. He ran three times through all the rosters on his desk, and then said, with the air of a man who might be slowed down but could never be stopped, "I think, sir, if you will ask Mr. Hicks, in the hut across the way, that he will have the information you want. Yes, sir, Lieutenant Hicks."

I thanked him and went looking for Lieutenant Hicks.

"Well, sir," he said very courteously, "I don't just recall at the moment the name of the street. But right over there are the quarters the Port Director had before he moved off the Base, and Commander Scott, who shared them with him, is still there. Just ask Mr. Scott."

I found the Commander sitting in his shorts on the side of his bunk digging his fists into his eyes and trying to wake up after a nap.

"The Port Director? Oh, sure. He lives on . . . Doggone it, I have an awful time with these Filipino names. Wait a minute, now. Begins with M . . . Mariveles? No. Malacanan? No . . . Tell you what, sir, the Personnel Office is closed, but the Personnel Officer is having chow right now in the wardroom. Right over there, see? He can tell you for sure. Just walk in and ask for the Personnel Officer."

But I didn't feel like barging into the Navy wardroom unescorted, so I stood at the screen door and made a reconnaissance. I was observed, however. A tall figure at one of the tables came over and opened the door.

"Come in!" he boomed. "Come on in!"

But I had spotted the two stars on his collar.

"Pardon me, sir," I said. "I was supposed to have dinner with the Port Director tonight, but I've forgotten where he lives, and I was told someone here might know . . ."

"Hell," he said, "You'll never find him now. Come on in with us."

So that night I had dinner with the Admiral. His table wasn't bad, either.

Father Ed Whelly, of the Albany Diocese, who was Chief of the Chaplain Section of Base X, came over to my desk one morning with a sheaf of papers in his hand.

"Do you think you deserve a medal?" he asked.

I stared at him. "A medal? What for?"

"That's the way we all feel. But General Baker is retiring and going home, and he wants to hand out a few decorations before he goes. I'm going to submit a negative report for the Chaplain Section."

As it turned out, there were many who felt that they had deserved well of the Republic. Bronze Stars were pinned on manly chests all over the Base. And though our modesty prevented our sharing in the higher honors, all the Chaplains received Letters of Commendation for distinguished service. The General departed in a warm haze of benevolence, to the strains of "For he's a jolly good fellow." His successor was General Trudeau, of Vermont, then a Brigadier, and a faithful Catholic whose presence in the first pew at Mass every Sunday warmed the Chaplain's heart and provided a sturdy example for lesser ranks.

It did not pay to leave valuables lying around unguarded. The civilian riff-raff working as laborers in our Army buildings and compounds would steal your eye-teeth. Of course we were a constant temptation to them; it was the old case of the haves and the have-nots, and it must have seemed to them that anything they took we could replace without difficulty—which was almost invariably the case—whereas they had little or nothing. My glasses were the first things to go. Later, I had a more serious loss: I left my breviary one day on the seat of my jeep, and when I returned it was gone. It had been in a leather case, and no doubt the thief thought it was something very valuable, like binoculars. He must have been sadly disappointed when he found that it was only a book, and only one of a four-volume set useful to professionals only. But in the Philippines, where religious shops had been burned or destroyed, it could not be replaced, and for many weeks I had to recite in its place the fifteen decades of the Rosary which were the official substitute. It was a real deprivation. I had never liked the Rosary, or found it easy to pray, whereas the breviary had been a consolation and an inspiration. I remember how, when I was crossing the Indian Ocean on the long way home, it suddenly came to me that the next day was the First Sunday of Advent, the beginning of the Winter Season, and I did have, in my footlocker below decks, the winter volume of the breviary. I went below, got the book, and read Vespers with the gratification of a man who, after living off K-rations for many days, is given a full meal.

> "As with the riches of a banquet shall my soul be satisfied, And with exultant lips my mouth shall praise you."

One morning two non-coms from an Army ship (no contradiction there; the Army had, actually, more small vessels in commission than the Navy) visited me with a real tale of woe. According to them, their company was in a bad way—morale very low, work suffering, relations between officers and men strained, and so on. It was a long story and apparently a straight one. I promised to go aboard and see the C.O. I did and was pleasantly received, had a good supper (Navy chow), spent a genial hour with the officers and another with the C.O. He listened to my version of the complaints and smilingly dismissed them one after another as exaggerations of minor matters, tempests in a teapot, hallucinations of a few disgruntled enlisted men—not at all representative of the majority of men in the outfit. He sold me a pretty good bill of goods. As I walked down the deck with him on an inspection tour of the ship, however, one of the enlisted men asked if he might speak to me. I asked the C.O. to excuse me, and five minutes later there were some sixty men about me. It was not a mob; no one was hysterical. If anybody spoke out of turn the first sergeant would silence him with "at ease, there."

I listened for two hours to all the non-coms and half the enlisted men aboard. Then I went back to the C.O.

"Major," I said, "I'm a chaplain. I can't tell you how to run your outfit. But I would like to tell you that you have a serious morale problem here, and I would recommend that you do something about it, in a hurry."

I told him that I had talked to the same non-coms he had been boasting about as the best soldiers in the Army, and repeated their complaints about the incompetence and partiality of one of the company officers. Finally I said,

"It's your baby, sir, and I'm putting it right in your lap."

Well, he saw me to the small boat that was to take me ashore, and promised action. He didn't know it, but I had wangled an invitation to dinner a week later in order to learn whether any action had been taken. However, when I returned the problem had been given a *deus-ex-machina* solution. The C.O. had gone to the hospital with a bad case of jungle rot, and was sent home. The new C.O. was very acceptable, and kept the obnoxious captain, who had been driving the men crazy, within bounds.

Sundays were on the strenuous side. June 17th was a typical one. I picked up the generous Father John McNicholas at the temporary Jesuit residence and drove some eight miles out to Grace

Park to celebrate Mass with some Engineers who had just arrived from the States. I decided to give them some tips on overseas duty, and felt like a real veteran as I talked. Then we came into the Base for my second Mass at ten-thirty, where I had a goodly congregation of about two hundred and seventy men. Father John helped me with confessions in both places, and of course we heard many more than I would have been able to hear alone. We returned to the Jesuit residence for dinner, and at four o'clock I had my third Mass at the Base. Afterward I rushed through supper and went to De La Salle College to open a week's "mission" for the WACS who were billeted there. I was a bit stale by this time, so the sermon wasn't very good, and I wondered whether many of the girls would come back. But the number in attendance (about sixty) held up through the following week.

Weekdays were not exactly idle, either. A log of one of them might read like this:

1. It's considered *infra dig* for an officer to hitch-hike, but there's nothing in the Army Regulations to prevent him from standing on a corner and looking wistful. By using this technique I manage without difficulty to get a ride to the Base from some passing jeep.

2. Breakfast at the Base with a quick look at the headlines of *The Daily Pacifican* (the equivalent in our Theatre of the European Theatre's daily newspaper, *The Stars and Stripes*). Then to the office for a brief conference with my Protestant and Jewish colleagues.

3. A procession of petitioners: (a) a soldier who has just learned that his brother has the same APO as himself and wants to locate him. (b) A very young soldier who, on a month's acquaintance, wants to marry a Filipino girl. I discourage him eloquently. (c) Another soldier who wants a transfer to a new unit because he has been "busted" from corporal to private. He is a Quartermaster truck driver, and he says that he was punished because he gave a ride to a civilian (this was against regulations). He pleads that the civilian was a poor old widow whose only son was killed in the liberation of the city. I call his C.O. and learn that he was busted, actually, for exceeding the speed limit after having been warned

three times. (d) Another soldier whose marriage to an Australian girl has been approved by the Army. Can he go back to Australia and marry her? I call my friend Captain Geary in the Adjutant General's office and find that, according to USASOS Memo no. 30, dated 30 March 45, he can. (e) A sailor from a Navy cargo ship at present tied up in the harbor. Can I get him a manual on automobile mechanics which he might study in preparation for his return to civilian life? (f) A Protestant chaplain, just landed with his unit from the States, wants Mass next Sunday for his Catholic men. I promise to get him a priest from among these still waiting for assignment in the 5th Replacement Depot at Angeles. (g) Joe Doakes wants an emergency furlough, and Sam Boakes' wife at home is threatening to divorce him, while Tom Joakes has managed to get a Filipino girl pregnant and her family is demanding that he marry her. Then Father Spoakes, from one of the hospitals in the area, comes in for supplies (bread, wine, candles, literature) and Major Hoakes calls from the Area Command to say that he wants that overdue report by noon "at the latest."

4. I drive furiously to see old friends in the 759th Engineers, have supper with the officers, remonstrate gently with one when his language gets a little too picturesque, hear confessions and celebrate Mass in the mess hall, preach briefly about their opportunity to offer to God, in union with the offering of Christ in the Mass, a costly and precious gift, their personal purity.

5. I visit the nearby hospital to see one of the Engineers, who has picked up hepatitis.

6. At the office again, a merchant seaman drops in for confession, and then a priest I don't know calls to learn what happened to a box of supplies sent him from the States and signed for by my clerk. A young officer, a graduate of our Rockhurst College in Kansas City, comes in to talk over a problem. He has just been promoted, and to celebrate he gives me sixty pesos (thirty dollars) for the Jesuits in Manila. An enlisted man who has never made his First Communion comes in for instructions. Alone at last, I pray the night Office and look at the pile of neglected letters on my desk. But the mosquitoes and other insects attracted by my desk lamp are a nuisance, and the heat is intense, and I am beginning to feel more

than a little superfluous to the war effort. It's time to wangle a ride home. And Father Heinie Greer will probably have to tip the bed over at six-thirty tomorrow morning to get me out of it.

This pace never really slowed, and there were no holidays, so that by September I began to have once more the feeling that has been with me most of my life as a priest—that I was trying to move through an endless crowd, while hands without number plucked and tore, not at my clothes but at my flesh. I did, as a matter of fact, leave the service forty pounds lighter than I had been when I was commissioned, but that was owing to tropical heat and the inroads of hepatitis as much as to hard work. Hard work I have never minded, so long as I could finish one job and start another in some kind of orderly succession. But who, in the twentieth century at least, can work in that fashion? Our problem is to give our attention simultaneously to a dozen, a hundred projects, all clamorous for our undivided attention, all to some extent deserving of it. Happy the man who can discern the merits of each and allot his energies accordingly, who can (particularly when he is dealing with persons, not things) deal with each patiently, kindly, but economically, saving a bit of himself for the others that are sure to come.

My consolation, when I felt so hemmed in, so harried, was my memory of the Lord in his public life. They pulled at him, they made absurd demands of him, they shouted and wept and snarled, they refused to understand anything that did not advance their own interests. I used to recall the importunates who, unable to get into the house because of the crowd, lowered their paralytic through the roof-hole into his lap. Because he was their servant, he did not rebuke or order them to take their turn; he gave them what they wanted and even sent them off in a glow by praising their faith. I used to remember how he sat exhausted on the lip of a well in Samaria; his disciples had the energy to walk on into the town to buy food, but they had not sat up night after night (not they!) with the likes of Nicodemus, answering objections, parrying accusations, trying to open the eyes of those who refused to see. If a priest is to discover his identity in the present "secularized" world, it must be by plunging into service like this, spending himself without counting the cost, struggling to love by meeting the real needs of the beloved. We are not better than our Master.

It was usually impossible to see or evaluate the fruits of our labors, and we had to acknowledge that in most cases we were unprofitable servants, but sometimes, for our consolation, the Lord let us see what He could do through us. A friend of mine in the States, a nun, wrote just after I arrived in Manila to ask my help for her brother's family. Her brother, an officer in the regular Army, had been stationed in the Philippines and had married a Filipino girl; there had been three children, but the father, after fighting on Bataan, had been captured and then had gone down aboard a torpedoed ship that was taking him to a prison camp in Japan. Could I find out where the mother and children were and help them? It took some doing, but at last I located them in a suburb; they had rented their house to get a little income and were living in the cellar. All of them were perilously close to starvation, and the oldest child, a boy of twelve, had incipient tuberculosis. I got him into a hospital and then arranged to have them receive the father's back pay and pension; later they went to the States and basked for a time in the healing warmth of the father's family.

A vocation is so infinitely more than an opportunity to follow a career or accept a job. A mere job-holder can walk off the premises at five o'clock and forget his occupation until next morning; even a professional man can step out of his role when the long, busy day is done and be for a time anonymous. But a vocation consumes one. I have never been able to free myself, for instance, of concern about people's reactions to my priesthood. Does Christ prosper or fail because of me? Is it harder or easier for men to accept him? Sometimes, like poor old Jeremiah, I have rebelled against this total appropriation of my time, my energies, my whole person. Why do I always feel that I must get people to do what they'd rather not do——read the Scriptures, participate actively in the liturgy, make a good confession? Why keep trying to steer even casual conversation toward more meaningful topics? It's just meddling, isn't it—satisfying some unconscious psychological need of my own to make people think as I do? So I would decide, sometimes, like Jeremiah, to relax, wait for clients to come to me, give them a decent reception, and let it go at that. I used to say,

> "I will not think about him,
> I will not speak in his name any more."

And then, as with Jeremiah,

> "There seemed to be a fire burning in my heart,
> imprisoned in my bones.
> The effort to restrain it wearied me.
> I could not bear it."

That gray little man, Harding Fisher, who was our novice master, knew very well how to appeal to boyish temperaments like mine. He never raised his voice, but his flashing eyes revealed the fires in his own soul and lighted fires in others. It was obvious, when he presented St. Ignatius' contemplation on the Kingdom of Christ, that personal, total love of Christ was the hinge on which swung his entire being. The subsequent contemplations of the "Long Retreat" were so many corollaries he drew from it. He let the challenge sink in for several days, during which we went over together scenes from the birth and young manhood of the Lord, and then, one evening—who was it who said that the time to reach men's hearts is in the evening?—he gave us the contemplation on the Two Standards. He pictured the endless struggle for the souls of men between the forces of light and darkness, the skilled, experienced infiltrators who stole into the ranks from both sides and sought to win adherents. He made us feel the strain and urgency of the battle, the need of tireless vigilance and constant activity if we, an elite squadron, hoped to win it for our King. He inspired enthusiasm, but sought also to make it durable, to root it forever in an appreciation of the infinite goodness, generosity and charm of the Person of Christ, who would ask of us no hardship he had not himself endured and who would share with us the spoils of war in proportion to the share we had taken in it. During the following week Father Fisher brought us from the Last Supper through Gethsemani to the judgment seat of Pilate, and at last to the foot of the cross. And there he left us for a time, suggesting only that we study what the Lord had done for us and ask ourselves what we should do for him. In view of such an experience, it was no wonder that we emerged from the retreat genuinely changed men, blinded to be sure by the new revelation, clumsy and awkward and stiff as we tried to live the new life and walk in the new ways opened to us, but eager, enthusiastic, and—as I said before, destined to be consumed by our desire. Poor Edna St. Vincent Millay, that troubadour of the flaming twenties whose later years were so sad, wrote a sonnet whose occasion and context I never learned, but some lines from it might serve to explain the restlessness of the apostolic heart:

> My earnestness, which might at first offend,
> Forgive me, for the duty it implies:
> I am the convoy to the cloudy end
> Of a most bright and regal enterprise;
> Which under angry constellations,
> Ill-mounted and under-rationed and unspurred,
> Set forth to find if any country still
> Might do obeisance to an honest word.
>
> Duped and delivered up to rascals;
> bound and bleeding, and his mouth stuffed, on his knees;
>
> Robbed and imprisoned; and adjudged unsound;
> I have beheld my master, if you please.
> Forgive my earnestness, who at his side
> Received his swift instructions, till he died.

CHAPTER 15

Bishop Without Portfolio

IT WAS GENE ROBILLARD WHO, FIFTEEN YEARS AFTER THE WAR, asked the constantly recurring question, though he phrased it in the insouciant slang of his own college days.

"Father," he said, "How'd you get off on this liturgical kick, anyway?"

Other questioners over the years had not put it so kindly. They asked if I shouldn't have entered a monastery instead of joining the Jesuits, or whether I had not turned a legitimate but rather irrelevant hobby into a monomania.

Each of us who worked for liturgical reform during the preconciliar years could tell, I suppose, a different story as to how we had become interested. In the case of my friends among the Boston priests, it was largely owing to the influence of a seminary teacher, Father John Sexton, who taught church history at St. John's Seminary and wove into his lectures his own profound love of the liturgy. In the case of the Chicago priests, it was owing chiefly to the influence of Monsignor Reynold Hillenbrand, who was Rector of St. Mary of the Lake Seminary at Mundelein and years ahead of his time in realizing the needs of the contemporary Church. Of course it's a nice question, one that involves the mystery of temperament as well as the much deeper mystery of divine grace and human response, why the same influence lighted a fire in some hearts and left others cold.

In any case, I remember that when I arrived at the novitiate I was asked if I had brought a missal.

"A missal?" I said, "What's that?"

I had spent four years in a Catholic high school and never heard the word. But that was in 1925, before the hand missal became popular. We had prayer-books—*The Key of Heaven* for girls and *The Young Men's Guide* for boys—which contained devotions for various occasions and sometimes even the Epistles and Gospels for the Sundays. No publisher, as far as I know, however, had brought out a complete missal in translation. Actually, the prohibition against printing a translation of the Latin Canon had been dropped from the *Index of Forbidden Books* only twenty-five years before.

But after my father had located and sent a missal, I found that it was a miniature though exact replica of the altar missal used by the priest. The only English words in it were those hand-stamped on the title-page, "Printed in Belgium." No matter. I fell in love with it. I had never heard, I suppose, of many of these feasts of our Lord, or of most of these saints. Certainly I had not known how they could be celebrated with such appropriate readings and chants from Scripture. In our parish at home we had assembled for the observances—Christmas, Lent, Holy Week (especially Good Friday), and of course all the Sundays. On these days the Gospel was read to the people, but nothing else. And on other days even the Gospel was not read aloud. It was a subsistence diet, eked out with what we remembered from catechism classes and what we heard from the pulpit, more particularly at the time of the parish "mission" or at Lenten devotions. We did not starve, but our fare was meager. And we did not suspect that in the stores of our Mother the Church there was an abundance which was never set before us. It was the wealth of the liturgical year—what one of the Fathers has called "the riches of Christ."

God has revealed himself to us, little by little at first and then supremely in the Person of Christ, "the image of the invisible God." It would be unnatural if, once we have come to realize this, we should not ponder from every possible vantage point each of these manifestations, laboring to extract from them every last scrap of information. So we go, if we can, on pilgrimage to Palestine, to see at first hand the places made holy by the visible presence of God. So we turn and turn again the pages which record God's interventions in human history—the things God said, the things God did. In imagination we stand at Sinai with the frightened refugees from

Egypt, seeing the seared face of Moses, the stone tablets smashed, the lightnings at the mountain-top. Or we sit with the Twelve at the Supper, having our feet washed, eating the bread-that-is-not-bread, drinking from the cup of fellowship.

It soon comes home to us, however, that what God has revealed by his words and actions is not simply information, the basic data on which theology might ruminate and erect a system or a creed. We see that God has revealed himself, a Person who thinks and desires. Like other persons, God wishes by what he says and does to communicate himself. Like other persons, he looks for a response. He hopes, if we may put it that way, that by word and action we may reveal ourselves to him as persons who think and love. When we realize this we become aware that God approaches us with respect for our freedom and a desire to prove himself deserving of our love. This is overwhelming when we experience it, of course. It is like being singled out for attention by someone we thought would never notice us.

Such personal meetings with God can occur either when we come together with our brethren or when we are alone. It is obvious that the Christian can enjoy both and should have both, and that there should be reverberations from one such experience to the other.

When the community which is the Church of Christ assembles to act officially, as it were, and when it carries out the rites that are characteristic of it, Christ who founded and sustains it is there in the midst, according to his solemn promise. Christians so united meet God in Christ. They join in the peerless worship he offered during his earthly life and continues, as head of their race, to offer. Seeing in Christ "the goodness and kindness of God our Savior," they respond eagerly to this new presence of God among them and submit themselves to the grace whereby they are conformed to Christ and so made holy.

"I know that my Redeemer lives," said Job. We Christians, who meet him and are made one with him in these encounters, know it, too. His priestly intercession for our race continues through the generations. His ministry to the fallen, the blind, the destitute goes on in our own time. Mary Magdalene meets him, and

Nicodemus the questioner, and Nathaniel the simple-hearted. The will of God, that every human creature be saved and come to the knowledge of the truth, is achieved in the sacred signs whereby the Word is made flesh and dwells among us.

So, in the sign of water, Christian life begins, which is to say that we are plunged into the dying and rising of Christ. From the tomb in which our "old man" lies we stand up a "new man" in Christ, a child of his Father in heaven. The power that raised Lazarus from the dead has shown itself mighty here, too. But this immortal must now live amid mortality. This child of eternity must learn to live in time, and to sanctify time. So the redemptive strength of Christ, which transcends time, is made present to us by other signs: bread, and oil, and the spoken word; gestures and postures; facts and feasts. By meeting Christ thus in all the vicissitudes of his life we go far beyond the theoretical knowledge of our faith. We come to know Christ as we know our friends, through trustful exchange. We learn what every creature must sometime learn, that for us there is no good apart from our Creator, but equally that "in everything God has made us rich in Christ."

The year of grace, as we call it, is thus not only an inexhaustible source-book for our prayer, a perennial "Contemplation for Obtaining Divine Love." It is not only an effective preaching of the basic doctrines of our faith. It is also a re-enactment of the mysteries which God has made the source of all our holiness, and by which we pray (on the Feast of St. Ignatius), that we may be sanctified in truth. As the Second Vatican Council put it, "Recalling thus the mysteries of redemption, the Church opens to the faithful the riches of her Lord's powers and merits, so that these are in some way made present for all time, and the faithful are enabled to lay hold on them and be filled with saving grace." The liturgical year becomes in this way a sacrament of Christ's availability to us. We keep our holy days, our seasons of joy and penance, knowing that in them "Jesus of Nazareth is passing by."

Isaiah might have been thinking of the liturgical year, and of Christ's putting himself at our disposal in it, as well as of the profound change of heart every man must undergo if he is to be a genuine Christian, when he wrote:

Oh, come to the water, all you who are thirsty:
though you have no money, come!
Buy corn without money, and eat,
and at no cost, wine and milk.
Why spend money on what is not bread,
your wages on what fails to satisfy?
Listen, listen to me, and you will have
good things to eat
and rich food to enjoy.
Pay attention, come to me,
listen, and your soul will live.
With you I will make an everlasting covenant
out of the favors promised to David . . .
Seek the Lord while he is still to be found,
call to him while he is still near.
Let the wicked man abandon his way,
the evil man his thoughts.
Let him turn back to the Lord
who will take pity on him,
for my thoughts are not your thoughts,
my ways not your ways—it is the Lord who speaks.
Yes, the heavens are as high above earth
as my ways are above your ways,
my thoughts above your thoughts.

For most of us, a lifetime is scarcely long enough to bring about a conversion so total that we habitually think God's thoughts and walk God's ways. We need to hear, again and again, year in and year out, St. Paul's exhortations to "put on the Lord Jesus Christ," to "have that mind which was in Christ Jesus." But simple hearing is not enough, either. We need the flooding grace that purges us of meaner loves and lifts us to summits where we love purely. We need to meet, often and intimately, the Christ through whom God spoke his word of love to us. This Christ lives on in the Church, and prolongs his redemptive work in her sacred signs. As St. Leo said, "what was visible in the life of Christ has passed over into the sacraments"—not the seven sacraments only, but that whole tissue of life, visible and invisible, which we see in the prayers, rites, absolutions, and consecrations of the holy Church.

But the Christian's prayer is not always offered in community. Since we are persons addressing a Person, it is fitting that sometimes we should do this when we are alone. We should speak to God out of the depths of our own highly individualized souls—saying things we alone can say, or at least saying them as we alone can say them. Moreover, our experience in the community prayer is sometimes so charged, so intense—as when in the course of an hour we offer, let us say, the Midnight Mass of Christmas—that we need and want to savor it at leisure, to ponder and discuss it with God. By the same token, the more we pray alone, the richer will be our participation in the prayer of the community. For the community prayer, after all, is the sum total of individual prayers. We must think sometimes if our conversation is to be worth listening to. We must pray in our hearts, alone, if we would pray well with our brethren. Holy Communion, for instance, will mean much to us if we have reflected on the plan of God for human unity and have asked pardon for the obstacles placed in its way by human perversity, including our own. The Feast of All Saints will gladden us if we have prayed that God's Kingdom may come. Lent will find us receiving with our brethren the ashes of mortality in a rite that will be meaningful insofar as we have determined on a more fervent life, and sought God's purifying and strengthening grace to that end.

There is a constant and quite natural interplay here, as we should expect from a person whose life is at once solitary and social. But each kind of prayer draws its substance from the same source: the history of salvation. When the community assembles, it "calls to mind the passion, resurrection, and ascension of the Lord Jesus Christ." It comes together, in fact, to re-enact those saving mysteries as well as the others, less climactic, which prepared the way for them. And when Christians go apart for individual prayer their thought and aspiration are nourished by the same history of God's love for human beings. Both individual and community know that that history is not yet finished, it is being written still, day after day. The interventions of God continue, the Christ of the New Testament is the risen Christ, living now in his Church and laboring still at this work of salvation. So both individual and community know themselves as part of that work and that history, both deduce from the pattern of the past the judgments and mercies of God's accustomed way of acting. Both are "certain that the one who began this good work" in them "will see that it is finished when the Day of Christ Jesus comes."

I know now that as a novice I had not such accurate or complete awareness of the year of grace, or of the liturgy in general. I came to it through the back door, so to speak. I was enthralled by its poetry. My missal introduced me to the Bible, to the calendar, to ritual splendor and symbolism. The practice of religion had been a serious matter, even a grim one, at home; suddenly it was bathed in light and warmth. True, the daily Mass was offered in absolute silence most of the time, and we novices were accorded only the role of privileged spectators. But now I could follow the lovely texts and feast on them. I was not drawn to the devotions that were urged on us—to the Sacred Heart, to our Lady, to St. Joseph and the Holy Family and the others. The prayers associated with these devotions, and the terms in which they themselves were couched, seemed to me rhetorical, sentimental, subjective. I felt guilty about this, and wondered if I belonged in a life that, we were told, could not be sustained without such helps; my contemporaries seemed to find them congenial and satisfying, so, I worried, the fault must be mine. It would be many years before I could resolve this difficulty, but meanwhile I had my missal—nothing else, alas, not the breviary or any part of it, not the active sharing in rite or office now taken for granted—and I began to know, beneath its beauty of language and imagery, the strength and solidity of the Church's prayer. It was long afterward that I read Pius X's famous saying, "the liturgy is the primary and indispensable source of the true Christian spirit," which was the only authoritative dictum that we "liturgists" could quote for many years, and I subscribed to it not because it was said by a Pope but because I had personally come to experience its truth.

Fr. Ed Whelly, who was the ranking chaplain in our office in Manila, was transferred to the higher headquarters of PHIBSEC, so I became the only Catholic chaplain in the Headquarters of Base X, and found myself as nearly a bishop as I shall ever be. I hadn't the episcopal authority, much less the consecration, but I had the headaches. I was supposed to provide for the religious needs of all the

Catholic military personnel in the area between Base M in the north and Base S in the south. It was a sprawling, densely populated diocese, with hundreds of "parishes" and many of them on the move in or out. Many lacked pastors, so there was a scramble every Sunday to provide Mass for them. The Fifth Replacement Depot, in which we had languished for five weeks at Oro Bay, was now located at Angeles, forty miles north of us, and chaplains from the States sat there for weeks after their arrival, waiting for orders. At one time thirty-five priests were there, so I had a reservoir to draw from on Sundays, if I could get phone messages through to them accurately, and if I could arrange transportation. There were also American civilian priests, like the generous Maryknoller Father Bob Sheridan, who had been released from internment camp at Los Banos but delayed his return home in order to help in any way he could. I should have liked, as "bishop," to inaugurate a few simple changes in the way the liturgy was celebrated, but this would have been to exceed my modest mandate, and few of my priests would have sympathized. Odd how it took a General Council, with some three thousand real bishops in attendance, to let us share our own language so that the congregation might know what was going on. And yet not so odd, either, because such minor changes are only surface manifestations of the profound attitudinal changes that the Council brought about. Those Christians to come, who will never have known the older attitudes, will be hard put to understand what all the bother was about.

The "diocese" had other problems. One of them, prostitution, was as old as the oldest army of occupation. By midsummer, however, it had grown to frightening proportions, and an effort was launched to railroad a bill through the Philippine Congress which would set up a legalized red-light district in each of the principal cities of the Islands. The arguments advanced by the congressional committee, which had approved the bill and only reluctantly yielded to a demand by a congresswoman from Mindanao for a public hearing, were that it would prevent the spread of venereal disease and also assure decent citizens that GI's would not come knocking at their doors. The congresswoman invited Father Jim Barnett, a Jesuit from the New York Province, who had worked hard to find a solution for the same problem in New Caledonia, to present the views of the American chaplains, and urged us to attend the hearing. About fourteen of us, Protestant and Catholic, went.

Father Barnett was superb. He took care of all the diplomatic niceties; the chaplains were not, he said, trying to dictate to the Congress how it should vote, or even speaking officially for the American Army. We were there only at the Congress' invitation, to present moral and practical arguments that in our view made the bill undesirable. Still in a very low key, he went on to cite the United States Surgeon General, Dr. Parran, and other authorities, to show that the proposed legislation would fail of its purpose, and that its only effect, a lamentable one, would be to legalize prostitution in this largely Christian democracy.

At this point a fiery young major in the Filipino guerrillas leaped to his feet and delivered himself of an oration. He waved his arms and thumped the desk in the best Hitlerian tradition, shouting that the bill was a social necessity, that the Army as a whole approved it. The Chaplains, he said, live in an ideal world, anyway. At last he left, feeling, no doubt, that he had spoken his noble piece and demolished us, but Father Barnett countered his presentation and was supported by the Director of the Board of Health of the City of Manila. Then, suddenly, the major reappeared and took the floor again, shouting that the honor of Filipino maidens had to be protected. But he made one egregious slip. I am sure that he intended to be complimentary, but his remark boomeranged on him to his utter bewilderment.

"Soldiers," he shouted, "are knocking at the doors of respectable citizens, looking for satisfaction. The chaplains would have this continue. I cannot understand their attitude, although it must be said to the credit of the Chaplain Corps that so far not one chaplain has been among those who have come to the doors."

He got no further. With a reflex bound every one of us was on our feet, demanding that the insult be withdrawn. The oldest among us, a Protestant with the rank of full colonel, nearly lost his head. Amid the clamor he got the floor.

"Am I to understand that the Major is really a member of the Philippine Army? What is the Major's name, please? Can it be understood that he represents the mind of his superior officers? I shall take up this insult through military channels!"

The fire-eater turned white under his brown skin and lost all his aplomb. The chairman tried to intervene. Our colonel stood his ground, demanding that the remark be stricken from the minutes and that the major offer an apology. At last it came, and it should be said that he made it a very handsome one, expressing sincere regret that in the heat of debate he had been carried away.

Well, it was a very exhilarating passage at arms, and apparently it carried the day, because the Committee reversed itself and brought in no bill. We chaplains could not be overly happy, however, because our efforts to get the Army to use its off-limits power were unavailing, at least up to the time I left Manila, and the situation was thoroughly nasty.

My chancellor, vicar-general, and secretary at this time was Tippy Maher. Tip was not long on such secretarial skills as typing and filing, but he was a gracious receptionist, a generous collaborator in the manual work that occasionally fell to our lot, and a merry companion whose wit often lightened my fatigue, and whose unaffected piety made me glad. He knew, if he had never studied it, the *ars dicendi,* and his pungent way of putting things, orally and in writing, made me, whose business was so dependent on words, a bit envious.

"Father," he said the morning after the Japs had shelled the beach at Lingayen, "Do you know how long it is between the time you hear the whine of a shell and the explosion?"

"No," I answered. "I guess I haven't been watching the time."

"It's just the length of a Hail Mary," he said.

Not for nothing had he been the poet laureate of his company.

"Tip has a new pome, Father," his buddies would say when I visited the Engineers in New Guinea.

"Read the pome, Tippy."

Tip celebrated in somewhat heroic stanzas the death of Franklin Roosevelt, the victory in the Philippines, the birth of a son back home to one of his buddies. His meter may have limped, his rhymes clashed, his imagery occasionally faltered, but he had the authentic fire.

When Father Whelly left Base X, his place as chief of the Chaplains' section was taken by a Protestant lieutenant-colonel. We got on very well, except for one untoward incident that almost wrecked our relationship. Tip did not return our jeep on time one night, and when he did get in he was taken to task by the Chaplain. Tip protested that I had authorized him to keep the jeep, and of course he referred to me as "Father Leonard." At last the Chaplain broke in,

"He's in the Army now. From now on you will call him 'Chaplain Leonard.'"

Tip looked him in the eye, then said softly, but very firmly,

"I'm sorry, Chaplain, but ever since I was a small boy I've been accustomed to call priests 'Father,' and I don't intend to stop now."

Then he went out to another office and phoned me. He was afraid that there might be fireworks next morning. When he returned, the Chaplain apologized for his abruptness, but still insisted that when I entered the Army I had surrendered all rights to any title except "Chaplain." Tip stuck to his guns.

During this little contretemps I was at a meeting of our "diocesan synod," which we celebrated weekly at La Consolacion, and I told the other priests what had happened. Next morning, shortly after the day began, Father Daly, from 14th Corps, appeared and greeted my superior.

"Good morning, Chaplain. I'm Father Daly."

A little later Father Ed Tanski came in.

"Good morning, Chaplain. I'm Father Tanski."

Then Father Whelly arrived, with Father Coleman in tow.

"Good morning, Chaplain. I don't believe you've met Father Coleman. Father, this is Chaplain ———."

Inasmuch as Father Daly was a lieutenant-colonel, and the other two were majors, there wasn't much that my superior could say, and the subject never was brought up again. Looking back, one can only regret such incidents. The Protestants could not have been expected to realize what the title "Father" meant to us, or why we preferred it to "Chaplain." We, on the other hand, should have known that "Father," for the Protestants, was not only not an evangelical term, but it implied that we were a caste by ourselves, exclusivist and superior, and naturally they did not like it. Happily, we live now in more tolerant times, when, if titles are still matter for awkwardness between Christians, there is a greater disposition to find unobjectionable substitutes, or to dispense with them altogether. Only a bigot would see in this a retreat from orthodoxy.

Bigotry, or at least intransigence, was a large enough part of my own outlook in those days, however. Joint services were strictly forbidden by the Military Ordinariate as leading to religious indifferentism, and I never thought of the regulation as anything but proper. I opposed strongly a move by the Base Commander to take over the Church of the Augustinians, the oldest in the city, and use it for the services of Catholics and Protestants alike. One of our priests held that the church was already desecrated by bloodshed—the Japs had killed a number of priests in it—and hence had lost its consecration. But I knew that the Filipinos and the Catholic GI's would be scandalized, and believed myself that "heresy" in such a building would be profanation.

The priests of my generation grew up, for the most part, in Catholic enclaves—Irish, or Polish, or German. We were trained, then, in a Tridentine and therefore polemical theology, which fought and re-fought the four hundred-year-old battles of the Reformation. We knew many nice Protestants, we used to say, but Protestantism as such was the enemy, and we could have no part of it.

What is it that happens, at long last, to usher out tired old ideas, to get us to forget the ancient bitternesses? Surely it was not, for us Catholics, simply the generous stance of John XXIII, putting our carefully rationed charity to shame. John, I think, only expressed what so many in the world had come to feel, that it was time for a reassessment. I used to notice that most of the GI's, being twenty years my junior, did not share my prejudices altogether.

And the war, all over the world, shook so many out of their fortified positions and threw them together in new alignments that fresh attitudes might have been expected. Just the traveling that was done, in Europe, but especially in Africa and Asia, broadened our horizons and let us see that our outlook was a limited one indeed.

A small example: I had often passed the Chinese cemetery in Manila, but one day, showing a visitor around the city, I decided to visit it. The dead were buried in marble vaults or mausoleums above ground, surmounted by pagodas, and framed photographs of the deceased were mounted on the vaults. There were some perfectly gorgeous pagodas, adorned with ornate scrolls, minute tracery, inlaid tile, and delicate pastel scenes painted on the tile. One picture, often repeated, reminded me of the Coral Sea through which we passed on our way up the coast of New Guinea to make our first landfall after three weeks at sea. While I was thinking about all this elaborate ornament, and attributing it to Chinese ancestor-worship, I noticed with a start that practically every one of the graves had some Christian image or symbol on it; there was even one statue of the Sacred Heart, a hideous plaster thing probably imported from Barclay Street, and looking wildly incongruous in that oriental setting. All the dead in the cemetery had been Catholics, obviously, and yet in these burial customs there was what seemed to me a distinctly Chinese veneration for ancestors. Some time later I saw the Campo Santo in Rome, with its profusion of ornament, and the incredible cemetery in Milan, which resembles a sculptor's gallery, and the hundreds of lights flickering in the twilight on graves in Italian cemeteries on All Souls Day, and had to revise my opinions again.

The rainy season began in Manila, but the muggy heat continued. Unlike Finschhafen, where during the rainy season the skies opened and stayed open for days on end, it rained in Manila only in showers of a half-hour's duration, but there were three or four such showers each day, and they were sudden and copious enough to drench the unwary and flood the streets. During the occupation the Japanese had done nothing about cleaning the sewers, so that every drain was clogged and the streets often looked like canals. One afternoon I had a visit from two nuns, Augustinians from Belgium, who had been in the Islands as missionaries for thirty-four years. They told me amusing and pathetic stories of the occupation, and talked of their hopes and anxieties for the future of the Church in the Philippines. One of them was the Mother Procurator of their community, and she had me in roars with her accounts of how she had got around some tough Army officers for food and water and other necessities.

"Would you be Irish at all?" I asked her.

"No."

"Did you ever hear of the Blarney Stone?"

"No."

I tried to explain the properties of the Stone, but I'm not sure she understood altogether. However, it was pouring rain, so I borrowed a jeep and drove them home, and on the way Mother began to tell me how hard it was going to be for her to move about now that the rainy season had come, and she without a raincoat. I laughed, saying that I could now hear the authentic Irish tear in her voice. I gave her my raincoat, warning her to pull the silver bars off the shoulders so that she wouldn't be arrested for impersonating a WAC officer. Poor things; they had almost nothing but were as merry as if they owned the universe.

Father Ray Schueth, from Peoria, invited me to join a party of Catholic Chaplains going to Corregidor; Fathers Paul Hettinger and Mike Haddigan from the same diocese, the Redemptorist Father Burke and the Trinitarian Father Mulcahy were the others. We left in a "crash boat," a large motor launch, and arrived at "the Rock" after a journey of three hours. I had been anxious to see the place because of its grim history, but actually there wasn't too much to see; the Army had had little but a few barracks there before the War, and of course these had been leveled in the two savage bombings the little island had sustained. We were most interested in the famous Balintawak Tunnel in which the Americans had taken shelter, after the withdrawal from Bataan, in '42. A hill rises up very steeply in the center of the island, and this tunnel had apparently been dug so that supplies could be moved easily from one side to the other.

We could go into it only a little way, though daylight was visible at the other end, because the most recent American bombing had filled it with rubble—discarded ration cans, telephone wire, the rusted ruins of a generator, cement from the roof of the tunnel, and human bones. It was a gruesome place, and later, in the deep brush, we saw the bodies of Japanese, burned to death by flame-throwers, and not yet so completely decomposed but that they were polluting the air several hundred yards about them. Much later, a year after I had returned home, I saw an item in the newspaper which told how Company M, of my old 342nd Regiment in the 86th Division, had discovered on the island several Jap soldiers who did not know that the war was over. I wonder where they were the day we visited Corregidor!

On the way back to Manila I looked around the boat and thought how much I enjoyed the company of priests. *Time,* in the first year of the war, had carried a slur to the effect that the bishops and religious superiors were sending their "plugs" into the chaplaincy and keeping their "race-horses" at home. Well, I thought, if the priests I've met overseas are a sample, I'll take all the plugs I can get. I was constantly being given new evidence of their simple humility, genuine zeal, sense of humor, and esteem for their brother priests. We scattered after the War, of course, and have seldom met since, but I hope that the memory of those days, when without obligation they suffered cheerfully the heat and the rains, the discomfort and the danger, with the sole motive of being useful to the children of God, comforts them still and sustains them in whatever trials they may now be asked to endure.

One or another duty at the end of July kept me from writing my usual letter home, and I suddenly realized that my greetings to my mother, whose birthday we celebrated on August first, would not reach her in time. Should I send a cable? It might frighten her; Western Union envelopes at our door had usually meant calamity. At last I decided to chance it. Two weeks later Eleanor wrote describing what happened.

"Mama had quite a birthday. Your cablegram was the greatest surprise. When the phone rang I answered. 'May I speak to Mrs. William J. Leonard?' Because of the unfamiliar voice I inquired, 'Who is calling, please?' 'Western Union.' I passed the receiver to Mama, who by that time had become more than a little curious. I was all ears and trembling from head to foot, with my eyes pinned on Mama to see if I could read her facial expressions. Naturally I thought of the worst. There was a moment's silence while the operator delivered the message. I said a fervent Hail Mary and then got the happy thought that maybe you were coming home. When Mama smiled I thought it must be good news, but an instant later tears were rolling down her cheeks. She gulped two or three times, then found her voice long enough to say, 'All right. Thank you.' Knowing women as you do you won't be surprised to hear that the tears began rolling down my cheeks, too. I couldn't get a word out of Mama, so, watching her cry, I continued to weep with her. 'What is it, what is it?' I kept saying, but she couldn't speak. I had no idea all this time what the message was, but I was almost certain that it was good news. Finally Mama drew a deep breath and said, 'Love and birthday greetings to the best mother in the world.' Then the two of us cried our eyes out for fully five minutes, and at last I said, 'What on earth are we crying for?' We laughed then. It was all over. We had had a crying good time!"

It was all over for me, too, so far as cablegrams went, after I read El's letter. I would thenceforth stick to United States Mail, even if it were delayed.

Suddenly people started to go home. The War had ended in Europe, so the demand for manpower on two fronts was not as loud, and the long-termers in the Pacific, slightly dazed but with stars in their eyes, began to leave us. Not a few of them had been overseas for four years, on one blessed "island in the sun" after another. A colonel I had become friendly with dropped in to say goodbye. He had been married in 1941 in San Diego, and shipped out a week later.

"Where are you going when you hit the States?" I asked.

He made a gesture indicating direct, non-stop flight, "San Diego."

"Well, I sure can understand that," I said. "But it isn't what I would do if I had my way."

"What would you do?"

"Oh, I think I'd go from here to India, and then through the Suez to Egypt and the Holy Land, and then over to Greece and Italy and France, and finally to England, Scotland, and Ireland. Of course I won't be able to do anything of the kind."

"Don't say that. You never can be sure."

"No, you can't be sure. But you can make a pretty accurate guess."

"Don't say that!"

The departures had their psychological effect on the rest of us. It was particularly hard for those who, knowing of suffering at home, had not been overseas long enough to justify their return. During the previous months I had managed to get a WAC home on emergency furlough. She had plenty of reason, but getting people out of our theatre was not easy. I personally took her application around to the various headquarters to save time and to argue the successive Adjutants General into endorsing it. Finally I succeeded in getting the last signature at the highest headquarters, and the Major asked if I wanted to finish the job by getting the girl air transportation. This I thought would mean a long delay, but the sergeant at the Air Transport Command asked how soon she wanted to go.

"I think she'd leave in ten minutes," I said.

"OK," he answered nonchalantly, and typed out a ticket that put her on a plane at nine o'clock that night.

But I'd succeeded in getting a break like that for only one other person, a soldier whose young wife died suddenly and left a two-year-old baby to be cared for. For all other cases it had been "Sorry." Tippy's mother had been quite sick, and he himself had been so highly nervous that I finally ordered him to see a medic, but he had only sixteen months overseas, and the rule was that there would be no "rotation" until after eighteen months. What difference did two months make? None, in point of fact, but the Army really tried to send home those who had served longest, and some policy had to be set. That was where the chaplain's grief began—trying to get them to see that the common good supersedes the individual's, and that our great objective was to get everyone home as soon as possible. It was hard to convince them, though.

Then Tippy's wife cabled me to say that his mother had had a heart attack, and would I please get him an emergency furlough. Tip was a wreck when the news came, and I was stumped. But suddenly I had an inspiration. I sought out the medic to whom I had referred Tip, and he gave me a statement certifying that Tip was a very emotional and nervous boy, on whom this suffering would be certain to have a very adverse effect. I began a tour of headquarters. The request had to be endorsed by Tip's company commander, and then by the Adjutants General of PHIBSEC, AFWESPAC, and AFPAC. If it had been allowed to proceed in the normal way, the correspondence would have taken ten days to two weeks, so I carried it around myself, saying Hail Mary's as I approached each of the officers in charge. This took almost two full days, but at three-thirty on the second afternoon I emerged from AFPAC victorious. Tip's orders were cut and he flew out of Manila sixty hours after the news had arrived.

CHAPTER 16

It's All Over

THE UNSPEAKABLE NASTINESS, THE AGONY THAT WAS THE WAR came to an end in August, after six years. It ended with the coldly calculated Russian declaration against Japan, and the atomic bombing of Nagasaki and Hiroshima. Since then the bombing has been condemned as heinously immoral; it has been singled out as if somehow it could be considered apart from all the weary horrors which preceded it and which might conceivably be justified. To me Hiroshima was only the awful climax toward which men moved through atrocities like those at Warsaw, Coventry, London, Munich, Dresden, Auschwitz, Leningrad, Bataan. None of it was justifiable by standards of reason or decency, and certainly not by Christian standards. Humanity seemed to have got itself on a garbage chute, and went down from one level of filthiness to the next. *Facilis descensus averni.*

We heard that people in GHQ and in informed Navy circles were laying bets that the Japs would surrender before the week was out, but the rank and file found this too fantastic for belief. Our first intimation that it might be possible came as we were finishing a long evening at La Consolacion and thinking of going to bed. Father Clem Ryan, a Jesuit of the Missouri Province who had been on the staff of the Chaplain School for two years and was then with a hospital in Manila, came to the door shouting that the war was over. We didn't believe him, but we turned on the radio. The Marines' song, the Artillery song, the Air Corps song, and "Anchors Aweigh" were played over and over, and at last the announcer broke in with the story of the Japanese offer. The bells in San Beda and San Sebastian were ringing madly by this time, and the streets were filled with rollicking GI's, but still it seemed incredible.

Next day everyone was speculating furiously and waiting for news of what the Allies would do about the offer. That night—it was, actually, about two in the morning—we were shaken out of sleep by a bedlam in the Bay. Every ship's whistle was blowing, anti-aircraft guns were filling the sky with tracers, searchlights were skipping ecstatically among the clouds. Again the radio gave us the developments. The Allies had accepted the surrender—on condition. More waiting then; would the Japs accede to the conditions? We hugged the radio. On the night of the 14th, Chaplain Marty Hardin, my old tent-mate from the Ninth Ordnance, visited us, and joined the expectant group.

"It won't come tonight," I said.

"How can you be so sure?" asked Marty.

"Because tomorrow is the Feast of the Assumption. You'll probably call it Mariolatry, but wait and see."

Next morning, as we were driving down Ascarraga Street, newsboys were rushing out on the sidewalks with flaming red headlines: "IT'S ALL OVER."

"There you are," I said to Marty.

As the song said, "the lights went on again, all over the world," and the boys would come home again, all over the world, but though I made it the topic of six sermons, three on the holy day and three the following Sunday, I still couldn't grasp it. It might have been easier if there had been some change in our status and routine, but we went on doing the same things, and felt we might continue to do them for a long time yet. Still I tried to thank God, for myself, but most of all for the men who would not have to storm any more beaches or languish in prisons, for the women who would not have to cringe under bombs or weep for the beloved they would never see again. The problems we faced in the post-war world were gigantic, but we could not even begin to solve them until we had the peace.

Archbishop Spellman, who as bishop of the American Armed Forces kept visiting various theatres of the War, finally made it out to the Southwest Pacific late in August. He was due to arrive, we were told, on a Monday, but came instead on Sunday morning, so there was no reception committee to greet him. But someone got in touch with Father Dinny Coleman, of the New York Archdiocese, who took him around the ruins of the Walled City. And who should be visiting the Walled City at the time but the opportunist Joseph T. Nolan, of Winthrop and Boston College and the *Stylus*. Joe, just arrived from the States, attached himself to the Archbishop's entourage and smiled at the newsreel photographers who by this time, with their infallible nose for news, had got on the scene. Then he came to my Mass at the Base. During the sermon he stood behind a post, in order not to distract me, so that I did not see him until he came up for Holy Communion. After Mass we threw our arms around each other, and then talked through dinner and far into the night at La Consolacion. I will never forget that Joe had been offered his choice of theatres by the Navy, and had chosen the Southwest Pacific, as he told me with great simplicity, in the hope that he might meet me.

All the priests I could hurriedly reach by phone, sixty-four in number, came together Monday night to meet the Archbishop. He sat among us, looking in his black suit and Roman collar like a penguin in a group of seagulls, and finally asked almost timidly if he might remove his coat. After he had given us the news of the Ordinariate and the Church at home, he got down to business.

"What can I do for you?"

We were a little nonplused for a moment. Then a priest from one of the hospitals spoke up,

"Could you offer Mass for the patients at my hospital?"

"Of course." Pencil and notebook appeared. "What time?"

"Er—would eight o'clock in the morning be all right?"

"Fine. Now where can I go in the evening?"

In no time he had made engagements that would keep him on the run for ten days, at the Fifth Air Force Headquarters, the Seventh Fleet, the 38th Division, six General Hospitals, the Philippine Army Headquarters, Santo Tomas. I was surprised at his tremendous energy; I remembered him as the gentle, rather stately and almost shy Auxiliary Bishop of Boston. In those days, of course, he was living in the shadow of Cardinal O'Connell, who brooked no brother near the throne, and who—the story went—even called on the carpet any priest whose picture appeared in the newspapers. We left the meeting shaking our heads over the Archbishop's schedule. He was going on Thursday to Samar and on Friday to Cebu, returning to Manila until Tuesday and then leaving for Okinawa, Biak, New Guinea, Australia, New Zealand, the Fijis, and home. Most of us would have wilted half-way through such a program.

We combined our Catholic celebration of V-J Day with the Archbishop's visit, and arranged a Mass of Thanksgiving at Rizal Stadium. Father Jim Murphy, of Boston, procured and directed the Color Guard, consisting of personnel from the Army, the Navy, and the Filipino Army.

I got General Trudeau to thaw out for the occasion white gloves that had been "frozen," and the Guard looked as smart— well, almost as smart—as a Stateside parade in full dress. Father Jim McKelvey, of Brooklyn, took care of the liturgical ceremonial and the appurtenances of the altar. My job was the altar itself.

My Finschhafen altar, which had been crated by Bill Graham the previous November, taken to Lingayen shortly after our arrival there, and carried down to Manila by the 959th Ordnance Company, had lain in their company area ever since. I went out to see it, and we stripped off the crates to find that the mahogany block and the planks that formed the table had become a nest for thousands of termites and their eggs, while the brass shells were pitted and eaten away by rust. Alas for the glories of this world. Sergeant Martinelli and Warrant Officer Chris Spicuzza, who had worked so hard to make the altar in the first place, looked at the ruin and then at me.

"Well," I said at last, "can we salvage anything or shall we let the forces of destruction have their way?"

It was decided to make a try, and when I returned two days later there was my altar almost as good as new. Marty and Chris must have worked like demons on it. Then my new assistant, Bob Cahill of San Francisco, and two Navy volunteers worked all Sunday afternoon setting it up in the Stadium. Promptly at six-thirty, with sixty-five hundred of the military present, the Color Guard entered the arena and marched toward the platform on which the altar was set. The Archbishop, with the Apostolic Delegate, Archbishop Piani, and Bishop Hayes, with Fathers Ed Tanski, Joe Smith, and Dinny Coleman and several Filipino priests as chaplains, followed.

After Mass the Archbishop spoke for about fifteen minutes; the sermon was well-written, but the presentation was not very dynamic, and the occasion called for a real orator. Well, St. Paul speaks of the diversity of gifts, and if the orator's charism had been denied him the Archbishop had great talents for administration as well as a generous heart. I think I would not have felt the flatness of the sermon so much if there had been more participation in the Mass by the congregation, if the event had been more of a conscious Eucharist and less of a dress parade. At any rate, my altar had served a last good purpose overseas. From first to last it had been a soldier's symbol, and now it had helped to express our gratitude for release, for peace, for hope.

With the signing of the surrender document aboard the U.S.S. Missouri, and the departure of many units for Japan, Manila became a rear-echelon base, and there was an enormous let-down. The war was won; the élan of the crusade evaporated. "When do we get out of here?" was the cry on all sides. Again, one did not deny the veterans their right to yearn for home; Major Jim Maloney, for example, was in his forty-first month overseas. For the others I thought of installing a wailing wall in my office; on one day I had twelve petitioners seeking my assistance in getting them home. I managed to listen, to gesture helplessly and grin, trying to get them to grin, too. I pointed to Bob Cahill, sitting at the next desk.

"There's a man who spent three years on Espiritu Santo. How long did you say it took to walk around that island, Bob?"

"Three-quarters of an hour, Father."

"You know," I used to say, "My friend Father McNicholas has a sign on his desk. It says 'When one reaches the end of his rope, he should tie a knot in it and hang on.'"

Only when they pulled that line, "I can't stand it; I'll blow my top," did they get a chewing.

A certain amount of griping is endemic to the Army, and indeed the self-pity any group of men can generate is astonishing. But after I visited the hospitals and saw the number who had really cracked up with brooding, with homesickness, I thought it worthwhile to mention the subject in a Sunday sermon.

"Look," I said, "Let's all resolve to talk about something else besides the number of points we have. It's not healthy. What would you be doing if it weren't for the war? You'd probably be standing on the drug-store corner at home, wishing you could take a trip. Well, this is your trip. You're seeing new places, different people. You're having experiences you could never have except for the war. It's not costing you a dime, and you're in no danger. And when you get back to that drug-store corner, what will you be talking about? The good old days in Manila, of course. Don't forget that your buddies back home are going to be talking your ear off about how they won the war in the European Theatre, and you'll be glad to have a few stories that can match theirs. Maybe you can go them one better. Incidentally, if you're blue because you have only seventy-nine points, or only fifty-six, don't come to see the chaplain. He has only forty-five."

In September I had a phone call from Batangas.

"Father, it's so good to hear your voice."

"Who's this?"

"This is Frank Gale, Father."

The 86th Division had finally followed me to the Pacific.

A week later I was able to get away long enough to visit them, but at Batangas things were normal. No one knew where they were. I went to the Sixth Army liaison offices, and the Eighth Army liaison offices, and the Base Area Command, and finally blew a fuse with a major.

"Eighteen thousand men sitting in your back yard, and no one can tell me where they are!"

He got down off his high horse and grudgingly made a phone call that enlightened me—and him. A few minutes later I walked in on Chaplain Bill Bolton and got a tremendous welcome. Then Colonel Perry, the Division's Adjutant General, came in, and I settled down to hear the story of the 86th's adventures after I left them. They were transferred from Camp Livingston to California en route to the Pacific, but when the Germans started the offensive known as "the Bulge," the Division got an SOS to go the other way. They landed in Le Havre, fought through Cologne, closed the Ruhr pocket, and rushed on through southern Germany, stopping just short of Hitler's mountain hideout at Berchtesgaden. Actually they had only forty-one days of combat, but acquitted themselves well despite their lack of experience. Then they came back to the States, had furloughs, and reassembled in Oklahoma for eight weeks of jungle training. This, however, was cut short after thirteen days, and they went on to California for the second time. The day they arrived at Camp Stoneman peace was proclaimed, and all men with seventy-five points were screened out. Then they sailed, and five days later, too late for them, a directive was issued that no men with forty-five points or more would be sent overseas. So they were not in a cheerful frame of mind, especially since nothing more interesting than garrison duty was in prospect, and recreation areas like Nice, Paris, and Rome did not exist in the Pacific.

My reunion with Frank Gale was a delight on both sides. In fact, the 342nd Regiment, from Colonel Pete Heffner down, gave me the welcome of a returning prodigal. I heard all the stories and all the gripes, had dinner with Headquarters Company, and at last Captain Arthur Dion, the Adjutant, sent me back to Manila in his jeep, with Colonel Aassen and Captain Jim Kennedy for company.

Early in October I learned that I had been assigned to an inspection team, to visit and report on the condition of cemeteries in the Base area, and to locate, if possible, any American graves that had not been known up to that time. Somebody among the brass hats had received complaints that the cemeteries on Luzon were not being given adequate care, and, with visions of a congressional investigation probably dancing before his eyes, had issued "immediate action" orders for a report on their condition. It was, of course, a piece of nonsense. The Luzon campaign had been officially closed only a few weeks before; the peaceful invasion of Japan was still being mounted; Filipinos were still hungry; the black market was extorting fantastic prices. It seemed a part of reverence to concentrate for a time on the living and to let the dead bury the dead. In addition, every care had been taken to bury honorably the dead of the 1945 campaign, while the work of locating and removing to established cemeteries the bodies of the victims of '42 was proceeding as rapidly as could reasonably be expected. But we had orders, and so we—Lieutenant-colonel Thomas O'Donnell, of Brooklyn, Cap-

tain Charlie Gobel, of Wichita, and myself—went rolling and bump-
ing for eight hundred and fifty miles in the brand-new jeep we had
drawn for the purpose.

Charlie and I alternated at driving and bouncing on the hard
back seat of the jeep. It was hard telling which was worse; we both
had long legs, and sitting for hours in the driver's seat paralyzed
them; on the other hand, driving afforded some distraction, whereas
the rods of springless steel that were the back seat offered none.
They simply walloped your posterior and your kidneys and shook
up your stomach.

Charlie is one of those wonderfully quiet, unselfish fellows
whom you have to watch or they'll carry all the painful burdens
themselves. Several times, when I knew the back seat must have
about done him in, I pretended to be drowsy and got him to drive.
The Colonel, because of his years and rank, had an option on the
right-hand front seat. He could twist and turn a little there, and ease
the kinks somewhat. But there wasn't much comfort for any of us.
The country roads of Luzon had received no maintenance from the
Jap regime, and three years of tropical sun and rain had pitted them
with holes and ruts. We grew to like the rough, unfinished provincial roads, bad as they were, better than the scarified remnants of
macadam. Here and there we were able to get on the cement National Road, still intact, but its narrow, glaring white ribbon was
torturing for the eyes by day, and at night thundering QM trucks,
careless of the minority rights of small vehicles, edged over on our
side of the road and scared us. If we had slipped off the cement we
would strike a muddy soft shoulder and could find ourselves cata-
pulting ten to fifteen feet down into the rice paddy ditches. We
counted eight jeeps and trucks lying on their sides or overturned
completely in the water, and an MP told us two GI's had been
pinned beneath their cab and drowned. I used to think without
pleasure that it would be tragic irony if we, a team of cemetery
inspectors, should climax our inspection by ending up in one.

The old, fixed cemeteries at Fort McKinley and Fort Stotsen-
burg had been overgrown with jungle grass, and at McKinley the
Japs had dug shallow foxholes on some of the grave-sites. But a
little care, which was already being expended, would make things

right again. It was the isolated burials of '42 that bothered me. The ones, for instance, that Carmen Santa Cruz showed us. We came into her town one afternoon—it was on our list as the location of some American graves—and were directed to her home by the first Filipino we met. She came down to us wreathed in smiles, her very young baby on her arm. Could she tell us where the Americans had been buried?

"Ah, the Americans. But of course."

And she led us, and a growing horde of children that had swarmed about us when we arrived, to the schoolhouse where she had been a teacher until the Japs came. Then they had quartered their American prisoners, who were doing slave labor, in the schoolhouse, and she had known them all well, ver-y well. She had kept a list in her house of all their names, which they had told her and she had written down. She would give us the list except that she had already turned it over to the "Offeece of the Provost Marshal in Ma-neela." Then she took us behind the schoolhouse to a patch of marshy ground, where the coarse grass squshed beneath our feet, and she stood by the five wooden crosses planted there, her smile just as wide but with something like motherly pity brimming in her dark young eyes.

"Here are the Americans," she said gently, "One of the prisoners have escaped, so the Japanese have shot these, and I place here the crosses."

I turned away in pain; Charlie, as was his gentle wont, said nothing; the Colonel asked a few perfunctory questions; and the gay swarm of children skipped about crying "Hel-lo, Joe" and laughing at the deliciously absurd syllables. Waves of heat beat down on us as we walked back to the dusty jeep and drove away. Carmen stood among the children and waved us goodbye.

In the next town over a hundred Americans had died of disease, and were buried in a rice paddy. We saw their graves from a distance; now, during the rainy season, they were covered by three or four feet of water, and nothing could be done to remove the bodies to an established cemetery. When the dry season came the Graves Registration men would remove them.

On southern Luzon we visited a Prisoner of War cemetery. Many of the Japs, who were still surrendering, came in so scrawny from malnutrition and so disease-ridden that they lived only a few days, and were buried in the POW camp in a well-kept cemetery. We saw many of the living Japs in the stockade. It bothered me, after our experiences of the day before, to see them smoking cigarettes, living in comfortable tents, and eating good chow. God forbid, I said to myself, that we should ever treat them as inhumanely as they had treated our men, but the contrast seemed altogether too sharp, especially after one had wandered about in this country for a bit and tried to reconstruct what happened in '42. At a place called Lumban the scene of the burials was again a schoolyard, where some ten Americans, members of a road-building gang, lay in their hasty graves. In the same town, in the municipal cemetery, were fourteen more, shot by the Japs in retaliation for the deaths of some of their own men, killed by the guerrillas.

A feeling of awful futility comes over one as he looks down on graves like these. If I needed any evidence of the reality of original sin, I think I could find it in the madness that overtakes reasonable beings and makes them kill one another, when on every count it would be desirable that they get along peacefully together. One can never surrender the hope that some day the human race will emerge from childhood and be mature enough to settle its differences by arbitration, but a reading of history gives no grounds for optimism that it will occur soon. As Pope Pius XI exclaimed in sorrow, "this old world, that has shed so much blood, and dug so many graves."

It was several days later that we found ourselves on the far side of a respectable mountain in Tayabas Province, without rations, blankets, or arms, and the sun sliding swiftly down the last slope of the sky. Arms we would probably not require, although there were bandits and Communistas in some provinces; blankets we could get along without, though they would make softer beds for SOS softies; but rations were indispensable. In that moment of decision a weapons-carrier, the first Army vehicle we had seen since noon, whirled by, and before its dust rose like a smoke-bomb to hide it, I saw "1 Cav" stenciled on its rear.

"Get after him, Charlie," I said, "He's our meal-ticket, and our lodging for the night, too."

A half-hour of dizzy flight in the weapons-carrier's wake, up-hill, downhill, around hairpin turns, and we swung off where the sign read "Rear Echelon, First Cavalry Division," and a handful of disgruntled officers and men who had not gone to Tokyo passed the empty days. Chow time was over, but the cooks, with that spontaneous generosity which distinguishes combat outfits from SOS troops, whipped up three platters laden with eggs, ham, and potatoes, topped it off with canned peaches and steaming coffee, and apologized for the extempore fare. Charlie and I laid our aching muscles on canvas cots that night, languidly, from long habit, tucked in the mosquito netting, and lost consciousness for ten blissful hours. The Colonel, who had not done so well on the springless canvas, was poking us at seven o'clock.

"Long way to go today," he kept saying. "Up and at 'em."

It was a long way. We were hurdling holes along the Pacific side of the narrow isthmus which connects the Camarines Provinces with the rest of Luzon, and saves Legaspi from being on another island, when we came on a wire-stringing crew of three GI's from the 68th Signal Battalion. They were members of a small detachment living in a nearby town, and suggested that we might get some rations from their mess sergeant.

"Just ask anybody in town where the House of Pure Culture is."

In the Philippines a request for directions produces an invariable answer. The man or boy says simply, "I go with you," and swings his leg into the jeep. So it was here, where a swarm of adolescents all knew the House of Puericulture and fought for a place in the jeep. When we found him, the mess sergeant offered us our choice of his stock, but we took only K's, not wanting to be delayed by cooking. It was high noon, all the same, when we came to a doubtful fork in the narrow road; the high grass almost concealed the sign, and a part of the sign had been shot away by small arms fire. The Colonel took out the map and set his glasses astride his nose.

"Beats me," he said finally. "This ought to be it. Let's try it."

But in the seaside village two miles further on, our first inquiries elicited only much regretful head-shaking. The young pastor was newly assigned here; he was very happy to see another priest, and gave us bananas but no information.

"Maybe if you were to see the mayor . . ."

I found the mayor sitting in the door of his little shop, beside his stock of coconut candy, odd cakes of American soap, and fly-blown copies of *Life* and *Yank*.

"Ah, yes, the place of burial of the Americans! But it is already thirty-five kilometers to this place. And it is impossible to come there." His heavy shoulders rose in a shrug. "The roads. The bridges. No more. You must go with banca. Seven men will be needed. Five days will be consumed. Formerly good roads, but in Japanese times . . ." Another shrug.

When I returned to the jeep the Colonel had another lead.

"Let's look up this—what's his name?—Mr. Ayala. He's supposed to know what the score is."

But Mr. Ayala was not at home, and the ladies of his household could not say when he would return.

"Guess we're licked," said the Colonel. "We can't go on any five-day trip in a native boat right now. Besides, there are still Japs hiding out down there. This looks like a job for Graves Registration in Batangas."

We turned the jeep and drove away, but six miles down the road another jeep overtook us and four Filipino MP's saluted crisply. Would we mind to return to the village? Mr. Ayala had returned home and desired to talk with us.

"Can't lose," decided the Colonel. "Let's go back."

Mr. Ayala was standing at his door when we drove up.

"Please to come in," he insisted anxiously.

We went in and sat down on rude chairs around what would have been the dining-room table except that there was only one room in the house. Mr. Ayala was excited and voluble, and it was difficult to piece his story together. Gradually we began to understand. He had been one of a group hired by Graves Registration to locate and remove American bodies buried in the place spoken of by the mayor. But there had been one other body which the GRS had not known about. His friend, Felix Villamiel, knew about it, because Felix had also been a prisoner of the Japanese, and had escaped with an American, "Jeem Roossell," in June of '42. Together they had hid in the swamps, and when Jim Russell died in August of dysentery, Felix had buried him and carefully marked the grave. Then, when the Americans returned to the Philippines, Felix had dug up the remains, and he had Jim Russell's gold signet ring and two letters written by Jim to his family to prove identity. And he wanted only that his friend Jim should be buried honorably with the other Americans.

"But where," I said finally, "is Jim's body now?"

Mr. Ayala smiled proudly, and pointed to a canvas sack hanging from the rafters.

"There only," he said.

Egad. Nothing was left, naturally, except bones, but the idea of keeping the bones hanging over the dinner table until they should be claimed was a little ghastly. Of course Mr. Ayala didn't see it that way; in fact, he and his friend Felix were doing their utmost to see that their Americano received his due meed of honor and reverence. We didn't take the remains along; instead we notified the GRO at Batangas to include them in his next trip south.

On Monday morning we set out in a Coast Guard cutter for Corregidor. At the dock we were met by the GRS people, who showed us what they had been able to accomplish toward locating the American graves in the rude and hasty cemeteries set up before the surrender in May of '42. Most of the wooden crosses had rotted, and those that remained were charred by flame-throwers used by our invading paratroopers in March of '45. GRS had found a number of dog-tags, but many had been lost or detached from their proper graves, so the work was slow. We talked to a Lieutenant Goodman, who had been on Corregidor in '42 and had assisted in burying the dead. He had volunteered, after being released from prison in Manchuria, to stay for a while and help in identifying the graves.

It was hard, in the bright sunshine, to reconstruct what had happened in those painful times, when burying parties, led by the chaplain, used to go out at night from the tunnel to dig graves and hastily bury the dead, when the bombing was incessant and food was scarce and disease had attacked almost everyone on the Rock. What a bitter time it must have been: no hope of help from the States, surrender imminent, the arrogant and triumphant Japs flaunting their power in our men's faces.

We had chow with the GRS company in the ruins of the old Fort Mills Barracks on the very top of the island, and I talked for a while with H Company, of my old regiment in Louisiana, which was now doing garrison duty and supervising some hundreds of Jap POW's working there. Then we left for Mariveles, a town at the southern tip of Bataan, from which the evacuation to Corregidor was made in '42. Here there were four cemeteries, three American and one Filipino. Father Joe Tockert, from Wichita, assigned to a unit working over there, had cleaned up one of them and intended working on the others. To get to the last one we had to walk about three miles through the mud of a former airstrip, and just before reaching it there was a shallow but very swift stream. The bridge had been destroyed, but I waded the stream and found, with the guidance of a Filipino boy, the cemetery. Grass taller than myself had entirely overgrown it, and I had to push the stalks aside and peer to find the remnants of the crosses. So this was the end of the trail for so many Americans. I was full of sadness for old, unhappy, far-off things, and battles long ago. The Colonel hadn't much imagination, and was chiefly concerned with the long, hot walk back through the mud, but all I could think of was the succession of bitter days which ended in disease and wounds and death on the fringe of the tropical jungle. Poor fellows. May they rest in peace.

In such a situation one cannot escape, either, a premonitory chill,

> In after days, when grasses high
> O'er top the stone where I shall lie . . .

and must swiftly counter with

> "I am the resurrection and the life.
> He who believes in me, even if he dies,
> will come to life."

We boarded the cutter again and headed for Manila. I wasn't hungry—naturally, perhaps—but when the skipper proposed chow and we went below to a heaping dish of spaghetti and chile con carne, it was wonderful how rapidly the dead faded from my mind. Therein lies a moral for the philosopher.

I was beginning to be restless. Manila had been interesting—the only assignment I had in the Army that I really enjoyed—but now the interest was fading. And the unrelenting heat was draining my energies seriously. I remember sitting in a breeze from the bay so strong that I had to put paperweights on every paper on my desk, and at the same time watching my tan shirt turn dark with sweat. The sameness of the tropical islands was wearing, and I pined for four seasons, with all their infinite shadings and variations. Frost and October haze; chill November rains on sidewalks under street-lamps; a June evening under the fragrant lindens along the Bapst Library walk; white-caps off Cohasset in July; even the crunch of snow on cold days, with invigorating breaths of really fresh air . . . New England, I said to myself, I have much maligned thee in the past; take me back and I'll sing thy praises.

I applied for transfer to Japan, but there was no opening in any of the bases that were being established there, and I didn't really want to go with a small unit. I could see myself moving in, building another chapel, then settling down to a quiet parochial life. It would have been small beer after Base X and I had no stomach for it. Meanwhile the Army was promising to discharge eight hundred thousand men by December, but I had no wife, no children, no decorations, and only sixteen months overseas. It looked like a long, long stay in Manila. My friend Phil McNiff, whom we now referred to as St. Philip the Prophet because of his early and start-lingly accurate prediction of the war's end, promised that I would be singing Christmas carols in Cambridge with him and Mary and Brian on St. Stephen's Day, as we had done for many years. This time, I thought, Phil had overreached himself. He didn't really understand the situation, especially in the South Pacific.

Then it happened. My Provincial wrote, ordering me to request relief from active duty in order to return to teaching. The men of the armed forces were coming home and back to college, he said, and my services would be needed in the classroom. I was dazed. The Provincial must be out of his mind, I thought. But would he have told me to ask for inactive status unless he had some assurance that I would get it? An immense hope dawned. Possibly, just possibly . . .

It took me five days to get the request framed in the appropriate military language and documented with the required supporting papers. General Trudeau protested, but finally approved it. Then the personnel officer in PHIBSEC, the next higher headquarters, balked at the statement in the application that there was a surplus of chaplains in the Philippines. But PHIBSEC went out of business that very week, and we began to deal with AFWESPAC. No snags developed there, but AFPAC, the next headquarters, would be critical. On October 16th the Theater Chaplain told me that he had approved the application, and on Saturday afternoon, October 20th, Jimmy Hatley, the chief clerk of our Chaplains' Section, came to my desk, saluted very formally, shook hands, and presented me with a sheaf of papers which, he suggested, I should immediately take to the Utilities Section for framing. There it was, in black and white!

> "By command of General MacArthur, Ch (Capt) William J. Leonard, 0544318, is relieved present assignment and attached 21st Replacement Depot. He will proceed by water transportation to Separation Center, Fort Devens, Mass., for return to inactive status."

There was a lot more, but those were the essentials. I leaned back and stared at the document. Only a year before Father Jerry Collins and I had sat at Finschhafen and speculated on how long it would be before we could look for release. The Japs at that time gave every promise of holding on indefinitely, and we agreed that we would be overseas for two years more, and in the Army for at least three. Now, except for the matter of getting home and out, it was all over for me. "All over." I kept turning the succulent syllables in my mouth.

Getting home, however, presented some difficulties. I went to the 21st Replacement Depot, about ten miles out of town, to check in for "processing," which meant more papers, a physical examination, shots. The place was depressing. I was a "casual" again, and could look forward to being treated, as "casuals" were in all Replacement Depots, like a recalcitrant child. Worse still, there were hundreds of men who had been in the 21st for five or six weeks, with no prospect of boarding ship in the immediate future. They had been promised by every authority in the Army that they would be home for Christmas, and they could see their chances fading. And they had been taken out of their units, where they might have been kept busy and distracted to some extent, to sit idle in the Depot. When I arrived I saw an officer sitting dejectedly near an Orderly Room.

"Sir," I said, "Can you tell me where the processing office is?"

He answered from the depths of weary disgust. "When I came in here twenty-five days ago it was down there by the PX, but I don't know where the hell it is now."

At the processing office, when I found it, I inquired about the possibility of a delay en route from San Francisco. It had struck me that, since my Army experience had afforded so little chance to see the places I really wanted to see, I might drive from San Francisco to Boston and at least see a bit of my own country. But the processing officer snorted.

"Out of the question. Impossible."

I went back to Manila thoughtfully. "Impossible" in Army language meant that it couldn't be done unless you knew the right people. But I did know the right people. Hm-m-m-m. The old dream surfaced and hung before my eyes, bright and alluring.

My friendship with Colonel Henry Amy, commander of the Troop Movement Section, had begun some months before, when he arrived in Manila and became a faithful worshipper at my Sunday Mass. His brother, Father Paul Amy, S.J., had been a teacher at Boston College High School when I was a boy there. I had been able to help him with some matters that were giving him concern, and he had told me to come to him when I received my orders home. Now I climbed the stairs to his office in the Customs House.

"Look, Father," he said. "Stop worrying about your trip home. You're not going on one of those troopships. I'm going to wait until a freighter comes in and put you aboard her. It will be a little slower, and you'll be the only passenger, but you'll have a chance to sleep and eat some decent food, and maybe your mother will know you when you get home. How does that sound?"

"Well, Colonel," I answered, "I appreciate your kindness. But it isn't exactly what I had in mind."

"Oh, it isn't, eh? What did you have in mind?"

I told him I wanted desperately to go home by way of Europe.

"But, Father, you can't do that. You'd have to have individual orders."

I looked at him. "That's why you're wearing those eagles on your shoulders."

He stared at me for a moment, shook his head, and then picked up the telephone. I clenched and unclenched my hands while he argued with the Commanding Officer of the 21st Depot. At last he hung up, sweating.

"You'd better be nice to me the next time I come to confession," he said.

"Colonel," I laughed, "You're a gentleman. I won't forget it."

On the way out I stopped to chat with Captain Dick Thomson, the Colonel's assistant.

"What are you going to do with that altar of yours?" he asked.

"I don't know—hadn't given it any thought."

"Could I have it?"

Dick was not a Catholic, so I said, "What would you do with it?"

"I think my university would be glad to have it—as a war souvenir."

Dick had graduated, as I recall, from the University of Idaho. I pondered. If his university would be glad to have it, maybe mine would, too. And it was much more likely that it would be used at my university for its original purpose.

"Dick," I said, "I think I'd like to have it at Boston College."

He was generous. "Okay, you get your friends in Ordnance to crate it and I'll see that it follows you home."

So they did, and he did. But more of that later.

There was one more hurdle, and it was a high one. No matter what orders you had from the Army, you didn't travel by water without the concurrence of the War Shipping Administration. I had no connections in the WSA, which was in the hands of civilians, so I approached that office with trepidation. And indeed, as I entered a young man, evidently in charge, was laughing at a crestfallen captain.

"Not a chance, Captain. Not a chance."

Ouch. This didn't sound good. But the young man said "excuse me a minute, sir" to me and disappeared into the adjoining office. While he was gone I turned over idly the pages of a college yearbook that was lying on the counter. It was the yearbook of the College of St. Thomas, in St. Paul, Minnesota. I blush a little when I think now of the idea that leaped into my mind, but I was desperate. The young man reappeared and said briskly,

"Now, sir, what can I do for you?"

"Tell me," I replied, "How is Father Flynn?"

He looked suspiciously from me to the yearbook and back. "What Father Flynn?"

"Father Vincent Flynn, the President of St. Thomas."

"How do you know him?"

"Oh, he took his degree in English at Harvard, and I'm from Boston. We were pretty good friends while he was in Cambridge."

I could have had the whole War Shipping Administration, with sugar on it, but I settled for a ticket that put me on the *U.S.S. Roswell,* a fast Victory ship bound for Singapore and Calcutta, and sailing in four days.

Nothing left now except good-byes. Joe Nolan and I spent the last three evenings together; I felt guilty about leaving him behind, but he would have Sandy Jenks and Jack Schindler to keep him going. And, though neither of us knew it at the time, his ordination and first Mass were in the future, eight years later. And Sandy would come back to Boston College to do that dedicated work of teaching and counselling which he carried on for forty years. I toured the Base offices to shake hands and get the ribbing, half envious and half humorous, that I expected. And I said goodbye, with affection and lasting gratitude, to Father John Hurley and the other Fathers at La Consolacion. Mike Maroulis, a young sailor from Newark whom I had received into the Church in May, came to see me off. And, five minutes before the ship swung out into the stream, Jack Lyons, who had been in my class at Boston College, arrived breathless at the dock. He had just discovered my whereabouts and come to see me, and at the office they told him I had boarded the ship.

I stood on deck—it was the Feast of Christ the King—and watched Corregidor and the high hills of Bataan fade into the distance. It was the end of the chapter. Except that AFWESPAC published a directive a week later—Joe Nolan wrote me about it—decreeing that individual orders would no longer be authorized and that all personnel would return to the States across the Pacific. It was not too little, but it was too late. One bird, at least, had flown.

CHAPTER 17

Travel Is Broadening

AT LEAST FOR THOSE OF US WHO WERE BORN NEAR IT, THERE IS HEAL-
ing in the sea. When nerves are raw, when the sap of life runs low,
it is good to look across ineffable blue distances from the deck of a
ship, or to walk a beach that borders the deliberate rhythms of the
tide. My "parting shot" from the Army in the Pacific was an anti-
influenza injection; it carried something else I would be hearing
from later, but its immediate effect was to give a small fever that
made me want to sleep. This gave me a chance to recoup a little the
vitality poured out during all those hot and harried days in Manila.
It was an excuse, too, for being alone, to enjoy privacy for the first
time in two years. The men aboard had not yet found me out, and I
did not encourage visitors for a few days.

It was pleasant to travel the sea without fear. Our anti-aircraft
gun tubs were not yet emptied of their weapons; however, all but
three of the guns had been dismantled, and at night we rode with
running lights at the masthead and all ports open. We could sit on
the deck and not be afraid that the glowing end of a cigarette or the
flare of a match would be the tip-off to a submarine and the prelude
to flaming disaster. Our first night out I enjoyed standing on the
after-deck and watching the patches of white wake, gleaming with
pale phosphorescence, slide by the stern into the dark water behind
us. Scuds of heavy rain-clouds ringed the horizon, but as I looked
aloft I could see the stars tossing to right and left of the crow's nest.
"Alone," I told myself exultantly,

> Alone, alone, all, all alone,
> Alone on a wide, wide sea.

It was a grand way to "let your soul catch up with you," especially if you had a pipe. I was not the only passenger aboard the *Roswell.* Major William Wipf (he instructed me, when we met, to pronounce both final consonants—if I could), had somehow managed to leap or scramble over all the barriers and to get passage. He had been in the European Theatre, where he saw England, Scotland, France, Belgium, and parts of Holland and Germany, and then had volunteered for the Southwest Pacific. Now he wanted to see the Mediterranean countries, and as much as he could in between. At first, remembering Kipling's "he travels the fastest who travels alone," I was afraid any associate would be an encumbrance, but the Major turned out to be a model of the Good Companion, even-tempered, considerate, jolly, resourceful, and we got further together than ever we might have by our own unaided efforts.

Our situation then, however, was tentative and even precarious. If the *Roswell* were routed out of Calcutta to the West Coast or Japan or elsewhere, we intended to leave her and pick up another ship going to Suez, and at the northern end of the Canal we would try to get off again, look around a little in that part of the world, and pick up whatever transportation offered itself. It would be strictly catch-as-catch-can, with as many stop-overs as we could manage. We had no idea how it would all turn out, and some crusty colonel along the way might wreck our plans by peremptorily ordering us home straightaway, but Manila was virtually equidistant from the States whether one traveled east or west, and we convinced ourselves that we were carrying out the spirit if not the letter of our orders, which simply told us to go home. If one route were more scenic and more interesting than the other, we felt that our benevolent Uncle Sam would prefer that we choose it. We did, in any case.

And so we coasted down the South China Sea, between Viet Nam *(O caro nome!)* and Borneo, while familiar names, echoing from Kipling and Conrad, G.A. Henty and biographies of St. Francis Xavier, ran through my mind: Bangkok, Rangoon, the Malabar Coast, the Straits of Malacca. I felt like the young man in Conrad's *Youth,* approaching ports with eager curiosity and a sense of lifting the veil. Even then however, I was sure that I would not be captivated, that I would not come home with the light of "the gorgeous

East" in my eyes, or, like Kipling's returned soldier, sighing for the countries east of Suez. My roots, my intellectual and spiritual roots at any rate, were in the Mediterranean lands. Whenever I thought of wandering around in the Holy Land, or the Isles of Greece, or Italy, I would gulp. Could I do it? I would surely try.

After a few days of hibernation I began to get acquainted with the ship's company. Aside from the Skipper and the Chief Engineer, who were both old salts, the officers and crew were quite young; the First Mate was only twenty-three. Everyone was very decent to the Major and myself. Our first day aboard the Chief shook hands, and later, when we were talking on deck and he learned that I was a priest, he said quite unaffectedly,

"Let me shake your hand again. I've known a lot of Catholics, and not one of them ever gave me a dirty deal."

I was more than a little touched, and thought how simple and generous was the nature of this Mr. Kuhn, who could say a thing as nice as that sincerely and with no desire to curry favor. Most of the crew, once you had steeled yourself to disregard a certain coarseness, showed a kindred simplicity, though in their cases it was allied to ignorance—few of them had been educated beyond grammar school—and became naiveté. On Hallowe'en I drifted about the ship, announcing that Mass would be celebrated for All Saints at seven o'clock next morning on the fantail. A percentage of the men were Catholics, but in their long months at sea, with no chaplain aboard, they rarely took part in the Mass or received the sacraments, and I was not surprised when my congregation was a slender one. I made it my business to seek out the absentees and try to get them to come to Mass the following Sunday, but most of them either hid from me or started an argument on some point of doctrine or practice, wanting to make their defection look intelligent.

There was one lad, whose cabin was near mine, whom I persuaded to assist at Mass on the Holy Day. But on the Sunday he was missing, and I did not see him until evening when, observing him taking a snack in the officers' pantry, I said, jokingly and without thinking of his absence in the morning,

"There's a strange man in the house."

On Monday evening, as I was finishing a letter home, he came in.

"I want to talk to you."

"Fire away," I said.

"Why did you tell all the men aboard that I am a strange man?" he asked pleadingly.

"Did I?" I asked, having quite forgotten the casual joke of the previous night.

"Yes, you did," and he recalled the incident.

I laughed and explained that it had all been quite genial. But his conscience had been giving him no end of trouble. On Thursday, when we anchored in Singapore Harbor, he had done some trading over the side of the ship with the natives who came alongside selling various homegrown articles, and had promised three packs of cigarettes for a pair of sandals. When he had hauled the sandals over the side in a basket, he sent down only two packs, and the other boys had ragged him about it. I guess he didn't sleep much that night, and concluded that he couldn't honestly go to Mass on Sunday morning. When he was called, therefore, he purposely lay abed for ten minutes so that if I asked why he hadn't been there he could say he hadn't got up on time. Then his conscience bothered him about that, he avoided me all day, and the first time I saw him I called him a strange man. Well, he worried all day Monday, consulted with several of the men about it, and finally decided that he just had to get it off his chest.

O, what a tangled web we weave . . .

Slowly I was being re-introduced to American ways and objects. We had apple juice for dinner, and it called up the lacy blossoms and exquisite fragrance of New England orchards in May, their russet and crimson fruitfulness in October. The Chief had an American dog which was even a fellow-citizen, a Boston terrier. And one afternoon I caught myself staring at a fixture on the wall of my cabin, wondering in a subconscious sort of way what it was, and really not giving it much thought because there were so many fixtures and gadgets aboard the ship whose purpose I couldn't figure out. Then I woke up. It was a *radiator.* One of those things you turn on to heat a room.

We had no sooner dropped anchor in Singapore Harbor than we were surrounded by canoes and other small craft. The occupants were brown Malayans, not unlike the Filipinos in appearance, but their English was a slurred speech that sounded like Chinese, not the labored, precise, Iberian English one heard in the Philippines. They offered pineapples, cigars, bananas, cloth of a cheap sort, and especially sandals—hundreds of pairs of them, with straps of leather or some similar skin and crepe rubber soles, evidently a local product. They wouldn't take any money, but insisted on American cigarettes, which would bring them, I was told, at least two dollars a pack in the city. Their trade with the crew was brisk and lively.

The Skipper was going ashore to pick up his orders; with him he took the Chief Engineer and the Third Mate and several others. Major Wipf and I stood expectantly at the head of the ladder which had been thrown over the side, anticipating an invitation to go along, but the Skipper swung a heavy leg on to the ladder and started down without a word,

"Say, Captain," I said, "Wouldn't you like some company?"

But he went on his way without vouchsafing a reply, and all we saw of Singapore we saw through a pair of binoculars. Our disappointment was keen. The waterfront looked interesting: there were several large buildings in the style of British Houses of Parliament—the Customs House, probably, and similar maritime buildings. Among many steeples two in particular drew my attention: a Gothic cathedral, which would have looked perfectly at home in a French town, and, not far away, a Byzantine church with rounded, globular towers. Neither one looked in place at the tip of the Malayan peninsula, where one would have expected something markedly oriental, but the Gothic was especially out of place. At least the Byzantine, with its teardrop towers, was not Western. I began to think of what a burden we had placed on our missionaries. Not only did we ask them to preach Christianity, "to the Jews a stumbling block and to the Gentiles foolishness," but we insisted that they present it in its exclusively Western version. The Mass and the sacraments were by Roman fiat celebrated only in Latin. The vestments, the sacred art, the architecture were European, alien. Native clergy were few, and bishops were appointed from the ranks of the missionaries. It was no wonder that, in spite of heroic efforts, enormous expenditures of lives and money, the great masses of Asia had not had the Gospel preached to them.

The Skipper and his party returned, the native traders departed, but we still hung over the rails in the late afternoon, watching the abundant life in the harbor. It was almost time for evening chow when a little craft—they are called "bumboats" out there, and they ply with small freight between the shore and the shipping—drifted between us and the setting sun. Because it was sunset, and the hour of prayer, the Moslem who lived on the boat and made his precarious living from her spread his prayer rug and, facing toward Mecca, began his evening devotions. It didn't bother him in the least that hundreds of eyes were gazing down at him. He hadn't a shred of what we Westerners call human respect. And his posture, outlined against the gold and crimson of the sunset, was so unaffectedly reverent that there wasn't a jeer or a snicker from the onlookers. There wasn't even the discomfort one sometimes feels when he has intruded on another's devotions. As the flare in the West softened and faded, as the crew went below for supper, it seemed to me that one man in the world, without being aware of it, had just given the most effective witness he would ever give of the faith that was in him.

It may be that one of the unlooked-for benefits of the Second Vatican Council will be the restoration of a sense of reverence. Our young people have the virtue of honesty (if indeed, untempered by charity, it can be said always to be a virtue; they certainly feel that it is). They do not seem to have the virtue of reverence, and perhaps the Council's decrees on the Liturgy may help to give it to them.

Exactly what is reverent and what is not may be difficult to determine in a given case; standards vary from one age to another. Our novelists, poets, journalists during the last fifty years, impatient with prissiness, with compliment, with outworn forms, have striven for fresh realization and forthright expression; and much of this, though it has shocked the older generation, has been salutary, inasmuch as it has given us a new awareness of reality. There remains much, however, that is lacking even in basic reverence, and particu-

larly where God Himself is the subject. Here one encounters allu-
sions or remarks that are overtly blasphemous, or if they have not
that formal malice, only the writer's muddle-headedness saves them
from it.

It is an excellent thing to make reparation for blasphemy, as
our Holy Name Societies have done, but it would be better to prevent it. The Council's Constitution on the Liturgy, by cutting away
a good deal of pointless ritual, by permitting the use of the native
languages, and especially by insisting on the theological reasons for
all its legislation, has done much to create a climate of reverence.
Once the liturgy is understood and the people are given their full,
active share in it, formalism will decline and the habit of intelligent
worship will have its chance to influence all our attitudes.

Human acknowledgment of the Holy has been constant during
the history of our race. Wherever one looks in our records, one
finds humanity bowed in reverence. Painting, sculpture, music, architecture, poetry report this acknowledgment down to our day, and
it would be easy to compile an anthology of statements from the
captains and the kings, the sages and the saints, as to its importance
and value. But the contribution of our own age to this chorus of
praise has not been large.

In the popular consciousness, too, the idea of worship seems to
have faded. Among non-Catholics, who have no precept of regular
church-going, one meets the attitude often which considers religion
as primarily humanitarian; its function is to elevate the human spirit
in some undefined way, or at least to bring comfort. "Worship together this week," plead the subway ads, implying that if you do
you will be happier. People feel that they are religious if they work
for civic welfare or are simply neighborly, or if they "don't hurt
anyone." Among Catholics, for whom regular church-going is not a
matter of option, there emerges too often the mentality which seeks
to receive rather than to give. Church-going, where it has not de-
generated to the mere satisfaction of an obligation, offers a chance
to ask for favors, to win graces, to store up merits.

And while one must admit that there is nothing essentially
wrong with asking favors, winning graces, or storing up merits, this
certainly cannot be the prime purpose of religion as it has been un-

derstood throughout the centuries. Rather one must assert that the purpose of religion before all else is to worship God, to acknowledge his might, his wisdom, and above all his holiness.

When we creatures brought out of nothingness make this acknowledgment, we are responding with the profoundest depths of our nature. We are offering thanks for a gift greatly conceived and lavishly bestowed. We are being completely and maturely human, in accord with the reality of things, for we cannot call ourselves mature persons unless we see reality as it is. Simply we should not have been if God had not called us into being, and we should not be completely ourselves unless we were willing, even eager, to profess our debt. If it is difficult for us to imagine ourselves as not being, as possibilities only, then this is evidence of the generosity of the gift which establishes us so firmly in being that we cannot picture ourselves outside it.

For such a gift gratitude is the only possible response. The God who made us, we sense, did so not from any need of his own— what need could he experience whose power leaps the chasm between being and non-being, whose love, in Dante's phrase, first moved the sun and all the stars? Rather He wished to share with us some infinitely small jet of His own being, to bring into existence creatures who might live, partially at least, as He Himself lives. And this generosity, this prodigal endowment by which we are made, and made conscious of ourselves and the world we live in and even of things beyond the visible world, is so astounding that it must elicit from us a tribute of thanks. At the very least it must move us to speak of our Father with awe.

We can be instructed here especially by Holy Scripture. The sense of reverence is everywhere in Genesis; for instance, in the Bedouin simplicities of that patriarchal religion to which the Jews looked back so wistfully in later centuries as the honeymoon period of their faith. God and men speak together familiarly, Father and sons, yet God is never named without honor and loving reverence. "Yea," said Abraham, "Though I be dust and ashes, yet will I speak to the Lord." Most instructive is the admonition given to Moses when out of mere curiosity he seeks to approach the burning bush, and is told to put off the shoes from his feet and to approach with reverence, "for this is holy ground." Later, when David the King has gathered together gold, silver, brass, marble, and precious stones for the building of the temple, and has invited his people to add their own offerings, he utters that splendid prayer which teaches us so much about our obligation and our privilege of worship:

> May you be blessed, Lord, the God of Israel our ancestor, for ever and for ever! Yours, Lord, is the greatness, the power, splendor, length of days, glory, for all that is in the heavens and on the earth is yours. Yours is the sovereignty, Lord; you are exalted over all, supreme. Riches and honor go before you, you are ruler of all, in your hand lie strength and power; in your hand it is to give greatness and strength to all. At this time, our God, we give you glory, we praise the splendor of your name. For who am I and what is my people to have the means to give so generously? All comes from you; from your own hand we have given them to you. For we are strangers before you, settlers only, as all our ancestors were; our days on earth pass like a shadow, and there is no hope. Lord our God, this store we have provided to build a house for your holy name, all comes from your hand, all is yours. O my God, you search the heart, I know, and delight in honesty, and with honesty of heart I have willingly given all this; and now with joy I have seen your people here offer you their gifts willingly. Lord, God of our ancestors, of Abraham, of Isaac, of Israel, watch over this for ever, shape the purpose of your people's heart and direct their hearts to you.

Later still, the Prophet Isaiah feels himself transported into the very presence of God and hears the angels chanting their unceasing song, "Holy, holy, holy is the Lord of hosts. His glory fills the whole earth." In this presence he senses most keenly his own unworthiness and the need of reverence while he stands, a sinful man, before the All-holy. The Book of Psalms, that lovely collection of inspired songs which teaches us at once both what and how to pray, has an aspiration for every temperament, every mood, every human need. It ranges from crashing alleluias and triumphant "praise hims" to deep misery and plaintive cries for help. It cajoles, re-proaches God because he has kept silence and not answered prayer; yet, whether the psalm be a tender simplicity like the 131st or a piece of world-weary sophistication like the 90th, awareness of the infinite distance that separates Creator and creature is never lost. Our contemporaries, with their fondness for the direct, the shocking, might learn from this book how to avoid what is merely trite and conventional without sacrificing reverence.

Considering how we men and women are situated in the midst of an absolutely lavish creation, alluring and beguiling in its own right, perhaps the most genuine worship we shall offer will be our free choice of God over anything he has made. We are to prefer him and love him over everything that is not he. This means that we are to surrender to him. And here we come to the heart of all worship. God approaches us as a lover, laden with gifts, wooing us, seeking us for himself. It is of course staggering that he should want our surrender, that he should as it were seek our approval. But there is no answer to the question as to why he has made us except this, that we may come to know him, acknowledge all he has given us of himself, and in response give ourselves to him completely.

For us, then, anything that does not praise God is fundamen-tally irrelevant. We must not allow ourselves to be distracted. Our basic concern in life is to settle how we can contribute according to our powers to what the generations before us have done for God's glory. Even if we had never sinned, if we stood in no need of par-don, adoration would be our first duty. Adoration comes before sin, and therefore before impetration. And while we are obliged of course to be aware of our fellows, and to do all that love prompts us to do for them, humanitarianism—the "horizontal" aspect of wor-ship—is not the only nor the first obligation. If I were the only human being in the world, I should still be required to worship God.

And indeed I find myself admirably equipped for this high purpose. I am a person; I can think, I can love, I can with my five senses perceive God's presence in the world. I myself and all the creatures about me are so many testimonies to his having passed this way. In all the things I have found beautiful, in whatever has pleased my mind, my senses, there he is. His tremendous beauty, so ancient and so new, lies about me on every avenue or by-path of my life. Unless I blind myself or harden my heart, I shall be able with sincerity to echo Newman's familiar hymn:

> Praise to the Holiest in the height,
>   And in the depth be praise;
> In all his works most wonderful,
>   Most sure in all his ways.

The next leg of our journey took us out of Singapore Harbor, through the Straits of Malacca, and across the Bay of Bengal to the Hooghly River, one—and the most navigable one—of the many mouths of the sacred river, the Ganges. On the afternoon of November 5th I noticed that the ship had stopped and was wallowing a little in the small sea that was running, so I went on deck to see what was going on. A small ship, the size of an old-time schooner, was chugging a hundred yards off our bow, and had put over a boat, manned by eight oarsmen and a coxswain, and carrying a portly figure in a striking white uniform. This was the pilot, whose job it was to take us through eighty miles of the Hooghly's shoals and sandbars up to Calcutta. The oarsmen were Indians, who wore only shorts, but each had on his head a round, brimless hat like a page boy's. The coxswain, perhaps to indicate his rank, was clad from his neck to his toes in a light cloth of blue, close-fitting. After considerable effort they managed to pull alongside, and the pilot awkwardly swung his weight on to the ladder—a good feat even for a young man when the seas are rough—and began to pull himself up. This involved a great deal of thrashing and hoisting, and the sight of so much magnificence laboring against the grey ship's side was comic. The smiles exploded into laughter, though, when the pilot, endeavoring to clamber over the rail, hung for a moment bottoms up, and we could see that that sector of his splendid uniform was badly in need of repairs. The Royal Navy—he was a Britisher—lost something of its dignity.

We got under way again, and kept moving until twilight, when we hove to and anchored. The river would have to be negotiated by daylight. We were definitely in it now, though no land whatever was visible at sundown; the mouth of the river, the Skipper said, was almost a hundred miles wide. But we could distinguish the river from the ocean by the color of the water, which was now a muddy brown. Our log read 2,985 miles from the breakwater at Manila. The Major and I, pacing the rusty red deck after dinner, took counsel and resolved if at all possible to jump ship at Calcutta. We had lost out on our sight-seeing at Singapore, and did not want to miss anything else. But we knew we might have to wrestle a bit with the Troop Movement people to bring it off.

The *Roswell* tied up at the King George Dock in Calcutta next afternoon, and the Major and I went ashore. We walked up and down Chowringee Road, that river of teeming humanity, brushing off the importunate beggars who screamed, "Bakhsheesh!" and clung to us like flies, staring at the peddlers who hawked their wares everywhere, at the CBI shoulder patches, the uniforms of all the British forces, the Hindu and Moslem costumes. It was a violent transition from the sea's grey solitudes.

By courtesy of the Red Cross, which provided a six-by-six truck and a knowledgeable guide for visiting service men, and by dint of our own efforts, we saw the town for three days. There was the mosque, with its minarets and its five clocks showing the hours of prayer, its startling emptiness of ornament or furnishing save for the marble floor and the lectern from which the Koran was read. There was the mosaic and filigree Jain Temple, with its repellent idol. We visited the Nimtalla Burning Ghat, watching in fascinated horror as relatives and friends built a pyre for their dead and stood by while flames consumed the body. One fanatical black man prayed aloud as he rubbed the ashes of the dead into his genitals, asking, no doubt, for the fertility of the departed. We saw the High Court and Eden Gardens, but the Victoria Memorial Museum was closed: its pure white marble had been painted black as a safeguard against air raids, and now the paint was being removed. The Major and I took our first ride in a rickshaw; the poor devil who pulled it had a sore on his foot which made him limp as he ran, and we both felt guilty over using a human beast of burden, so we stopped far short of our destination, the Anglican cathedral, gave our man all the change we had in our pockets, and walked the rest of the way. St Paul's was Tudor Gothic, very lovely, with a splendid simplicity of altars in the sanctuary and the lady chapel. But it was empty. When I saw the Jesuit Church of St. Thomas later in the day, I thought its sanctuary horribly cluttered with statues and ecclesiastical whatnots. But people prayed there at all hours. I visited St. Xavier's College, our school, tried vainly to get the point of cricket as played by the small fry in the yard; then I spent some hours in the Oxford Book Shop, appeasing a long hunger for books. And I closed the day delightfully by having tea and dinner with the Jesuits at St. Thomas' Presbytery, a real crossroads where I found, in addition to the Belgians who served the Church, an Irish Jesuit who had somehow got over "the Hump" from China when his mission was destroyed by the Japanese, nine American priests of several dioceses and religious communities, an explosive little Italian Franciscan, likewise a refugee from the Japs in China, who had no English but with whom I had an amusing conversation in Latin, and two English chaplains—one resplendent in a monocle and a heroic Oxford accent. And one night I walked back alone to the ship—a silly thing for a well-dressed man with money in his pockets to do—and got my first intimation of what real poverty is when I stumbled several times over bodies lying on the docks—living bodies, which had nowhere else to sleep.

On our Red Cross tour there was an alumnus of the University of San Francisco, who when he learned of our ambitions suggested that we hitch rides from Military Air Transport all the way home. It seemed a splendid way to cut the knots of our perplexity, especially when it was announced that the *Roswell* would carry a cargo of unexpended ammunition back to the States. After the War ended (and the real danger was over), military personnel were not allowed to travel on ammunition ships, so Major Wipf and I were ordered off. We went out to the Dumdum Air Base and asked for a ride to Delhi, but were turned away. "No orders, no flight." It looked hopeless until I discovered that the base chaplain was Father Marty O'Gara, a Jesuit contemporary with whom, many years before, I had spent several summers. Marty, who perished six months later when the plane he was flying home crashed off the Amalfi coast, knew a sergeant who knew another sergeant who knew—anyway, I celebrated Mass next morning (it was Sunday) for two hundred men in the Base Chapel, preached for ten minutes, and then rushed off with the Major to Barrackpore, where a B-25 bored into the sky and landed us nine hundred miles away, in Delhi, three hours and a half later.

We were impressed by Delhi. There was, for example, the huge Council House, an immense rotunda that looked from the outside like a football stadium, where the Upper and Lower Houses of the Legislature met. Close by was the Viceroy's House, a palace flanked by congressional office buildings and magnificently overlooking the whole city, especially the vista closed by the Gate of India, with its eternal flame. The symbol of ultimate British authority was adroitly and powerfully stressed. At the city's Kashmir Gate was a monument to the British victory over the Sepoy mutineers. But the Red Fort was a monument to an even older imperialism; it had been the luxurious place of the Akhbar Dynasty, the Great Moguls. Jewels were inlaid in the walls; extensive waterlines had been laid to cool and beautify houses and gardens. Old Delhi was something else again. Some of the streets through which we rode must surely have been off-limits, for we saw no other military, our own or allied. They were swarming with animals, carts, Hindus, Moslems—screaming, dirty humanity, abjectly poor but insistently alive. Our driver shouted and sang to the horse, the bystanders, and the traffic that got in his way. After supper that night we sang, too—barbershop harmony with a group of officers—but under our merriment was the gnawing consciousness that our hot seat was growing hotter. When we sang, "We are poor little lambs who have gone astray," the Major and I looked at each other. We were now on nobody's "morning report," and maybe we were technically AWOL. Besides, Delhi was not a usual port of call for the Air Corps, and there would be nothing, we were told, going west to Karachi or Bombay. We decided, after a discussion with the chaplain, Father William Byrnes of Richmond, that we had better go to Agra by train and try there—it was the location of the Central India Air Depot—to get a plane back to Calcutta, where we might give our status some legitimacy.

But first I wanted a kashmir jacket for Eleanor, so next morning, I pushed open the door of a very posh shop in "the Ring." The proprietor, wreathed in smiles and bowing from the waist, greeted me. It was most kind of me to enter, but what, he asked with deprecating gestures, could a wealthy American officer expect to find in his humble shop, among his wretched, sleazy goods? I pricked up my ears. I had read something about Oriental bargaining. Maybe I could play that game, too. So I answered that I felt presumptuous and rude in venturing to come in amid all this magnificence, when my resources were so slender. The proprietor's eyes gleamed a little; this might be more interesting and civilized than the usual encounter with Americans, who demanded the price of an item and took it or left it. He invited me to have coffee with him on his balcony, where we discussed for a long time the war, the Russian menace, the decline of Britain and the future of India. Only by gradual and slow degrees and with profuse apologies did he steer the conversation around to the mysterious motive that might have brought me to his lowly door. I said at last that I had a charming sister at home who was very dear to me, and I would love to bring her some gorgeous thing—a kashmir jacket, for instance—as a sign that I had thought of her while I was visiting his beautiful country. Of course it was idle to think of such matters because I could never hope to have the sum that such a purchase would require. Well, he did have a kashmir jacket, to be sure, but it was a poor thing, and he was certain that I wouldn't consider it even though he would give it to me (because of our friendship) for the paltry price of forty-five rupees. When he brought it out I exclaimed over its lovely fabric and workmanship, and wondered how he could bring himself to part with it, even at the price he had named; I was grateful, of course, but it was far beyond my poor means. Well, we danced to this music for a long time, and at last I came away with the jacket, leaving him fifteen rupees and my Parker 51 fountain pen. For some reason the Parker 51 had the value of jewelry in Asia at that time, and I'm sure that after I left he went round the corner and traded it for twice what it had cost him.

The railroad station in Agra was a long shed with many wooden benches; when we arrived at seven in the evening every one of them was occupied by people who could claim no other shelter, and one had to step carefully because the cement floor was covered by those who had come too late to get a bench. It was cold, too; I was glad to put my tropical bones under two blankets at the ATC Transient Quarters. Before that, however, we persuaded our GI jeep driver to take us out to see the Taj Mahal. The moon was full, and ritual demanded that the Taj be seen first by moonlight. It was enchanting beyond our expectations; the shimmering dome seemed to float in the moon-drenched air. Next day, with the assistance of an informed Moslem guide, we marveled at the jewelry of design inside and out—the marble screens, the inlaid emeralds, lapis lazuli, cornelians, mother-of-pearl. I counted fifty-three gems in a tiny stone flower. Our guide took us then to the Agra Fort, an assembly of gorgeous buildings erected, once more, by the Moguls, and I resolved to read all I could about Akhbar the Great, Shah Jehan, and Aurangzebe. Late in the afternoon, in fact, hearing that it was not far from Agra, I borrowed a jeep from the chaplain, Father John Higgins, of Fall River, and drove out to see Fatehpur-Sikri, the city, now deserted, where Akhbar had held court, and where the Blessed Rudolph Aquaviva lived for three years while he worked for the conversion of the Emperor. Akhbar, though he was illiterate, was highly intelligent, and believed that if he could invent a syncretist religion and impose it on all his subjects he would be able to hold his empire together. I saw the throne-room where Akhbar had presided over discussions of religion; he sat in the centre while representatives of the Hindu, Moslem, Zoroastrian, and Christian faiths sat in the corners. Father Aquaviva was the Christian, and persisted in his hope of winning the Emperor even though his superiors became very skeptical about the Emperor's sincerity. At last Father Aquaviva was recalled to Goa and assigned to another mission, where, in six months, he was martyred. I gave thanks to God, as I drove away in the twilight, for the heroism of my Jesuit brother— not so much for the six months as for the three years.

Father Higgins generously gave us dinner; he had, moreover, got us a ride on a B-25 leaving for Calcutta early next day. We took off while it was still dark and went riding into the morning as dawn broke over the hills at the edge of the Indian plain. Today would be critical for our plans. We could be assigned to a transport routed non-stop to the States, and if so the bud would be nipped just as it was beginning to flower. Or we could be put aboard a ship that was scheduled to make a Mediterranean stop, and then we might be able to invent a reason for leaving the ship. Or we might just be hauled up on charges of being AWOL, if some brass hat wanted to throw his weight around. We got a haircut and a shine and repaired to the Hindustan Building. At the Troop Movement office thirty officers sat at desks.

"Wait a minute, Major," I said. "Let me make a reconnaissance."

He wanted to know what I hoped to gain by that, but I walked through the room reading the officers' name-plates and finally stopped before one desk.

"Captain Casey?" I asked, "I'm Father Leonard."

"Oh, hi, Father."

I hoped my relief wasn't too visible. "This is Major Wipf. We came in from Manila aboard the *Roswell,* but had to get off. Now we're looking for a ride home."

A twinkle came into the Captain's eyes. "The *Roswell* has been in for some time now, hasn't it?"

"Well, yes. We were—so to speak—delayed en route."

"Uh-huh. Well, I guess we can get you home all right. Can I see a copy of your orders?"

"Er— we were rather hoping you could put us on a ship that would be making a stop somewhere in the Mediterranean. Neither of us has ever seen that part of the world."

Now the twinkle broadened into an Irish grin. "I get it, Father. Tell you what you do. Go out and live at the Karnani Estates— that's the Officers' Club—and I'll call you as soon as I have anything."

He called next day to say that we had been assigned to the *Mandan,* a Victory ship bound to New York, with a stop at Port Said for refueling.

"Well, that's great," I said. "Thanks a lot."

"Yes, but look, Father, how are you going to get off at Port Said?"

"I have no idea," I answered. "We'll try to dream up something."

The *Mandan* did not sail on Sunday, as she was scheduled to do. Some of the crew had been in a tavern where a man was killed in a brawl, and the ship was not released until their depositions had been taken. It was one o'clock Wednesday morning when a tug took us in tow, snaked us under a drawbridge with only three feet of water on each side—a most workmanlike job—got us into and out of a lock with the same cool efficiency, and left us on the Hooghly with a river pilot to take us down to blue water. It would be thirty-six hundred miles—fourteen days—to Suez through the Arabian Sea, off Ceylon, and the Indian Ocean to the Red Sea and the Canal.

The trip was tedious, in the main. Rest, however gratefully welcomed at times, passes at last into restlessness. At Calcutta I had laid in a supply of reading that helped to fill the hours; I wrote letters home and to Manila; I offered Mass on the after cabin deck, where, on the Last Sunday after Pentecost, the high wind soaked the deck with spume, and I had to step aside periodically when a stream of water came my way. Result: one much-muddied alb, and only eight men showed up to hear St. Matthew on the end of all things. By now *Time* and the *New Yorker* were referring, with a curious, frightened insistence, to "the Atomic Age," and one would have thought the world's final dissolution a most apposite topic. But there were more pressing matters in people's minds: we were carrying fifteen Army and three Navy officers due for demobilization, and they were thinking and talking incessantly about civilian life. What would it be like? What would they do? It would have been strange if I had not shared something of their uncertainty—trying to picture myself in a classroom two months hence, giving an occasional off-campus lecture, a week-end retreat . . . it didn't rouse much enthusiasm in me, though I certainly wanted to be out of the Army. I wondered whether the advocates of a house-cleaning at B.C. and other Catholic colleges would continue to be shrugged off after the war. Would some of us still be considered idealists, faddists, fanatics? Had enough young men come out of the seminaries with new ideas? Would we still prepare our students to answer the objections of long-dead Protestants, and deny them any appreciation and share in the Christian life and worship? I'd seen enough war and touched enough American manhood in the raw to have become almost bitter toward the stand-patters. Wouldn't they see? One of my first jobs on returning, I resolved, would be the devising of a new curriculum in Theology, so that I could stump for it before the aura and authority of the returning chaplain ("he knows what's needed") might fade. Teaching would be most challenging if a few doors could be forced open, but a return to the old grooves would be unbearable.

Major Wipf and I did our sentry-duty on the deck each evening after dinner. The all-absorbing topic of our conversation was how we might succeed in being "bumped off" the ship at Port Said. Maybe we wouldn't even be given shore leave when we got there. Maybe there would be no Troop Movement Officer in Port Said, and if there were, how could we offer him a reasonable excuse for leaving the ship?

"At least you have a cold," said the Major. "You could demand to be hospitalized. I'm too healthy."

Even as a boy in high school, I hungered to visit Europe. When I joined the Army I took it for granted that my service would be in the European Theatre, where, under very adverse circumstances to be sure, I might see at last the lands out of which had come the literature, philosophy, history, art, and theology which had been my education, my inspiration, my recreation. Every name that cropped up in European war communiqués used to shake me with envy and regret that my job was in those ineffable Pacific islands. Now it would be tormenting to be so close and yet not see such places as Jerusalem, Athens, Rome, Paris, London. Well, tomorrow or the next day would tell the story.

"If we get off the ship," said the Major, "We make a first down and get four more. If we don't, we lose the ball and the ball game."

Of course there was another consideration. The *Mandan* was due in New York on December 20th. I could picture myself ringing the family doorbell on Christmas Eve. What a Christmas that would be! But by January I knew I would be kicking myself all over Massachusetts. There would be other Christmases; it was very unlikely that there would be other chances for a European junket. We had no guarantee, to be sure, that at Port Said we should not simply be clapped aboard the next ship, and so lose both Europe and Christmas-at-home. It was a gamble I had to take.

Came the First Sunday of Advent, and I could begin praying the Breviary again after a six weeks' absence from it. *Laetabor ego super eloquia tua, sicut qui invenit spolia multa.* I re-read *Exodus,* too, as we entered the Suez Canal, and one afternoon the Skipper leaned over the bridge and shouted,

"There's Mount Sinai over there, Chaplain!"

I think he was wrong; Sinai is too far inland to be seen from the Canal. But I stared through binoculars at the hill he pointed out, and at the barren slag on every side. If the Chosen People came this way, they had need indeed of manna and water gushing from a rock.

Four days out of Manila, on the *Roswell,* I had had violent stomach-cramps that made me walk the deck of my cabin for four hours of the night, hugging my innards and in amazed reproach demanding of my hitherto irreprehensible digestive organs what the hell went on here. There was another revolt in the interior before we reached Calcutta, and two or three more between Calcutta and Port Said. I didn't like them; they kept me up nights, and they suggested a possible Fifth Column in what had been a loyally efficient corps of domestic servants. But I couldn't explain them, so I told myself they were due to some transient tensions and tried to forget them. They did give a little more color, of course, to the case I intended to present when I applied in Port Said for transfer from the ship.

Small boats warped the ship slowly over to the fuel wharf at Port Said on December 3rd, and shore leave was granted after a moment's dull fear that it wouldn't be. The Major and I stood on the bridge that spans the Canal and debated.

"You can use your cold and your cramps," he said, "but the only excuse I have is this broken denture."

We went looking for the troop movement office. It was manned by a solitary lieutenant, who was aghast at our request.

"Don't you want to go back to the States?"

We stood firm in our demand for medical attention.

"But this ship is due in New York just before Christmas!"

The Major said that he couldn't go without eating for two weeks, and I blew my watery nose strenuously.

"Well, I dunno. Let me talk to Cairo."

He reached for the phone, and talked to someone in the American Middle East Headquarters.

"Yes, they insist. Okay. Yes, sir, I'll type that on their orders: 'removed from ship for medical attention at own request.' Yes, I told then that, but they still insist. Yes, sir. Good-bye."

Outside, the Major and I shook hands and did a little dance. A first down, by inches!

We left Port Said next day in a mail truck and took the desert road to Cairo. The tawny desert lay all about us, broken by sudden oases like Ismailia. We saw barges with tall sails on the irrigation canals, and villages, as filthy as anything in India, where the people huddled for warmth in sheltered, sunlit corners. Late in the afternoon we drove into a real "stateside" set-up at Camp Russell B. Huckstep, in Heliopolis, ten miles outside Cairo. At the base hospital our suntan uniforms easily distinguished us as the odd sticks from the Pacific who had turned down a chance to go home, and the doctors and nurses came out to have a look. It was a close thing, probably, that they did not put us in the psychiatric ward. As it was, we sensed that a very careful eye was going to be kept on us. That night, in the medical ward, I walked the floor for four hours with abdominal cramps. They told me I might have a touch of malaria.

Egypt was, for me, as much richer than India as India had been richer than the Philippines. Here, in the Nile valley, history has a tongue and speaks: of the ancient dynasties, of Joseph and his brothers, of Moses and the Exodus, of St. Mark and apostolic Christianity, of the Crusades and the Napoleonic conquests. We met Colonel Al Hayes, from Winthrop, the Staff Judge Advocate of the Theatre, who, after I had been discharged from the hospital and assigned to the casual section, had us for dinner at his "fur-lined foxhole" (an apartment on the banks of the River) and sent us in his car to see the Sphinx and the Pyramids. In Matariah we visited the fig tree, aged and gnarled, under which the Holy Family rested—so the legend went—during the flight from Herod. We took the Red Cross tour through Old Cairo. There was the Mosque of Amr, built in 640

A.D. by one of Mohammed's earliest followers, and not used now except on the last Friday of Ramadan; near the pulpit was a pillar of gray stone on which there was a mark like a whip lash, and the story is that when the mosque was near completion Mohammed lashed the pillar and bade it fly to Cairo. Two other columns, supposed to be curative, were surrounded by rails now to keep the faithful in search of cures from licking them with their tongues; we were shown the bloody indentations worn by their tongues in the past. There was the tiny Coptic Orthodox Church of the Holy Family, built over the crypt where the Family supposedly lived. The resident priest gave us a lecture on the site, and told us that the Nile now floods the crypt during most of the year; he was trying to raise money to repair the leaks. There was the Synagogue of Ben Ezra, where Moses prayed and where the Prophet Jeremiah lived after the Fall of Jerusalem; the guide pointed out to us a copy of the Torah, inscribed on a gazelle skin, which he said dated from the time of Jeremiah. We went to the City of the Dead, a Moslem cemetery, and the Dead City, a wasteland, unutterably dreary, of ruins left after tracts of ancient Cairo were destroyed by fire and the sword in 1168 and never rebuilt. We saw, from the outside only, the Citadel, erected by Saladin in 1176; the Egyptian and British flags were the latest in a succession of flags flying over it. I had a day in the Museum of Egypt with King Tut's amazing sarcophagi and jewels and the relics of earlier dynasties as well as those from the Greco-Roman period. There was the sumptuous Shepheard's Hotel, since destroyed in riots and now, I think, rebuilt, and, in vivid contrast, the baked mud houses of the filthy slums. We strolled through the bazaars, admiring brass, ivory, and leather work of beautiful but prohibitively costly workmanship, and wondered how all these artisans stayed alive. The streets were filled with gharries, push-carts, limousines, jeeps and the jabbering of a dozen languages; we met Italians, Frenchmen, Britishers, Jugoslavs, Russians, Armenians—not to mention the native Arabs, Jews and Copts, all of whom seemed to have learned the ancient cry of "bakhsheesh" or its equivalent in their own language, and shouted it persistently in American ears. I recall one fat Egyptian who, over coffee, looked exultantly forward to the day when "the British will be kicked out

of Egypt, and you will see Egypt rise." I felt like saying that he
didn't have to wait until the British left before getting rid of that
stinking pile of dung in his front yard. A hopelessly Occidental reaction, no doubt.

Meanwhile we had begun to negotiate cautiously for our on-
ward journey. Christmas in Bethlehem would have been a privilege,
Christmas in Rome almost as good, but Christmas in Egypt, or
worse, on the high seas, held no attraction. No ships were due, so
our orders were cut for air travel, and we haunted Payne Field, hoping against hope that we could somehow get a "priority" that would
take us home for Christmas, or even—so stubborn was our determination—a stowaway berth on a flight to Rome. The days dragged
by, and we killed time in the usual casual camp style. One dreary
December night a sergeant said,

"There's a convoy of trucks going up to Alexandria tomorrow,
Father. Would you like to go along?"

I perked up. Anything for diversion, and Alexandria—I remembered St. Clement, St. Cyril, St. Catherine (she had been fired
as patroness of philosophers during my time at Weston when Father
Robert Swickerath, our professor of church history, shot her authenticity full of holes)—Alexandria would certainly be worth a visit. It
was an all-day ride through the desert, with relics along the road of
the British war with Rommel, and the broken window in the cab of
my truck admitted far too much of the cold wind. We came into the
city at dusk, but I walked the main street anyway. The shops were
brightly lighted, and people were out in spite of the rain. In fact,
certain people were very much in evidence; I was accosted and
propositioned every hundred yards. This was, too, I remembered,
the city of Cleopatra. Next morning I took a very early taxi to
Ibramieh and celebrated Mass with the Irish Franciscan Sisters.
They gave me an egg for breakfast, and I felt guilty. It was probably the only egg in the house. The convoy left Alexandria at nine-
thirty, giving me nary a glimpse of St. Cyril or St. Clement, and no
sight of the city except the pretty waterfront and romantic-looking
citadel at the harbor mouth. There were fifty-seven trucks in the
convoy, and we were instructed to drive through Cairo fifteen feet
apart at forty miles an hour. We did, too, on the busiest streets, with

the Egyptians dashing recklessly between trucks. My heart stopped at some of the near-misses.

It's unbearably trite to say so, but I was convinced anew that the world is a very small place. One of the auxiliary chaplains at Camp Huckstep turned out to be my old friend Father Frank Anderson, a New England Jesuit who had been out in these parts for ten years, teaching at our college in Baghdad and, during the war, serving as secretary to the Apostolic Delegate in Cairo. Even more surprising was my encounter with Father Bill Coppens, a high school friend who became an Oblate and was sent to the missions in South Africa. When the war came he enlisted in the South African Army and spent four years in North Africa and Italy. These friends and others they introduced us to helped much to alleviate the tedium of life in the casual camp. Some weary GI, I reflected, must have coined the definition of a casual: a transient en route from there to there, with no friends here. And I remembered the black-eyed Moslem urchin who sang to us in Calcutta (some of the casuals there must have taught him the chant):

> No poppa, no momma,
> No whiskey, no soda,
> No mail, no ship—
> Bakhsheesh!

It became obvious that our Christmas would be spent in Egypt. However little we relished it in prospect, the day was delightful, probably the most memorable I had known, and probably because Christmas is Christmas wherever Christian men may spend it. As an American, I felt very young in this country, but as a Christian, and especially on Christmas Day, I felt older than the sands, older than time. Because only Christmas can give meaning to the maze of memories, follies, short-lived joys, betrayals of conscience that are Egypt or, by analogy, any man's life. Only Christmas can plant an oasis in the desert of blasted human aspirations. Only Christmas can bring into this very bewildered world the light that enlightens every man.

The day began when Father Talsky, the Catholic base chaplain from Milwaukee, Father Anderson and I heard confessions for almost six hours, and then celebrated Midnight Mass in the Post

Theatre for about five hundred men. In the morning, alone except for a few soldiers who dropped in and out, I offered unhurriedly and without distraction my own Christmas Masses. I have changed my thinking and would not now celebrate alone after sharing in the community Mass, but in those days it had not occurred to me to question the practice, or to wonder about offering three Masses in succession. I did revel in the scriptural readings appointed for the Masses, and in the lovely antiphons that cried out for a choir to sing them. In fact, singing seemed so much in order that when after Mass I heard a piano tinkling in the Officer's Club I could not pass it by, and went in where there was the traditional eggnog and much howling of "Sweet Adeline" and "Down by the Old Mill Stream." "What a caterwauling do you keep here!"

The Post was entertaining for the day five hundred Greek and Jugoslav war orphans from a camp near Port Said; most of them had dinner with the enlisted men, but each officer had several children at his table. I found myself with three little Greek girls, very shy. They spoke, of course, no English whatever, while my Greek, very rusty now after fifteen years away, was the ancient classical tongue of Plato, Sophocles, and Homer, not the modern spoken tongue. My only conversational success, therefore, was in learning the children's ages; they were respectively *deka, hendeka,* and *dodeka* years old. We filled them to the brim with turkey, potatoes, asparagus, dressing, and mince pie (they couldn't hold very much, since the GI's had been giving them fruit and candy all morning, and I suspect that there were revolts in several little interiors that afternoon), and sent them off to a showing of Walt Disney's "Dumbo" at the theatre. In the evening, at the Catholic Club in Heliopolis, we had supper with Fathers Anderson and Coppens and several American sailors. Everyone had to contribute to the entertainment; Father Anderson, who was a good tenor in the Weston choir, sang, and I remember reciting Belloc's "Song of the Pelagian Heresy." We listened to Father Anderson's very interesting insights into the Middle East, and wrangled a bit over who won the war, the Army or the Marines, and concluded at last a very pleasant evening with a toast to Egypt: "May all of us get out of it, since none of us wants to stay in it." Getting out of it: that was the problem. On the 26th and again on the 27th

we went to Payne Field. No planes in; "probably storms in the Atlantic." We played pool, and ping-pong, and sat through Class B
movies, and discovered for ourselves what the GI's meant by
"sweating out a plane." On the 28th we tried again; there were still
no trans-Atlantic planes, but flights were going out to Europe. The
Major suddenly seized my arm. "Let's try your friend Colonel
Hayes!"

"He's in the Judge Advocate Section," I answered. "They have
nothing to do with transportation."

"Yes, but he might know somebody."

"It's a long shot."

"It's better than sitting here."

So we went to Cairo, and found Al Hayes in his office.

"Al," I said, "Do you know the G-4?"

"Yes, I know him."

"Does he owe you anything?"

"Well, I've done him a couple of favors."

"How about two tickets to Rome?" Al sat back and surveyed
us for a long moment, then shrugged.

"I'll be back in a minute," he said.

He was gone fifteen minutes, but when he returned he threw
two pieces of blue paper on the desk, and said,

"Get out of town fast, will you?"

In the Breviary that day, the Feast of the Holy Innocents, I
read the words, "Out of Egypt I have called my son," and next day,
as we sat waiting to board our plane, I read at Matins the opening
lines of St. Paul's Epistle to the Romans, "God is my witness . . .
how unceasingly I make mention of you, always imploring in my
prayers that somehow I may at last by God's will have a prosperous
journey to get to you . . . that among you I may be comforted together with you by that faith which is common to us both, yours and
mine."

CHAPTER 18

Roman Honeymoon

OUR PLANE TOOK OFF AT SEVEN IN THE MORNING, JUST AS THE sun was rising. From the air it was easy to see that Cairo owed its being to the great River; the city was a huge, green oasis in the midst of the yellow desert. Off to the east was Palestine, the Promised Land, which, like Moses, I had been forbidden to enter. Beneath us, in a little while, were the Patmos of St. John and the Delos of Apollo, and Sappho's and Byron's Isles of Greece. At eleven we came down into Athens, or rather, into Athens' airport, which was ten miles outside the city, and from which we could see the ancient seaport of the Piraeus.

Athens! I had read Greek for seven years, from Xenephon's *enteuthen exelaunei* to the *Hespera men gar en* of Demosthenes; the forty-eight books of the *Iliad* and the *Odyssey;* the plays of Sophocles, Aeschylus, Euripides; the philosophy of Plato; the lyrics of the Anthology. I could, I felt, have spent a couple of months in Athens alone. Alas (or *omoi,* which would be more appropriate), before he landed the pilot announced that we would have one hour, no more, on the ground. I walked rapidly to the gate, and found there the sentry, a tall, lanky GI.

"How long does it take to get into the city?" I asked eagerly.

"'bout twenty minutes."

I calculated. Twenty minutes in, twenty minutes back, if all went well. That would give me twenty minutes to see Athens. I groaned, and—thinking of shrines, ruins, monuments—said,

"Is there anything interesting around here?"

"Well," he answered, "There's a place down the road where you can get a pretty good beer."

The pilot, sensing that several of us were grievously disappointed, offered to circle the city several times after we had become airborne, but, since we did not know what to look for or where to look, the maneuver gave us small satisfaction.

We flew west, above the clouds this time, where the air got thin and we put on oxygen masks, but we dropped down as we approached Italy. The pilot swung around the heel of the boot and came up the western coast, giving us a splendid view of Capri, Naples, Vesuvius, Sorrento, the Anzio beach-head, and the magnificent reclamation of the Pontine Marshes that was one of the few memorable achievements of Mussolini. About five o'clock I jabbed the Major and shouted,

"There it is!"

I had just seen the dome of St. Peter's, unmistakable in the soft afternoon sunlight.

At Ciampino there were Army buses waiting, and on the road we asked discreet questions. Where could we find billets? Would the billeting officer make difficulties for us? We might have spared ourselves the anxiety. We were out of Egypt, the land of bondage, and were free men now. The clerk at the Albergo Maestoso, on the Via Vittorio Veneto, glanced absent-mindedly at our orders and assigned us rooms on the fourth floor. We had a pleasant dinner in the hotel, visited the Red Cross in the Piazza Barberini to learn about tours of the city, and went to bed. I was exhausted, but pinched myself awake for a second to be very clear about it. I was in Rome!

The mellow conversation of a hundred church bells, the most gladsome sound I had heard since leaving Manila, awakened us next morning and reminded us that we were in a Christian town. I felt as I did on my boyhood Christmases, when the floor beneath the tree was piled with gifts waiting for my eager fingers to unwrap them. There was the Rome of the Caesars, the Rome of St. Peter and the martyrs, medieval Rome, the Rome of the Counter-reformation (which would be, for me, Jesuit Rome), and today's Rome.

"Let's get going," I said to the Major.

My honeymoon with the Eternal City lasted for eleven days. Later I would see flaws in the beloved, but now I was dazzled, blissful, intoxicated. For three days the Red Cross took us to the great basilicas, to the Colosseum, and the Forum, to Horatius' Bridge and the Royal Palace on the Quirinal, and the Gesú and St. Peter-in-Chains and the Catacombs, and then, alone or with the Major, and with the help of a dozen generous cicerones, I went back for a lingering visit to many of these fascinating places and saw others that were not on the grand tour but were of absorbing interest to me. It was very cold; my fingers ached as I offered Mass at St. Paul's-outside-the-walls, at St. John Lateran, at the Blessed Sacrament chapel in St. Peter's, in the Borghese chapel, at St. Mary Major, where Pope Pius XII had offered his first Mass forty years before, at the tombs of St. Ignatius and St. Robert Bellarmine in the Gesú. I had a sepulchral dinner with the Jesuit community at the Gregorian University, where the food was meager indeed and we sat in overcoats listening to some chanted reading in Italian from the lofty pulpit, and I had to sprint to get out of the house before the doors were closed, irrevocably, at ten o'clock. Father Joachim Daleiden, a Chicago Franciscan who was the Rome Area chaplain, loaned us his jeep for an entire day and we went to Castel Gandolfo, where Father Walter Miller, a Jesuit astronomer from the New York Province, showed us through the papal apartments and chapels. We saw the Gardens of Domitian, formal terraces with orange and olive trees—the Halls of Domitian, we were told, had been bomb-shelters during the Anzio campaign—and looked down into the amethyst pocket of Lake Gandolfo. Frascati and Rocco di Papa lay on the slopes of the Alban hills, and in the distance were the Sabine hills and Mount Soracte. *Vides ut alta stet nive candidum?* Father Vincent McCormick, then Assistant to the General of the Jesuits, told me he had seen Soracte snow-capped only once in his ten years in Rome. The Red Cross took us to Tivoli and the Villa d'Este and Hadrian's Villa; we watched one of the famous Roman sunsets across the Campagna, and rode back with everything in sharp relief against the afterglow: little towns like Monticelli snuggling in the hills, aqueducts striding across the horizon on their looping arches, ancient keeps like Aeneas Sylvius Piccolomini's fort and Alceone Castle grimly guarding the approaches to Rome. I was losing my heart to Italy, as I had suspected I would.

Father George, a Dutch Benedictine archaeologist who was temporarily chaplain of the Catholic Club in the Via della Conciliazione, snorted when he heard of our superficial visit to the Catacombs of St. Sebastian, and offered to show us something worthwhile: the Catacombs of St. Callistus on the Appian Way. I was enchanted with their simplicity, as compared with the Renaissance munificence of the Vatican and the baroque of the Gesú. I liked the deep galleries of graves and their touching inscriptions, and noted with a sense of vindication that the altars in these primitive chapels were all "facing the people." Father George insisted that the catacombs were never used for anything but cemeteries; they were not hiding places for the persecuted Christians; this was a notion propagated by such romances as *Fabiola* and *Quo Vadis*.

Father John Ford, a Jesuit from my own Province, who was teaching at the Gregorian, took me on New Year's Eve to Solemn Vespers at the Gesú, where, because it was the vigil of the Jesuit titular feast, the church was crowded and a group of laymen presented a chalice to our Father General. Some of the things the choir sang were so operatic that I turned to Father Ford in naive perplexity.

"Wasn't that stuff outlawed thirty years ago by Pius X?"

His eyes twinkled.

"There's a story," he said, "of two statues here in Rome. One is of St. Peter; it faces the city, and the inscription on the pedestal says, 'Here the laws are made.' The other is of St. Paul, and it faces outward toward the world. The inscription on it says, 'There the laws are kept.'"

It was the tiny beginning of a considerable disenchantment that would not strike me with its full force until I went to the Vatican Council twenty years later. Meanwhile, I had heard that it was possible—if one were very patient and didn't mind a wait of several days—to put through a personal phone call to the States. When I asked about it at the telephone building the sergeant said, unconcernedly,

"Put you through now if you like."

In an hour I was talking to my mother and father and Eleanor for the first time in two years. There is something about the timbre of loved voices that a thousand letters cannot duplicate. If they had said nothing of any consequence—and it was hard for any of us to do more than exclaim—I should have been rewarded. It was midnight when I finally hung up and started for the hotel. I had taken only a few steps when a volley of shots rang out. From habit, I hugged the walls, wondering if an insurrection were in progress, but I should have known: the Italians were celebrating the New Year with firecrackers.

"*Auguri* to you, too," I grumbled.

On the second and third of January my sight-seeing was slowed down a little by queasiness at the stomach and (a totally new experience) loss of appetite, but I put it down to tourist fatigue and went to bed early. There was so much more I had to see: the Janiculum, the North American College on "Humility Street," the Castel San Angelo, in whose grim dungeons died Father Ricci, the last Jesuit General before the Suppression, the Biblical Institute, the Borghese Gallery. And on January 7th the Major and I had a private audience with the Holy Father. We were ushered up the long stairs by the Swiss guards, who clicked their heels and halberds on the marble floor and saluted, and we waited for a few moments in an anteroom draped in crimson, talking with one of the chamberlains. He was a Venetian lawyer, who had a brother a Jesuit and a son in our novitiate, and he came for this duty to the Vatican each year for two weeks. At a signal we walked through four more anterooms to the reception room; the Major, who was a Protestant, was feeling by this time the psychological tension anterooms are designed to create.

"What do I do when we see him?" he whispered.

I was not nervous at all, I thought, but quite suddenly the door opened and the Pope darted—if one may use that verb for so tall a man—into the room. I was startled, fell on my knees, and during the interview was so nervous that I talked more than he did. But Pius was very gracious, speaking almost in a whisper but with great kindness and a tremendous personal interest, even though he was seeing at that time hundreds of visitors each month. His English was correct, but bore a strong Italian accent.

"You are the Jesu-eet Father? And you are from what part of Amer-ee-ca?"

"Boston, Your Holiness,"

"Ah, Bos-ton. I have been there. Arch-a-beeshop Cooshing. He is very zealous. And there are many fine Catholics."

"Yes, Your Holiness," I said in what I thought he might find a welcome change from the routine interview, "But we are very disappointed in Boston."

"Dees-appointed?"

"Yes, you see we did have a Cardinal."

His eyes opened wide. "But the cardeen-al-ate must be dees-tree-buted all over the world. And Amer-ee-ca already has five cardeenals."

It wasn't the time to ask how many cardinals Italy had. And anyway, the Pope turned to Major Wipf.

"And you are from what part of Amer-ee-ca?"

"Hibbing, Minnesota, sir."

Well, the Holy Father couldn't say he had been there, but he did ask in a most interested way if the Major were married, how many children he had, and what he intended to do after he left the Army. Then our audience was over; Pius ended by calling down on us a tremendous blessing; he seemed to reach up to heaven with his long arms for it, and it included ourselves, he said, and our families, and all we held dear, and especially my own apostolic work. With a parting smile and at the same speed he was gone, then, into the next room, where others awaited him. Pius XII is out of fashion these days, almost as much as Victorian literature and manners, and one hears only of his patrician ancestry, his cold and tragically mistaken diplomacy, his unbending aloofness. All I can say is that if these things made the whole man, I must have met someone else. I saw, of course, the Roman nose, the marble pallor; what impressed me and what I shall always remember was the gentle manner, the kind and interested eyes behind the thick glasses, the impression he gave that he had been waiting for years for me to come to see him, and that he would have loved to talk with me longer if there weren't all these other demands on his time. *Oremus pro Pontifice nostro Pio.*

I went next morning to the Air Booking Office in the Piazza d'Esedra, and the girl there promised to put me on a plane for Marseilles any time I wanted it. How ridiculously easy, after Calcutta and Cairo! The Major, who had seen northern Europe, was going to Casablanca and home; I hated to break up our gate-crashing partnership, so filled with fun and conspiracy and near-failure, but I hadn't seen northern Europe.

On the 9th I lunched at the North American College with Monsignor (later Bishop) Markham of Boston who was with the Catholic War Relief agency, Bishop Hurley of Florida, Monsignor (later Cardinal) Brennan and Monsignor Carroll of the Vatican State Department, four chaplains from Germany, and Monsignor Luigi Ligutti, an American who had single-handedly organized the Catholic Rural Life Conference at home and has since done outstanding work in the FAO of the United Nations. The Bishop made him the target during lunch of much joshing about his bucolic interests and his "hicks"; some of the barbs were rather pointed, and it was clear that the Bishop saw small value in the work. The way of the pioneer is a painful one; lonely he who has ideas in advance of his contemporaries!

"Have you said Mass in the Catacombs yet?" Monsignor Ligutti asked me after lunch.

"No, I haven't."

"Well, why don't you get a jeep and we'll go out tomorrow morning. I haven't been there in years."

So I borrowed Father Daleiden's jeep again and we went to the Catacombs of St Callistus, where Monsignor celebrated Mass in the Chapel of St Cecilia and I in the Chapel of the Popes. This was in the days when our textbooks told us that concelebration was a "rite peculiar to the Oriental Churches." What they meant was that it was a peculiar rite which the Orientals might somehow justify but with which good Latin priests could have nothing to do. In these happier times we Latin priests, too, may gather around the altar like the Twelve newly-ordained at the Last Supper and "do this" to remember our common Lord and to knit stronger the bonds that unite us in Him. All about me as I read the Mass, twenty to thirty feet beneath the ground, were flat marble slabs, covered with inscriptions and Christian symbols, that closed the graves of early Popes like Fabian and Eutychian. The two lists of saints in the Canon of the Mass struck me with great force. "That You would give us sinners some part and company with these." Just some!

The Monsignor and I got back to the city too late for breakfast at the hotel, so we repaired to the Red Cross for coffee. Instead of the cinnamon buns they had been serving, that day they offered doughnuts—something I'd never eaten with relish or without suspicion. Against my better judgment I put away two of them before parting with the Monsignor and going out for another look at the Borghese Gallery and its amazing luxuriance of beauty; Bernini, Titian, Tintoretto, Raphael, Giotto, Fra Lippo Lippi, Fra Angelico. These Italians!

The next day was the first anniversary of our invasion of Lingayen. It seemed to me during the night that a similar battle had broken out in my interior. I was up all night and very sick all day. Major Wipf got worried and called Father Ford; I would not hear of hospitalization at first, but they called in Captain Harkins, a medic from Lewiston, and I was at last overruled. The diagnosis at the 34th Station Hospital was gastro-enteritis (treatment: sulphur drugs, liquid diet), but two days later it was changed to hepatitis, and the judgment was confirmed when my eyes and skin took on a rapid discoloration such as atabrine had failed to bring on in eighteen months of daily dosage. Treatment: rest, a fat-free diet. How long? The medics, with their air of "get-yourself-ready-for-the-worst," said six weeks at the least. Six weeks! How was I going to explain my presence in Rome for that length of time? But I was too sick to care very much about that. Where had I picked up this bug? The doughnuts had triggered the outburst, but rebellion had been in the making since—yes, ever since I left Manila. And in Manila they had given me shots just before . . .

"Doc," I said to one of the medics, "Can you get hepatitis from shots?"

"Well, not from the shots themselves. But from an unsterilized needle, maybe."

Ah, ha! Those Navy corpsmen must have been the villains. Well, of course I would not have wanted to go home without some souvenir of the lovely tropics. And if I had to get sick, I could imagine few better places than Rome. Suppose—I shuddered—suppose it had been Egypt!

I had to write home and explain, without creating too much anxiety, that I would be (again) a little delayed en route. This was my letter:

"From my bed of pain,
    And my cot of rue,
This plaintive prayer
    I send to you.

"Egad, isn't that lousy. Sounds like a greeting card. Let's try again.

"Out of the blankets that cover me,
Drab as an olive from head to foot,
One wistful wail I send to thee:
'write me a letter or I'm kaput.'

"Or, to get out of the *fin-de-siècle* and speak with the *haute monde,*

"Sickness.
Army sickness.
Writhing serpents frustrate in caduceus.
'Swallow this, please.'
'Have your bowels moved today?'
SEND ME A LETTER!

"I remember a white-haired, rosy-cheeked, lovable old cherub of a man who carried mail at the Mattapan Post Office the summer I worked there, and every morning he used to sing delectable Irishries I've never heard repeated. One of them I recall—the only one:

"When I was young I used to be
The finest lad that you could see,
The Prince of Wales he wanted me
To join his bloomin' Ar-r-my.

"The song went on to give specific reasons why, like any true son of Ireland, he spurned the offer. But when I was young, I joined the Ar-r-my, and thought to get out of it early and scot-free. The Army chuckled and agreed too easily, too winsomely, and now, in my old age and on a foreign shore, hath left me naked to mine enemies. (Practically naked, except for an ill-fitting bathrobe and pajamas not guaranteed against slipping.) The point of all this blather is that I am hors de combat, come a cropper, offside and out of the play. It's me liver, me darlint liver, as Sean O'Casey would say, the only liver I've got, that's up and doin' as if it were the masther of the house instead of a humble chore boy. It's goin' on three months now since it's been fractious, but I was that taken up with what was passin' before me eyes that I had no time for it. (Quick change of set from the Liffey to the Thames.) And now it's had its day, and put me on me back, and in an 'orspital, a bloody 'orspital, where they talks of keepin' me, so they do, for six weeks or more. It ain't roight to treat a bloke what's done 'is toime in that fashion, is it now? (Change of set to Louisiana and high, squeaky voice of complaining negro.) Lissen here, Missus Ma, and you, too, Marse Daddy, I ain't heard a pip outa you since three months ago. Howzabouts you-all settin' down an' makin' up for lost time, on account I'm sho' nuff gonter be here long 'nuff to get yo' letters?

There were times during the next two months when I thought that if people at home asked me what I saw in Rome, I'd say, "an apartment house," because that was all I could see from the window in our ward. The hospital in Mussolini's time had been a Navy *caserna,* across the Tiber some three or four miles from St. Peter's. Nausea and a disgusting sense of repletion kept me on intravenous feeding for the first three weeks; I used to say that all those needle pricks should add up to a wound and get me the Purple Heart. My weight dropped to 144 pounds, and I was too languid to mind the incarceration much. Father Ford and Father Bob Dyson, a professor at the Biblical Institute, both New Englanders, came often to see me, and I was grateful especially because there was no public transportation at that time in Rome, and they had to walk a long distance. They kept me supplied, too, with books and periodicals. Father Zack Maher, who had been during the war superior of the American

Jesuits, came over from our Curia; so did Father Vincent McCormick and Father Durocher, the amiable Treasurer of the Society, a Canadian, and Brother Sullivan, from our Chicago Province, who had very kindly arranged our audience with the Pope, and Father Joy, an Irish Jesuit at that time assigned to Rome. Father Daleiden dropped in often; so did Major Ed Ryan and Captain John Brennan, both dentists on the hospital staff. But my most regular visitor was Father Tom Nolan, a Maryknoller from New York City, whose wonderful grin lighted up my door every day but one during those two months. His mission in Korea had been destroyed by the Japanese, and when he managed to get home he joined the Army—which of course sent him to Europe instead of to the Far East, where his experience might have been useful. In any case, his jollity and his obvious solicitude were useful to me, and the memory of his brotherly kindness is a heart-warming one still.

In the ward my liver began to return to peace-time levels of production, and my jaundiced skin began to itch furiously as it peeled off, and the days began to drag—a sure sign of returning health. I was given steak three times a day, but it was boiled in water, like an egg, and tasted like shoes. My room-mates came and went: an Ordnance captain with an infected foot, an Air Corps captain with dysentery, an Infantry lieutenant with the flu. The conversation turned infallibly to religion, and I tried desperately to go in by these men's doors that I might come out at my own. The world had changed with the war, I began to see, and the old Apologetics that I had learned, with its neat summaries and its relentless logic, no longer appealed. Christianity in syllogisms was as tasteless as my steak. I found myself talking now from the Gospels, from the history of salvation, from the existential concerns of people who wanted to be free, to live in peace, and to feel that their lives added up to some perceptible meaning. I talked about the new community of nations that had just been formed in San Francisco and how it squared with the Christian summons to establish a human community by entering into our inheritance—a share in Christ's sonship of the Father. By building and consolidating this community we would achieve our own perfection, because when we surrender ourselves to the love and service of others we discover and fulfill ourselves. The world's goods are not to be repudiated, but used wherever and however they can make our lives more livable, more human.

The officers were skeptical. They had seen selfishness at close range, in themselves and everyone they knew. How do you get this community?

"Well," I said, "You ask for it—often, and in earnest. We don't really make community; it's a gift, and we can only receive it. But we can open our hearts to it when it's offered, and nourish it so that it grows in us. We can draw back in fear from anything that threatens it. We can do our darndest to heal its wounds, instead of opening them wider."

"Yes, but this isn't what religion is all about, is it—the Church and the Pope and all that stuff?"

For answer I would quote a line from St. John's Gospel which I suppose I must have read a thousand times in my young manhood, but which had only recently struck me like a lightning bolt: "Jesus was to die for the nation—and not for the nation only, but to gather together in unity the scattered children of God."

I don't remember exactly how I interpreted and amplified the quotation at that time. But if I were in the same situation now I would probably say something like this:

That God intended human society is evident not only from human nature of man and its needs but also from history. God gave each of us companions: husband or wife, children, relatives, binding them to us in stable union. At first we thought of other people as aliens and enemies—fundamentally because we did not know them as human like ourselves. We were distracted from their essential human nature by superficial differences like color, speech, possessions, traditions. It has taken us a very long time to realize that beneath these differences are people whose origin, destiny, and essential characteristics are identical with our own. We have been slow to realize this, of course, because our tendency toward union with our fellows was warped or blocked by that aboriginal catastrophe which darkened our minds and impaired our power to do what we ought. In the beginning a man had been able to recognize in a single bound of his mind that he and his wife were, as we say, made for each other: "This at last is bone from my bones, and flesh from my flesh . . . This is why a man leaves his father and mother and joins himself to his wife, and they become one body." But his sin is no sooner committed than the union is damaged. He blames his sin on his wife: "It was the woman you put with me; she gave me the fruit, and I ate it." Then his elder son, in a fit of envy ,murders his brother. The subsequent history of our race is a sadly familiar one; Pius XI invoked God's mercy on "this old world, which has shed so much blood and dug so many graves."

God set about restoring human unity when he called Abraham and made him the father of a race that would be God's people. Ultimately every other race would benefit from this, because from this people would spring, in the fullness of time, the Christ, the principle of unity, under whom as head God had determined to join the human family together once more. But in the meantime this people would provide the world with an example of "brothers living together in unity" and itself become conscious of the great good of peace.

If, however, a common ancestry and the inheritance of the Promise was enough to make a few people brothers and sisters but excluded everyone else from the community, more had to be done. It was done by Christ, whose full achievement is summed up by St. Paul, writing to converts from paganism:

> Do not forget, then, that there was a time when you who were pagans . . . had no Christ and were excluded from membership in Israel, aliens with no part in the covenants with their Promise; you were immersed in this world, without hope and without God. But now in Christ Jesus you that used to be so far apart from us have been brought very close, by the blood of Christ. For he is the peace between us, and has made the two into one and broken down the barrier which used to keep them apart, actually destroying in his own person the hostility caused by the rules and decrees of the Law. This was to create one single New Man in himself out of the two of them and, by restoring peace through the cross, to unite them both in a single body and reconcile them with God . . . So you are no longer aliens or foreign visitors; you are citizens like all the saints, and part of God's household.

You are part of a building that has the apostles and prophets for its foundations, and Christ Jesus himself for its main cornerstone. As every structure is aligned on him, all grow into one holy temple in the Lord; and you, too, in him, are being built into a house where God lives, in the Spirit.

The genuine Christian community, in its mutual love, is an image, however flawed and tiny, of God's love for his human creatures. "As I have loved you, you ought to love one another." Here selfishness is vanquished, not merely for the sake of tranquil human relations and the common advantage, though these are desirable enough for themselves, but also because the members of the community are consciously trying to imitate Christ, to obey the law whose observance he made the criterion of true Christianity. Here men and women labor for the general good because in Christ they are sons and daughters of the one Father and therefore brothers and sisters.

It might be objected that the wars, jealousies, petty factions, hatreds which have disfigured Christian history make it clear how little attention has been paid to the ideal of the community. But, while acknowledging shamefacedly all these sins, we should not forget the gigantic efforts expended to establish and consolidate it. Who but God can measure or give account of the labors in education, the relief of the poor, the care of the sick and the handicapped, the rearing of orphans and the sheltering of the aged, the ransom of captives and the burial of the plague-stricken? What else can we think of except a profound and lifelong dedication to human unity when we hear the names of Francis, of Vincent de Paul, of Elizabeth of Hungary, of John XXIII?

The prevailing mentality of the last few centuries, which stressed the maximum development and achievement of the individual rather than the maximum contribution he or she might make to society, obscured the ideal of the community. But the time to make a happy change has never been so ripe. The Christian community, as a governing idea in theology and asceticism, has been gaining ground among us for a hundred years. At first the insight of a few little-known theologians, it began to enlist more general interest after the turn of the century. The astounding and frightening events that followed then so hard on one another, the World Wars, the Depression, the concentration camps, the nuclear bomb, the emergence of new peoples in Asia and Africa—only served to propagate this idea more widely, until it began to be the single dominant theme of all theological and ascetical writing. It inspired the teachings of the Second Vatican Council, which will determine the basic outlook of Christians for many years to come.

It is not at all a new idea. Christ taught it tirelessly under multiplied metaphors: the Kingdom, the banquet, the net and the fishes, the sower and the seed, the temple built of living stones on a single cornerstone and foundation, the shepherd and the sheep, the vine and the branches. Paul taught it to the dockhands of Corinth through the imagery of the head and the members of a single body. The Fathers of the early Church, notably Augustine, made it the vehicle of their extensive teachings in doctrine and morality. But in the ages that followed it was obscured—overlaid through a succession of historical accidents, seemingly, that stemmed from the reaction to the Arian heresy, the new stress on the divinity of Christ, and the virtual effacement in the popular mind of Christ the Mediator, Christ the Head of his body the Church. Now that the Christian people are entering a new world, a world desperately seeking how it may be one, most providentially God our Father has led us back to this ancient yet endlessly vital truth and conditioned our minds to accept it as his blueprint for the good society.

At the head of the community he has set his Son, who justly takes that preeminent place because of his inexpressible dignity and because by his victory on the cross he has won title to it.

> He is the image of the unseen God
> and the first-born of all creation,
> for in him were created
> all things in heaven and on earth:
> everything visible and everything invisible,
> Thrones, Dominations, Sovereignties, Powers,
> all things were created through him and for him.
> Before anything was created, he existed,
> and he holds all things in unity.

Now the Church is his body,
he is its head.

As he is the Beginning,
he was first to be born from the dead,
so that he should be first in every way;
because God wanted all perfection
to be found in him
and all things to be reconciled
through him and for him,
everything in heaven and everything on earth,
when he made peace
by his death on the cross.

Christ is not, however, head of the community only in the sense that He rules it. He is head in a relationship of vitality: the members derive their life from him. "Cut off from me you can do nothing," is the categorical assertion recorded by St. John, who affirms the same thing in a positive way in his First Epistle: "Anyone who has the Son has life." This is obviously a more perfect union than any in which the head and members are bound together simply for the attainment of some good purpose, as in a republic. The common life here is a reality like that shared by the members of the human body. Of itself, moreover, it is vigorous and immortal, since it derives from him who conquered death: "God has given us eternal life, and this life is in his Son."

The members of this community are any who, having been called by God, respond by identifying themselves with it. There is no discrimination based on place of origin, on race or color or endowment. There is no criterion for rank or preferment except that of service to others in love. Like the members of the body, each has his contribution to make to the health and beauty of the whole, so that no member is without dignity. And the community has a single purpose: the worship of God. St. Peter, in what might be called the first papal encyclical, determined this purpose for all times: "You are a chosen race, a royal priesthood, a consecrated nation, a people set apart to sing the praises of God who called you out of darkness into his wonderful light. Once you were not a people at all, and now you are the People of God; once you were outside the mercy, and now you have been given mercy."

The sacred community at worship together is not only fulfilling its loftiest purpose and its holiest privilege, but it is providing for all its members a constant instruction as to its own nature. It is clear, for example, that any child of God, irrespective of nationality, race, color, wealth, or social status, may participate. There will be some gradation or rank, because God Himself has established a hierarchy in the community, but it will be a hierarchy of service, since some of the body's members render a more necessary service than others. One member will read, for instance; another will fetch and carry; others will provide special music. At the head will stand "the president of the assembly," who represents the invisible Head of the community. As Christ gave the most conspicuous and costly service, so he who acts in Christ's name will pray in the name of all, consecrate for the good of all, and distribute to all the wealth of the community. No one will be silent or inactive. A strong, true voice will help to carry weaker ones. A particular talent for, say, decoration or musical embellishment will be offered and accepted to enhance the beauty of the assembly's gift to God. A great silence will fall when God's word is proclaimed in the midst of his people, but then silence will be shattered as the people rise and join all their powers in thanksgiving, in enthusiastic renewal of their covenant with the faithful God. From the ordered collaboration of their worship the community can learn what it is and how it is to work together in other concerns.

It is appreciation of the sublimity of this community worship that will send the members away into their private lives determined to act like redeemed men and women. It is anticipation of their return to participate again in the community worship that will make them want to live Christian lives so that they can add their contribution to the common offering. Unless they are to be utter hypocrites there can be no cleavage between what they profess in their assembly and what they do elsewhere, no taking back from the altar of sacrifice what they put there once for all in willing surrender. Rather, as we pray on Ash Wednesday, they will want their lives conformed in every particular to the symbolic offerings of the community, given in union with Christ its Head. They will practice an asceticism so designed, so focused—a twentieth-century asceticism, if we may so describe it without detracting from its genuinely Christian character. It will have as its serious purpose the gradual purification and enrichment of one's own gift so that the quality of the common gift will be enhanced.

"For their sakes I consecrate myself," Christ said on the eve of his Passion. Here is a real love of one's brethren, given a costly expression.

Along with this there will inevitably be a burning zeal to help one's brethren know and love God better, so that the community may increase in numbers and in charity, and the worship of God may be more widespread and more intense. Such a zeal will find obvious outlets in works of love like instruction, given either as patient answering of questions or as formal education, in efforts to make justice the standard for decisions taken by civic leaders and business executives, in bearing witness amid the vicissitudes of life by serenity, confidence in God's love, and profound faith. Our young people, nurtured from childhood in a loving community atmosphere, will make service, not simply personal advantage, the criterion of their choice in determining their life's work. A more outgoing mercy will characterize our present impersonal neighborhoods, parishes, organizations set up to help the needy. The stranger in our midst, from a foreign country or another race or a dissenting creed, will have a warmer welcome. More and more the community in Christ will be seen and felt to be the shelter against the cold of modern life which God our Father has erected for his children in these times.

It will be difficult for us to unlearn some of the mental habits which militate against the spirit of the true community—the idea of conquest, for example, audible sometimes in statistics about converts or about missionary expansion; any expression of "triumphalism" in word or gesture, in architecture or monuments or music or ecclesiastical pomp. These things offend not only against poverty of spirit and the humility which recognizes that anything it possesses is a gift, but against the community itself, which is Christ in the contemporary world, bent on loving and helping people rather than on vanquishing them. God sought to make Himself lovable; He appeared in this world in "goodness and kindness," his solicitude and courtesy and disregard of merely legalistic barriers between people won hearts and disposed them to accept his service. The Christian community must in the same way make itself lovable to the men and women of our time. "Not by dialectic did it please God to save the world," said St, Ambrose, and the world today will not be saved by syllogisms, either, much less by harshness, or lack of sympathy—sympathy even for that suffering which denies God or mistakes hedonism for the good life.

One certain way to alienate affections is to show no interest in what people are enthusiastic about. The people of our times are enthusiastic about the community; unless we talk to them in this idiom they will not understand us, they will think us out of date and perverse in our lack of decent human feeling. Similarly, people today are justifiably enthusiastic about their achievements in science and technology; research goes on tirelessly in every field; scholars collaborate and applaud one another's success generously as the assault on ignorance continues unabated on every front. Unfortunately, Christian approval for all this has been tardy and grudging. Not only have particular discoveries been challenged; intellectual curiosity itself has sometimes been censured or disparaged, and our participation in contemporary intellectual life is not yet as full as our numbers warrant. Whatever reasons may be alleged to explain or palliate this, it remains true that a community which would appeal to the modern mentality must show itself sympathetic to accomplishments and actively interested in enlarging them.

What the community could well strive to contribute to the welter of emerging knowledge in so many areas is a synthesis, a theology of the temporal order as it exists today. The average Christian life in our time, Karl Rahner has pointed out, is lived in a diaspora, as far removed in time from the Christendom of medieval days as the Jew of Alexandria or Rome was in distance from the Holy City of Jerusalem. And just as God permitted many devout Jews to migrate into the cities of the Mediterranean world so that their Messianic hope might become known to the Gentiles and the way might be prepared for the coming of his Son, so we may think that a kindred purpose impels the penetration of the community into contemporary thought and life. Augustine provided a synthesis for his time; Aquinas, eight centuries later, provided one for his. It is in the nature of syntheses to break down, and any we might construct to-day will one day be found as inadequate as theirs are now, but this should not prevent us from trying to shape a pattern of relevance, a system or disposition of human knowledge and activity as we have come to understand it in the twentieth century and as we know it to be governed by "the God of all knowledge." Perhaps we are in a situation analogous to that of the ancient Jews in their captivity, to whom the exhortation was addressed,

> Declare his praise before the nations,
> you who are the sons of Israel!
> For if he has scattered you among them,
> there too he has shown you his greatness.
> Extol him before all the living;
> He is our Master
> and he is our God
> and he is our Father
> and he is God for ever and ever.

At last I was allowed out of bed, and then, after a month's deprivation, to celebrate Mass, and then, five weeks to the day after my ignominious downfall, I was permitted to go outdoors. It was a beautiful day in February, warm—what the Romans call *La Primavera,* the beginning of spring. Everyone was in the streets; women knitting in the doorways, old men hungrily soaking up sunshine, kids running after balls and getting under the hoofs of horses. Cherry trees were white with blossom; near the Foro Mussolini the lawns were starred with daisies. It was gorgeous, and I walked for ten blocks.

"Any bad effects?" asked the doctor.

"Nope. I was glad to get back to bed again, though."

He laughed. "You're going to that Consistory if I have to push you there in a wheel-chair."

The Consistory, the ceremony at St. Peter's in which the new Cardinals would be "created," had been my target. On the morning of the 21st, I met Fathers Joy, McCormick, and Tom Fay (a contemporary from my Province, at that time a chaplain in Belgium), on the Borgo Santo Spirito, and walked with them to St. Peter's. The streets were crowded with other hurrying figures: nuns, laymen, dozens of monsignori and priests, even a bishop, who was accompanied by a boy of about twelve absurdly got up in cassock, Roman collar, freckles, and huge tortoise-shell glasses—evidently a pupil at some one of the "apostolic schools."

One enters St. Peter's on great occasions as one does a football stadium at home; your ticket tells you which gate you must use. We went in by the "Door of St. Martha," and found ourselves in the transept, just left of Bernini's *Confession*.

When you go to church in Rome you must forget most of the customs and courtesies you grew up with. For one thing, you must cope with the Roman crowds. If you pause to let a lady precede you she will probably tramp on you, even though her dress and appearance seem to mark her as a person of some refinement. After I had been elbowed, shoved, and passed by for some minutes I decided that the proverb "when in Rome" would never in my lifetime be more perfectly verified. I lowered my shoulders as if I were going off tackle and followed Father Fay, my burly blocking-back, as he ploughed open holes for me. Father McCormick, who knew his Rome, was by this time many yards ahead of us.

We came finally to the "tribune," a tier of seats built under the magnificent statue of St. Andrew and only twenty feet from the papal throne. Our tickets entitled us to places here, but the tribune was already jam-packed and we saw the futility of trying to get in. As we turned away we caught sight of an American officer waving us to come over to his section, then we recognized him as a priest and the group sitting in his section as the American chaplains—two hundred of them. So we heaved and tugged our way over there; the vantage-point was not quite as good, but we had an excellent view of the throne if not of the nave, and there were benches to sit on.

It was quite early, with three-quarters of an hour still to go before the Pope's scheduled entrance. All about us people jabbered, laughed, waved to friends. We might have been in a theatre.

"Gosh," said one of the priests, "Never think you were in church, would you? Wonder if anyone is saying a prayer?"

At that point three other priests, sitting silently by and reading their breviaries, raised their heads and looked at him. We all laughed. But the crowd showed little of the propriety we were accustomed to.

Finally huge spotlights began to go on in the nave; there were batteries of them every fifteen feet, and when they were all lighted it looked like morning sunshine. Promptly at nine-thirty (Pius was a stickler, they said, for starting things on time) there was a blare of silver trumpets, and we heard the crowd near the doors go wild. There were storms of handclapping and shouts, *"Viva il Papa!"*

We looked at one another in disgust. These Italians! Had they no idea of the fitness of things?

The Pope's progress down the great nave could be determined by the bursts of applause and cheering that grew nearer and nearer, and our Anglo-Saxon discomfiture grew with them. At last, as I looked by the bald head of the Crown Prince Umberto (now known as "the Lieutenant-General"), the Pope came in sight, vested in red with a tall golden tiara on his head, and riding on the *sedia gestatoria*. We Americans were suddenly fired with the spirit of the thing and shouted *"Viva il Papa"* with all our lungs. The Italians had been right, of course; there are times when we should share in the spontaneity of heaven.

The Holy Father was not long about seating himself on the throne, and Monsignor Respighi, the Master of Ceremonies, quickly got things moving. One by one the "old Cardinals," those who had been created before this Consistory, came up to kiss the Pope's hand and be greeted by him. We had no list of their names, but one of the chaplains near us had studied in Rome and remembered many of them. Each received a wave of handclapping from the crowd, but one in particular was applauded wildly.

"Say, Father," I said, "Who's that?"

"Cardinal Faulhaber," he answered.

When all the old Cardinals had been greeted, a group of laymen in formal dress presented themselves at the foot of the throne. Each spoke for some moments, asking the Holy Father to canonize four "Blessed" whose causes they had investigated and with whose sanctity and merits before God they were satisfied. They were professional lawyers in the service of the Vatican for this type of investigation. They used microphones, and the loudspeakers carried their voices beautifully, but my Italian, alas, was not good enough to follow their speeches. I had good reason for wanting to understand; two of the Blessed, John de Britto and Bernardino Realino, were Jesuits, and the fourth was Mother Cabrini of Chicago.

The most interesting part of the ceremony began with the "obedience" of the new Cardinals. There were many more non-Italians than usual among them, and the Roman crowd was so curious to see the foreigners that each one, as he appeared, stood in a spotlight of concentrated attention. I suppose, too, that in everyone's mind (and especially in the minds of the Romans) there was the absorbing thought, "Maybe this will be the next Pope."

The first Cardinal to mount the long steps to the throne was the Armenian Patriarch of Cilicia, Agaganian. I don't suppose I'd even thought of Cilicia since reading Xenophon's *Anabasis* in second year high school. Inasmuch as he was wearing the Oriental head-dress, and so indicated that he came from an unfamiliar corner of the world, little in the thoughts of Latin Christians, he evoked the glories of eastern Christendom and the tragedy which divided most of it from us. He was followed by our own American, Cardinal Glennon of St. Louis, who in spite of his eighty-three years walked firmly up the steps and drew a hail of applause from the chaplains. It was an applause we repeated, naturally, for Cardinals Mooney and Stritch, but particularly for our Military Delegate, Cardinal Spellman.

But even our enthusiasm for our countrymen gave way to and was lost in the surge of applause that we and everyone gave to certain of the Cardinals: the Chinaman, Tien; the first cardinal from Australia, Gilroy; Mindzenty, the Hungarian who was jailed by the Nazis and now had to fight the Russians, who refused to let him come to Rome until the last moment; and the two Germans, von Preysing of Berlin and von Galen of Münster, who battled the Gestapo and the S.S. for twelve years. Von Galen was a giant, standing about six feet five inches; he had a great white head and shoulders and a face that was grim with purpose; he was nicknamed "the lion of Münster." A story was being told of the day the Gestapo came to arrest him. He asked if he might get his hat and coat from another room, and reappeared in a few minutes clad in full pontifical vestments, his mitre on his head and his episcopal crozier in his hand. "I'm ready," he said. But they didn't dare take him out into the street, where hundreds of people had gathered, in that costume, and left him where he was.

When it was all over the Holy Father stood and, in a voice which rang in every corner of St. Peter's, pronounced the solemn benediction. Then he ascended the *sedia gestatoria* again and was carried out of the church, looking intently and smiling at every group he passed, repeatedly blessing each while the applause and cheers rolled about him. He had been quite tired and suffering from a cold, we heard, but today he had a look of quiet satisfaction, as if he were saying, "this was a good day's work." *Viva il Papa!*

Cardinal Spellman gave the chaplains a luncheon at the Grand Hotel; he talked to us, and so did General Mark Clark and Bishop (later Cardinal) O'Hara and Bishop McCarty of the Ordinariate, later Bishop of Rapid City. For me it was a poor luncheon (I had become wary of overseas foods) but a glorious reunion with many old friends, especially Father Bob Walton. Bob had gone from the 86th Division through Indiantown Gap to the First Division in Europe. Many years later, after he had become a Right Reverend Monsignor and the pastor of a comfortable parish in Kansas City, he threw it all up and went off to supplement the thin ranks of priests in the mountains of Bolivia. But that's another story.

I was not a free man yet. My legs were still untrustworthy, and my icteric index had not yet come down to the point where the medics would let me go. So it was back to bed again, though I was allowed to go out for a couple of hours each day, and gradually for a whole afternoon, or, if there were no tests scheduled, for a whole morning. The hospital was in the least interesting section of the city, so, having conned my map and the only guidebook I could put hands on—it was Father Chandlery's *Pilgrim Walks in Rome,* a gracefully written but now much outdated work, with too frequent lamentations over the *Risorgimento* and too many condemnations of Garibaldi—I would catch the hospital truck to some point in the center of town and start my peregrinations from there. The truck might go in through the Piazza del Populo or it might climb the hill leading through the Villa Borghese, where mimosa and budding willows gladdened the eye, and enter by the Porta Pincia. In the latter case, we would roll on down the Via Vittorio Veneto, Rome's Fifth Avenue, lined by swank hotels and cafes and embassies, and crowded on sunny afternoons with strollers and people sitting in café chairs on the sidewalk.

The truck today, let us say, goes only to the Red Cross at the Piazza Barberini, so I climb out there and begin my walk up the hill toward the Piazza d'Esedra. Elderly but rosy-cheeked women sit on the sidewalks, backs against the buildings, with a little fire and a pan of roasted chestnuts. They are always munching; I wonder if they don't eat more than they sell. In the shop windows are displayed good things of all kinds, but the prices are prohibitive; the cheapest price for a man's hat is a thousand lire, and the hat looks pretty shoddy. Women's shoes start with felt toes and cardboard soles at sixty-five hundred lire and mount up clear out of sight. The windows are very attractively dressed, the store fronts more "modern" than anything staid old Boston had before the War.

A series of billboards at an intersection carry new advertisements, chiefly for movies. *"Ricordate la Famiglia Sullivan?"* asks one, and promises even greater thrills from *Il Canzone del Bernadette*. Another shows four GI's tearing off with rollicking laughter in a jeep; the title for the show is *Un Americano in Vacanza*. Political posters are everywhere, long adjurations beginning *"Attenzione!"* or *"Italiani!"* or *"Romani!"* and signed by every shade of political opinion. A recent poster, plastered over an Army Special Service announcement of a concert held last November and a placard inviting people to visit the crib in one of the churches at Epiphany, reminds all and sundry that in North Africa are the graves of a million Italians, but it doesn't go beyond that, it makes no demands. The Italians love to publish their allegiances; everywhere, and most startlingly on the embankment that confines Father Tiber within bounds, one sees signs chalked and painted on hoardings, blank walls, sidewalks: *"W de Gaspéri!"* *"W la Partita Communista!"* *"M la Democrazia Cristiana!"* "W" is the symbol for *"viva!"* (thumbs up), "M" for *"a basso!"* (thumbs down). One day I saw hundreds of copies of a new poster, a coat of arms with the motto

"*Che ci molesta morrá,*" and it seemed to manifest an arrogance out of keeping with a defeated and disorganized Italy, so I spoke to one of the ward-boys, with whom I was trying to practice my Italian, about it.

"Guiseppe, ieri in tutti le strade del città ho viduto notizie molte," and I described them.

He hadn't seen them, but thought they might be symbols of an "*associazione di buon' ordine,*" because at night there was a good deal of looting, and public sentiment was aroused. But he went out and asked about it, and came back sadly shaking his head, he feared it was an emblem of Fascism—"*per que é ancora molto fascismo in Italia.*"

So I was right in my reaction to fancied arrogance. But, as if to avert rash judgment on my part, he went on to remind me that "*in tutti le gente sono molti buoni e molti cattivi,*" a sentiment I could scarcely disagree with. Poor Italy! One afternoon I took the Via Sistina, a rather narrow street with books and antique shops and genteel millinery stores in whose windows one noted the discreet card,

> English spoken.
> On parle Francais.

At its end was the top of the Spanish Stairs (Keats had his rooms at their foot), with the obelisk that once stood in Sallust's garden and the towering church of Trinità di Monte, the Hassler Hotel and a most impressive view of Rome looking west to St. Peter's. It was the favorite view of St. Ignatius and St. Francis Xavier when they first came to Rome. In the Trinità was a good "Descent from the Cross," and in the adjoining Convent of the Sacred Heart is the "Mater Admirabilis" of which the Sacred Heart nuns at home used to speak. At the Hassler one day I had lunch with a captain who had been a patient in the hospital for a few days; he was in the OSS, and told me some amusing and some rather grim tales about the mores of the very highest Roman society. This was in the days before *La Dolce Vita* published them to the world.

Every street, however unpromising, seemed to hold some historical interest. One day I was returning to the Red Cross by what seemed a rather drab, narrow street, the Via San Nicolà da

Tolentino. A plaque on the wall of one of the buildings caught my eye. "Here," it read in Italian, "the American sculptor St. Gaudens had his studio, 1871-1875." Afterward I discovered in my guide book that the "German College" founded by St. Ignatius to educate priests for Germany was lodged, for a time at least, on the same street. Ten years in this city would mean only ten years of returning to the same places and saying "Well, how about that?"

Back at the Red Cross, one has a coke and waits for the truck. Children, ragged enough in good sooth but assuming a suspiciously pathetic face, hold under your nose a card on which is written in English, "One of seven starving children. Please help." A man comes up and says with oily cordiality,

"Good evening, Captain."

Eying him, you reply "Good evening."

In a moment you learn his racket; he's selling cameos, or silver bracelets. When you shake your head he comes close and whispers,

"You like sell watch?"

"No."

"Sell cigarette, maybe?" (Cigarettes bring three thousand lire a carton in the black market.)

"No."

Coaxingly, "No?"

You point to your pipe. "I don't smoke cigarettes."

"Ah . . . Captain, you like buy German marks?"

You remove your pipe and ask with emphasis, "Now what the hell would I want with German marks? Beat it, will you?"

So he goes off, smiling and bowing like Hamlet's Osric, but it's only a moment before a fourteen-year-old is pulling at your elbow.

"Hey, Joe, you sell American money?"

" Nope."

"I give you good price, Joe. Three hundred lire for one dollar."

"No."

"Aw, whatsamat', Joe? Three hundred and fifty lire?"

Just as you're meditating which insecticide would be most effective, the truck swings up to the curb, you look eloquently at your tormentor and climb aboard. On the Corso a beautiful underslung sports sedan, painted a delirious blue, honks your driver impatiently out of its way and goes by in a sleek rush, leaving you wondering why UN officials must have such luxurious transportation, and who's paying for it. The GI's on the truck are whistling and waving at the pretty girls, and singing their parody of "Lili Marlene,"

> O Mr. Truman, won't you send us home?
> We conquered Naples and we have taken Rome,
> We licked the master race and now there's lots of
> shipping space.
> Oh, please to send us home, and let the boys at home see
> Rome.

Back at the hospital. And so to bed.

My solitary tours continued into March. One afternoon I passed the tremendously elaborate monument to Victor Emmanuel in the Piazza Venezia (the GI's used to call it "the ice-cream monument") and went up the long, broad stairs leading to the Capitol Hill. Here, though the Church and convent of Santa Maria in Ara Coeli rise up with you on your left, you are leaving for the most part ecclesiastical Rome and going back to the Rome of the Caesars. A heroic equestrian statue of Marcus Aurelius stands in the centre of the majestic piazza designed by Michelangelo. Behind it, dominating the hill, is the palace of the Mayor of Rome, built—by Michelangelo also—over the place where the ancient republic and empire of Rome had its record office and where St. Jerome said he saw the record of our Lord's birth still preserved in the fourth century. Completing the square to right and left are museums, in one of them a statue of Constantine, now in fragments, so huge it recalled the lines,

> Why, man, he doth bestride the narrow world
> Like a Colossus, and we petty men
> Walk under his huge legs and peep about
> To find ourselves dishonorable graves.

The other parts of the museum would not be open until two o'clock, the guard told me, so for a moment I hung over the iron railing, looking down on the arch of Septimius Severus and the scattered relics of the Roman Forum, wondering what to do. Then I remembered that I had never really seen the Forum. There hadn't been time in that first crowded week to do more than look at it from afar, as I was doing now. So down I went by the Church of St. Martina and the Mamertine Prison, a filthy little hole where both Peter and Paul had been confined, paid my twenty lire, declined the proffered services of a guide, and entered the Via Sacra. And then it happened. I was mesmerized, bewitched, transported. For one thing, I was almost the only person in the whole area. Rome sleeps from one to three-thirty, and tourists were few with the troops gone home and civilians still denied peace-time travel. It was one of those afternoons the photographers call "cloudy-bright"—not sunny, yet not dull. Nor was it warm, in fact, the breeze was a bit sharp. All in all, it was very much like an afternoon in one of those belated springs we used to have in the Berkshires. When, on the inscriptions and on the signs erected by the Army's Special Service, I saw old names like Vespasian, Augustus, the Vestal Virgins, Minerva, the illusion was complete. I was in the Berkshires of twenty years before, in that two-year period we called "the Juniorate," when the world of Rome and Greece had at least equal reality with the one we were living in.

I pause to amplify and emphasize. Fifty of us seminarians lived on that hill in Lenox. We left it only to take walks through the countryside or to visit the dentist in nearby Pittsfield. We were not allowed newspapers, magazines, new books, or radio. Lindbergh flew the Atlantic, but we learned of it two years later. Murder cases rocked the country, but we never heard of them. We had visitors once or twice a year. Meanwhile, except on holidays, Latin was the everyday language about the house, savagely disputed debates questioned whether Caesar or Cicero had done more for Rome, public expositions of Virgil's poetry were given, and light reading was advised along the lines of Mommsen's *History of Rome*. During the years 1927-1929 we were a colony of imperial Rome, far indeed from the mother country, but, like the English colonists in India or Jamaica, trying for that very reason to be more like the mother country than the land of our exile.

I wandered happily on, wishing with all my might that one of that old crowd could be with me, and finding that fragments of the old sonorous verse and prose were rising unbidden to my lips. They were, to be sure, fragments that are the ragtag and bobtail of memory for anyone who has ever studied the classics, but they were sweet because of the unexpected flush with which they returned, and I (being safely alone) chanted them aloud:

> *Jam satis terris nivis atque dirae*
> *Grandinis misit pater, et rubente*
> *Dextera sacra jaculatus arces,*
> *Terruit urbem.*

How Father Bob Reynolds (himself an old Army chaplain, I thought with amusement) used to shout that! And how he used to make us write imitations of it!

"Gentlemen," he would plead with us, "This Latin prosody is a wonderful thing. Don't let it become a lost art!"

But he was in his grave, alas, and the prosody was—or soon would be—in with him.

> *Integer vitae scelorisque purus . . .*

> *Si quid est in me ingeni, judices—et sentio quod sit*
> *exiguum . . .*

Wonder if the old smoothie thought anyone believed that?

> *Mitte sectari rosa quo locorum*
> *Sera moretur.*

Old Horace seemed to have lingered longest in a fast-failing memory. But what wonder? He was the father of so much grace, the inspiration of so many subsequent *lyra elegantiarum.* There is nothing in the Cavaliers to surpass the hopeless tenderness of his lament:

> *Quis desiderio sit pudor aut modus*
> *Tam cari capitis?*

There were the lines that really meant something at Shadowbrook, where spring was so very late and the ice clung to the lake one year until April 27th:

> *(Solvitur acris hiems grata vice veris et Favoni,*
> *Trahuntque siccas machinae carinas . . .)*

The second line always made me think of Jim Geary and Joe Shea pushing the rafts out into the lake for the swimming that most of us would do much later, when the water had warmed up. Could that, and all the irrecoverable youth and rapture (tempered by despair not seldom!) really be twenty years ago, and I be actually in the old, old Rome, saying of my private loss what Tennyson said of the world's?

> Now thy Forum roars no longer,
> Fallen every purple Caesar's dome.

I went on and up over the ruined Palatine, a succession of unrevealing excavations, and came back to wind my way around the far end of the Forum. Here I was a bit annoyed to find the seventh-century church of Santa Maria Antica, with its Byzantine frescoes— a Christian intrusion, if I don't speak irreverently, on the paganism of the place and my mood. But I was soon back on the Via Sacra, and there the perfect quotation, part of which I had recalled and the rest of which I had been struggling for, leaped into my mind:

> *(Ibam forte Via Sacra, sicut meus est mos,*
> *Nescio quid meditans nugarum, totus in illis.)*

Only, thanks be to Jupiter and Juno and Mars and Vulcan and Horace's own Lares and Penates, I didn't have to wrestle with the bore who made his walk wretched. Mine was one of those perfect things.

In spite of such diverting expeditions, things were beginning to pall. The hospital routine was dreary, the lack of privacy grating on the nerves.

> *(La chair est triste, hélas, et j'ai lis tous les livres.)*

Father Bob Gannon, then President of Fordham University, came to see me; Father Jim Geary and Bill Graham, both home and out of the Army, wrote good letters; Father Bill Keleher, the new President of Boston College and a classmate of my own, wrote a heart-warming letter assuring me that my room and my job were both waiting for me. My feet were beginning to get itchy again.

By great good luck I got a ride one morning on the hospital truck straight to the church of St Agnes, out on the ancient Via Nomentana. I had always had a strong attraction to Agnes, because of Keats' and Tennyson's lyrics, perhaps, but much more because of her story. In the Breviary on her feast, St Ambrose sums it up in a style reminiscent of Tacitus:

> Tradition says that she suffered martydom at the age of thirteen. Detestable, indeed, the cruelty that spared not so tender an age, but great was the power of faith that could find even children as witnesses.

Here, after her martyrdom, Agnes' family buried her, and Constantine built in the fourth century the church which, with some restoration from time to time, is as he left it, a very attractive little building built on the level of Agnes' tomb, so that it must be approached from the street by a long flight of almost fifty marble steps. On the way down one sees on the walls of these steps inscriptions and Christian symbols found in the catacombs beneath the church and fastened here.

A very pleasant, lovable old man, Father Stefano Mancini, one of the Canons of St. John Lateran, showed me around the church and the catacombs. He spoke seven languages, and his English was almost faultless. I liked his story of how Cardinal Stritch, of Chicago, had begged the Holy Father to give him St. Agnes' as his titular church; the Cardinal had a great devotion to her, and Agnes was his mother's name. The Canon also showed me the tiny church of Santa Costanza a short distance away. On the altar there was an inscription saying that it enclosed very rare relics indeed: some of the Blessed Virgin's hair and clothes worn by our Lord in his infancy. Father Mancini shook his head over this; he had asked, he told me, to have the inscription removed, but got nowhere.

"Well," I said, "If it's a superstition, at least it's a pretty one."

"In the Middle Ages," said Father Mancini, "people made legends about the holy ones they loved. St. Jerome and the fly that perched on the line where he had stopped reading, so that he could always find his place. St. Bridget who hung her cloak on a sunbeam so that it wouldn't get dirty on the ground. Nowadays people make legends about the things *they* love. In the States you have Santa Claus, no? And Mickey Mouse?"

I knelt to pray for a while, but was distracted, pleasantly, by a persistent and very heady fragrance. Flowers on the altar, I supposed. But it was Lent, and the altar and the sanctuary were bare. Maybe a flowering shrub in the garden; mimosa has a pungent scent. At last I walked around the entire church and looked into the garden. No flowers anywhere. Odd. Father Mancini had gone, so I couldn't ask him about it, but that afternoon, when I got into bed and reached for Chandlery's guide-book, I read that "visitors to St. Agnes' Church are often mystified by a pervasive fragrance that seems to have no visible source." Oh, well, another superstition, no doubt. Except that I had stumbled on this one myself.

> There are more things in heaven and earth, Horatio,
> Than are dreamt of in your philosophy.

Father Daleiden dropped in to see me at the hospital.

"What are you going to do when you get out?"

"I don't know, really," I said, "Go down to the casual camp at Naples, I guess, and ask for a berth on a ship."

"Do you like that prospect?"

"It gives me the horrors. Two or three weeks in virtual captivity, then fourteen days or more of seasickness for my poor old stomach."

"Well, what would you like to do?"

"Oh, I'd love to see a bit of northern Italy, then go up the Riviera to Lourdes, then to Paris . . . maybe England and Ireland . . ."

"Tell you what," he said, "I have some time coming to me, and I have a jeep. Why don't we just take off next week and see how far we get?"

I thought the idea was fabulous. Father Vincent McCormick, when I went to the Curia to say good-bye, didn't think so. He listed all the dangers of the road, my still incomplete convalescence, the discomfort of travel in a springless, unheated jeep.

"Very imprudent. Very."

I went across the corridor and knocked on Father Zack Maher's door.

"Just want to say thanks and good-bye, Father."

"How are you going home?" he asked.

I told him. "Father McCormick doesn't think it's such a bright idea."

Father Maher was too charitable to snort, but I could read between the lines.

"Ever seen those places?" he asked.

"No."

"Expect to be in Europe again soon? "

"Heck," I laughed, "It took me thirty-eight years to make it the first time."

"Then go ahead," he growled.

I was formally discharged from the hospital on March 15th, and celebrated by attending Mass at the Sistine Chapel. It was the seventh anniversary of the Holy Father's coronation, and he had invited Cardinal Agaganian to offer the Mass in the Armenian Rite. The Sistine is a small chapel, and after space had been set aside for the ministers of the Mass, for the Holy Father and his entourage, for the Cardinals and the accredited diplomats, there was very little room for small fry like myself. I squeezed in somehow and stood with my back to the rear wall. It was a thrill to see the Pope again, and the brilliant assembly in that gorgeous setting. The vestments worn by the Armenians were glorious—green-gold, canary, a ravishingly delicate blue. And, since it was an Oriental rite, much more elaborate and pageant-like than our sober Roman rite, it was not long before clouds of incense obscured Michelangelo's paintings on the ceiling, while really rich singing poured on the ear all during Mass. The Holy Father had obviously studied the rite; he knew exactly when to stand, when to sit. Unfortunately, I knew no Armenian, and had stupidly neglected to bring with me a translation of the liturgy. After two hours of standing and wondering exactly which point of the Mass we were at now, I began to feel some interior qualms. It wouldn't do, I told myself, for an American officer to get sick here, so I edged toward the door. A Swiss guard smiled knowingly at me.

"Troppo cantare, eh?"

"No," I said, *"Malato."*

His handsome face became solicitous. *"Ah, malato?"*

And he propelled me through the crowd out to the stairs where I could sit down. It struck me for the first time that this must be why so many good people back home chose to attend the low Mass in the basement and "duck the High Mass" upstairs. When they did go to the High Mass, they were taken, as I had been today, by the pageantry and the music, but after an hour or so of wondering exactly what was going on in that unknown tongue and those graceful but perplexing rites, they wanted out, as the GI's put it. *Troppo cantare.* It took us an awfully long time to do anything about it.

I was billeted again in the Majestic Hotel but spent most of my last days with Father Tom Nolan, whose kindness followed me even here, and Father Bobby Dyson. The latter had been on summer holidays in England when the war broke out, and stayed there during it. He had some vivid descriptions of the London fires and the nights in the Underground during the blitz. Over dinner at the hotel I put to him the question the Catholic GI's had been asking me.

"This is supposed to be the headquarters of the Church, isn't it? Then why don't the Italians go to Mass on Sundays?"

Father Dyson shook his head. "It is not the same."

"Why isn't it the same? They have the same obligation."

"You must live here for a long time before you understand."

"Okay, you've lived here a long time. If you understand, tell me about it."

He shook his head again. One could not compare, he said, Italian with American Catholicism. The Italian Catholics had never been a minority, never been scorned or persecuted. They felt no need to be militant; it did not seem to them that they were on parade, that their Church was being judged by their actions. They kept the Faith according to their lights; there had been many saints among them, and their family life was the best in the world. The foreign soldiers did not see this side of them at all.

"Well, there should be one law for everyone."

He smiled. "You have been around the world. Haven't you found that people differ very much, one country to another? Even at home, think of the cultural differences between a Yankee farmer in Maine and a half-Spanish ranchero in New Mexico. There can't be one law for everyone, at least in matters of church discipline, and maybe we have made too much of going to Mass on Sunday, not eating meat on Friday. Some of our people at home seem to think that if they keep those commandments they have fulfilled the whole law. Our Lord never said 'By this shall all men know that you are my disciples, that you eat fish on Friday.' He said, 'By this shall all men know that you are my disciples, that you have love one for another.' I sometimes think we have emphasized the wrong things."

I walked halfway home with Bob, and parted reluctantly from him in the Piazza Navona. He always seemed to me, even in the two or three years he had taught at Weston, a pathetically brave figure, very lonely. Now, at the Biblical Institute, he loved his books, but it was a desperately solitary life. Some day, perhaps, I shall write a chapter on the scholars like him I have known: warmhearted, exquisitely cultured and courteous, hunched for years over a desk, known only to a handful of students. Bobby came home many years later, when his days were numbered, and died among us. I like to think of seeing him again.

My Roman honeymoon was over. It had expanded from the ten days I anticipated to almost three months, and during that time a good deal of the gloss had been rubbed off the bride. I couldn't avert my eyes forever from the dirt, the noise, the venality of so many, from street-urchins to empurpled monsignori, the suffering of the poor. But I have visited no other city where I was so much at home in the spirit, whether my mood was antiquarian, or religious, or companionable. I have never seen a city in which people could live a more completely human life, on every level. Some day, perhaps, the supermarkets and the gas stations, the neon lights and billboards, the tracts of endless apartment houses would move in and reduce all that rich variety to dreariness. *Tu autem, Domine, miserere nobis.* I paid one last visit to the Piazza d'Espagna and looked at the clumps of yellow mimosa on sale at the foot of the Stairs, at the horse-drawn carriages, at the spire of the Trinità, at the roofs and domes of the city. Then it was time to go.

Ave, Roma immortalis!

CHAPTER 19

The Grand Tour

THE JEEP HAD A WOODEN HOUSING BUILT OVER IT, AND A HEATER after all, so we managed to keep warm on the road, but no ingenuity on the part of builders or renovators could supply for the missing springs. We jolted over 1,131 miles in the next eight days, and I discovered that much of my lost avoirdupois had come off the bones I sat on. Deprived of their normal cushion and exposed to the inequities of mountain roads, the bones set up a very articulate protest.

There were four in our party: Father Daleiden, Father Joseph Forst, a Chicago Franciscan who had come over with Cardinal Stritch for the Consistory and stayed to see the Franciscan shrines in Italy, Ted Wietrop, a G.I. who was Father Daleiden's assistant, and myself. Father Forst, in spite of his sixty-two years, was the merriest of the group, and had us crying with laughter over his stories just when the miles were longest.

We rolled through Terni and Foligno into Assisi and lunched belatedly off K-rations as we sat on the steps of Santa Maria degli Angeli. Then we visited the Portiuncula Chapel and the room where St. Francis died, before going up the hilly road to pray at his tomb in the great church there. Brown and black habits and tonsured heads were everywhere, but the abiding impression was of serene and even radiant faces. Something of Francis, that most perfect disciple of Christ, lingers still in the Umbrian air. One could wish, perhaps, that the enormous piles of masonry might have been foregone in favor of a more characteristic simplicity, but the huge crowds of pilgrims must be accommodated somehow, and it was natural for St. Francis' sons to want to glorify their father and the city that held such precious memories. Still, there was a more convincing authenticity at San Damiano, the convent of St. Clare, where we saw her cell, her garden and her place, marked with a cross, in the tiny refectory. From the little porch, where, the story ran, Clare had held up the Blessed Sacrament to frighten off Saracens who were invading the convent, we looked down into the valley and saw hundreds of fires twinkling in the dusk. Tomorrow would be St. Joseph's Day, and it was Umbrian custom to light "St. Joseph's Fires" on the Vigil.

We knocked at the door of the hospice maintained by the American Sisters of the Atonement. The Superior was cordial but apologetic.

"We'd be glad to give you dinner, Fathers, but there is no food in the house."

"That's okay, Sister. Could we have a large pot with some hot water?"

She was mystified but gave us what we asked, and we dumped C-rations into the pot to produce a steaming bowl of pork and beans, very welcome on that chilly evening. As the aroma drifted through the house, I'm sure that the hungry Sisters' mouths must have watered. When we drove off we left a case of C-rations behind us, and felt we had appropriately ushered in the feast of St. Joseph the Provider.

It would be my privilege to visit Assisi again and again in the years to come, and, finding always the same quiet, radiant gladness, I would understand why Alfred Noyes, imagining in his novel a world almost utterly destroyed but trying to start life over, located its beginnings in Assisi. What does go into the makings of Christian serenity, one wonders. It could not be indifference to the misery of others, or any madcap insouciance in the face of the mystery of one's own life and death. How does one balance time's inexorable ravaging of his energies, friends, substance, against the hope—aptly compared in the Gospel to the steady burning of a candle against the dark—which knows in whom it has put its trust?

> For though the fig tree blossom not,
>   nor fruit be on the vines,
> Though the yield of the olive fail
>   and the terraces produce no nourishment,

Though the flocks disappear from the fold
    and there is no herd in the stalls,
Yet will I rejoice in the Lord
    and exult in my saving God.
God, my Lord, is my strength;
    he makes my feet swift as those of hinds
    and enables me to go upon the heights.

Evenness of temper, a natural sanity and willingness to accept reality, would not seem able of itself to produce the specific Christian serenity, though it might be a valuable predisposition. It might issue, instead, into mere stoicism, a hardening of the heart. And if such psychological harmony were required, how many could be expected to have it? Most of us suffer from some imbalance: wracking by emotions out of control, a withdrawal into the self-fortress in order to avoid being hurt, a blind and greedy reaching for goods that, even by the standards of common sense, are not worth the efforts expended on them.

On the natural level, what would seem necessary is self-mastery, discipline. We must put ourselves far enough away from things to survey and esteem them correctly, then make our choices, and school ourselves by stern exercise to live by them. This may strike many of us as harsh, but the alternative is endless drifting, discontent, futility. Even granting that choices are made correctly, however, and adhered to rigidly, something else would seem to be needed. All the determination one can muster will not guarantee that things will go as one plans them. What happens when our dream turns to ashes? When what looked like a legitimate and even laudable ambition is frustrated? How does one keep from going sour, cynical?

Ultimately, by a Franciscan recognition of one's poverty, perhaps. Poverty of knowledge: we cannot see from our precarious perch in the centuries the vast plan of God, or how our little lives contribute to it. Poverty of wisdom: we do the things we should not do, and fail to do what we should. Poverty of purpose: we yield to sloth, or to self-pampering, just when we should be strongest. Poverty of resources: our lives are affected by forces that simply lie beyond our capacity to control them.

But this poverty would only make us wretched unless we could draw without limit on another's riches. "He who was rich became poor, that by his poverty we might become rich." Where I am ignorant, God knows all things. Where I am stupid, he is unerring. Where I falter, he is constant. My resources are meagre; his are infinite. Moreover, he loves me and has gone to staggering lengths to prove it. If I trust him, if I lean on his fatherly strength, am I unreasonable?

On the surface of the Christian soul, as on the surface of the sea, there will be turbulence from time to time. In the depths there should be peace—not, God help us, the stagnant torpor of stoicism, but the serenity of tides and currents setting powerfully to their end, and conscious that they will attain it.

Loreto was next on our itinerary, and we found it by going over the Apennines. The basilica was large, with an elaborate facade, and set in an impressive piazza. An ordination was going on of Capuchins who served the basilica, but, after watching for a few moments, we sought out the *Santa Casa,* the little house in which, according to pious legend, the Lord had been conceived, and which had been miraculously wafted by angels from Nazareth to this very spot in order to save it from profanation by the Saracens. Now it was encased in richly carved marble behind the main altar, with many hanging lamps and the inscription *Hic Verbum caro factum est.* The legend is generally discredited today, I think, but probably it served a purpose in a less critical age. The Incarnation did take place after all, and in some such unpretentious cottage as this, among the unsophisticated. One could easily detach and lay aside this pretty fable, like a tinsel wrapping, and ponder with fresh awareness the stupendous fact.

I had read somewhere that Richard Crashaw, of the English school of "Metaphysical" poets, had in middle life become a priest and served here, but I could find no tomb or plaque in the basilica, and none of the clergy had ever heard his name. Early in the afternoon we took the winding road again across the mountains to Foligno, then turned north, skirting Perugia, to Riccio and Arezzo and, at last and in darkness, to Florence at nine o'clock, tired, cold, and hungry. In the morning, after Mass in the Franciscan church oppo-

site the Excelsior Motel and breakfast off K-rations in Father
Daleiden's room, we did some languid sight-seeing. There was so
much here—Dante and Michelangelo, Giotto and Donatello and
Raphael—and our schedule permitted so little time to see it that our
efforts were half-hearted. I remember magnificent mosaics in the
ceiling of the baptistry at the Duomo, Andrea del Sarto's frescoes in
the courtyard of Santa Maria Annunziata, the statuary in Santa
Croce—along with the tombs of Machiavelli and many modern Fas-
cists. We had a glimpse of the Ponte Vecchio and then drove up
through olive terraces to Fiesole. I enjoyed seeing the convent of
St. Bernardine there, his cell and the garden with its canaries, but it
was the view that made me decide I would choose Fiesole above all
other places in Italy to live in. Florence and the valley of the Arno
lay at our feet, smiling, warm, memorable. It was in that valley, I
recalled, that Shelley first heard the West Wind blowing.

Off we went, to Pontassieve and the rugged Passo di San
Benedetto, over the mountains again, the road looping-the-loop like
a roller coaster and we looking up at snow-capped peaks and down
into bottomless ravines. At dusk, we came through Forli into Ravenna, and found a group of Polish soldiers who spoke German and
showed us to the Byron Hotel, refusing indignantly to accept any
remuneration for the service. They were certainly out of place in
Italy, we thought. The sheets in my bed were clammy and cold, and
the room was an ice-box, so I slept in a GI blanket that Father
Daleiden had thoughtfully included in our baggage.

I myself would probably not have included Ravenna in our
tour; I had missed or forgotten its historical and artistic significance.
St. Apollinaris and St. Vitalis had never been very distinct on my
horizons, nor Galla Placidia, either, and it was only after I had puzzled over the name *"San Apollinare in Classe"* that I recalled that
the seat of the Roman Empire had been for a time in Ravenna. I
was unprepared, therefore, for the beauty of what I was to see—the
lovely hexagonal church of San Vitale, for instance, with its columns of Greek marble opening like the pages of a book, and the
magnificent mosaics at San Apollinare and in the tomb of Galla
Placidia.

At San Vitale I was curious about the balcony that looked down on the church and asked our guide what its purpose had been.

"Matroneo," he sniffed.

Ah-ha. The women in those days had been relegated to the balcony, and men had carried on the worship of God. Times had changed, I reflected. If public worship now depended on the activity or even the presence of Italian men, there wouldn't be very much.

Dante had eaten the salt bread of exile in Ravenna, and died there. Later the repentant Florentines tried to recover the body of their illustrious citizen, but the Ravenna Franciscans stole it from the side of the tomb which abutted their property, and held it until 1865, when a sumptuous memorial was erected and made a national monument. The cities of Italy vied with one another to decorate the tomb for the sexcentenary in 1921, and I was glad to see American names on the list of foreign contributors: Henry Van Dyke, Charles Grandgent. But when World War II broke out the body had been placed in a new casket and buried under a mound of earth. Dante was to have rest neither in life nor in death.

I offered Mass that morning in the Cathedral, where I found the cleanliness of the altar and the linens unusual and refreshing, but was disconcerted when the server, following the universal Italian custom, washed my hands at the Offertory and then threw the water on the stone floor. In the sacristy guest-book I was pleased to find the names of two old friends: Father Anselm Strittmatter, the Benedictine liturgiologist (1933), and Father Robert Gannon, S.J. (1928). Over coffee at the hotel, afterward, I talked to several Italians who were afraid of Russia and the *Communistas*, and wanted to know what America planned to do about them. I shrugged. The Russians, our erstwhile "gallant allies" were showing themselves very intransigent, very bellicose, and we on the other hand, were demobilizing our armies and dismantling our war machine as rapidly as possible. I could offer little comfort to the Italians, who had had no real stomach for the late War and who envisioned themselves, justifiably, caught between the two giants if war should come again.

There were enough reminders of war along our road to Ferrara and Padua. Mussolini's wife was still interned in one of the concentration camps we passed. We came often on burned-out tanks, strafed automobiles, bombed freight cars, shattered houses. Roads and bridges had been patched by the engineers of the British Eighth Army. Soldiers' graves were frequent—a stick with a German helmet hung on it was their only identification. I thought with contrition and a plea for help of all the widows and orphans west of the Rhine, and of the futility of the whole sordid business.

In Padua we visited the enormous basilica of St. Anthony, where Lenten devotions were going on and a Dominican with a strident voice but obvious popular appeal was the guest preacher. At the Franciscan house there was embarrassment at the sudden appearance of four unexpected visitors. They were pressed for room; would I mind very much going to the Jesuit residence? I was delighted to learn that there was a Jesuit residence in the city; it was a small house where the Provincial of our Venetian Province lived, together with some scholastics and lay students who were at the University. I had a most cordial welcome from the community, and enjoyed recreation, when, on hearing my halting Italian, they shifted into Latin. The Father Minister, grateful but perplexed, brought in a can of beans from the case I had given him,

"*Be-ans?*" he asked, staring at the label, "*Nescio be-ans. Suntne pro usu interno vel usu externo?*"

One of the scholastics was concerned about the Communists he was meeting in his classes. They argued, he said, that the American people were dissatisfied with their form of government, and that this was evident from the labor strikes that were then frequent and violent in the United States. What was the best answer? I asked him if he had talked with any American soldiers.

"Very many," he replied.

"Did you ever meet any who didn't want to go home?"

"Oh, no!" Then he nodded his head slowly. "I take your meaning."

We set off for Venice the next morning. It was all there, just as it had been described and painted and photographed for us in a thousand books and pictures, but it was incredible, just the same—a city risen from the sea. We sailed up the Grand Canal in one of the launches that serve as trolley-cars for the Venetians, passed under the Rialto, and debarked at the Piazza San Marco with, I'm sure, our mouths wide open. There was the Lion of St. Mark on his pedestal, the Byzantine domes and richly frescoed facade of the Cathedral. There were the thousands of pigeons, fed by the populace and chased by romping dogs and children; scared by some distant explosion, they rose in a beating cloud of wings. We went through the splendid Palace of the Doges and crossed the Bridge of Sighs to see the dungeons, looked into the glass shops, gave tablets of Domino sugar out of our K-rations to the kids who begged the rich Americans for cigarettes and gum. Then we crowned the experience by taking a gondola across to the Church of Santa Maria della Salute and on a tour of the canals. The Grand Canal, our GI guidebook assured us, was "a rubber-neck's paradise"; we passed the houses were Browning died, where Byron began *Don Juan,* where Wagner composed the second act of *Tristan and Isolde,* and then the house of Desdemona and the Ca d'Oro or Golden House, cited by our GI scribe as the most typically Venetian and elegantly Gothic palace in the city and built in 1421.

The sun had come out for a while during the afternoon, but it was still raw and cold when we got back to Padua, and my room was so bleak that I finally went looking for the kitchen. The Father Minister, coming in to make sure that preparations for dinner were going well, looked his surprise at seeing me by the stove.

"*Sicut Sanctus Petrus, Pater,*" I said, "*Stans et calefaciens se.*"

He laughed, but I wondered what had become of the "sunny Italy" I had always heard about.

March 23rd was a long day in the jeep, broken only by a stop of three hours in Verona, where I came to the end of a long pilgrimage by visiting the tomb of Romeo and Juliet. The guide we hired to show us the tomb was an expansive and voluble Veronese, who with heroic gestures and in explosive Italian acted out all he told us, including the whole action of the play, and ended by quoting Shakespeare in Italian: "And I will raise her statue in pure gold!" He dismissed with scorn the story of the reconciliation between the Montagues and the Capulets—"a fantasm of Shakespeare's!" The sarcophagus he showed us as Juliet's coffin was disillusioning; it was shaped like a tub, the edges broken, the top gone. I had a chilly suspicion that it was in reality a horse-trough now serving to bolster the legend and satisfy romantic tourists, but he piled up authenticating detail: the sarcophagus had lain in the vault until 1842, when John of Austria (what was *he* doing here, I asked myself; I thought he was at Lepanto) stole the coffin-top, which was the golden figure of Juliet, and scattered her remains, dead then for five centuries. That would explain the present disenchanting appearance of the coffin, he said. Hmmm.

The Germans, our guide told us, had used the vault as a central telephone exchange from 1943 to 1945, and he himself had taken shelter there against American bombers. On two occasions near-misses had bounced him "like a rubber ball" from one side of the vault to the other. He gave us when we were leaving tiny pendants as souvenirs. On them was inscribed "*Se ami, credi in Giulietta,*" which made me think of the poignant lines in the play:

> But trust me, gentlemen, I'll prove more true
> Than those who have more cunning to be false.

"Now," said the guide, "You must go back and touch the pendants to the coffin of Juliet." We asked the reason for that.

"Ah, it is a *bella cosa.* You will be lucky in love."

When we indicated that this was a bit peripheral to our main interests, he was really distressed, seized the pendants and ran back to the coffin, then returned with a smile of pure benevolence. He had insured our future.

We saw the reputed house of Juliet, small, very old, but with an attractive balcony that made it the plausible site of the balcony scene in the play. Romeo's house was behind the tombs of the Scaligers, hard by the Church of Santa Maria Antica, on a dirty street, and a goldsmith had his shop on the first floor. We went to the Church of St. Zeno the Moor (there was a statue of him, with a black face), where the pretended funeral of Juliet was said to have taken place; it was in the Capulet section of the town, and there were many walls along the street such as Romeo might have leaped over when he gave Mercutio and his other tormentors the slip. Then we saw the Arena, a cone-like stadium which was started under

Augustus in 20 B.C. and finished by Diocletian in 280 A.D. Dante, who lived for a time in a room under the Arch of the Scaligeri, was supposed to have got his idea of the circles in Hell from standing at the top of the Arena and looking down. Verona—"fair Verona, where we lay our tale"—was badly smashed up; it had been an important railroad center, and our bombers visited it often. I remember lecturing after the war on *Romeo and Juliet* to a class of freshmen, all but four of whom were returned veterans, and describing the city as I had seen it. Next day one of the class brought in some snapshots of the city as *he* had seen it, from the nose of a bomber.

It was a long, long ride on aching bones through Brescia to Milan; we passed through Dezenzano near Catullus' Sirmio—

> Row us out to Dezenzano,
> To your olive-silvery Sirmio—

along the shores of Lake Garda, where Generals Clark and Truscott of our Fifth Army had their headquarters, and sumptuous yachts as well. The Albergo Nord in Milan was the "officers' hotel"; we found its supper of hamburg and beans a little plebeian after some of the meals we had had, Italian style, along the way, but the rooms were warm and we had a chance for a bath.

Next day we saw the magnificent cemetery, filled with such bronze and marble statuary as made it seem rather a museum than an acre of repose for the sleeping dead. Hundreds of people were passing in and out, and nuns asking charity for the poor were six-deep at the gate. We looked in on the Scala (Toscanini was coming back in April) and the Sforza Castle, and then went to the old Church of Santa Maria delle Grazie, in whose adjoining Dominican friary is the original painting of Leonardo's *Last Supper.* Painted in tempera on a wall of the refectory, often restored, it was now faded again. Save for this wall, almost the whole building had been destroyed by bombs.

The Duomo was staggering. Our guide told us there were twenty-three hundred statues on the outside walls; they produced a fabulous effect of stone lace. We admired the stained glass, and the guide said that the secret of its blues had died with the artist who created them. Solemn Mass in the Ambrosian Rite was going on at the high altar, presided over by Cardinal Shuster, and I wanted very much to watch, but the guide insisted on our rushing through to see a gas station where, after he had been shot with his mistress and some of his ministers in a town forty miles away, the bodies of Mussolini and the others were brought and hanged head downward. The place was chosen because it was here that fifteen young Partisans, a year or so before, had been shot without a trial, and the people venerated them as martyrs.

After the Special Service tour was over our party went to the Church of St. Ambrose, which the Saint himself built and where he baptized St. Augustine. The bapistry and font, both greatly restored, were shown us, as well as the pulpit from which he preached his sermons—eloquent and hard-hitting, as I knew from my breviary. Under the pulpit was a grotesque comic, a statue of Arius bent as if he were supporting the pulpit on his back; the vanquished heretic made to support the weight of orthodox doctrine. Over the main door was a tapestry showing Ambrose at the door of his cathedral refusing entrance to Arian soldiers, who lay prostrate at his feet, and I remembered Newman's description of the scene.

In the crypt beneath the church we came on what was to us a gruesome discovery. The skeleton of Ambrose, flanked on either side by the skeletons of Sts. Gervase and Protase (martyrs whose relics Ambrose had recovered), lay in gorgeous vestments, exposed for veneration. Does such an exhibition do honor to the saints? We Americans are so afraid of death, so determined to conceal corruption, that we are probably not the best judges. The Italians are a more realistic people. We returned to the crypt next morning to offer Mass; visiting priests were accorded the privilege of reading the votive Mass of St. Ambrose, but it was the lovely Feast of the Annunciation, and we were sure that Ambrose himself would have urged us not to pass that by.

We crossed the mountains for the fifth time on a tangled ribbon of looping road, and reached Genoa early in the afternoon. There my very pleasant companions turned south to Pisa, Leghorn, Florence, and Rome, while I went in search of the Railway Transportation Officer to get a "warrant" for a ride to Marseilles and

Lourdes. But the British had largely gone home, and the RTO was a civilian who spoke English with an American accent.

"Where are you from in the States?" he asked me.

"Boston," I replied.

"Boston!" he shouted. I thought he was going to embrace me. He had been in the Boston Symphony Orchestra, went on the Orchestra's world tour in 1936, married in Italy, and his wife coaxed him to stay. Now he was aching to go back. There was no difficulty whatever about the "warrant"; in fact, he gave me a compartment to myself, and pasted on its glass door a sign which read *"Riservato al Commando Alleato."* I wandered about Genoa for a couple of hours; the people in the streets were shabbily dressed, and, I was told, very hungry. Food was scarce and impossibly dear. Movies were playing, though; *L'Incendio di Chicago, con* Tyrone Power, and Bing Crosby in *La Mia Via.* The city had been shelled by the British "Home Fleet" in 1941 and heavily bombed later; the Cathedral of San Lorenzo was damaged and other churches, as well as the Opera House, totally ruined. I dropped in at the Jesuit residence and chatted with the Father Minister and seventy-five-year-old Father Luchetti; then it was train-time.

There were no bulbs in the electric sockets in my compartment, so, after staring dreamily out the window until the light faded, I fell asleep with my head on my duffle-bag. It was one o'clock in the morning when we arrived in Ventimiglia, the border-town and the end of the line for the Italian train. I stumbled into the "Hotel Suisse," got a room, and went on sleeping until nine-thirty the next morning. The past week had been dream-fulfillment but a little strenuous for one so recently put back into circulation.

I sauntered down the main street, having foregone breakfast, to the sea, and there walked what must at one time have been the social promenade of the town. But there had been a German garrison here, and the French fleet had stood off and blown it—and most of the town—sky-high. The principal buildings were wrecked, homes were in ruins, palm trees were sheared off as I had seen them in the Pacific. The sad futility of it was apparent, but I was in one of those relaxed moods when past and future matter little, and one accepts gratefully the good things offered by the present. The warm sunlight was comforting; I listened to the rolling surf and inhaled greedily the salt smell of the beach. Fishermen had their nets out and were mending them at the far end of the promenade; a boy was playing with two dogs on the rocks; a very sweet and unmistakably Italian woman's voice was singing behind a high wall. When I went back for dinner I had no need of the waiter's *"buon' appetito."*

Not all the "displaced persons" were in camps. On the beach again after dinner, I talked with a man who had been an officer in the Greek army. He was captured by the Italians in Albania, fought with the Partisans against the Germans, and had just been discharged. There was no reason, he said, why he should go back to Greece; his wife and child were killed in a bombing, and anyway, he was afraid of Russia. So he planned to go to Brazil, where he hoped to resume his profession. And what was his profession? He was a teacher of ballet.

On the French train there was a burly sergeant from Providence, returning from a furlough.

"Where ya headed, Father?"

"Marseilles," I said.

"Ever been there?"

"No."

"Skip it. It's a bandit town."

I respected the practical sagacity of sergeants. "What would you recommend?"

"Get off with us at Nice. I'll fix you up with a room; then you can go on to Lourdes."

In that fashion I crashed the haut monde, the refuge of English novelists: the Riviera. There were a hundred and eight hotels in Nice, and the U.S. Army had taken over all of them as a rest and recreation area. At the height of its "season" there were over fifteen thousand GI's there. I was quartered in the sumptuous Hotel Negrisco, and for my billet I was given the bridal suite. "Here's a fine revolution, an' we had the trick to see it."

Father Jerome Toner, a Benedictine whom I had met in Rome, was the area chaplain, and offered kindly to show me the sights next morning. We drove down the Promenade des Anglais in his jeep after he had obtained passes from the MP's for us to visit Monaco, which was an independent principality and off-limits to GI's. There were three roads to Monaco, varying in altitude; we went over on the lowest and came back on the middle road; the highest was closed by landslides. There was no taxation in Monaco, no industry. The whole state lived off the Casino and its visitors. We visited the cathedral and the aquarium, the latter an interesting collection of fish, nets, harpoons, stuffed seals, and then one of the management, a friend of Father Toner's, showed us around the Casino. Even at that early hour several tables were busy, playing *trente-et-quarante,* black jack, and other games. twenty-four thousand francs was the limit in one room, sixty thousand in another. In a third room, not functioning at that time, the sky was the limit. I was struck by the intentness of the players, men and women; our presence was not even noticed. The entire Côte d'Azur had an air of brittle unreality, expensive honky-tonk; Ventimiglia and the Riviera dei Fiori were much more to my taste.

On the train to Marseilles I found that my sergeant was still a power to be reckoned with. Although the train was crowded, I was once again assigned to a reserved compartment. But two priests came by looking for seats, and I invited them to join me. They were Polish, so our conversation was a polyglot mélange of English, Latin, French, and Italian. One of them had been confined in Dachau for five years; he said that everyone sent to the concentration camp had been required to learn some trade. His had been masonry, and he worked for many weeks on a project whose purpose he did not learn until it was finished. It was a gas chamber for mass executions. He also told me that more than a thousand Polish priests had been executed or died of hardship at Dachau.

At Marseilles I found that the RTO at Nice had called and asked that I be put on a sleeping car for Toulouse. This was becoming too easy! At five o'clock next morning the conductor wakened me. I checked my luggage at the station and set off into the black and unfamiliar streets of the city, looking for a church. The first I came upon was built over a garage; its bells rang but its doors did not open. It was almost seven o'clock when I spotted a priest hurrying along and with his aid found the Church of St. Sernin, where I managed to convince the astonished and doubtful clergy that I was a priest in good standing and celebrated Mass. At a half-awake café nearby I persuaded the hostess to give me a ham sandwich, since she had nothing that an American would consider breakfast food, and drank two cups of what (humorously, no doubt) she referred to as coffee. It had the merit of being hot.

The town was a rather drab provincial capital that made me think of Flaubert, but I did like the names of the streets: *"Rue Bertrand de Born, Troubadour, XIIIme Siecle," "Rue d'Hirondelle."* Other streets were named for *"Écrivains"* and *"Bibliotheques."* I found myself worse off for language than if I had never tried to speak Italian; the two got hopelessly mixed up, and I was constantly saying *"Grazie"* when I should have been saying *"Merci."* A little knowledge is a dangerous thing.

Four hours on another train put me in Lourdes, a corner of Languedoc that must have been as unknown to fame as Nazareth until Our Lady came there. In this season especially, before the pilgrims began to arrive in their thousands, there was a great and contemplative silence, an atmosphere of prayer. All the shops were in the village, outside the area of the shrine; there were no amusements except two small movies. Convents of about thirty religious communities, together with an orphanage and hospitals, surrounded the shrine; behind them were only the mountains of Languedoc and the far, snow-capped peaks of the Pyrenees. The grotto was amazingly simple: just a cleft in the rock, the familiar blue and white statue of Our Lady, and an altar beneath. I'd seen more elaborate imitations at home. The church built above and around the grotto was large, but its architecture and the local gray stone of which it was built were not pretentious. I was glad I had made the long pilgrimage across France, and felt a deep, serene gladness and confidence, as if I were indeed in the presence of the Mother of God.

Mr. and Mrs. Felix Douly ("Dooley" a hundred years ago) were a French-Irish couple who operated a religious article shop. They got me a room in the only hotel open during the winter and arranged for me to celebrate Mass at the grotto in the morning. A bishop from Colombia preceded me at the altar, and whispered the text as if he were alone in the world. When my turn came, and he knelt in the sanctuary, I read the Mass in a loud voice, hoping he might take the hint, but probably I succeeded only in distracting him from his highly private devotions. There was no active participation except by the server; everyone was praying the rosary, and I saw only one missal beside the one on the altar. That was propped up in front of an invalid in a wheel-chair, piloted by a nun. The invalid must have been either a rugged individualist or a liturgical pioneer. I wanted to ask which, and to shake hands if he were the latter, but he was wheeled off while I was removing the vestments. A pity— "liturgists" were a rare species in those days, and we drew aid and comfort from one another.

I made the Stations of the Cross up a steep hill that afternoon, and visited the museum of the shrine, where I saw a few relics of St. Bernadette (her habit and shoes), pictures of the great pilgrimages, and pictures also (some before-and-after) of the people who had been cured during the past ninety years, together with their medical records and affidavits by physicians. That night I slept well, although from the many bites on my body I decided next morning that I had not been the only living being in the bed. It seemed more than a little incongruous that, of the many beds I had occupied since leaving home, the one at Lourdes should have been the only one that left its mark on me.

On the train to Paris I chatted pleasantly with Lieutenant Henri Aragnol of the French Navy, who shared his ration cards with me so that I could buy bread and cheese for lunch. The view from the windows was interesting: the rugged mountains in the south-east, the industry around Bordeaux, the rolling farms near Poitiers, the neat gardens, row on row, and separated from each other by ancient walls, as we approached Paris. Spring had arrived with me; I gratefully shed my topcoat, first, and then the sweatshirt I had been wearing since I left Rome. And I looked with unqualified approval on the bright pink blossoms that hung from peach trees in the orchards along the way.

Paris, even in the aftermath of the war, was dazzling. I hated to admit it, but I found the city far more beautiful even than Rome. Rome could not match those avenues, vistas, parks, glorious buildings. Few Italian exteriors were impressive; their beauty, like that of the King's daughter, was within. During the next few days, operating at first from my luxurious billet in the Hotel Louvois and then from the prosaic ATC barracks at Orly Field, I took the Red Cross bus and did the standard tour: the Place de la Concorde, the Madeleine, the Eiffel Tower and the Arc de Triomphe, the Invalides and the Tomb of Napoleon. On my own I spent hours in Notre Dame, the Latin Quarter, the Tuileries and the Louvre, Montmartre, Versailles. But it was sight-seeing, not a home-coming. The French I asked for directions were courteous—much more so than I was to find them ten years later, when they made it evident how much they disliked Americans—but I missed the warmth of the Italians, who had been *troppo gentili,* easy to engage in conversation, responsive. I may have been by this time, also, a bit jaded by all the great palaces and temples I had seen since November. And, finally, I ran into a little difficulty in negotiating my further travels—not serious, but enough to make me remember Egypt.

I took the area chaplain to lunch and sounded him out on getting me passage to England. He was chilly—the first priest I had met who was not spontaneously helpful.

"But look," I said. "My orders tell me to go home. They don't set any date for arrival. And if I go to England I'm still on my way."

He said it was not standard operational procedure for troops on the Continent to go home through England.

I tried again. "I've got sixty-nine days' accumulated and terminal leave coming to me. They won't be any use back in the States. I've taught English literature for six years and I expect to go back to it. England is right over there. Why shouldn't I take my leave time in England?"

There would be problems about food and currency. He advised me that I might get into trouble. The safest course was to go down to LeHavre and ask for a ship. I couldn't budge him, and the conversation turned to other things; he described his seminary days in Europe, and told me of a long trip he had made through Austria and the Balkans.

"For about a month," he chuckled, "No one knew where I was—not the rector, or the provincial, or anyone else."

"Hmmm. Then you should be sympathetic with this safari of mine."

"Oh, no. I wasn't in the Army then."

We parted, and as far as he knew I went to LeHavre. Actually, I went out to Orly Field and talked to the chaplains there. Father Jim Kirwan of Hartford and Father Collins of Los Angeles took me to dinner with Lieutenants Andy Kelly of Pittsburgh and Cliff Bueche of Texas.

"Don't worry about the area chaplain," they said. "He's bucking for a silver leaf. We'll see that you get to England."

I met a Captain Lauer, of the Military Police, who gave me a ride to Versailles. We stopped on the way to see his outfit, the Prisoner-of-War Information Bureau, and I was again amazed at how well we treated prisoners. Captain Lauer showed me statistics on the mail handled, the money and personal property put into safe deposit, the records kept up to date. Precious little like what was done by the Germans for us—much less the Japs. Whenever we entered a room the first P.O.W. to see us would shout *"Achtung!"* and the purely mechanical, instantaneous response was astounding.

At the palace I declined the services of a guide and proceeded at my own pace, using a guidebook and tagging along sometimes with groups of school children who were being lectured on what they saw. I noted the same sequence of reception rooms, drawing nearer and nearer to the awful presence on the throne, that I had seen at the Vatican, the Quirinal, and Castel Gandolfo, and my democratic sense was getting tired of it. The decoration was splendid, but the grounds outdoors, with their artificial ponds, canals, and terraces, suited my mood better, and I walked to the Petit Trianon and to Marie Antoinette's little hamlet, an idyllic pastoral village with all the lovely features and none of the drawbacks of rustic life: the pond and the mill, the columbarium, the Queen's boudoir-cottage. It was pretty but fragile, and the Mob had smashed *that* way of life in the Revolution. I could not wish it back.

I went to Chartres and fell in love forever. Here was a shrine of Our Lady that gathered up all the poetry and pageantry of the High Middle Ages and translated it into a soundless music, into stone that sang her praises. The superb glass had not yet been restored to the windows from which it had been taken during the War. When I saw it ten years later I realized how much I had missed on this visit; Chartres without its windows is like a lovely human face without eyes. But there was more light in the cathedral, and I was able to see better such things as the glorious frieze that runs around the back of the choir, depicting episodes—real or tenderly imagined—in Our Lady's life.

Pelting rain and strong winds on April sixth made it doubtful at first whether the flight that Father Collins had arranged for me would take off. When the wrack did begin to blow away our pilot, Lieutenant Ransford, suddenly received new orders sending him elsewhere, so he turned over his wife to me, as he put it, for safe-keeping. She proved a charming girl, South Carolina born, who had spent four years of the War in England. Our crossing, bumpy at first, became smooth as we climbed above the clouds, and the sun came out as we flew over northern France. At the Channel near Dieppe there were bomb-craters and shattered homes. I kept watching for but missed the white cliffs of Dover; then we skimmed over neat fields and a corner of London to an airport at Bovingdon. I had no currency, so Mrs. Ransford paid for my sandwich and coffee; I enjoyed listening to the English accent on every side, "This way, please. Right you are." I took leave of Mrs. Ransford at the Athenaeum Hotel and went looking for the London Area Chaplain, Father Vin Hart, a Redemptorist, who gave me a warm welcome and took me to dinner at the officers' mess with Father Durand, of the LaSalette Fathers, Father William Walsh, of Portland, Oregon, and Father Steve Barron of San Francisco. They proposed, then, a hockey game at Wembley Park between a team of Americans, champions of the ETO, and a Canadian team. The Canadians won handily, of course, 14-3, but it was good to see the game and note the good humor of the English.

"Oh, lovely, lovely," said the chap next to me, applauding a play. Then there was an announcement over the loud-speaker, "Will the parents of John Sykes kindly come at once to the box-office and re-possess their son?"

I chewed the rag with Fathers Hart and Durand until after midnight in my room at the Cumberland Hotel, near the Marble Arch.

It was not far from Tyburn Tree, where another wily, slippery, but far holier Jesuit, Edmund Campion, had, after he was betrayed, been hanged, drawn, and quartered for the Faith. Getting into the country had been for me absurdly easy, after all, though I had had a moment of acute discomfort when my orders were asked for and inspected. One more land-fall and I could go home content.

In the morning I walked to our church in Farm Street and celebrated Mass. The roof of the church had been blown off during the blitz, but a temporary one was already in place. I talked with Brother Taylor, the refectorian, Father Devas, the Superior, and Father Martin D'Arcy, the Provincial. Meeting Father C. C. Martindale, whose lives of the saints I had devoured when I was a novice for their literacy and sprightly style, was an unlooked-for pleasure. He was then old, and suffering from circulatory troubles, but cheerful and very cordial.

"You've been a chaplain? Let me shake your hand. You've talked to men. I never have."

He was thinking of the barrier to intimacy supposedly created by our wearing of clerical garb and suggesting, perhaps, that a real apostle would dress like other men. I had reservations on this; for one thing, I knew how many distinguished men and women he had led to faith, and the story was already current of how, returning to England from Denmark, where he had been interned during the war, he had heard the confession of every Catholic sailor on the ship— even burrowing on hands and knees into a coal-hole to catch up with one reluctant mariner who was trying vainly to elude him. Nor had I experienced any great difference in the essential attitude toward me of men in the service from what I had known as a civilian. It seems to me that whatever awkwardness the Roman collar may cause in the beginning of a relationship can be quickly dissipated by genuinity and warmth. Clothes do not make the man, and putting on a necktie is no guarantee of apostolic effectiveness. I was ready to admit even then, however, that I vastly preferred a black suit, or even an Eisenhower jacket, to any kind of skirt, and that included the skirt of a cassock.

On Mount Street I saw a milk-wagon full of bottles, and reflected that I had not tasted or seen milk for two years. Berkeley

Square, like most public parks and gardens, was devastated—torn up for anti-aircraft guns, bomb shelters. There were many gaping holes among the buildings fronting the streets, and many buildings still standing which were completely gutted inside. The Red Cross tour that afternoon took us to Hampton Court Palace, built by Wolsey and given by him to Henry VIII. It had been the home of all Henry's wives from Anne Boleyn on, and then of Edward VI, Mary, Elizabeth, James I, Charles I, Cromwell, and William and Mary; Victoria had given it to the public. We had an informed and entertaining guide, though I remarked his use of the characteristic English understatement: the paintings were "not bad, really," and the stained glass in the Great Hall was "rather decent." I liked better the exclamation of a sixteen-year old girl who jumped up on a wall to look out on the "Long Water," "Oh, a smashing view, wot?"

By good chance I met in a restaurant Captain Tim Lynch, a young Irish medic serving in the British Army and waiting for transport to India. He thawed out over Welsh rarebit and beer and became a wonderfully genial companion during the next few days. We went together to the Tower, where we joined a group shepherded by a hearty guide in the uniform of the Tower Guard: a vivid red suit, with "G VI R" on the breast, and an Elizabethan hat. He showed us the "Bloody Tower," where the two princes were killed by order of the Duke of Gloucester, and many notables, including our Father Parsons, Guy Fawkes, and Sir Walter Raleigh, had been imprisoned. We saw, too, the "Traitors' Gate," through which passed St. John Fisher, St. Thomas More, and Mary Queen of Scots, and the spot where Anne Boleyn and others of Henry's unfortunate cast-offs had been beheaded.

In Westminster Abbey, which we thought a glorious building but somewhat anomalous—more a hall of fame than a church, and full of memories of the departed faith—our guide was a seventy-one-year-old former lecturer at the University of London, a retired officer type who might have stepped out of Thackeray. We liked the Byzantine style of Westminster Cathedral. Some of it was still unfinished; marble, for instance, was being laid on the pillars only as funds permitted. To tell the truth, I rather regretted the marble; the red brick pillars had a virility that appealed to me. All in all, the

Cathedral was a pretty substantial achievement for a Catholic population of only a couple of million.

My evenings were given over to a splurge of theatre-going that made up for the enforced abstinence of two years. I started on Sunday with a screen version of *The Corn is Green,* a fair play that was lifted to excellence by the acting of Bette Davis. On Monday I saw *The First Gentleman,* a period piece about the reign of the Prince Regent before Victoria. The story was slight but the cast, especially Robert Morel, was superb. Tuesday evening Tim and I saw the Old Vic Company in the first part of *Henry IV.* The performance was professionally smooth and flawless, with Lawrence Olivier a superb Hotspur and Ralph Richardson a magnificent Falstaff. On Wednesday we went back to the Old Vic, this time for an unforgettable presentation of *Oedipus* in Yeats' translation. Olivier had the title role, Sybil Thorndike was Jocasta, the chorus was first-rate. The house was plunged in silence during the entire play. I was astounded by the power of the old piece, which I had read in Greek years before, but which had never before moved me to the pity and fear specified by Aristotle as the truly tragic emotions. The evening was then nicely rounded off with a presentation of Sheridan's *The Critic,* with Olivier as Mr. Puff. I was amused by several penetrating comments (like the remarks of Puff that proved our modern publicity men rather old hat, after all) and I had my own memories of Father Bob Reynolds' mad production of the play when we were Juniors. It was good comic relief after the tragedy. On Thursday Father Hart and I went out to Hammersmith to see Paul Vincent Carroll's *The Wise Have Not Spoken;* the title, I believe, was taken from one of the Padraic Pearse's lyrics. I had liked Carroll's *Shadow and Substance,* but this play disappointed me. Carroll took up O'Casey's old burden and gave the palm to Communism. The acting was not very good, and the characters were distressing.

The next four days were given over to expeditions that were ridiculously short in view of all there was to see, all I wanted to see, but I felt, still, an alien without an authentic visa in this country, and I was never sure that my credentials would not be challenged. I would have to give some of these places what my grandfather, when he was sweeping the floor, used to call "a lick and a promise," and hope to come back for a careful inspection later. My first choice was Canterbury. It was April, after all, and the unfailing freshness of Chaucer's spring-song came to mind, as it always does:

> Whan that Aprille, with his shoures swote,
> The drought of Marche hath perced to the rote . . .

I took the train, feeling that it would be more appropriate to join pilgrims floundering through the deep spring mud of His Majesty's Highway. Two English soldiers shared my compartment, but they were cold as ice, so I admired the "tendre croppes" of the Kentish countryside in silence; there were miles and miles of hops and orchards. The ancient Cathedral had been damaged somewhat by bombing, but things were being put to rights slowly—there was a great shortage of manpower in England now. I admired the lovely nave, the choir, the sanctuary, the spot where St. Thomas had been martyred and the shrine whose stones were worn by the knees of a million pilgrims. St. Anselm had been buried here, and the Black Prince, Lanfranc, Henry IV, Cardinal Pole; there was the chair of St. Augustine, now used for the enthronement of the Anglican Archbishops of Canterbury. The cloisters of the "Precincts" were so beautiful that I hated to leave them.

On the train again next day, I read the *Catholic Herald,* and happily came on a reference to St. Edmund's House, so I sought out the place in Cambridge and was most cordially met by Father Britt-Compton, of the Westminster Archdiocese, who was teaching geography at the University, and Father John Petit, the Rector. I was to meet the latter, subsequently Bishop of Menevia in Wales, often in later years, at the International Liturgical Congress at Assisi in 1956, and at both sessions of the Council, and when he came to America seeking alms for his impoverished diocese. Father Britt-Compton expended every energy to show me the principal sights of the University; the lovely "courts" or quadrangles, the beautiful Gothic colleges (with Saxon or Norman survivals here and there), the "Backs" or lawns of colleges along the Cam, the "Halls" or refectories. The chapel of King's and Trinity Great Court were particularly impressive, but best of all was the academic peace of the whole place in the bright spring sunshine. It was easy to understand why so many had loved Cambridge with all their souls—and Oxford, too, as I decided when I went there on the following day. (I have never forgotten how Newman, before leaving Oxford forever, kissed every tree on the grounds at Littlemore, a gesture that might seem weakly sentimental if one had never seen Oxford or known Newman.)

At Campion Hall, the Jesuit residence, I was nicely received by the Master, Father Thomas Corbishley, and the Bursar, Father James Cammack. A scholastic, Mr. Winterborn, kindly took me to see Magdalen, Merton, New College, "Tom Quad," "the High," "the Meadows." After supper I talked in the handsome common room with a stimulating group; Father Lester King, who was lecturing at the university on psychiatry, Father Andrew Gordon of the Catholic Worker's College, Father Kevin Booth, a historian, Colonel Ted Larkin, an Australian psychiatrist with the British Army, Mr. Mahony, who was painting murals in the Lady Chapel, and Father Leslie Walker, who was writing a book on Machiavelli. It was all pleasantly topped off by a walk with Father Cammack along the tow-path in the moonlight.

Campion Hall itself was memorable; it had been designed by the architect Edwin Luytens, who had died only two years before. Frank Brangwyn's "Stations" in the chapel had a wonderful freshness and power. And Father Martin D'Arcy, the founder, had brought together an amazing collection of pictures and statues—gifts from his friends—to adorn the house. The vestments were valuable and historically interesting, if not especially suited to the liturgy. I was glad to see autograph poems by Maurice Baring and Chesterton on the sacristy walls. The names in the guest book convinced me that living here would be of itself an education.

CHAPTER 20

A Little Bit of Heaven

THE TRAIN TO HOLYHEAD TWO DAYS LATER WAS CROWDED WITH people going for an Easter holiday to Ireland, and I stood during most of the eight-hour trip. On the ship the faces were markedly Irish, and soft accents replaced the clipped British speech; it was not long before I, too, was inverting sentences and repeating the verb instead of saying "yes" or "no." After all, I came by it naturally— or, as my aunt used to say, "Sure, where would he left it?" Indeed, I was deeply moved when we made out the coast of Ireland; except for one uncle and aunt, I was the only one of the family, on either side, who had ever visited the ancestral home-land. We docked at Dunleary and rode by electric train to Dublin; at the gate there was a sea of eager faces, searching for loved ones, and I wished some-one were waiting for me. It was the last twinge of loneliness I was to feel in Ireland.

There were curious glances as I made my way through the crowd since I was the only one in uniform; the British, when they came here, were required to wear civilian clothes, and Americans of the military were rare. On O'Connell Street the shop windows were strong on local products but short of imported goods—"hello," I said to myself, "what's this?" In a window there were displayed such pastries and other delectables as I had not seen for many moons, and especially not in England. I went in and had a feast, thinking meanwhile of the ironies of history. A hundred years be-fore, my ancestors had fled the Great Hunger brought about when England seized the wheat crop and the potatoes failed. Now Eng-land was half-starved and Ireland was flowing with milk and honey.

At our house in Upper Gardiner Street, when I found it, I asked for hospitality. But a provincial congregation was being held there, and the Provincial himself came down to apologize. Every room was taken; would I mind very much going to the house on Lower Leeson Street? I said I would be glad to be accommodated anywhere, and a few minutes later I had one of the warmest welcomes of my life at the residence of our Fathers who were teaching at University College. Next morning the Superior, Father Frank Shaw, professor of early Irish history, and Father Con Murphy, just back from five years' service as chaplain with the British Eighth Army, gave me a tour of University College and University Church, built by Newman a hundred years before. We crossed Stephen's Green, then, to see Nelson's Pillar and the Post Office where Pearse and MacDonagh and the other poets of '16 had made their glorious, hopeless last stand against the Black and Tans. It's a great pity, of course, that the Pillar has had an "accident" since and has "fallen down." These things will happen.

I had lunch at our house with Father Aubrey Gwynn, the historian, Father Kennedy, an ornithologist and also Minister of the community, and Father Connolly, the editor of *Studies*. It was more sight-seeing then; Trinity College, where I saw the Book of Kells and other beautiful things, the National Museum, where the Tara Brooch and Celtic crosses and many relics of the Irish past are on display, and the Royal Irish Academy.

A wild idea entered my head at this time; why not fly home from Shannon? But I hadn't the price of the flight, if I were to travel privately, and—as I learned on discreet inquiry—to charge the Army for it would involve such delicate and protracted negotiations that I abandoned the idea. I'd have to go back to England, and perhaps even to France.

But I was not going anywhere until I had visited Tipperary. My mother had sent me the address of her aunt, whom she had never met, so I took the train at Kingsbridge and traveled through country that the pouring rain made ineffably dreary: farms and bogs, with an occasional station in some isolated hamlet. The connecting train at Thurles was slow; it covered twenty miles in two hours. The engine was burning "brickettes" of pressed turf in place of coal, which was at that time unobtainable, and we stopped, I thought, at everyone's back door for a chat with Pat or Molly. At Clonmel I alighted and looked about. The station was there, but nothing else except a horse and wagon. The driver a pint-sized, unsmiling man, looked down on me.

"Well," I said, "Where is it?"

"Where's what?" he answered.

"Clonmel."

"Down yonder."

"How does one get there?"

"Well," he said with careful mimicry, "If one wishes, one gets up on one's wagon and one rides down."

I laughed and climbed up beside him. But he did not relax. After a time I asked,

"Is that the parish church?"

"It is," he said, and his use of the verb gave his answer a truculence which I am sure was less real than apparent.

"Tomorrow is Holy Thursday, isn't it? I think I'll just join the congregation."

"Why wouldn't you?" he asked.

"Well, I'm a priest."

There was a long silence. Then "You're a *what?*"

"I'm a priest."

"A *Catholic* priest?"

"I don't know any other kind," I said, a little impatiently, and jumped off the wagon at the Hotel Ormonde. It was not his fault, of course, that he had never seen a priest in anything but black, and I should have been more tolerant.

Lisronagh, where my aunt lived, was five miles out in the country, and the only way to get there was to hire a car and the driver who went with it. But the driver was not altogether sure of his way, so we stopped at a crossroads store for directions.

"Would any of you know Mrs. Tynan?" I asked.

"Just take the next turn and go to the end of the boreen," they told us. I didn't notice particularly at the time, but as soon as I mentioned my aunt's name a small boy took to his heels. He was her great-grandson, and he was running to tell her that a man in a strange uniform was asking for her. So when I reached the little house, looking, with its thatched roof, like a set for an Irish play, she was at the gate. And she resembled my grandmother, who was wonderfully kind to me when I was a little boy, so much that my heart turned over. There was the same gray hair, pulled straight back and tied in a knot at the back, the same severe black dress, the same high buttoned shoes. But then I didn't know how to introduce myself.

"Are you Mrs. Tynan?" I asked.

"I am," she said, and again the manner of repeating the verb instead of saying "yes" made it seem as if she were saying, "if it makes any difference to you."

"You had a sister, Catherine, who went to America many years ago?" I said clumsily.

"I had."

"And your sister had a daughter in America, also named Catherine?"

"She had, then."

"Well." I said carefully, "Her daughter, Catherine, is my mother."

"Oh, my dear," she said softly, and embraced me.

The poverty of the little house was very real. There were only three rooms: two bedrooms and a larger kitchen-living room. The floor was stone; the hearth served both for warmth and cooking. We sat down.

"You'll be telling them in America how you sat with the old woman by the fire," she said.

"Have you always lived here?" I asked.

She told me that she had been born here, as had my grandmother. Their parents had built the house after their marriage. *Their* parents, and God knows how many generations before, had lived in a similar house thirty yards away.

"And I'm going eighty-three," she said, "Would you believe it?"

I wouldn't have. She was bright and keen, her sight and hearing were perfect, and her little figure was slender and erect. Moreover, although in her eighty-three years she had never been further away from this little house than Clonmel, she was interested in affairs, and listed to the "wireless" every day.

"That Mr. Truman of yours," she said, "He's a fine man."

Harry had mentioned God in several of his speeches.

"I had thirteen children," she told me.

"Thirteen!" I exclaimed. "Where did you put them all?"

"Ah, sure, dear, I didn't know myself sometimes where they all were. And after the thirteenth child was born, my man left me."

I was shocked.

"And I never saw him again. Now wasn't that hard?"

There wasn't a trace of bitterness in her voice, and I thought suddenly of my mother's sweetness in disappointment and sorrow. What a lovely strain of womanhood this was.

After some time she asked, "Had you not a brother who was a priest?"

I realized at once that my uniform had disguised me from her, too, but, God forgive me, I teased her, and said no, which happened to be true.

"You had not. I thought . . . When your Uncle John was here he gave me a photo. I'll get it." She went off and rummaged in a drawer, and then came back with a photograph. It was a picture of my family, taken on the lawn at Weston the day I was ordained.

"Now," she said, "Is that not your mother?"

"It is," I said.

"And is that not your father?"

"It is, indeed."

She wrinkled her forehead. "And you had no brother who was a priest?"

At last I took pity on her. "Look at the young priest in the picture, Aunt Stasia."

She looked at it.

"Now look at me."

She did, but nothing registered.

"Well," I said, "That's *me*."

"Oh, my dear," she breathed, "Is it a priest you are?"

"Of course," I said, "Didn't you see these crosses on my coat?"

"Ah, dear," she said, "I thought you were wearing them for protection."

We had tea, then, with my aunt's youngest daughter, who was the only child now at home, and her two sons.

"Jimmy will be in soon," said my aunt.

"Who's Jimmy?" I asked.

"Ah, he's blind, poor little fellow. And we do for him."

The "poor little fellow" turned out to be a seventy-nine-year-old neighbor. Another visitor was a young woman who had taken in six of her dead sister's nine children and was "doing for" them. She had the two oldest of the six with her, pretty girls of eight and nine, and they sang songs for us in Gaelic.

"Well, those songs are lovely," I said finally, "But I don't understand Gaelic. Do you know any songs in English?" They sang several, all of them songs of grief and exile ("lonely I wan-durred") and lamentation. At last I said, "Of course Ireland has had sad days. But it's going to be better now. Do you know any glad songs?"

They couldn't think of one, and I recalled that description of the Gael:

All their wars are merry and all their songs are sad.

I came back the next day, bringing two pounds of black market tea. Tea was a necessity in the Irish household, but at that time they could buy only three-quarters of an ounce a week. We all went off to "the Forge," to meet the other side of my mother's family. Here my grandfather had been born, and many generations before him; the family name of Smith derived from the Forge. Back at Aunt Stasia's, I asked if there were not some little thing I could get for her. She said she would like to buy a headstone for herself and those buried before her in the Powerstown cemetery. I hope it is under my stone that she sleeps there today.

By the grace of God I met at breakfast two gentlemen from Dublin who became my dear friends: Professor Hamilton Delargy and Senator Michael Hayes. Delargy was the famous folklorist who had brought together an archive of material relating to Irish social history that is unsurpassed in the world; he lectured at University College. Hayes, after a youth spent fighting the wars of Irish freedom, became Speaker of the Lower House in the Dail and then Senator; he was also professor of French Literature at the University. They were in Tipperary to visit Delargy's "collectors" there—people who gathered songs, anecdotes, proverbs, riddles, and the like from the lips of the old folk, writing them down or taping them on recorders. There wasn't much sympathy for this activity in some quarters; I overheard a backstairs conversation between the maids in the hotel:

"Who would those two be?"

"Oh, they're down from Dublin to listen to the blather of the old crones."

"Faith, they'd be better settin' out a few potatoes."

They invited me to join them on Good Friday for a tour of the countryside, and we drove between walled estates and by an occasional Norman-looking castle to the "V," a road that twists up through the hills toward Waterford. The weather was sharp and frosty, but bright, and the country was absolutely lovely, with green fields, lanes, brooding hills, farmyards and animals, and primroses as yellow as anything in Wordsworth. On the road we met horses, donkeys, and, now and then, a Morris or an Austin. Clonmel, they told me, meant "swarm of honey"—a pretty name—and "Slievenamon" meant "Hill of Fair Women." In my ignorance I had believed that the latter name held a reference to "the Good People," who, under King Brian Connors, lived in the interior of the mountain, but, after meeting my Aunt Stasia, I was ready to accept the real meaning. We stopped near the summit and climbed Sugar Loaf Hill, whence we had a splendid view of southern TIpperary's smiling farmland.

"No wonder they fought for it," said Delargy. He told us that a cairn of rocks we came on was probably a burial site going back to pre-Christian or even pre-historic times, and that men had lived in this part of Ireland for at least seven thousand years. I put in my pocket a small stone to give my mother. When I was a small boy we went to a concert and heard a tenor sing "In the Valley Near Slievenamon," and she told me that was where her parents had been born.

I would have liked to drive on to Lismore, thirteen miles further, where my father's people had lived, but the round trip would have strained our slender "petrol" ration, so we decided to visit the Cistercian monastery of Mount Melleray and follow the Stations of the Cross. The Father Guest-master took us on a tour of the monastery. He had a curious, faraway voice, like the ghost in Hamlet, and he took mournful pains to impress on us the austerity of the monastic life.

"This is the dormitory," he said. "I don't know why they call it that. We don't sleep very much." and a few minutes later, "This is the dining room. I don't know why they call it that. We don't eat very much."

"Gosh," I muttered to myself, "I hope he doesn't take us to the chapel."

At the end of the tour Michael Hayes, as the parliamentarian among us, undertook to thank the Father Guest-master for our visit. It had been most instructive and edifying, he said; we would long remember this Good Friday. And he hoped he was not presumptuous in expressing the special appreciation of his friend from America, Father Leonard.

"*Father* Leonard?" asked the Guest-master.

"Yes," answered Michael, enjoying himself. "He is a priest and a Jesuit."

I could see the Guest-master running back mentally over some of his earlier remarks, but he recovered quickly.

"A Jesuit, eh?" he wailed. "They say that's the higher life, but of course we think ours is the higher life."

Michael and Hamilton snorted periodically all the way back to Clonmel. "That stuff about 'the higher life'—where does he get it?"

But before leaving I remembered that Tim Lynch had told me to ask for his brother if I ever got to Melleray. He was a pleasant-faced novice in a habit that had certainly seen better days.

"You don't know me," I said to him, "But I toured London with your brother, and we became good friends."

"How do you do?" he said in the same faraway, detached voice that the Guest-master had used. Maybe, I told myself, they picked up that tone from chanting the Office, or from reading at table. Maybe—I hoped not—it came from an unconscious disdain for the concerns of worldly men. I decided, at any rate, that I had no vocation for the Cistercian life.

That evening I walked with Michael and Hamilton along the banks of the River Suir. It was immeasurably peaceful; a swan floated by, four oarsmen and a coxwain passed us in their shell, a young man and a girl—"walking out," in the local phrase—went up the path, their heads close together. All of an April evening.

I left word to be called at six-thirty, but no one called, so I entered the church in time only to hear the last three "prophecies" of the Holy Saturday liturgy. I was distressed by the inattention of the congregation—one old lady was piously making the "Stations"—but more by the complete lack of desire on the part of the officiating clergy to make the rite intelligible, or even audible. We heard nothing except a confused, distant murmuring at the blessing of the font; there were no lights at the Gloria. Even the wonted thrill of *Vespere autem sabbati* was missing. It poured rain all day; I considered that the Irish have a beautiful green island, but the price is a bit high.

We had high tea at Michael's home in Dublin, and a memorable evening of good talk and laughter with his wife and children and Mrs. Delargy. Father Shaw took me next morning—Easter morning—to see Milltown Park, our seminary. The sun shone intermittently, but it was raw and cold, and my teeth chattered during lunch so that I could scarcely eat. So Father Shaw built a fire in my room, and stayed to talk; Father Gwynn joined us, and the discussion ranged far and wide: Irish nationalism, the inability of the present government to keep young men and women from migrating in search of opportunity, the career of DeValera, how much time should be given by Jesuit professors to out-of-class contacts with students. After dinner and in celebration of the day, there was coffee and punch (Father Connolly was always delegated to make the punch, since he had a heavy hand) in the recreation room. At the end of the evening I stood and said how grateful I was for their warm reception of me and how much I hoped I could return one day. Whereupon Father Connolly rose to his feet and delivered an oration: it had been their distinct pleasure, he said in spontaneous but rolling periods, to entertain such an outstanding representative of the Society in America; they had all profited beyond measure by my coming, which was unforeseen and therefore the more appreciated; they would await my return with eager anticipation, and it could not be too soon. Everyone hammered on the table at this point and shouted "hear, hear" and I went to bed laughing. If there is something to be said, trust an Irishman to say it magnificently.

I was back in London the following night, listening with a sense of shock, after Dublin's rich accents, to the chirping of English voices. And then there was the familiar, weary shuttling from office to office, trying to get Army people to make decisions when they would rather pass the buck. I consulted Father Durand, called Paris about a priority for flying (there wasn't any), considered going to LeHavre for passage on a ship leaving in a few days, and finally elected to stay in London and take ship from Southampton on May sixth. That evening I went round to see Father Vin Hart at the Mount Royal Hotel, and found with him Father Bob Walton, just in from Germany on leave. It was great.

"What are you going to do?" I asked him.

"Going to Scotland."

"Good," I said, "Let's go to Scotland."

It was settled, but first we went to see John Gielgud's production of *Lady Windermere's Fan*. It was stagey and melodramatic, but the acting and the sets were excellent, and it was fun to picture oneself at the premiere of the play forty years before and to contrast the tastes of the two generations. What the two wars had given us in the way of sophistication! The crowded house seemed only mildly amused by Wilde's brittle epigrams.

In Edinburgh the following night we saw *The Merry Widow,* a play my parents recalled with great affection. In this presentation at least, it was dripping sentiment, only a cut above burlesque, with leg-show and tired vaudeville gags, and the old music scattered here and there. The audience, however, was easily pleased, being perhaps less sophisticated than we, or more war-weary. A comparable London or New York audience would have been bored; certainly the judicious would have grieved.

I own that I came to Scotland with some prejudices. I remembered John Knox, and Masonry, and some instances of Scottish dourness I had encountered. The beauty of "the Royal Mile" in Edinburgh and the staunch affection shown to the relics of Mary Queen of Scots mollified me considerably, but the weather was atrocious, rainy and raw, and the people, hungry and tired of rich Americans, did little to make us feel welcome. When we entered a shop on "the Mile" the proprietress asked crustily what we wanted. When we said we'd like to look around she told us that sight-seers usually visited John Knox's house next door. I couldn't help but notice, too, how thoroughly evidences of the Catholic past had been obliterated in St. Margaret's Chapel and St. Giles' Cathedral—much more carefully than in England.

We debated a trip to Inverness or the Lake District, but the weather was so dismal that we gave it up and went to Glasgow. Probably this was a mistake; we found only dirt and black weather. Even a walk along the bonny, bonny banks of Loch Lomond only drove us back to the hotel where we might find some of the native distillation and get warm.

"Bob," I said, "There's only one thing to do. Let's go to Ireland."

The ship for Belfast that night was crowded. We stood until ten, then found seats in the dining salon, but that was cold, and we were driven out at four-thirty when they began to set up for breakfast. At seven-thirty we went ashore. I asked a group of passing workmen where we might find a church, and was directed to a spire nearby. Then I remembered that I was in Ulster, and asked,

"Is it a Catholic church?"

Their faces hardened. "*That's* down the other way."

Their bitterness perplexed and distressed me, and after Mass we were treated to more of the same from the sacristan of the Catholic church. The atmosphere was oppressive, and we were glad to board a train for Dublin. Here the weather was no better, but I saw my friends again, and their warmth made us forget how perishingly cold we had been.

In London, once more, I decided to make sure of my berth on May sixth and visited the Transportation Officer. Sure enough, my name, for reasons neither he nor I could establish, had been scratched. The words should have stuck in my throat, but a bit of bluster seemed to be called for.

"I've been trying to get home for seven months," I said. "There must be something you can do."

He was a civilian and a good fellow. He called Southampton, talked a moment, then turned to me.

"Can you get to Southampton by five o'clock?"

"Sure," I answered, without the vaguest idea of how long the trip would take.

"OK. You're on the *Lake Charles Victory,* sailing tomorrow."

It was a wild rush then to pack my luggage, get a haircut, check out at the billeting office, pick up a bottle of wine at the chaplain's office, and get a sandwich before the Southampton train left Waterloo Station. All my departures seemed to be like this.

So it was goodbye to England, goodbye to Europe, goodbye to all my ex-lex junketing. The tug snaked us away from the pier and down the stream. There was jubilation among the soldiers lining the rails. A few wistful GI's who were not going home and some English girls waved farewell from the dock; a jeep, with two girls in it, pursued us down the long pier, stopping every now and then to wave.

We were at sea for eight days. It was cold and dreary on deck, stuffy and uncomfortable below decks. The Atlantic was capricious, petulant, and at times boisterous; many of the GI's were seasick, but I, though a poor sailor, was spared that ultimate misery. One more week, I told myself, of open living quarters, open sleeping quarters, open latrines. Movies were shown, but none of them seemed to have much resemblance to human life as I had known it. And the books I had bought in London and Dublin palled on me. I offered Mass each morning in the dispensary, and conducted a "General Service" for the Protestants on Sunday. Gambling went on hour after hour among the GI's—on deck if there were a sunny corner, or on the floor of a sleeping compartment in the hold. How the enlisted men must yearn, I thought, for the day when they could throw away those filthy fatigues they wore.

On the night of May tenth we were five hundred miles out; a couple of Air Corps lads, who must have thought they were still on a bomber, tried to get a glimpse of Cape Cod Light. Everyone talked of the landmarks he wanted to see, but actually the last leg of our journey was made at night, and we awoke on May twelfth in New York Harbor. At the pier in Hoboken a sleepy band played patriotic airs and Red Cross girls passed out cartons of milk that were greeted with cries of delight by the GI's. I had come home at last, but the thrill was not there.

Processing at Camp Dix was swift enough, and I was soon in Manhattan, staring with a stranger's eyes down the stone canyons and feeling guilty, after the poverty I had seen abroad, about the opulence in the shop windows. At our house on 84th Street I had a cordial welcome from old Jesuit friends and spent the night. And next morning, when I was called to the door, I ran downstairs into the arms of my mother and father, hugged Eleanor, felt Fran's strong handshake. At last, and at last, I had come home.

CHAPTER 21

Not by Dialectic

THE SUCCESS OF OUR HIGH SCHOOL DEBATING SOCIETY WAS DUE
to its faculty adviser, Mr. Philip Clarke, a young Jesuit who brought
to his task enthusiasm, capacity for hard work, and a thick Irish
brogue. It was reported of him that he read his Edmund Burke daily
for half an hour; certainly he wanted for himself and for us the
faculty of speaking in public with clarity and coherence, and after
that with all the grace and force God might give us to obtain. He
worked hard to build up the Society's membership and to keep interest in its meetings, and, looking back now across seventy years, I
can appreciate how much talent he assembled and with what skill he
kept it working. The Society debated everything: local issues like
the amalgamation of autonomous cities and towns under one mu-
nicipality, national questions like Prohibition or our entry into the
League of Nations. Meetings were never dull; it was taken for
granted that the appointed speakers would be carefully prepared, and
they were; if you did well in an intramural debate you might make
the New York trip or even the public prize debate. But the real fun
began when the question was "thrown open to the house." Mr.
Clarke showed you, a timorous beginner, how you might write a
two-minute speech, stand and give it from memory during that open
period, and sit safely down again before losing your breath. Then
of course someone would be sure to challenge the soundness of "the
previous speaker," and you would rise hotly to defend yourself; in
the most natural way your stagefright began to disappear. It was an
unusually gifted and keen group of boys, and they went far in self-
development, but Mr. Clarke deserves most of the credit. Even
when we had forgotten our speech or failed to take advantage of an
opponent's obvious lapses, he began his criticism gently, "Ye had a

foine spache, Linnord," he would say; "ye brought out two good arguments and 'twas aisy to see ye'd worked hard. But . . ." And I came to wait for that "but," pronounced as "put" and uttered with explosive emphasis.

A priest in the Army gets inevitably into many debates; in the beginning of his chaplaincy they provide a stimulating challenge. For the first time, perhaps, he is meeting men without the diplomatic immunity accorded to the Roman collar, and they speak with a candor and conviction which a politer society might not countenance. It may be on the deck of a transport, or in a pyramidal tent at night when there is no movie and solitaire or letter-writing has palled. I remember one debate with a long Oklahoman on the edge of a foxhole in Luzon. There was a full moon—"Bombers' Moon," we called it, a quaint little variation of our own on "Wabash Moon," "Carolina Moon," etc. The air raid warning had sounded to pull us out of bed, and we sat on our helmets waiting for the Japs, in one of the oddest settings for a religious discussion I have ever heard of. For twenty minutes we discussed the merits of the Reformation, and then the unmistakable whir of "Washing-machine Charlie" overhead sent us scrambling into our hole. I remember laughing as I burrowed down beside my opponent; this would of particular necessity be a "no-decision debate." The Jap went over, aiming for the nearby airstrip at Mangaldan, and we peeked out to see the show as our ack-ack sent up all the flak it had. But they missed him, and he went on his way without accomplishing anything. When we tried to walk back to our tents we found that the sharp edges of the helmets we had been sitting on had cut off the circulation in our legs, so we had to hang on to each other like a couple of topers making their unsteady way home. No debaters ever made a less dignified exit from the platform.

But as the months roll by the challenge fades. Rarely is a new argument adduced. The debates with Protestants all ended in the acceptance or rejection of the authority of the living Church; the debates with agnostics ended inconclusively with something like the possibility of miracles or the contradictions of biology. Occasionally, indeed, there appeared the odd stick who advanced the view that the only bright moments in life are the sinful ones, and I realized that Oscar Wilde was mighty yet. But in general I got ready to put on the old record and spin it once again, trying to live up to St. Paul, "Proclaim the message, and, welcome or unwelcome, insist on it. Refute falsehood, correct error, call to obedience—but do all with patience and with the intention of teaching." Too often I came away feeling that my opponent, if silenced, had not been convinced; the decision was given me but not the prize. And such victories were hollow indeed. Echoing over the years came the criticism, "Ye had a foine spache, Linnord, but . . ."

"Not by dialectic," said St. Ambrose, "did it please God to save the world," and his chief convert bore him out. St. Augustine entered the Church not only because he listened to Ambrose's eloquence, but because the public chanting of the Psalms melted his stubborn heart. How often I wished that I might invite an interested non-Catholic to come to Mass or to Vespers; perhaps a congregation united in audible and intelligible prayer might undo my ineptitudes and inspire him to become one of them. Sometimes, after I had been with a unit for a few weeks and had been able to institute Dialogue Mass, I could issue such invitations, but for the hundreds of casual encounters this was not possible: the men I met were not attached to my unit and, ten to one, I would never see them again. Nor could I send them elsewhere. Only one of the priests I knew in the Pacific encouraged active community participation. He was Father Bill Rogers, of Chicago, the chief chaplain of the 33rd Division, and he said that Dialogue Mass was the best thing he had ever started.

Yet when we priests talked with one another, as we did every time we could come together—in all our memories will linger those evenings of comradeship on the fringe of the jungle or in some provincial village where the Army paused before lunging forward again—we always started with the admission that our men were not the Catholics they should have been. I recall now one such meeting, in the little town of Villasis, on Luzon. The very zealous chaplain of the Army hospital there, Father Harold Whittet, of St. Paul, had at the cost of much effort conducted a Mission for his men, and afterward invited to dinner all of us who had helped him. He was grateful for our assistance, but depressed about the Mission; only a third of his Catholic personnel had come to the services. And I remember how the other priests had sought to cheer him. "You did well to have so many!" "Heck, if I had a third of my Catholics at Mass regularly on Sunday, I'd be happy." "They all come around when we get near combat, but in a rest area I just don't see them."

Well, what about the missing two-thirds? Discounting those who had come from families Catholic in name only, and who had been deprived of training and good example from their parents, discounting also those whose characters were naturally weak and who took the line of least resistance, making every allowance for the thoughtlessness of youth, one may still wonder about the many hundreds whose families were devout and who themselves were regularly at Mass and the Sacraments in civilian life. What happened to them? My own conviction is that many of these stopped coming because it was too much effort to continue doing something they did not understand and had so small a part in.

I remember the great public celebration we Catholics had in Manila for the official V-J Day. Mass was offered in Rizal Stadium; the altar and sanctuary were elaborate, the color guard was meticulously correct, the music was rendered by a full-voiced choir. And yet, as I stood and looked about at the congregation, tier upon tier to the number of seventy-five hundred, I sensed in them a lack of personal identification with what was going on before them. They rose, knelt, and sat in accordance with custom; some fingered rosaries; a handful received Holy Communion. What for them were the plaintive, wistful Kyrie, the glad cadences of the Gloria, the profession of faith flung defiantly at a skeptical world? Did they hear the exhortation addressed to them to pray that the sacrifice might be acceptable? Did they subscribe to its offering with the great amen? They heard a blare of bugles and an intermittent jingling of bells; they bowed their heads and beat their breasts because they had always done so; when all was over they sang "Holy God, We Praise Thy Name," their only active contribution, and filed out.

It might be objected that they were there, after all, and that they were there because they believed in the Mass as the unique expression of Christian worship. They knew that objectively God was being supremely honored by what they saw. One may concede all that and still feel that their personal involvement should have been much more extensive. These were adult Christians, baptized and so endowed with the capacity to give God a singular adoration. The least of them were reasonably intelligent and had learned such skills as reading and writing, or the use of fairly complicated modern weapons. Surely they were capable of more than passive spectatorship, and surely, if they had been encouraged and trained patiently to active participation, they would have heard all our catechizing re-stated in the most appealing and persuasive way. They themselves would have recited—nay, acted out—each Sunday the doctrines we could only touch on occasionally in our brief instructions.

Debating is a strenuous mental exercise, an intellectual swordplay that sometimes lays bare the truth of the matter, but often only gives an agile mind and a fluent tongue a chance to outpoint or disarm the opponent. Seldom if ever does it touch the heart or move the will. And when one of the contestants is interested much more in winning his opponent than in winning the argument, when he is deeply, painfully convinced of the truth and importance of his ideas, when he breathes silent prayers all during the debate for grace to say the things that will move this particular soul, then debating can be a frustrating occupation. One will begin to look for better methods, for a catechesis majestic and compelling to supplement one's own halting presentation of revealed truth.

At Boston College, over the south door of Bapst Library, there is a tympanum which shows a seated female figure giving instruction from a book which lies in her lap. This is our Mother the Church, proclaiming the Word of God. We priests must act as her ambassadors, since we have a mandate to speak for her, but we should get as many as we can to come to her feet and listen to her own voice, audible in her liturgy. When she prays she teaches, inevitably, and we learn as children learn, from listening to their parents talk. And when she teaches expressly, as she does, for instance, in choosing and proclaiming a particular passage from Holy Scripture on a given occasion, her doctrine has the authority and clarity of her Lord: "never did anyone speak as this man speaks." This is not, obviously, to go to the opposite and ridiculous extreme of advocating that we cancel catechism classes and send our children or our adult converts to Mass as a substitute. But let us acknowledge freely that our own instructions are something less than perfect, that the very sublimity of the Faith needs a reiteration we cannot possibly give it ourselves, that there are moments (and they occur especially when our people have assembled and prayed together on the Day of the Lord, in his house) when souls lie open and vulnerable, as it were, to the two-edged sword of his Word. Let us give room and scope for his swordplay. Our own words, by a humbling and gracious commission of his, may be the means whereby he attracts souls to himself, but we who know too well their fumbling inadequacy can only rejoice when we hear the voice of the Bridegroom speaking in our stead.

I remember that when we were novices the Novice-master reproved us one day for not keeping as well as we should the rule of silence. He reviewed all the motives which should have prompted us to observance, and then paused, smiling and pointing his eloquent finger at us, "You won't believe this now, but the day will come when you'll be tired of talking." How often I have recalled that prophecy, when the labor of matching words with ideas became almost too oppressive, and one could only remember the Lord sitting up, hour after hour, with nocturnal visitors like Nicodemus, who wouldn't understand and who wouldn't leave. The Lord was a debater, too; the lightning parry and thrust of his logic paralyzed the Scribes and threw their weapons clattering to the ground. He used the crushing summary that reduced them to silence. He used the *ad hominem* argument that unmasked their hypocrisy, showing what pious frauds they were in refusing their parents financial help because, forsooth, they had turned over all their resources to the Temple. He used an invective (it is summarized in that terrible twenty-third chapter of Matthew) whose corrosive acid stripped and burned his enemies and even now appalls the reader accustomed to hearing only of the gentle Christ. He threatened, coaxed, denounced, pleaded. And in the end, because debating had no effect, he wept, "Jerusalem, Jerusalem, how often would I have gathered your children together, as a hen gathers her chicks under her wings, and you refused." There was only one way left by which he could touch this people, and he took it. He died for them. Maybe we Army priests will discover one day that that was our most effective argument, too. We didn't have to enlist; we had been classified as ineligible for the draft, and might have stayed at home. But we went out by the hundreds, and many of us were killed, and all of us sweated and ate K-rations and endured whatever our men had to endure. *Tantus labor non sit cassus.*

Christian life, one might say, starts with a decision—at least from the human side. It is the decision to respond to God's call. Perhaps that call has been sounding in a person's ears for a long time; perhaps one has just become aware of it. In any case, a decision is asked for and made. It proceeds from a new attitude on the man's or woman's part—one might call it a new willingness to listen and respond—and it involves a decisive turning away from the past, from self-centredness, from sin. One cannot face the East without turning one's back on the West.

Parenthetically, one might wish that all of us were at all times eager to respond to God in this decisive fashion. God is delighted, as the history of David, for one, informs us, with a responsive heart, eager to learn, to be guided by suggestions, to leap at the voice of command. But by nature most of us are sluggish, or even wilful and stubborn, and at best inconstant. We go on hearing God's voice and paying as little attention to it as we give to street-noises. By contrast, how appealing is the picture of the boy Samuel trotting obediently to the bed of the priest Eli when he thought Eli had called him during the night: the little fellow, tousled and sleepy but earnest in his desire to serve, saying "Here I am; you called me." Later, when he realizes that it is God who calls him, Samuel has the same readiness, "Speak, Lord, your servant is listening."

Any of us may rightfully think that we have been called by name when God created us and gave us our unique personality, for by so creating us God summoned us from the infinite ranks of possible beings and sent us into life. There is, however, a more specific call addressed to us, the call to redemption and holiness and eternal life with God. For this one must have a responsive heart, ready to listen, swift to comply. "Today, if you hear His voice, harden not your hearts!" "He that has ears to hear, let him hear!" Such a call was trumpeted by John the Baptist to the contemporaries of Christ before Christ actually made his appearance among them, "Repent, for the kingdom of heaven is at hand." The verb "repent" is more accurately rendered "Change your attitude," and it means "Surrender something of your assurance, of your confidence in your own powers. Acknowledge that all your self-seeking has not brought you the peace you need. You cannot, you know, have it both ways; God sees through hypocrisy, and will have a whole heart or none. Change your attitude!"

No one embarks on the Christian life without so deciding to cast his or her lot definitively with Christ. "He that is not with me is against me." On the brink of such a decision the timorous hesitate, the ungenerous balk. But the voice of God is imperious and peremptory: "Risk everything you have! Have me even if you must have nothing else! Lose your life in order to find it!"

Some are called to join the laborers in the vineyard at the sixth, the ninth, or even the eleventh hour, and this decision is taken when their powers are mature and the alternatives are very clear. Most Christians are summoned early in life, and may wait for many years before they face the decision which will determine whether or not they continue their labors. All of us find ourselves periodically under the necessity of reaffirming our choice, blinding our eyes to the seduction of the moment, clinging indomitably to our hope.

For hours of crisis like these there must be help. It is not only the intellect, perhaps scarcely the intellect at all but the will that is torpid or mutinous. And so the generous goodness of God, his willingness to forgive and his eagerness to help us live the Christian life, must be presented as attractively as possible. In the past this summons has, very often, been presented either as a stern, imperious command to come to heel, under pain of eternal damnation, or as the conclusion of hard reasoning, an inescapable deduction from premises carefully set out. No one denies that such approaches to the soul are valid. God can, and sometimes in sacred history has, issued uncompromising commands. And it can be demonstrated with iron logic that a creature must be obedient to his Creator. The question is whether such an approach is the one God has usually employed in his dealings with us, and whether it is calculated to evoke the kind of response he wants, or, indeed, any positive response at all. Human beings are not uniformly ruled by reason, and a direct command often excites rebellion. God, who knows us so well, has mercifully chosen to draw us to himself by love. He wants a response that arises out of an answering love.

Sometimes the "Principle and Foundation" of St. Ignatius has been so presented as to make it seem that our service of God is nothing more than an obligation rigorously imposed and minutely supervised. The concept reminds us of the Puritan Milton's ambition, "to live ever in my great Taskmaster's eye," which is so directly opposed to everything we know of God our Father that it should strike Christians with horror. It is a fact that "we are created to praise, reverence, and serve God, and by this means to save our souls," but this is our privilege and opportunity as well as our duty, and the call to it should be presented for what it is, a supremely generous invitation.

Perhaps the reason why the invitation has been so poorly understood lies in the fact that its generosity is so little realized. It is enormously difficult to grasp or explain the fact that one is pursued by love, enveloped by love. At times, so small is our awareness, we tend to brush off or even resent the attentions of the lover. Instead of yielding to and accepting gratefully the proffered love, we push it aside because it asks a return, and we do not want to make this effort. Sometimes it is because we have not had the experience of being loved greatly and selflessly, as for instance by a mother or father; or it may be that we remember painfully how little love we gave in return, and shrink from a repetition of such churlishness. "I don't want to be loved!" we cry petulantly. Or it may be that we ourselves have loved deeply and have been hurt by the indifference we met; we do not want to run the risk of that anguish again.

Against all these pathetic defences the love of God beats like an ocean, tirelessly seeking to break through, to run over. It is wide and deep enough to lift and bear us up forever if we would only abandon ourselves to it. Somehow, then, people must be solicited gently, tenderly, to surrender at last. Perhaps they will yield if they can be brought to see how, as Jacob said, "God has been my shepherd from my birth until this day,"—leading them through pain and perplexity, out of the swamps and thickets into which they had wilfully wandered, to himself, to the country where they can find at last and in abundance the food and refreshment they crave.

Or perhaps it will help if people can be brought to ponder some segment of sacred history in which God overwhelmingly demonstrates his love for our race. The 78th Psalm invites us so to review the history of the Chosen People and God's patient wooing of them. Or there are the readings of the Easter Nightwatch, when in the half-light we wait for the Risen Christ and listen meanwhile to the recital of the great things God has done for us. "In the beginning God created heaven and earth. . . " "In those days the Lord slew the host of the Egyptian army . . ." It is very moving indeed to trace through the Scriptures, from the sin of Adam to the preaching of John the Baptist, the long preparation of the world for the coming of its Savior. One cannot miss the delicacy and persistence of God's love for our race.

The vocation of the Christian is a calling by name, like that of Abraham, Jacob, Moses, the prophets, and it is an invitation to enter into a covenant or pact. God offers to bind himself to certain obligations if we will agree to commit ourselves in similar fashion. There is touching evidence of God's love here not alone in the condescension by which the Infinite offers to be bound but also in the desire he manifests for permanent union, for a stable marriage, as it were, that will be proof against the ebb and flow of human moods and unite us to him forever. On one side we contract to believe, to hope, to love. God for his part agrees to forgive, and to share with us "that life which was promised once to Abraham and to his seed forever," his own life. This Christian covenant was foreshadowed by the pact to which God and the Jews subscribed at Sinai, and which was sealed with the blood of animals. The "new" covenant is sealed with the blood of Christ, and is therefore guarded by that *mysterium fidei* or pledge of fidelity which is renewed every time the blood of Christ is offered. The ancient Jews praised God for his fidelity: "He said he would do it and he did." St. Paul voiced the Christian ratification of this praise, "God is faithful, who has called you to the company of his Son."

We Christians are summoned by our vocation to baptism. We are invited to permit the Son of God to lay hold of us and join us to himself. In this mighty clasping we shall be forgiven, cleansed, and sanctified through the in-streaming of divine life. We shall be made, like Christ and in Christ, sons and daughters of the Most High, heirs of the promise and the kingdom. Into our flesh will be burned the paradox, the seal of victory in defeat, the dying and the rising of him who, once dead, dies no more, and who willed that where he would be his brethren would be, too. By accepting baptism we agree to die with Christ to the will of the flesh and our own will, to the "old man," as St. Paul calls our unredeemed nature, that we may rise with Christ to the new life of grace and glory. We accept the breath-taking possibility that like his our poor flesh may be transfigured and may shine like the sun, and in that hope we submit ourselves to be drowned in the waters of life. It is a winner-take-all risk, a superb and gallant act of faith, but "we know in whom we have put our trust."

The entire plan of God should be placed before people of good will, in all its sublimity, and from the beginning of our dealings with them. As their questions multiply and their appetite is whetted, this or that detail of the plan will need further exposition. But they should know from the outset what God offers them. So the Apostles, and Peter notably, preached the Good News in Acts and invited their listeners to baptism. It was an invitation to adventure, an appeal to generosity that sought not only to convince the mind but to move the heart. That it succeeded is evident from the amazing growth of the Church in the first centuries. "That very day about three thousand were added to their number." In our retreats perhaps we have waited too long, until the meditations on the Kingdom and the Two Standards, to introduce the note of enthusiasm for the open-handed liberality of God. It is of course necessary to make sure that the soul is purged from its attachment to sin, but will this be achieved more surely by a process of painful detachment, step-by-step, motivated by rational considerations of sin's malice, or by the sudden and cleansing flame of love which the generosity of our God calls into being? Sometimes one thinks that the early meditations of the Spiritual Exercises are presented as if there were value in having the exercitant feel shame for its own sake, and not that gratitude and love might spring from it. If it is objected that there are those who can be stirred only to fear God, this might have to be conceded in some cases, but my own conviction is that their number is as a rule grossly overestimated; the average human heart—more especially the heart of the person who makes a retreat—is not that hard, and if he or she has not surrendered yet to love it may be because its case has never been presented adequately. Or if it be objected that the emotion of love so fanned into flame will burn low and die out in a short time, the same can surely be said of the emotion of fear, as everyday experience bears witness.

Making a retreat, however, was impossible for us in the South Pacific. And it is realistic to admit that the great majority of Catholics at home cannot or at least do not take advantage of their opportunities to make a retreat even in peace-time. How will these be given the indispensable reminder that they are greatly loved? How will they renew once more their personal response to that love? No problem in the whole range of the pastoral ministry seems more urgent than this, and every ingenuity should be called on to solve it.

The weekly assembly of the faithful offers, one would think, the perfect occasion for such an exchange of love. Here the gracious Lord speaks, and his people reply; the generous Lord gives, and his people give in return. But—so far as is possible for human frailty—every shadow of custom, every vestige of perfunctory routine must be eliminated. The experience, for all present, must be new—as if it had never been realized before, as if there were never going to be a chance to have it again. Each such occasion must be planned for its maximum effect, and every authentic aid—elocution, music, setting, demeanor—must be pressed into service. The good news in God's word must be proclaimed as if for the first time (and we can rejoice that we have been given a larger variety of readings than we once had), with passion and urgency. Its meaning and relevance must be set forth clearly and forcefully. And the people must be encouraged, led, and assisted to make a response that will be genuine and wholehearted. There is question here of intimate communion with the most high God.

But the renewal of the assembly's covenant goes beyond a merely verbal expression. It is acted out in the sign language. The bread and wine that are brought to the altar, because they are purchased with the assembly's contributions, symbolize each one's gift of himself. As St. Gregory says, the sacrifice of the Mass is not celebrated with the requisite sanctity unless it includes an offering of ourselves, and the text of the Mass prays often that we may be conformed to the gifts we present at the altar. We are to "have in us that mind which was in Christ Jesus"—a priestly mind, a worshipping mind, a committed mind. The assembly should be taught, if need be, how its bread and wine are at Mass ineffably dignified and given a value they could never have of themselves, through being changed into the body and blood of Christ, and how in a similar way its own commitment is caught up into the worship of Christ the High Priest and invested with his excellence and merit. All Christians should know that as their gift of bread and wine undergoes at Mass a mighty transformation through the omnipotence of God, so they too come to Mass asking to be transformed by God's power into new beings. Their presence in the assembly is an acceptance of the transformation God's grace would bring about in them; it is a declaration of dependence on their Father, since they themselves could never achieve the hoped-for result; it asks that they be broken at this Mass and shaped anew into something nearer the divine plan. And their Holy Communion is God's return-gift, the total indwelling of divinity in the beloved Son, the solemn pledge not only of ultimate resurrection and eternal life but also of the gradual modulation of their powers so that these take the same direction as Christ's and fashion them into the "new man," another Christ.

So we came home, all the khaki-clad army, back through the Golden Gate or the Narrows in New York Harbor to God's country, back to L.A. and Sioux City and Fall River. We shucked our khaki and tried to pick up where we had left off. But on all our memories were etched unforgettable, incommunicable things. The Vivid Years . . . Our first morning in Lingayen Gulf, with the shell-cases of the Navy bombardment floating black in the water, and the sheared-off palm trees on the beach, and the low hills beyond, full of enemies, and us going down the scramble-nets to the landing craft. Would this be It? For many of us it was. There was one Filipino place-name which for me will always have a sound of menace and mourning. The town was a tiny one, little more than a hamlet and only one of four or five where we established cemeteries as soon as we got beyond the beaches. I had no chance to visit it, actually, until some months later, after the campaign had been closed, and when I did the cemetery had been evacuated and the bodies moved to Santa Barbara. Nevertheless I recall how, driving along the sunny, dusty highway, I suddenly saw the sign and felt once more the chill the town's name had always given me. "Binalonan." Like Keats' "forlorn," the word rings a passing bell in my memory, a bell calling to prayer for slaughtered youth.

Nothing so silent as the body wrapped in its shelter-half. No one so soft-spoken, so courteous and gentle as the personnel of Graves Registration supervising the cemetery. A great pity for the young dead mutes all voices and blunts all passion: something motherly, tender. Could not the compassion, the sense of being somehow involved in a corporate guilt and shame, have been born earlier, in time to prevent this? Was whatever we achieved or proved worth it? Was there no better way?

Sometime after the war I visited a rectory in Boston. I had been there before, and the young priest who opened the door gave me a cordial welcome.

"Come in, Father. We have another visitor I'd like you to meet. Father Ford, this is Father Leonard."

A long, gaunt Irishman unwound himself from the divan and came forward with his hand outstretched. "How do you do, Father?"

I looked at him. "Weren't you in the Philippines?"

"I was."

"Lingayen, wasn't it?"

He studied me for a moment, then pointed with a long finger, "Patrick's Night!"

"Patrick's Night it was," I said.

We fought the war all over again that night, and won it about two o'clock in the morning. Father Ford shook hands, and there was an Irish glint in his eye and Irish eloquence on his tongue.

"Good night, Father. We'll meet again on some foreign strand. Remember, we stood where thousands fell."

The phrase he quoted, originally Falstaff's, came from no hero, and we could not preen ourselves, either, for valor or skill or wisdom because we had survived. It was not luck, or chance, or fate; a Christian does not believe in such superstitions. It could only have been the choice of our Father, who had some use for us in the working out of his saving plan for the world, and who at the same time (for he sees small things as well as great) saw that we ourselves might grow in his love if he left us here a bit longer. When I remember some who fell—the gifted, the magnanimous, those to whom the world was or could predictably be indebted—I am tempted to wonder why we were left to stand. But I am content to accept my Father's choice; I cannot see into the depths of time and eternity; I cannot follow each thread that is woven into the enormous tapestry. I know he loves the world he has made. I know he loves me personally. He is strong enough to be Lord of my little history and Lord of the world's. He is faithful to his promises. And so the epilogue to the war, spoken by the survivors and the fallen: his will be done.

CHAPTER 22

And So Farewell

THE ORDNANCE ALTAR, ALL FIVE HUNDRED POUNDS OF IT, CAME across the Pacific and through the Panama Canal and arrived in Boston before I did, courtesy of Dick Thomson and my old friends in Ordnance. And it lay in my brother Fran's garage for two years before I found a use for it.

At the edge of the Boston College campus in those days there was a ramshackle, cheerless old house, since torn down, in which, the story went, the original owner had committed suicide many years before. During the years before the War the building was an anthropological museum, full of artifacts from Central America, and the most striking exhibit was in the fireplace of the old living room, where two mummified human corpses lay behind plate glass and made a grisly display. After the War, however, the Jesuit population on campus suddenly expanded, taxing the capacities of St. Mary's Hall, so seven of us moved in with the mummies. We called our new home "Typhoid Towers." The living room became the house chapel. A vestment case was moved in to conceal the mummies, but I thought of them as silent participants in our liturgies, perhaps placed there providentially to remind us to pray for them, and I included them hopefully among "all the dead whose faith is known to you alone," as the Eucharistic Prayer puts it.

"You'll need an altar," the Rector said.

"I have one," I said.

So with a truck and much grunting and groaning the altar came from Fran's house and was set up in the chapel. Over it I hung the red canopy and Clarence Staudenmayer's rosewood crucifix. Helen Amendola made a gorgeous red and gold antependium, embroidering on it the text *"Regimini militantis ecclesiae."* These were the opening words of the papal decree authorizing St. Ignatius to establish the Society of Jesus as a religious order in 1540, and could be translated "for the administration" (or "the regulation," or, with a tolerant bow to the enemies of the Jesuits, "the strategy") "of the Church Militant." They seemed to blend appropriately the original purpose of the altar and its new use by St. Ignatius' sons. And I hung a card in the sacristy, asking any who might celebrate Mass there to "remember the builders of this altar" in their sacrifices. That would be Steve Brennan, Bill Graham, Charlie McCormack and Les Shoemaker, Joe Rigotti, Bob Hauser, Tom Jones, Chris Spicuzza and Sergeant Martinelli, Jim Scannell and Leo Spinelli, Sammy Shapiro, Bob Carracher and "Skinny from Sheboygan," Johnny Mangiaracina, Captain Richman, and all those others who had helped with ideas and labor. Maybe they'd like to know, half a century later, wherever the winds of change have carried them.

After five years "Typhoid Towers" was razed to make room for a new dormitory, and I came home from a summer's lecturing to find that the altar had been moved to an inconspicuous corner of St. Joseph's Chapel, where with only occasional use it gathered dust and candle grease, and then migrated to several other undistinguished locations. Finally, after a three years' residence at Pope John XXIII Seminary, I returned to campus, discovered the altar in the cellar of Bea House, and realized that since as a war memorial it was not exactly in high regard, its next destination would probably be the dump. So I offered it to the U.S. Army Chaplain Museum, and within a week a truck appeared and carried it away. Since then the Museum itself has done its share of migrating, but now seems to be securely established at Fort Monmouth in New Jersey, and there the altar, with all its adornments and appurtenances, is the centerpiece of the World War II exhibit.

But the chapel itself—what happened to that? The last thing I saw in 1944, as we cleared the area in a frantic rush the morning after Christmas, bound for the ship that would take us in on the invasion of Luzon, was the steep pitch of the chapel roof. In all the years that followed I wondered: was it still standing? Could it possibly have survived the termites and the typhoons of forty tropical years?

In the movie *Twelve O'Clock High,* which film critics praised for its authentic sense of World War II, begins with a wistful sequence in which the former adjutant of the Air Wing returns, twenty years after the War, to the field in England from which his fighters and bombers had gone out to risk the flak over Germany, and to which many never returned. We see him, alone, step out of his rented car and look eagerly about; it's the same place, right enough, but it's not the same. The barracks are gone; the hangars are tumbling down; the strip is overgrown with grass. Strangest of all is the silence. Where engines roared and hundreds of men shouted, there is not a sound. He turns away at last, full of memories, sad, knowing, as Bob Hope—or was it Tom Wolfe?—said, "You can't go home again."

I was old enough, God knows, to have acknowledged the truth of that poignant observation. Nevertheless, I found myself, forty-three years after the war, making a last effort to disprove it. I was aboard Air Niugini's 727, looking down on the gray-green hills around Port Moresby, and feeling again a twinge of the dislike and apprehension that jungle country had inspired in me. I remembered the miseries of the Salamaua campaign, and thought I could pick out, on the Owen Stanley Range, the thread of the Kokoda Trail. In 1942 the Japs, having landed at Buna on the east coast, went swarming up that Trail, over the top (one of the highest mountain ranges in the world), and down the other side almost to Port Moresby, from which they would have had a clear shot at Australia. But we landed the 32nd American Division, the work-horse division from Wisconsin, and the 7th Australian Brigade, took the Japs head-on and pushed them up, up, up, over the top again, and down, down, down, into Buna. There, according to the legend, General Eichelberger, commanding the 32nd, wired to General MacArthur, "I can spit in Buna, but I can't take it." MacArthur wired back, "You will take it, or leave your body." Eichelberger took it, of course, but the cost was enormous: thousands dead or wounded, with malaria, scrub typhus, dengue fever, dysentery, psychological exhaustion, physical suffering (the men had left Moresby in tropical uniforms, and needed winter clothing at the top of the Range) as the price paid by the survivors. From a purely military standpoint, it was one of the finest exploits of the War. But the human cost is what overpowers the imagination, and I hear Pope Paul VI pleading in the U.N. chamber, *"Jamais encore!"*

My plane was coming in for a landing now in Finschhafen, and I was peering intently at the empty harbor and the desolate beaches, looking for something—anything—familiar. Finschhafen, they had told me, was a malarial area, and had not been developed as Moresby, Lae, and other provincial centers had been. So, I unthinkingly assumed, the place would look pretty much as I had last seen it.

At that time the Base ran along the coast for some fifteen miles. On both sides of the one road, built by our Engineers, were acres of tents, mess-halls, headquarters, a hospital, shops, offices. There was a Navy base for P.T. boats and a strips and hangars for the Air Corps, and the 33rd Division was bivouacked there, waiting for the word to move on Biak, Halmahera, and the Philippines. Gangs of natives labored under the surveillance of the Australians. But the population of the Base was largely Army service troops— ordnance, signal, quartermaster—struggling under the tropical sun or in the deep mud of the rainy season to empty huge crates of equipment from the States and to assemble it for shipment forward to the combat areas. At the height of its activities there were upwards of a hundred thousand men on the Base.

But when Father George Lawlor and I set out from the Lutheran Mission Hospital, where the volunteer American physician, Dr. Hershey, generously loaned us his car, there was only one recognizable feature—the single road along the coast. I was driving on the left, and using a stick-shift instead of the more familiar automatic transmission of recent years, but it didn't matter; we met almost no traffic. We dipped into the hollow where Base Headquarters had been, but saw only thick underbrush and mature palm trees. Then we were on the level again, where, I was sure, the nine hundred men of the 9th Ordnance Battalion had had their tents and shops— this must be the place, this was where I would find my chapel. But there was nothing—not even a bit of old metal rusting away under the gently waving fronds of jungle vegetation. I suppose the natives carried away whatever they could use after we left, and anything else simply disintegrated. We stopped, explored as best we could under the fierce midday sun—how had we ever done such heavy work in such a climate?—but I could not with certainty identify even the site of the chapel. I asked questions at a sort of general store near what had been the Navy Base, and at the Lutheran minor seminary, but got only a wondering and regretful shaking of heads. I knew we had gone too far when we reached Scarlet Beach. (The Japs had attempted a landing there, and had been repulsed with so much bloodshed that the place was given this grisly name, and it is still so called, though probably the natives today don't know why.) So we went back to try once more, scanning every foot of the way. Nothing. And if the kookabura bird had cawed its raucous laugh, I would have felt the mockery of the triumphant jungle. With a flash of sympathetic perception, however, Father Lawlor sensed my disappointment, and said, in a quiet, let's-be-reasonable tone, "You fellows came out here to establish peace, didn't you?"

"I suppose we did," I answered.

"Well," he said, "Look around you."

The breeze soughed softly through the palm trees, and I broke into a slow grin. It was true. The Japs had gone. We Americans had gone. The Australians had gone. The country belonged, as it should, to the people of New Guinea. Mission accomplished. So my chapel had vanished; it didn't matter. I took a last look at the silent, serene bush, said a quick prayer for all the comrades, living and dead, of those days, and drove back to the hospital. Dr. Hershey, with rare delicacy and kindness, thanked me for what we had done, forty years before, for New Guinea.